Logic Design and Computer Organization

Logic Design and Computer Organization

Morton H. Lewin

Professor of Electrical Engineering and Computer Science
Rutgers University

**ADDISON-WESLEY
PUBLISHING COMPANY**

Reading, Massachusetts
Menlo Park, California
London □ Amsterdam
Don Mills, Ontario □ Sydney

094272

This book is in the ADDISON-WESLEY Series in
Computer Sciences and Information Processing

CONSULTING EDITOR: Michael A. Harrison

SPONSORING EDITOR: James T. DeWolf
PRODUCTION EDITOR: Doris L. Machado

TEXT DESIGNER: Vanessa Piñeiro
ILLUSTRATORS: Arvak and F. W. Taylor Associates
COVER DESIGNER: Ann Scrimgeour Rose
COVER ILLUSTRATOR: Ann Scrimgeour Rose
ART COORDINATOR: Robert Trevor

PRODUCTION MANAGER: Herbert Nolan
PRODUCTION COORDINATOR: Sheryl Stenzel

The text of this book was composed in Autologic Melior by TriStar Graphics

Library of Congress Cataloging in Publication Data
Lewin, Morton H.
  Logic design and computer organization.

  1. Logic design.   2. Computer architecture.   I. Title.
TK7868.L6L48   621.3819′582   81-20636
ISBN 0-201-04144-8   AACR2

ISBN 0-201-04144-8
BCDEFGHIJ-HA-89876543

For Suki,
Cherie, Brandon,
Julie, and Gene

Preface

This book is based on material from courses I have been teaching for the past several years. It is intended for a two-semester sophomore- or junior-level course, although it may be covered in one semester at a graduate or advanced undergraduate level. It has no prerequisites, except for college-entry-level mathematics. In particular, it does not implicitly assume some "previous exposure" to computer programming or to digital circuits.

It is meant for both electrical engineering and computer science students. While it omits extraneous electrical details on circuits and technologies (for which non-EE students are generally not adequately prepared), it still retains a realistic approach to signals and timing.

Logic design is redefined to include several topics (for example, memories, register transfers) normally covered in introductory computer organization. Switching-theory topics, which logic designers rarely use, are omitted. The emphasis is on building components hierarchically, starting at the gate level. Each component is described with an interface and a function, and then with an examination of the alternatives for its internal structure. Logic design is taken to mean the study of all components up to the processor level. Computer organization begins at that point. While an intuitive, engineering approach is maintained throughout, formal methods are employed where applicable.

Chapter 1 introduces the basic logic elements (including tri-state gates, ports, and buses) and contrasts intuitive design techniques with the use of formal methods. Integrated combinational elements are covered (in Chapter 2) *before* sequential circuits are introduced (in Chapter 3)—to permit students to see, at a very early stage, how gate networks "compute." Chapter 4, on memories and register transfers, includes an introduction to stacks. Chapter 5 contains three nontrivial sample applications, which show how the elements described in the first four chapters are interconnected and used. The video display controller, in particular, is an excellent digital-system vehicle of significant complexity.

Chapter 6 dissects the logic diagram of an elementary hypothetical processor, while covering such fundamentals as instruction and data formats and addressing modes. Three approaches to the detailed implementation of control logic are discussed in Chapter 7—using a much more sophisticated, hypothetical processor as a common design vehicle. Chapter 8 provides an in-depth study of interrupt and I/O systems, covering typical I/O interfaces, direct memory access and introducing I/O processors. Finally, Chapter 9 treats those software components (supervisors, interpreters, and debuggers) that are closest to the hardware interface. Virtual memories and microprocessors are also covered.

To explain the alternatives to the implementation of control logic, I chose to employ a reasonably complex, hypothetical vehicle, which was still sufficiently tractable to permit the reader to visualize all of its components connected together and running. My general intention is not to be so "current" (for example, by using the latest integrated-circuit part numbers or by reiterating information found in the manuals of real processors) that the material presented becomes dated in a short time. I have tried to concentrate on those aspects of logic design and computer organization which I believe will remain "classical"—if such a word is applicable in such a rapidly changing field.

Many of the problems at the end of each chapter were extracted from "closed-book" examinations which I have given in the past. I employ such exams exclusively, because I believe that they best measure the information that students *retain*. I justify this approach by explaining that a typical technical job interview is rarely an "open book" experience. For this reason, I urge the reader to approach any problem that does not specifically refer to a portion of the text as if it were a closed-book problem. Refer to the pertinent discussion only after you have struggled sufficiently with the problem. In this connection, I also include (at the end of the text) *solutions* to all of the problems—assuming, again, that each reader will check a solution only after having made a diligent effort to develop his or her own.

I would like to take this opportunity to thank Professor Arthur W. Lo of Princeton University and Professor Theodore R. Bashkow of Columbia University, who were kind enough to review the manuscript and to make numerous useful suggestions for revision. In addition, I am grateful to those Rutgers University students (too many to mention by name) who uncovered errors in the manuscript while using it as a text.

Princeton, New Jersey   M. H. L.
September, 1982

Contents

Gate Structures

1.1 CODES AND NUMBERS

A string of symbols is a *code*. It conveys information. Its meaning is defined by an interpretation rule. This rule may exist either in the form of a table listing all permissible codes and their corresponding meanings, or as a clear statement from which such a table can be constructed. A code which has not been assigned a meaning is said to be undefined or unused.

Each symbol in a code is selected from an established set of available symbols. For example, every word on this page is a code. The letters of the alphabet comprise the set of available symbols, and a dictionary provides the meaning of each defined code. Clearly, in this case there are many undefined or unused codes. Some will become defined later as our vocabulary expands. The Morse code, used in telegraphy and blinker signaling, represents each alphabetic and numeric character with a unique sequence of dots and dashes. In this case, there are only *two* available symbols, and all of the defined codes are listed in a short "Morse Alphabet" table.

A *number* is a very important code. Each of its symbols is a *digit*. The number of possible values for each digit (i.e., the number of available sym-

1

bols) is called the *base* of the number system. A base *B* number system employs *B* digit symbols, beginning with the digit zero. Thus, the base-8 or octal number system includes only the digits 0 through 7, while the decimal (base-10) number system uses the digits 0 through 9. A number system may have a base greater than ten. In this case, digit symbols beyond 9 must be invented. For example, the *hexadecimal* or base-16 number system utilizes the sixteen digit symbols 0, 1, ..., 9, A, B, ..., F. The sequence of digits BE3F is a perfectly valid hexadecimal (shortened as "hex") number.

The most elementary number system is the binary or base-2 system. Only the digit symbols 0 and 1 (called "bits"—short for "binary digits") are available. This system is particularly important because a digital computer processes information represented or encoded in the form of bit strings.

Counting in a number system begins with the number of lowest value, namely a string of all zero digits. Normally, leading zeroes are *implied*. That is, they are not explicitly written. The least significant digit always increments as the count proceeds. Any other digit increments only when it receives a "carry" from the digit on its right. A digit advances from its maximum value back to zero by generating a carry to the digit on its left. Thus, for example, 277 + 1 = 300 in base 8, while 4BF + 1 = 4C0 in base 16. In base 2, we may enumerate all possible three-digit numbers (calling them three-bit codes and explicitly showing the leading zeroes) by using a counting process. This results in the following list of all possible three-bit combinations:

$$000 \quad 001 \quad 010 \quad 011 \quad 100 \quad 101 \quad 110 \text{ and } 111.$$

Note that there are eight such codes.

A base-*B* integer is expressed as a string of digits $A_n \ldots A_1 A_0$, where A_n is the most significant digit and A_0 is the least significant digit. Here A_0 is called the "units" digit, A_1 may be called the "B's" digit, A_2 the "Bsquared's" digit, and so on. The numeric value of this number is

$$\sum_{i=0}^{n} A_i B^i .$$

The *length* of a code is the number of symbols in it. If there are *B* choices for each symbol (i.e., if the family of available symbols has *B* members), then there are always B^N different possible codes of length *N*. These may be enumerated by assuming that each of the available symbols corresponds to a digit in the base-*B* number system. There are as many codes as there are *N*-digit base-*B* numbers. The "lowest" code contains the equivalent of *N* zeroes. The "highest" code has an equivalent value which is one less than that of the *N* + 1-digit number 100 ... 00, whose magnitude is B^N. Thus, *including* the lowest all-zero code, we count exactly B^N possible codes of length *N*.

To arrive at this same result from another point of view, divide the *N*-symbol code into two fields: one containing 1 symbol and the other containing $N - 1$ symbols. There are B choices for the 1-symbol field. For each of these, the $N - 1$-symbol field may take on any one of X possible values. The entire code therefore has BX possible values, where X is presently unknown. In other words, every time we add a symbol to a code (incrementing N), we *multiply* the number of possible code values by B. Since there are B different codes when N is 1, a code of length N must have B^N possible values. Thus, for example, there are 26^4 (which is 456,976) different four-letter words (from AAAA to ZZZZ) and, as you may know, there are 10^3 (which is 1000) different three-digit decimal numbers (from 000 to 999).

Since a computer stores and processes *binary* codes (strings of 1's and 0's), the case $B = 2$ is of particular interest. There are $\underline{2^N}$ different combinations (codes) containing N bits, from all zeroes to all ones. As you become familiar with computer terminology, you will find it easier not only to count in binary but also to recall common values of 2^N. Some of these are listed in Table 1.1. Notice a verification of the fact, derived earlier via a counting process, that there are eight (2^3) possible binary codes of length three.

All information processed by a computer is internally *encoded* or represented in binary form. An N-bit string may be used to represent any member of a set of (no more than) 2^N discrete objects, events, states, numbers, or things. For example, a four-bit code may specify one of sixteen (2^4) possible directions. A two-bit code may specify one of four (2^2) possible colors.

A code may be subdivided into substrings called *fields*, each with its own interpretation rule. Defining the meaning of such a code involves specifying the positions, lengths, and meanings of all of its fields. Such a specification is called a *format*. For the same reason that adding a symbol to a code multiplies the number of possible codes by the number of available symbols, add-

Table 1.1 Some Commonly Used Values for 2^N.

N	2^N
1	2
2	4
3	8
4	16
5	32
6	64
7	128
8	256
9	512
10	1024
12	4096
16	65536

ing a field to a code multiplies the number of codes possible by the number of values that that field may assume. Thus, the number of possible values for a code is equal to the *product* of the numbers of values possible in each of its fields. For example, consider a 26-bit code representing a command to a line-plotting device. The code includes a 10-bit X field and a 10-bit Y field defining the coordinates of the endpoint of the line to be drawn (beginning at the present position of the plotting pen). Note that it is implied that the plotting surface is organized in a 1024 by 1024 grid, since $2^{10} = 1024$. The command code also includes a 3-bit field specifying the color of the line (eight are possible) and a 1-bit field defining the thickness of the line (thin or thick). Finally, a 2-bit field determines one of four types of line structure—solid, dashed, dotted, or not plotted. The last option permits commands to move the pen to a new position without marking the paper. Observe that the total number of possible commands to the plotter is

$$(1024)\ (1024)\ (8)\ (2)\ (4),$$

which is

$$(2^{10})\ (2^{10})\ (2^{3})\ (2^{1})\ (2^{2}),$$

which is 2^{26} (adding the exponents), which is the number of values that a 26-bit binary code may assume.

Since writing down the value of a long bit string—for example, one of the 26-bit commands above—can be quite tedious and error-prone, a shorthand system is frequently employed in which the string is divided into equal-length fields (say, n bits each), and a single symbol (one of the 2^n that are possible) is written to represent the value of each field. In this book, wherever convenient we will use a hexadecimal shorthand notation, in which a single hex digit (0-F) will represent a 4-bit field. Table 1.2 lists all of the hex digits and their corresponding 4-bit codes. (It will not take you long to remember them.)

Hex-digit substitution begins on the right-hand (least significant) end, and the proper number of leading binary zeroes is added on the left-hand end to make the replacement process come out even. If these rules are followed, we can show that the resulting hex number is numerically equal to the binary number it represents. As discussed earlier, the rightmost digit of an integer is assigned position zero. Bit X in position I of a binary number contributes $X(2^I)$ to its total value. A field of four bits $WXYZ$ contributes $(8W + 4X + 2Y + Z)$ (2^I) if bit Z is in position I. Starting at the least significant end, this I value begins at 0 and increments by 4 for every new group of four bits. Since 2^I can be expressed as $(2^4)^{I/4}$, which is 16^K (with $K = I/4$), each four-bit field contributes $(8W + 4X + 2Y + Z)$ (16^K) to the total value. Note that now K starts at 0 and increments by 1 for every new field. Using the binary-hex equivalents shown in Table 1.2, we may rewrite this contribution as $H(16^K)$,

Table 1.2 The Hex Digits and Their
Corresponding 4-bit Codes.

Bit String	Equivalent Hex Digit
0000	0
0001	1
0010	2
0011	3
0100	4
0101	5
0110	6
0111	7
1000	8
1001	9
1010	A
1011	B
1100	C
1101	D
1110	E
1111	F

where H is the substituted hex digit. Thus, the amount contributed by a set of four bits is *equal* to that contributed by its corresponding hex digit. Hence, the numbers are equal. Similar arguments may be applied in other "conversion-by-inspection" cases in which the base of one number system is a power of that of another. For example, one can convert between octal and binary codes by inspection. In this case, each octal digit represents a field of *three* bits.

From the programmer's point of view, the elementary data unit processed by a computer is the *character*. Characters are the symbols found on typical keyboards. A file of data contains a sequence of *records* each of which consists of a sequence of characters. A computer program contains a sequence of *statements* each of which consists of a string of characters. Standard binary codes exist for representing the most prevalent characters. The most common of these codes is the ASCII (American Standard Code for Information Interchange) code. It represents each character with a 7-bit code, giving 2^7 or 128 combinations. Since most computers process codes whose lengths are multiples of 8 bits, each character is usually represented by a hex pair *MN*. The eighth bit (the upper bit—in position 7) may have any suitable use. It may be a constant (for example, 0) merely to permit convenient processing. It may be used in some future expansion of the code to double the size of the standard character set to 256 symbols. It is currently often used as a "check bit," to permit detection of intermittent errors when character codes are transmitted over error-prone paths. The most common check bit is the *parity* bit. It has one value when the number of 1's in the code to which it is attached is *odd*, and the opposite value when this number is *even*. A receiving device has a high degree of assurance that a received character code is correct if the parity bit accompanying it checks out properly.

Table 1.3 shows 96 of the 128 ASCII characters. With the exception of the DELete character, all of those shown are the *printable* characters. The other 32 (those, not shown, for which $M = 0$ or 1), are called *control* characters. A printer responds to a control character not by printing it but by performing some special control function, such as "carriage return" or "line feed." Note that a SPace may be considered a "printable" character (even though it delivers very little ink to the paper!).

Table 1.3   ASCII TABLE (M = Upper Hex Digit; N = Lower Hex Digit).

$N\backslash M$	2	3	4	5	6	7
0	SP	0	@	P	`	p
1	!	1	A	Q	a	q
2	"	2	B	R	b	r
3	#	3	C	S	c	s
4	$	4	D	T	d	t
5	%	5	E	U	e	u
6	&	6	F	V	f	v
7	'	7	G	W	g	w
8	(	8	H	X	h	x
9	)	9	I	Y	i	y
A	*	:	J	Z	j	z
B	+	;	K	[	k	{
C	,	<	L	\	l	|
D	–	=	M	]	m	}
E	.	>	N	∧	n	~
F	/	?	O	__	o	DEL

We may now envision a (variable-length) line of characters (a record in a data file or a statement in a program) as it is encoded internally in a computer. It consists of a string of hex digit pairs. A hex pair is also known as a "byte." It is eight bits long. Each byte is selected from Table 1.3. For example, the character string "IN", which might be extracted from a program statement or from a data record, is stored internally as the hex string 494E, which is actually the 16-bit binary code 0100100101001110.

1.2 SIGNALS AND PORTS

A computer consists of a network of interconnected electronic devices. Each device is itself constructed as a network of less complicated elements. In other words, computer components are organized in a *hierarchy*. We explain the operation of any device in the hierarchy by examining how its lower-level constituents are interconnected.

The physical (as well as the functional) properties of computer components vary over a wide range. Every computer device has input and output "terminals," which receive and send electrical signals. These terminals appear physically in a wide variety of forms, which include microscopic conducting pads on a tiny semiconductor chip, metal pins emanating from a small integrated circuit (IC) package, metal sleeves inside a connector, and flat, edge conductors on a printed-circuit board.

Terminals are interconnected using wires, which carry the signals. Wires are the paths over which signals propagate. Like terminals, they have a wide variety of physical realizations. In addition to their conventional form, wires are found as microscopic metallization patterns on an IC chip, flat conducting paths on a printed-circuit board surface, and parallel metal filaments within a multiwire cable.

An output terminal is the *source* of an electronic signal. A signal that appears on a wire (coming from an output terminal connected to it) propagates instantaneously over all connected paths to one or more input terminals, each of which *simultaneously* receives the same signal. (A signal actually propagates with the speed of light.) Thus, an output terminal generates a signal that instantaneously propagates to all of the input terminals to which it is connected. The signal has one source and many *destinations*.

The waveform in Fig. 1.1 shows the behavior of a typical computer signal as measured over some time interval. At any given instant the signal may have only one of *two* possible levels or values. One signal level represents a binary "1". The other signal level represents a binary "0". The signal is termed "digital" because it may have only *discrete* values. At any instant, it denotes a specific binary digit or bit.

We have arbitrarily assigned a 1 to the high signal level and a 0 to the low signal level. We could have adopted, just as easily, the opposite assign-

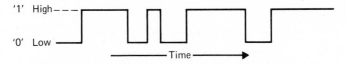

Figure 1.1 Typical digital signal waveform.

ment. In a family of compatible digital elements, all outputs are designed to generate, and all inputs designed to receive, signals which may only assume the same standard high and low levels. Thus, any input terminal may be connected to any output terminal.

The signal shown in Fig. 1.1 is considered *valid* when it has a well-defined 1 or 0 value. It is undefined or ambiguous only during the extremely short instant while it is making a transition between these levels. Ideally, this transition takes zero time to occur. A 0-to-1 transition is called a positive signal *edge*. Its actual transition time is called its "rise" time. Similarly, a 1-to-0 transition is a negative edge, and its very short duration is called its "fall" time.

A typical computer component has several input terminals that receive signals representing bits. It performs some function in response to these inputs. The definition of this function includes a description of how its output signals respond. We define the *interface* of a device by naming all of its input and output terminals and explaining the expected behavior of their corresponding signals.

Two signal waveforms that deserve special attention are shown in Fig. 1.2. Since one is the inverse of the other, they are called "complementary." Each signal is normally in a "quiescent" or "dormant" or "idle" state. For a relatively short time, it is "activated" or "asserted." It is called a *pulse*. Its initial transition is called its "leading" edge. Its final transition is called its "trailing" edge. The time period between these edges is called its *duration* or *pulse width*. Note that *either* signal polarity may represent assertion. A positive pulse has a positive leading edge. A negative pulse has a negative leading edge.

A pulse is commonly used within a digital system to initiate a specific operation or event. In particular, it may be used to cause a device to *sample* (i.e., look at, pay attention to, process) some *other* signals. At the instant when

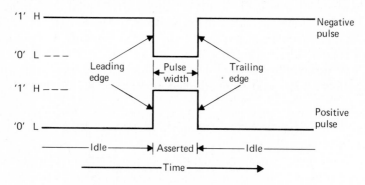

Figure 1.2   Positive and negative pulses.

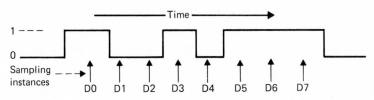

Figure 1.3 Example of serial bit string.

a signal is sampled or "strobed," it must have a well-defined 1 or 0 value; that is, it must be *valid*. Many signals within a computer are normally *ignored* by the components that process them—except for the short instances when they are sampled. The sampling instant is a narrow "slot" in time during which a signal's value is measured.

The sampling concept permits us to understand how a bit string or code is represented by one or more signals. A single, simultaneous sample of the values of N signals on N different wires defines a *parallel* bit string. Most computers process codes that propagate from one point to another in parallel. A single signal on one wire may also be used to represent an N-bit code if it is sampled N successive times. In this case, the signal represents a *serial* bit string. Typically, the sampling instants are equally spaced in time. For example, the signal shown in Fig. 1.3 represents the hex code E9 (11101001) if it is sampled at the instances shown, assuming that the least significant bit appears first.

Intermediate serial–parallel procedures may also be adopted. N successive parallel samples of M signals define a code of length N × M bits. For example, using the indicated sampling instances, the signals in Fig. 1.4 represent the hex code 594E. In this case, each sample defines a 4-bit parallel hex digit.

Note that a serial computer device takes N time intervals to process an N-bit code. A parallel device requires only one time interval but (as we will soon see) uses N times the "hardware" of the serial device. This well-known time-versus-hardware tradeoff is typical of every digital design problem. Unless otherwise indicated, we will assume that bit strings propagate *in parallel* from one point in a machine to another.

Every digital system includes two special output terminals whose signals always remain *constant*, one at the 1 level, the other at the 0 level. As we proceed, we will see many uses for these never-changing reference signals. (Their waveforms aren't terribly interesting, being simply horizontal lines extending indefinitely.) Typically, one of these terminals is called the electrical "ground" of the system, while the other is derived from the system's electrical power source. In this regard, we should emphasize that it is *implicit* (that is, while it is not shown explicitly in many logic diagrams, it should always

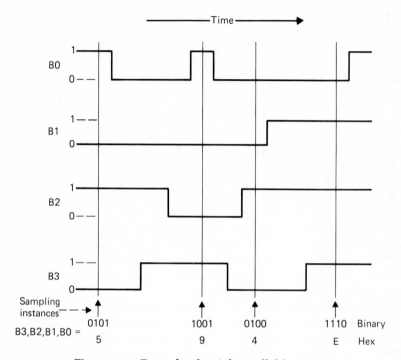

Figure 1.4 Example of serial–parallel bit string.

be automatically assumed) that every device operates only if it is connected to the system's electrical power source. Magnetic devices are the notable exception to the rule that every component must be "plugged in" if it is to work properly.

A *port* is a collection of terminals. Its *width* is the number of terminals in it. For example, an output port of width N is a set of N output terminals. It is the source of a parallel-bit string of length N. Similarly, an input port is the *destination* of a parallel-bit string. A *bus* of width N is a collection (a "bundle") of N parallel wires. It is a "track" over which a code (in the form of a set of parallel signals) propagates. A bus connects an output port to one or more input ports. All of these ports and the bus normally have the same width.

A wire is represented on a logic diagram by a line usually labeled with the name of the signal carried on the wire. The name is also the label for the output terminal that generates the signal. The expression "A = 1" means: "The signal named 'A' has a value 1" (i.e., it has a high level). The wires represented on a drawing by two intersecting lines are assumed *not* connected unless a bold dot appears at their intersection.

A bus is represented on a diagram by a (possibly bold or wide) line labeled with the number of parallel wires in it. It is also usually labeled with the name of the bit string carried on the bus. This name also labels the output port that is the source of the code. Each of the signals on a bus has its own subscript. We will use the notation $A[k : j]$ to name a parallel-bit string containing the individual signals

$$Ak, A(k - 1), \ldots, Aj.$$

Thus, a bundle of signals, all sharing the same name but having different indices, may be represented by a compact notation in which the subscript *range* is indicated within a pair of brackets. For example, DATA[3 : 0] stands for the set of bits DATA3, DATA2, DATA1, and DATA0. (The colon inside the brackets stands for the word "to.") When the lines representing two equal-width buses have a bold dot (or an equivalent connection indicator) at their intersection on a diagram, we interpret it to mean that *corresponding* wires are connected on a one-to-one basis. Thus, the two diagrams shown in Fig. 1.5 are equivalent.

A normal output terminal is *always* generating a signal—a "1" or a "0" level. If an output terminal is not connected to any inputs, its signal has no effect because it has no path over which to propagate. Except under special conditions, an output terminal may *not* be connected to another output. To see why this is so, suppose two outputs were connected and one was generating a 0 signal level while the other was producing a 1. Clearly, there is a conflict here. Its resolution depends on the detailed electrical characteristics of the devices involved. (This issue is discussed further later on.)

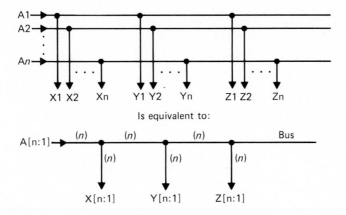

Figure 1.5 Bus connection notation.

Every computer component design is based on the assumption that each of its input terminals will receive a well-defined 1 or 0 signal at all times. Its operation is not predictable if one or more of its input signals is not valid. Thus, an input terminal cannot ordinarily be disconnected. It *must* be connected to some output terminal.

1.3 GATES AND PATHS

The most fundamental microscopic computer elements are called *gates*. Graphic symbols and names for the most elementary gates are given in Fig. 1.6. Each device has one output terminal and one or more input terminals. It obeys a very simple rule in interpreting its input bit pattern and deciding whether the value of its output signal should be 1 or 0.

The output B of the INVERTER is always the inverse of (the "complement" of) its single input A. AND and OR gates each have an arbitrary number of inputs. The output B of an AND gate is 1 only if *all* of its inputs are 1. If any of its inputs is 0, its output is 0. Thus, if a 1 indicates an output "assertion," the AND gate delivers an assertion only when it detects an "all 1's" input code. If we define a code "recognizer" as a device that has one output value when the input code it is designed to detect is *not* present and the opposite output value when that input code *is* present, then the AND gate recognizes the 11 . . . 1 input code. The output B of the OR gate is 1 if *one or more* of its inputs is 1. Its output is 0 only if all of its inputs are 0. Thus, the OR gate recognizes the "all 0's" input code and indicates detection of this code with a *negative* (0) output assertion.

The labels AND and OR stem from the following equivalent definition, in which the name of the gate being defined is substituted for all occurrences

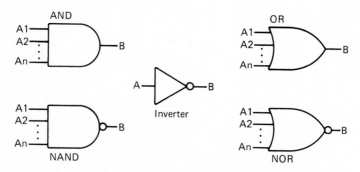

Figure 1.6 Symbols and names of the basic gates.

of the dummy # symbol:

B is 1 if A1 # A2 # ... # An = 1.   B is 0 otherwise.

The words AND and OR (as well as the word NOT) were originally called "logical connectives" in an area of study known as *propositional calculus*. This is the reason why the terms "logic" and "logical" are still used to refer to basic gate networks.

It is important to observe, at the outset, the *duality* present in the definitions given above. AND and OR are dual functions because one does for 1's what the other does for 0's, and vice versa. The fact that the output signal polarity which indicates "assertion" varies from device to device also deserves early emphasis.

A small circle in a gate symbol indicates an internal inversion function. Thus, NAND and NOR gates are AND and OR gates, respectively, with INVERTERs built in at their outputs. The leading "N" in the gate name is short for NOT, an alternative label for the INVERTER. That is, the inversion function may be expressed as B = NOT(A). (Since there are only *two* possible signal values, NOT of *one* value must mean the *other* value.) Using this notation, observe that NAND(An, ... , A1) is really NOT(AND(An, ... , A1)). Similarly, NOR(An, ... , A1) is the same as NOT(OR(An, ... , A1)). Note that AND and NAND are both designed to "identify" the same input code. They differ in the *polarity* of the output signal that indicates recognition. Similarly, OR and NOR detect the same input code but have opposite output assertion polarities. Note, in addition, that NAND and NOR are also "dual" functions.

Table 1.4 contains alternative definitions for the AND, OR, NAND, and NOR gates, assuming that each has only two inputs: A1 and A2. Any gate network whose behavior is described by such a "table of combinations" is called a "combinational" network. The table* lists all possible input codes

Table 1.4 Tables of Combination for the Basic Gates.

Input Signal		Output "B" Value for Function Named:			
A1	A2	AND	OR	NAND	NOR
0	0	0	0	1	1
0	1	0	1	1	0
1	0	0	1	1	0
1	1	1	1	0	0

*Originally called a "truth" table, when used in propositional calculus. The symbols T and F, representing the truth or falsity of propositions, were employed in place of 1 and 0.

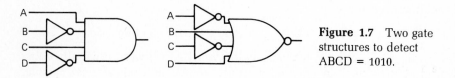

Figure 1.7 Two gate structures to detect ABCD = 1010.

and their corresponding outputs. The table always has 2^N entries, where N is the number of inputs to the network. Thus, the outputs of a combinational circuit, at any point in time, depend only on the input values that exist (i.e., are present) at that instant. This type of circuit is to be distinguished from a "sequential" network, whose outputs, at any point in time, depend not only on the inputs applied at that instant but also on the previous history of the circuit. That is, a sequential network possesses some ability to "remember" aspects of its past behavior. We concentrate first on elementary combinational gate networks.

With proper use of INVERTERs, we may devise a composite "gate" that recognizes any desired input code. For example, Fig. 1.7 shows two structures—both specifically designed to detect the condition ABCD = 1010. Each delivers a 1 output assertion only when this input condition exists. Each of these circuits is an elementary example of an interconnected network of gates designed to accomplish a desired function.

The graphic symbol and table of combinations for an EXCLUSIVE OR gate are given in Fig. 1.8. This device has two inputs and operates as does an OR gate, with the exception that when *both* inputs are 1, the output is 0 (hence the word "exclusive" in its name). A better description of its behavior is as follows: If the inputs are the same, the output is 0. If the inputs are different, the output is 1. From this point of view, the device acts as a *comparator* between its two input bits. One output level indicates that they are equal. The other says that they are unequal.

The EXCLUSIVE OR is fundamentally different from the other devices discussed so far. While it is considered a basic component, its internal structure is more complex than that of any of the other elementary gates. In fact, an EXCLUSIVE OR is normally fabricated as a tiny network of the other elements. Several alternative structures for realizing an EXCLUSIVE OR exist.

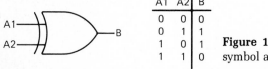

A1	A2	B
0	0	0
0	1	1
1	0	1
1	1	0

Figure 1.8 EXCLUSIVE OR gate symbol and table.

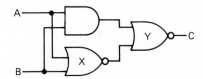

Figure 1.9 One EXCLUSIVE OR realization.

Figure 1.9 shows one of these. NOR gate Y has a 0 output if any (or both) of its inputs is 1. Otherwise, its output is 1. NOR gate X recognizes a 00 input code, while the AND gate recognizes a 11 input code. Each of these gates indicates recognition with a 1 output assertion, which in turn causes C, the output of the network, to be 0. Thus, the circuit is designed to have a 0 output if the two inputs A and B are the same. If this is not the case, the output C is 1. Other equivalent realizations will be discussed later.

Another fundamental element, whose graphic symbol is shown in Fig. 1.10, is the THREE-STATE or TRI-STATE gate. This device is important not because it performs any special logic operation but because it can effect the *connectivity* within a network. When its "control" input C is 1, its "data" input terminal A is effectively *connected* to its output terminal B, so that output signal B is always the same as input signal A. When control input C is 0, the device behaves as if an internal switch were opened—effectively *disconnecting* its output terminal B. In this state, the device ignores input A and its output terminal *carries no signal*. (This is the *only* exception to the rule that every output always generates a signal.) The gate's name originates from the fact that its output terminal B exhibits one of three possible conditions: signal = 0, signal = 1, and NO signal (i.e., "disconnected").

This is our first example of a device whose input terminals are not equivalent or interchangeable. Inputs A and C have distinctly different roles. The gate is termed "enabled" when C = 1 and "disabled" when C = 0, making it clear why C is called a "control" input. The term "data" input for A merely indicates that A may be any bit of any arbitrary data code. Its *transmission* through the gate is controlled by C.

This explains where the term "gate" originated. In one control state, the gate is "open" and the data signal is allowed to pass through it. In the other control state, the gate is "closed" and passage of the data signal is prevented.

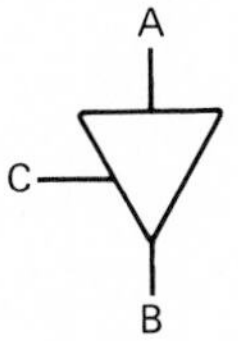

C	State of B
0	Disconnected
1	Signal same as A

Figure 1.10 TRI-STATE gate symbol and definition.

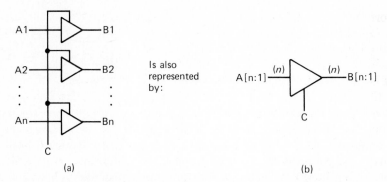

Figure 1.11 Equivalent notations for a bank of TRI-STATE gates.

A *bank* of gates is a collection of N identical gates. It has one output port and one or more input ports, all of width N. For example, a TRI-STATE gate is usually employed as one element in a bank of gates—all having a *common* control signal C. This structure is shown in Fig. 1.11(a). Since it is such a prevalent arrangement, we will use a shorthand notation for it, as shown in Fig. 1.11(b). The single symbol stands for a set of N identical gates, all of whose control inputs are "tied" (connected) together. The labeling on the diagram makes it clear that this must be the case.

TRI-STATE gate banks are normally used in conjunction with a bus, as indicated in Fig. 1.12. All signal sources (from ports X, Y, and Z) are directed to the same bus via individual banks of THREE-STATE gates. The bus connects to one or more destinations (input ports) not shown on the diagram. When one of the gate banks is enabled, its signals appear on the bus and propagate instantaneously to all input ports connected to it. All of the disabled sources are effectively disconnected from the bus. The system operates properly only if *at most one* of the control signals is asserted at a time. Knowing the character of a TRI-STATE gate, you can see why it is permissible, in this case only, to violate the rule that output terminals may not be connected together.

As our studies proceed, we will encounter several devices that incorporate *built-in* TRI-STATE gate banks at their output ports. A TRI-STATE out-

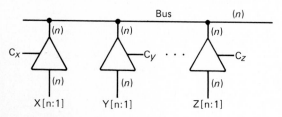

Figure 1.12 TRI-STATE gate banks used with a common bus.

put port has associated with it a special control input terminal, typically labeled OUTPUT ENABLE. (It is common to name a control signal with the type of action it evokes when it is asserted. Examples are control signals with names such as LOAD, COUNT, START, and SHIFT.) The assertion of the OUTPUT ENABLE signal permits the internally generated output code to reach the output terminals. When OUTPUT ENABLE is 0, the output port is effectively disconnected and carries no signals.

Consider the state of the bus in Fig. 1.12 when *all* of the THREE-STATE gates connected to it are disabled. With the bus decoupled from all signal sources, the input ports to which it is connected will not receive well-defined signals. This situation is normally avoided by an electrical arrangement in which special components called "pull-up" or "pull-down" resistors are also connected to the bus, causing each bus wire to carry a well-defined *quiescent* signal level (either high or low) when *no* signal source is "gated" or "enabled" to it. When the signals from an output port are coupled to the bus, they *override* these quiescent levels. Even though these special resistor elements will not be explicitly shown in most of our logic diagrams, their use will always be assumed or implied.[†]

In some component families, a disconnected input terminal may automatically assume a well-defined high or low signal level (usually because an internal pull-up or pull-down resistor is employed). If this is the case, it may be permissible to leave that input disconnected, in which case the input signal "defaults" to the wired constant value. However, this is normally *not* the case, and we will continue to adhere to the rule that input terminals may not be left disconnected. A constant input level is easily achieved by connection to either of the special constant "0" or constant "1" output terminals.

Speaking of wiring rules, consider what would happen if two or more active output terminals *were* connected together, forcing a single composite signal along their common output path. The resulting situation depends on the detailed electrical characteristics of the devices involved. For some component families, if any of the tied output signals is low, so is the combined output signal—even though some of the individual outputs would normally be high. What is formed by the connection is the logical equivalent of an AND of all of the signals, and it is called a *wired-AND*. Similarly, for other component families, if any output is high, so is the composite signal—even though some individual outputs would normally be low. What is formed is the logical equivalent of an OR, and the connection is called a *wired-OR*. Finally, in some cases, it is possible that conflicting output signal tendencies

---

[†]TRI-STATE gates are rarely used in configurations in which their outputs are *not* bussed together. If a single TRI-STATE gate output is the only signal source connected to one or more input terminals, the means by which a valid quiescent signal is guaranteed, when the TRI-STATE gate is disabled, should be explicitly shown. We will have little need to employ such a gate arrangement.

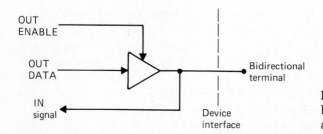

Figure 1.13 A typical bidirectional terminal arrangement.

could cause excessive electrical heating and permanent damage to some of the participating devices. For this reason, even though it may be possible to realize a "free" logic function merely by connecting outputs, we will refrain from doing so and will continue to consider it illegal unless TRI-STATE outputs (at most one of which is enabled) are involved.

Since a bus wire has a quiescent signal level, it is necessary to gate a signal to it only when the *opposite* signal level is desired. Some special output terminals (for example, those called "open-collector" outputs) are designed specifically to be "bussed" together. They have two possible output states. In one, the terminal is effectively disconnected, allowing the bus to assume its quiescent level. In the other, a signal that is the complement of this level is generated. Since these outputs are very similar to TRI-STATE outputs, we will ignore their use in subsequent discussions.

To reduce the number of pins associated with a complex device, some terminals are designed to be *bidirectional*. They have a dual purpose—sometimes acting as inputs and other times serving as outputs. A bidirectional terminal is usually mechanized internally using the arrangement shown in Fig. 1.13. As long as the THREE-STATE gate is not enabled, the terminal acts as an input. When OUT ENABLE is asserted, the OUT DATA signal is permitted to pass and the terminal serves as an output. Typically, a bidirectional terminal is associated with a common bus wire having other signal sources connected to it. Special care must be taken to ensure that these external sources are "aware" of *when* this terminal is acting as an output—so that conflicts of the type discussed earlier do not arise. The subject of bidirectional terminals is somewhat beyond our present scope. Examples of their use will be given later.

1.4 INTUITIVE DESIGN CONCEPTS

Formal techniques for the design of gate networks exist. Some are discussed in subsequent sections of this chapter. They are particularly useful to students, who respond favorably to well-defined established procedures, and to researchers, who use applicable formalisms to extend the theory of computer design. Most logic designers, however, apply intuitive ideas (originally based on the formal ones) to the design process. We discuss some of these here.

Intuitive concepts are particularly effective in checking the *plausibility* of solutions arrived at using formal methods. Some intuitive ideas—for example, the concept of code recognition, the notion of signal assertion, and the principle of duality—have already been discussed. The meaning of duality requires further amplification.

We may describe ANDing and ORing in more general terms, independent of the generic names of specific gates. ANDing involves detecting the simultaneous occurrence (i.e., the coincidence) of *all* input assertions and indicating this event with an output assertion. ORing involves generating an output assertion on the occurrence of *any* input assertion, effectively superimposing or "merging" all input assertions together. Each basic gate (AND, OR, NAND, or NOR) really ANDs together signal activations of one polarity and ORs together signal activations of the opposite polarity. Table 1.5 contains a statement that may be used to define any of the basic gates, once it is filled in with the indicated keywords. It will not take you long to verify its correctness.

Table 1.5   General Description of ANDing and ORing

The —(1)— gate ANDs together —(2)— assertion signals and generates a —(3)— assertion output.

It also ORs together —(4)— assertion signals and delivers a —(5)— assertion output.

1	2	3	4	5
AND	Positive	Positive	Negative	Negative
NAND	Positive	Negative	Negative	Positive
OR	Negative	Negative	Positive	Positive
NOR	Negative	Positive	Positive	Negative

The information contained in Table 1.5 can be expressed more conveniently in symbolic form. Imagine that an INVERTER is placed in the signal path at every input and output terminal of any one of the basic gates. Signal assertions of the polarity that had been ORed are now ANDed, and assertions of the polarity that had been ANDed are now ORed. Furthermore, the polarity of the output assertion is reversed. The composite "gate" that is formed (containing all of the INVERTERS) is *indistinguishable* from the *dual* of the gate we started with. Since an internal inversion function may be represented symbolically by a small circle, and since a *pair* of INVERTERS in the same signal path has no net effect on the signal, we derive the alter-

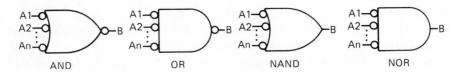

Figure 1.14   Alternate symbols for the basic gates.

nate symbols for the basic gates shown in Fig. 1.14. You should bear in mind that each of these graphic symbols is a perfectly acceptable alternate for the symbol of the same name that was introduced earlier. We will see uses for these alternate symbols later.

To gain added insight into how the basic gates are used, consider each of them from a signal-transmission point of view—as was done originally when the operation of the TRI-STATE gate was explained. In Fig. 1.15, the IN-VERTER is shown only to establish the notation $\overline{A}$ as representing the inverse of A. All of the other gates are drawn with two inputs. In every case, assume that input A is an arbitrary "data" signal while input C is used as a "control" signal—affecting how A is transmitted to output B. The C input path is intentionally drawn perpendicular to the A path to accentuate this interpretation of the signals. Note that *either* input terminal may act as A, with the other used as C. (Recall that this is not true for the THREE-STATE gate, whose two inputs have separately designated functions.) The statements below describe each gate by specifying how input A is transmitted to output B, for the two control cases: C = 0 and C = 1.

$$\begin{array}{rl}
\text{AND: If } C = 1, B = A. & \text{If } C = 0, B = 0. \\
\text{NAND: If } C = 1, B = \overline{A}. & \text{If } C = 0, B = 1. \\
\text{OR: If } C = 1, B = 1. & \text{If } C = 0, B = A. \\
\text{NOR: If } C = 1, B = 0. & \text{If } C = 0, B = \overline{A}. \\
\text{EXCLUSIVE OR: If } C = 1, B = \overline{A}. & \text{If } C = 0, B = A.
\end{array}$$

In every case, note that one value of the control signal permits the data signal to pass through the gate—either unmodified or in inverted form. In fact, in

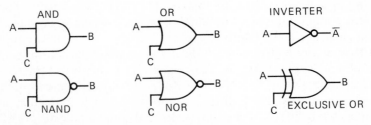

Figure 1.15   Gates from the signal transmission point of view.

the case of the EXCLUSIVE OR gate, *both* modes of transmission are possible, depending on the value of the control signal C. Thus, the EXCLUSIVE OR may be viewed as a "controllable inverter." The control signal determines whether the data signal passes through it unmodified or in complemented form. This interpretation is an alternative to the one (discussed earlier) that views the EXCLUSIVE OR as a comparator between its two input bits.

For the other four basic gates listed above, one of the control-signal values forces the output signal B to a constant level (either 1 or 0) *independent of what the data signal is doing.* Under these conditions, no matter how hard data signal A tries to affect output B, it is prevented from doing so. The gate is termed "disabled" because the data signal is "blocked" or "masked." Observe, however, that an output signal *is present* in this disabled state. (This is to be contrasted with the TRI-STATE gate's disabled state.) Thus, when the gate is "open" or "enabled," the data signal passes through it—possibly inverted in the process. When the gate is "closed," the output value is *held* constant by the control signal and the data signal is ignored.

It was mentioned earlier that a control signal is often named with the operation that its assertion evokes. For example, the C input to the AND gate above (or to the TRI-STATE gate discussed earlier) might have been renamed as PASS or TRANSMIT. Having already introduced the notation in which a bar over a signal name indicates an inversion of that signal, we also adopt the convention that the name of a negative-assertion control signal normally has a bar over it. Thus, if LOAD = 1 indicates assertion, so does $\overline{\text{LOAD}}$ = 0. Using this notation, the control input C to the OR gate above might have been renamed as $\overline{\text{PASS}}$.

A very common logic structure, shown in Fig. 1.16(a), contains a number of AND gates all of whose outputs are ORed together. If a pair of inversion "bubbles" is added in every internal signal path, the internal signals are not altered and the function of the network remains the same. Figure 1.16(b) shows the result—a network containing only NAND gates. Both circuits have identical functions. Using the same technique, the OR-AND cluster shown in Fig. 1.16(c) may be converted into the all-NOR structure of Fig. 1.16(d). These are early examples of the fact that every logic operation has numerous equivalent gate realizations.

To demonstrate the use of intuitive ideas in typical design situations, three sample problems are solved below:

■ **Example 1.1** Design a network having one output C, two arbitrary data-signal inputs A and B, and a control-input signal named SELECT. It should operate as follows: If SELECT = 1, C = A. If SELECT = 0, C = B. In other words, the SELECT control signal decides which of the data signals is "steered" to output C.

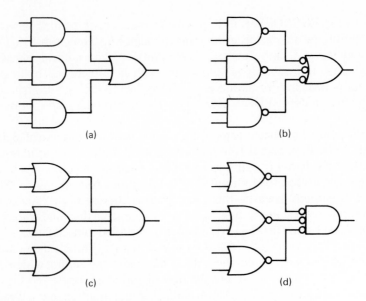

Figure 1.16   AND-OR/OR-AND clusters and their NAND/NOR equivalents.

We need one gate for each data signal to control whether or not it is transmitted. One of these gates should be enabled by SELECT, and the other by $\overline{\text{SELECT}}$. We also need to "merge" the outputs of these gates into the single output C, which will carry the passed signal. Several different gate clusters are possible. Any pair of the basic gates may be used to pass or block the data signals. We will employ a pair of AND gates. The enabled AND will pass its data signal. The disabled AND will ignore its data signal and will carry a constant 0 output. If we OR these two outputs together, we have a working solution, because when one input to an OR is 0, the other input signal is passed. The resulting structure is shown in Fig. 1.17(a). If the com-

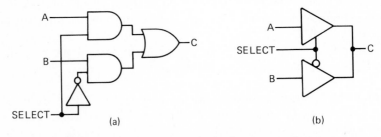

Figure 1.17   Example 1.1 signal-steering solutions.

plement of SELECT were also an available input signal, the INVERTER would not be needed. In many design situations (in particular, those involving FLIP-FLOPS, which are discussed later), signals and their complements are naturally available and some INVERTERs are not needed.

An alternative solution using TRI-STATE gates is shown in Fig. 1.17(b). (The lower gate symbol has a new variation—an inversion circle at its control input point. This notation is used to indicate a control input terminal which expects a negative-assertion signal. It also implies the equivalent of a built-in inverter. You will encounter this convention in many of the diagrams in this book. TRI-STATE gates with both control-input assertion polarities are available. So are inverting TRI-STATE gates, whose symbols include an inversion bubble in the signal transmission path.) This dual THREE-STATE gate structure clearly satisfies the stated requirements. For either polarity of the SELECT signal, one of the gates is enabled while the other is disabled. Note that a mechanism for achieving a quiescent signal at C is not necessary here because we are guaranteed that one of the two gates will always be enabled.   ■

■ **Example 1.2**   Draw the logic diagram of a four-bit comparator having two four-bit parallel input codes A[3 : 0] and B[3 : 0] and one output C. C is 1 only when the input codes are *equal* (i.e., when Ai = Bi, for all i). Otherwise, C = 0.

The EXCLUSIVE OR gate may be used to compare two bits. We need four of them, each comparing an Ai with its corresponding Bi. The two input bit strings are equal when *all* of the EXCLUSIVE ORs have a 0 output. To AND together these negative assertions and deliver a positive output assertion, we need a NOR gate. The resulting solution is shown in Fig. 1.18(a). Note that if the alternate symbol for a NOR gate were used and if the inversion circles were moved to the EXCLUSIVE OR outputs, the equivalent dia-

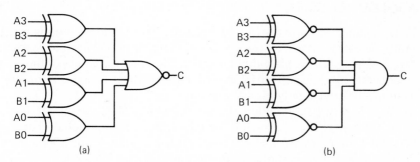

Figure 1.18   Example 1.2 4-bit comparator solutions.

gram in Fig. 1.18(b) results. An EXCLUSIVE NOR gate, whose symbol we have just derived, is also an available device. Its function is clearly defined by its symbol.   ■

■ **Example 1.3**   Recall our discussion (in Section 1.1) of the use of a *parity* check bit to permit detection of certain errors in a transmitted code. The sender of a code must first generate the correct parity bit prior to code transmission. Design an odd-parity generator having a parallel input code A[K : 0] and a single output P which is 1 if N, the number of 1's in the input code, is odd and 0 if N is even. For convenience, assume that K = 3.

If K were 1, an EXCLUSIVE OR gate with inputs A1 and A0 would suffice as a solution. For higher values of K, every time a 1 is encountered in the field A[K : 2], the parity bit which *would have been* generated should be reversed. This calls for use of the EXCLUSIVE OR as a controllable inverter. We require K − 1 additional EXCLUSIVE OR gates, each having as one input a bit in the field A[K : 2] and as a second input the parity bit from all *lower* bits in the input code. The result, for K = 3, is shown in Fig. 1.19. Note that this structure, like that for the comparator in EXAMPLE 1.2, is an *iterative* one. The same construction rule can be extended for any value of K. Devices containing repeated gate patterns are common in all aspects of computer design.   ■

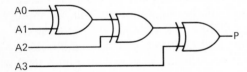

Figure 1.19   Example 1.3 odd-parity generator solution for A[3 : 0].

1.5 BOOLEAN ALGEBRA

A digital signal represents a binary *variable*. The name of the signal (for example, X) is the name of the variable. Here X is a "discrete" variable having only *two* permissible values: 0 and 1. The level (or value) of the signal represents the value of the variable. The mathematical formalism known as Boolean algebra treats only binary variables.

A variable may be a *function* of other variables. Thus, we may write X = $f(Y,Z)$ for example. The expression for the function **f** may include constants (only 0 and 1 are defined), variable names (for example, Y and Z), and *operators*—symbols that represent operations. An operation generates a resulting value from one or more argument values. Given the values of all of its variables, an expression may be *evaluated* by using these values ("plugging" them into the function) and performing the operations indicated. Every Boolean expression evaluates to a quantity 0 or 1. No other values are possible.

A variable in a logical (Boolean) expression may itself be a function of still other variables. Conversely, a subexpression within a function may be treated as an entity by giving it a new variable name.

Only three operations are permissible in logical expressions. A bar over a variable yields a value that is the *inverse* of that of the variable. Thus, if $X = 0$, $\overline{X} = 1$ and if $X = 1$, $\overline{X} = 0$. The other two operations are called "logical sum" (represented by the $+$ symbol) and "logical product" (represented by the $\cdot$ symbol, or implied by the adjacency of two arguments). While some similarities to conventional addition and multiplication are detectable in the definitions of these operations, it is essential that you recognize, at the outset, that *no* conventional arithmetic implications exist. (To stress this fact, some treatments of Boolean algebra use unique symbols for these operators. However, those specified above are the generally accepted standards.)

The symbol $+$ represents the logical OR operation. That is, $\mathbf{f} + \mathbf{g} = 1$ if either or both of the expressions $\mathbf{f}$ or $\mathbf{g}$ has a value 1; $\mathbf{f} + \mathbf{g} = 0$ only if $\mathbf{f} = \mathbf{g} = 0$. (You can see similarities to conventional addition—which you should immediately forget. You need to be comfortable with the fact that $1 + 1 = 1$.) The expression $\mathbf{fg}$ implies a logical AND operation on the values of expressions $\mathbf{f}$ and $\mathbf{g}$. That is, $\mathbf{fg} = 1$ only if $\mathbf{f} = \mathbf{g} = 1$. If either (or both) $\mathbf{f}$ or $\mathbf{g}$ has a value 0, then $\mathbf{fg} = 0$. $\mathbf{f}$ and $\mathbf{g}$ may be constants, single variables, or more complex expressions. In the latter case, pairs of parentheses or brackets may be used to delimit expressions whose values are to be ANDed. Since $\mathbf{f}$ and $\mathbf{g}$ may *themselves* be logical sums or products, we may extend the above definitions, obtaining the following:

$A1 + A2 + \cdots + An = 1$ if *any* $Ai = 1$. It is 0 only if *all* $Ai = 0$.
$A1A2 \cdots An = 1$ only if *all* $Ai = 1$. It is 0 if *any* $Ai = 0$.

A Boolean function is "plotted" by listing all possible combinations of values of its variables and, for each of these, specifying the function's value. Such a list is called a *table of combinations*. For example, Table 1.6 gives the table of combinations for the function $\mathbf{f} = x + y\overline{z}$. The table of combinations for a function of N variables always has 2^N entries.

Two Boolean expressions are EQUIVALENT or EQUAL if they both evaluate to the same quantity for all possible substitutions of their independent variable values. That is, they are equivalent if they have the same table of combinations. For example, the function $\mathbf{g} = x(y + z) + \overline{z}(x + y)$ is equivalent to the function $\mathbf{f} = x + y\overline{z}$ because both have the table of combinations shown in Table 1.6. (Please verify this fact.)

Table 1.6   Table of Combinations
for the Function $\mathbf{f} = x + y\bar{z}$

x	y	z	f
0	0	0	0
0	0	1	0
0	1	0	1
0	1	1	0
1	0	0	1
1	0	1	1
1	1	0	1
1	1	1	1

Every Boolean expression may be realized by a gate network, which mechanizes its function in hardware. For example, Fig. 1.20 contains the diagrams of two networks which implement, respectively, the example functions **f** and **g** given above. Since the two functions are equivalent, the two networks have the same external electrical behavior. Any other table of combinations similarly has many different equivalent physical realizations. In Fig. 1.20, network (a) is usually preferable to network (b) because it is simpler, more reliable, and less expensive. Procedures for finding a simplest gate network, for a specified logic function, come under the heading of "minimization."

The example above demonstrates that, in addition to its interest as an abstract mathematical entity, a Boolean function is a shorthand representation for a logic diagram of a real gate network. Given a Boolean expression, we can immediately draw a logic diagram that mechanizes it. Conversely, given a combinational logic diagram, we can trace through its various signal paths to define a logical expression for each of its output signals. Each such expression is convertible into an equivalent table of combinations, which is a detailed analysis of how the output signal in question will behave.

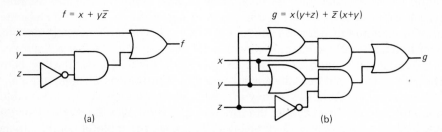

Figure 1.20   Logic diagrams for two sample Boolean functions.

In many analysis situations, constructing the table of combinations for a variable (after first writing down its Boolean function) may not be necessary. A word description of the function (from which a table could be generated) is often either preferable or adequate. For example, given the diagram in Fig. 1.17, we can specify a rule in one or two sentences that clearly explains the circuit's function. This rule was originally supplied in the presentation of Example 1.1. However, to demonstrate how a Boolean function and its equivalent table of combinations can be generated from the logic diagram of a circuit (using the example in Fig. 1.17), Table 1.7 is provided.

Table 1.7 Boolean Function and Table of Combinations Derived from the Logic Diagram in Fig. 1.17

SELECT	A	B	$C = SELECT \cdot A + \overline{SELECT} \cdot B$
0	0	0	0
0	0	1	1
0	1	0	0
0	1	1	1
1	0	0	0
1	0	1	0
1	1	0	1
1	1	1	1

The problem of synthesizing a gate network to meet a specific requirement (possibly provided in the form of a table of combinations) is interesting because it has a large number of potential solutions, and the use of a "minimization" procedure may be necessary. In Section 1.4, we approached the design problem intuitively, assuming that the solutions developed were reasonably efficient. Let us now consider such synthesis problems from a more formal point of view.

One method of designing a simplest gate network, to meet requirements specified in a table of combinations, is to devise any Boolean function that will work, and then to use known algebraic relationships (the theorems of Boolean algebra) to simplify this expression to its most concise form.

Finding any function that meets the requirements is not difficult. Suppose we use one hypothetical gate "recognizer" for each of the table's input combinations that requires a specific output polarity (for example, 1). Each of these gates is tailored to have an output assertion (for example, 1) only for *one* input code. If we OR together the output assertions of all of these gates, using one *additional* gate, we develop a circuit which, though not necessarily the simplest, will work. We can associate an algebraic *term* with each of the hypothetical code recognizers. For example, the logical product term $w\bar{x}yz$ (implying an AND gate with inputs w, $\bar{x}$, y, and z) has a value 1 only when $wxyz = 1011$. The term recognizes only this code. It has a value 0 for all other input codes. From a dual point of view, the sum term $w + \bar{x} + \bar{y} + z$ has a value 0 only when the input combination $wxyz = 0110$ arises. Thus, we may form a logical *sum of product terms*, each of which is designed to recognize (have a value 1 for) a specific input combination for which the table of combinations requires a 1. Similarly, we may form an appropriate *product of sum terms*, each of which is designed to detect (have a value 0 for) a specific input combination for which the table of combinations requires a 0. Each of these specially tailored expressions is called a "canonical" form. As an example, consider the table of combinations in Table 1.6 (ignoring the fact that we have already discussed some functions that implement it). It can be mechanized by the following canonical sum-of-products function:

$$\mathbf{f} = \bar{x}y\bar{z} + x\bar{y}\bar{z} + x\bar{y}z + xy\bar{z} + xyz$$

Similarly, its canonical product-of-sums function is:

$$\mathbf{f} = (x + y + z)(x + y + \bar{z})(x + \bar{y} + \bar{z})$$

Both of these functions are guaranteed to be equivalent because they were derived from the same table of combinations.

Neither of the functions specified above faintly resembles $\mathbf{f} = x + y\bar{z}$. Yet we know that this last function also realizes the table given. To derive it, we must use established algebraic relationships to simplify the canonical forms. We study these now.

Table 1.8 contains a list of some of the key theorems of Boolean algebra. Table 1.9(a) contains a sample proof of Theorem 9(a) to demonstrate the classical method in which each proof utilizes previously proved theorems. Note, however, that, since all of the variables have only *two* permissible values, an alternative proof procedure may be adopted in which the relationship under consideration is tested for all possible combinations of values of the variables involved. For example, Table 1.9(b) proves Theorem 13(a) by this method. This theorem is an elementary algebraic version of the duality principle, discussed earlier from the intuitive point of view. In words, it states that the complement of a product is the same as the sum of the complements. Its companion Theorem 13(b) states that the complement of a sum is equal to the product of the complements. Theorem 13(a) proves the equivalence of the two alternative graphic symbols for a NAND gate. Similarly, Theorem 13(b) proves the equivalence of the two graphic symbols for a NOR gate. Both of the Theorems 13(a) and 13(b) are known as De Morgan's Laws.

Table 1.8 The Key Theorems of Boolean Algebra.

1a $XY = YX$	1b $X + Y = Y + X$
2a $(XY)Z = X(YZ) = XYZ$	2b $(X + Y) + Z = X + (Y + Z) = X + Y + Z$
3a $XY + XZ = X(Y + Z)$	3b $(X + Y)(X + Z) = X + YZ$
4a $0 \cdot X = 0$	4b $1 + X = 1$
5a $1 \cdot X = X$	5b $0 + X = X$
6a $X \cdot X = X$	6b $X + X = X$
7a $X \cdot \overline{X} = 0$	7b $X + \overline{X} = 1$
8a $XY + X\overline{Y} = X$	8b $(X + Y)(X + \overline{Y}) = X$
9a $X + XY = X$	9b $X(X + Y) = X$
10a $X + \overline{X}Y = X + Y$	10b $X(\overline{X} + Y) = XY$
11a $XY + \overline{X}Z + YZ = XY + \overline{X}Z$	11b $(X + Y)(\overline{X} + Z)(Y + Z) = (X + Y)(\overline{X} + Z)$
12a $XY + \overline{X}Z = (X + Z)(\overline{X} + Y)$	12b $(X + Y)(\overline{X} + Z) = XZ + \overline{X}Y$
13a $\overline{XY} = \overline{X} + \overline{Y}$	13b $\overline{(X + Y)} = \overline{X} \cdot \overline{Y}$

$$14 \ \overline{f}(X, Y, \ldots, Z, +, \cdot) = f(\overline{X}, \overline{Y}, \ldots, \overline{Z}, \cdot, +)$$

Table 1.9 Sample Boolean Algebra Proofs.

(a) Using the classical method to prove Theorem 9(a)

$X + XY$	Given.
$X \cdot 1 + XY$	Substituting for first X using Theorem 5a.
$X(1 + Y)$	"Factoring" X out using Theorem 3a.
$X \cdot 1$	Theorem 4b.
X	Theorem 5a.

(b) Testing Relation 13(a) for all possible variable values

X	Y	XY	$\overline{XY}$	$\overline{X}$	$\overline{Y}$	$\overline{X} + \overline{Y}$
0	0	0	1	1	1	1
0	1	0	1	1	0	1
1	0	0	1	0	1	1
1	1	1	0	0	0	0

A generalization of De Morgan's Laws is indicated in Table 1.8 as Theorem 14. Recall that the "·" symbol explicitly represents the logical multiplication (i.e., the AND) operator. In words, Theorem 14 states that the complement of any arbitrary function may be written down, by inspection, by interchanging all + and · operators and complementing their operands. It is derived by dividing the given expression into two subexpressions, separated by an operator, and then applying either of Theorems 13(a) or 13(b), as appropriate. The problem is thus reduced to that of finding the complements of two *inner* expressions, each of which, in turn, is treated individually in the same manner. This process continues until the individual variables are reached. Table 1.10 gives some examples of the application of this theorem. Theorem 14 is particularly important because it permits us to immediately write down a *dual* theorem, once a particular algebraic relationship has been established. This is the reason why the theorems in Table 1.8 appear in two columns. Every (b) theorem is the dual of its corresponding (a) theorem. It is derived by complementing both sides of (a) and then redefining variable names to eliminate bars over variables wherever possible. (That is, if all X's in theorem (a) become $\overline{X}$'s in (b), we may rename all $\overline{X}$'s in (b) as Y's. Since Y stands for any *arbitrary* Boolean variable, just as X did originally, we may retain the same notation by replacing each Y with a *new* X.)

In addition to regarding any theorem in Table 1.8 as a mathematical relationship, it is sometimes useful to consider what it says about the gates that implement it. For example, we have already discussed the gate implications of Theorem 13. Mathematically speaking, Theorems 1 and 2 state that the logical AND and OR operations are *commutative* and *associative*, respectively. From the logic designer's point of view, Theorem 1 states that all of the inputs to any basic gate are equivalent or interchangeable. Theorem 2 states that the AND or OR of several signals can be accomplished in one, or in more than one, *level* of logic. That is, as an alternative to ANDing (or ORing) all input variables in one gate, we may AND (or OR) subsets of these variables in smaller gates and then AND (or OR) *their* results together. Theorem 3 defines the *distributive* property of the AND and OR operations. Note that a variable can not only be "factored out" of a sum-of-products expression. It can *also* be factored out of a product-of-sums expression. Theorems 4 and 5 define the transmission properties of AND and OR gates—originally discussed in Section 1.4. When the "controlling" input has one value, the gate is enabled and the "data" input signal X passes through it. For the other control input value the gate is disabled and the data signal is blocked or masked. Theorems 6 and 7 state that it is normally not very useful or meaningful to logically combine a signal with itself or with its complement. Once the X in Theorems 8 and 9 is "factored out" (using the rules specified in Theorem 3), these relationships merely reiterate what has already been said in Theorems 7 and 4, respectively.

To help you gain familiarity with the concepts of Boolean algebra, the burden of proving most of the theorems in Table 1.8 is left to you as an exercise. Sufficient guidance has been provided in the above discussions and, particularly, in the examples in Table 1.9. We consider now how these theorems may be utilized to simplify logical expressions.

Table 1.10 Examples of the Use of General Duality Theorem 14

Function Given	Derivation of Complement:	Complement by Inspection:
$f = A + B\overline{C}$	$\overline{f} = \overline{A}(\overline{B\overline{C}})$ $= \overline{A}(\overline{B} + C)$	$\overline{f} = \overline{A}(\overline{B} + C)$
$f = (A\overline{B} + C)\overline{D} + E$	$\overline{f} = \overline{[(A\overline{B} + C)\overline{D}]E}$ $= [\overline{(A\overline{B} + C)} + D]\overline{E}$ $= [\overline{(A\overline{B})}\,\overline{C} + D]\overline{E}$ $= [(\overline{A} + B)\overline{C} + D]\overline{E}$	$\overline{f} = [(\overline{A} + B)\overline{C} + D]\overline{E}$
$f = \overline{A}(B\overline{C} + \overline{D}E) + \overline{(F + G)}H$	$\overline{f} = \overline{[\overline{A}(B\overline{C} + \overline{D}E)]\,[\overline{(F + G)}H]}$ $= [A + \overline{(B\overline{C} + \overline{D}E)}]\,[F + G + \overline{H}]$ $= [A + \overline{(B\overline{C})}\,\overline{DE}]\,[F + G + \overline{H}]$ $= [A + (\overline{B} + C)DE]\,[F + G + \overline{H}]$	$\overline{f} = [A + (\overline{B} + C)DE]\,[F + G + \overline{H}]$

The following sequence of steps demonstrates not only how the sample logical expression in (b) of Fig. 1.20 can be reduced to that in (a). It also provides a template for the procedure you should adopt in documenting your solutions to problems at the end of this chapter. Each step contains a new version of the expression being simplified and a comment briefly explaining how it was derived from the previous version (citing the theorem that was used).

$x(y + z) + \bar{z}(x + y)$	Given. See Fig. 1.20(b).
$xy + xz + x\bar{z} + \bar{z}y$	"Multiplying out." Theorem 3(a).
$xy + x + y\bar{z}$	Combining middle two terms. Theorem 8(a).
$x + y\bar{z}$	First term was redundant. Theorem 9(a).

Note that, when convenient, the order of operands was reversed without citing an authority (Theorem 1 specifies that the operators are commutative), even though a strictly rigorous derivation would include such steps. It is quite clear, in this example, that the final result cannot be simplified any further. In other cases, it is not always obvious when an irreducible expression has been reached.

As a second example, we start with the canonical product-of-sums expression derived earlier from the table of combinations in Table 1.6:

$(x + y + z)(x + y + \bar{z})(x + \bar{y} + \bar{z})$	Given.
$x + (y + z)(y + \bar{z})(\bar{y} + \bar{z})$	"Factoring out" the x. Theorem 3(b).
$x + y(\bar{y} + \bar{z})$	Theorem 8(b) on first two parenthesized terms.
$x + y\bar{z}$	Theorem 10(b). Final result.

NAND, NOR, and EXCLUSIVE OR functions are not normally considered basic algebraic operations. Each is a compound function defined by an elementary Boolean expression. The EXCLUSIVE OR, in particular, is such a common function that the special operation symbol "⊕" has been assigned to it. From the canonical sum of products derived from the table in Fig. 1.8, we may write that

$$A \oplus B = \bar{A}B + A\bar{B}.$$

Applying Theorem 12(a) to the right side of this equation, we may also write that

$$A \oplus B = (\bar{A} + \bar{B})(A + B),$$

which is the canonical product of sums derived from the same table. Several possible realizations of the EXCLUSIVE OR function are shown in Fig. 1.21. Parts (a) and (b) are the logic diagrams of the two expressions above. Part (a) includes two gates which detect when the input values are *different*. Part (b)

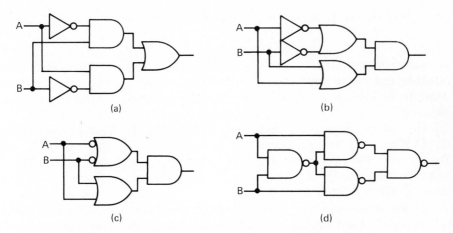

Figure 1.21   Several different EXCLUSIVE OR realizations.

includes two gates which recognize when the input values are the *same*. The output assertions (positive/negative) of these two gates are ORed together to develop the required output. Each realization contains five basic gates. Part (c) is derived from (b) by combining the INVERTERS and their OR into a NAND. By using the other symbol for the NAND, moving its inversion bubble forward, and adding a pair of inversion bubbles in the lower internal path, we convert (c) into the network of Fig. 1.9 (discussed earlier). Finally, using Theorems 10(b) and 13(a) "in reverse," we may replace each INVERTER in (a) with a NAND whose inputs are A and B. Thus, one NAND, whose output terminal is shared by both ANDs, replaces the pair of INVERTERs. After converting the AND-OR cluster to an all-NAND cluster, we derive the four-NAND-gate realization shown in part (d).

1.6 SETS AND MAPS

The canonical sum-of-products form of a Boolean function leads us to view it as the *set* of all input combinations for which it has a value 1. Each term in the expression, representing one of the members of this set, is a logical product of all of the input variables, specifically designed to have a value 1 only for the input code it represents. As a substitute for defining a function with a table of combinations, a shorthand notation is sometimes adopted which supports the notion that a Boolean function is also a set. It lists all input codes requiring a 1 output as a sequence of hexadecimal characters. For example, the table of combinations in Table 1.6 may be written as:

$$\mathbf{f}(x, y, z) = \sum (2, 4, 5, 6, 7)$$

The summation symbol implies a canonical *sum* of product terms—each representing one of the input codes listed. The variables on which the function depends are also listed so that bit positions in the input code can be properly assigned.

Throughout the ensuing discussion, please keep the duality principle in mind. What will be said about "products" and "1's" applies equally to "sums" and "0's". For example, from the canonical product-of-sums viewpoint, the complement of a Boolean function is the set of all input combinations for which it has a value 0.

As we have seen from previous examples, a simplified form for a function generally has fewer terms than its canonical form, and each of these terms generally has fewer variables. Yet, viewed as a set, it still contains the same number of input combinations. Therefore, a simpler algebraic term, with fewer variables in it, must "cover" more input combinations than a term containing many variables. For example, assuming the four input variables A, B, C, and D, the term $\overline{A}BCD$ covers (has a value 1 for, "recognizes") the single code $ABCD = 1011$. Any term containing fewer variables (for example, $\overline{A}BD$, $\overline{B}D$, or D) has a value 1 whenever its *specified* variables have the proper values. While this is true, any variables that are missing from the term may have *any* arbitrary values. The term is *independent* of these variables. Thus, for example, the term $A\overline{B}D$ has a value 1 for the *two* input combinations 1001 and 1011. The missing variable C may take on either value. Similarly, the term $\overline{B}D$ covers the *four* input combinations 0001, 0011, 1001, and 1011, each of which satisfies $BD = 01$. The missing variables, A and C, may take on any of *four* possible combinations of values. Likewise, the term D (missing A, B, and C) covers *eight* input combinations.

Implicit in the above discussion is the use of Theorems 7(b), 8(a), and their extensions. The first two extensions of Theorem 7(b) are as follows:

$$XY + X\overline{Y} + \overline{X}Y + \overline{X}\overline{Y} = 1,$$
$$XYZ + XY\overline{Z} + X\overline{Y}Z + X\overline{Y}\overline{Z} + \overline{X}YZ + \overline{X}Y\overline{Z} + \overline{X}\overline{Y}Z + \overline{X}\overline{Y}\overline{Z} = 1.$$

In other words, a sum of the 2^N different possible product terms, all containing the same N variables, is bound to have a value 1. For any combination of the variable values, one of the terms must have a value 1, causing the entire sum to have a value 1. [Observe that, for example,

$$(X + Y)(X + \overline{Y})(\overline{X} + Y)(\overline{X} + \overline{Y}) = 0$$

for the same reasons.] Similarly, the first extension of Theorem 8(a) is:

$$XYZ + XY\overline{Z} + X\overline{Y}Z + X\overline{Y}\overline{Z} = X.$$

Any of the variations of Theorem 8(a) is proved by factoring out the common variable (X, which may itself be a function of still other variables) and declaring the remaining expression equal to 1 by citing the appropriate version of Theorem 7(b).

Given a specific product term (such as $\overline{B}D$ above), we may find all input combinations that it covers (i.e., that cause it to have a value 1) by using Theorem 8(a) "in reverse." Thus, for example:

$$\overline{B}D \quad \text{implies} \quad \overline{B}D(AC + A\overline{C} + \overline{A}C + \overline{A}\overline{C}).$$

In other words, any term covers 2^M input combinations, where M is the number of variables missing from it. While the explicit variables in it must have their proper values, its missing variables may take on any possible combination.

From the set-theoretic point of view, the logical OR of two terms includes all input combinations covered by *either or both* of them. Note that an input combination may be covered by more than one term. If **f** and **g** are terms, the set **f** + **g** is called the *union* of sets **f** and **g**. A sum of products is thus the union of all of its terms. Similarly, the logical AND of two terms includes all input combinations for which *both* have a value 1. The set **fg** is called the *intersection* of sets **f** and **g**.

The simplest expression for a function contains the fewest terms, each of which contains the fewest variables. This translates into the smallest number of gates, each with the smallest number of inputs. Given the table of combinations for a function and viewing it as a collection of input combinations for which the output signal is required to be 1, we wish to find the simplest product terms that cover the *largest subsets* of the given set. Further, we wish to find the smallest number of these whose union (keeping in mind that the subsets may overlap) covers the required set. The final expression must satisfy every required 1 output without generating a 1 where the table of combinations requires a 0. The Karnaugh map method is one means of finding this expression.

Each map is specifically organized to graphically present the information contained in a table of combinations in a rearranged form, so that subsets of input codes that satisfy Theorem 8 can be easily identified. If N is the number of input variables, the map consists of a rectangular array of 2^N squares or boxes, each corresponding to a unique input code. Every cell has N orthogonally adjacent (perpendicular neighboring) cells. The labeling system is chosen so that the input code associated with a given square differs from that of any of its neighbors in only *one* bit position. To satisfy these geometric constraints as N increases, we must visualize certain adjacencies that are not obvious on a two-dimensional representation. In particular, we must imagine that a map's left and right edges are synonymous, as are its top and bottom

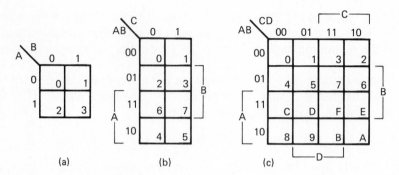

Figure 1.22   Skeleton maps for two through four variables.

edges. When $N = 5$, the map consists of two submaps, one pictured as being positioned directly behind the other. For $N = 6$, a rectangular array of four submaps is used. For $N > 6$, the graphical advantage of a map disappears, and we resort to an equivalent tabular method.

Figure 1.22 contains a set of skeleton maps, for values of N between 2 and 4. The hexadecimal label in the corner of each square is the input code associated with it. (The leftmost input bit in each code is assumed to be A.) You may verify this notation by examining the labels of the map rows and columns. The brackets around the borders of the larger maps are an alternative labeling scheme permitting easy identification of those rows and columns for which a given variable has a value 1. Using the conventions described above, you should be able to identify the N orthogonal neighbors of any cell, particularly one on an edge or in a corner.

We define a function by filling in all of the squares in a map with its pattern of 1's and 0's. When this is done, the map contains information identical to that contained in the table of combinations. For example, Fig. 1.23 provides the same information as that given earlier in Table 1.6.

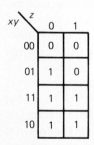

Figure 1.23   Map equivalent of Table 1.6.

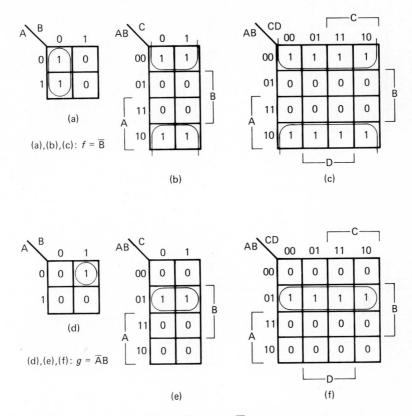

Figure 1.24   Maps for $f = \overline{B}$ and $f = \overline{A}B$ for 2, 3, and 4 variables.

Figures 1.24 and 1.25 contain several examples to show how various product terms are represented on a map. The labeling system was devised so that each appears as an easily identified rectangular *cluster* of exactly 2^M "1"-cells. Each cluster (encircled for emphasis) meets the criterion of one of the versions of Theorem 8(a), discussed earlier. The term corresponding to it is derived by finding those variable values that remain *constant* over it, and "factoring them out." Here M is the number of input variables which go through all combinations of values over the cluster and are therefore eliminated from the term (by the application of Theorem 8). The larger the cluster, the simpler is its corresponding term. Note that some clusters straddle the left–right or top–bottom edges.

To find a simplest expression for a function, we construct its map and then find the *smallest number* of *largest* clusters that completely cover it.

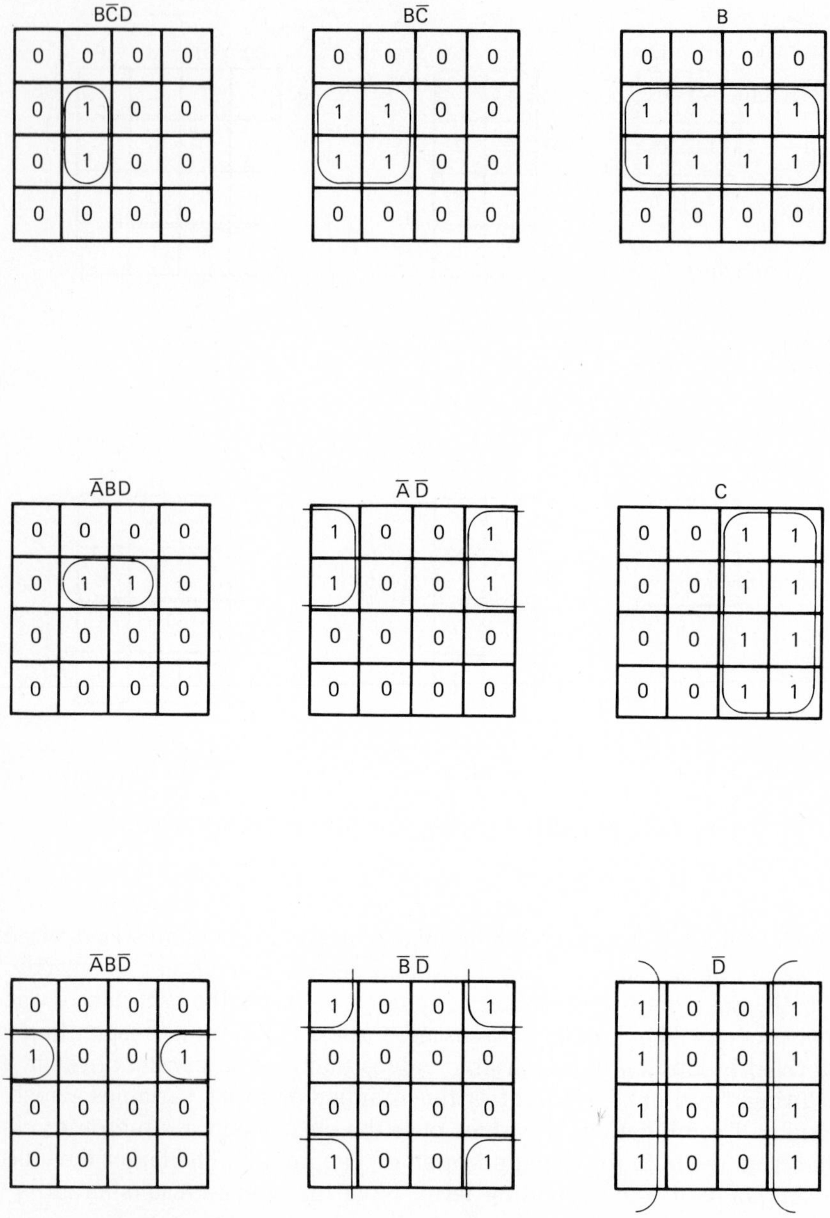

Figure 1.25 Various cluster patterns and their corresponding terms. [Maps are assumed labeled as specified in Fig. 1.22(c).]

Note particularly that clusters may *overlap*, in which case some 1's are covered more than once, and that a grouping is not "largest" if it is completely enclosed in a larger one. The final resulting expression is the *sum* of the terms corresponding to each of the clusters found.

The examples shown in Fig. 1.26 demonstrate the procedure. In (a), the map of Fig. 1.23 is solved to derive the same solution arrived at earlier by algebraic means. The other examples point out several things. First, a given problem may have more than one "simplest" solution. For example, (e) and (f) contain equally acceptable solutions to the same problem. Second, a cluster that is largest may not be needed to cover the required function when all "essential" clusters are taken into account. For example, (d) shows a case in which every member of the central set of four 1's is already covered by an essential grouping. An *essential* cluster is one covering an "isolated" square that cannot be covered in any other way. Generally, in approaching the map of a function, one attempts to find all of the essential groupings *first*.

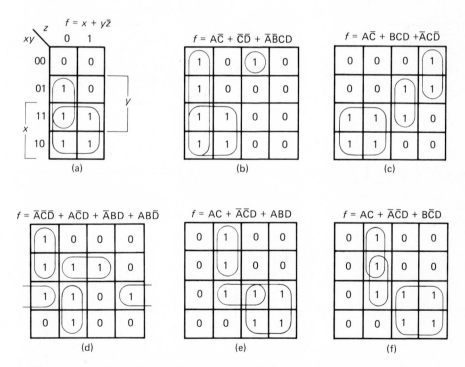

Figure 1.26 Typical sum-of-products map solutions. [Maps (b)–(f) are assumed labeled as specified in Fig. 1.22(c).]

In a similar fashion, a dual approach leading to a simplest product-of-sums realization can be adopted. Figure 1.27 shows example solutions to the same problems dealt with in Fig. 1.26. You are encouraged to be equally familiar with both viewpoints, even though the "1's" approach has been discussed in greater detail here. The strategy for finding 0 clusters is identical to that described for 1's. The procedure for constructing the sum term corresponding to a given cluster should be clear from the examples given.

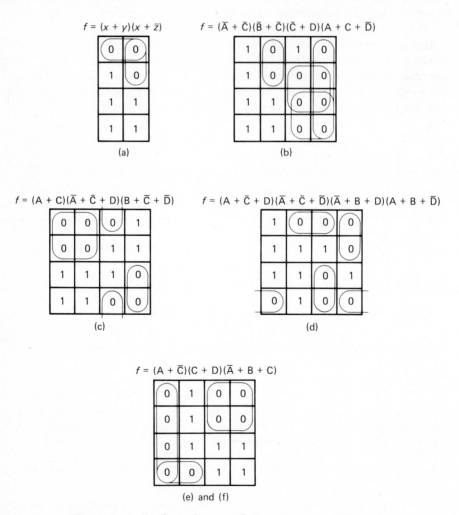

Figure 1.27   Product-of-sums solutions to maps of Fig. 1.26.

Note that the sum-of-products approach covers the function by ensuring that, for each input code requiring a 1 output, *at least one* product term has a value 1, causing the entire function to be 1 (since 1 + anything is 1). Similarly, the product-of-sums approach covers the function by ensuring that, for each input code requiring a 0 output, at least one sum term has a value 0, causing the entire function to be 0 (since 0 · anything is 0). Both approaches normally result in different but equivalent "minimal" solutions. Usually, one chooses that method which permits one to work with the smallest number of (1 or 0) cells.

It is possible for an input code to have an *unspecified* output value associated with it because *either* a 0 *or* a 1 would be acceptable. Situations of this kind will arise in our later discussions. For example, it is possible that a specific input combination may never occur. Under these conditions, we take advantage of the additional design freedom available by including in the map a special "don't care" symbol (for example, "d") in place of the 1 or 0. The "d" may be taken as either a 1 or a 0—as convenient. In particular, a "d" may be included within a map cluster if it helps to increase its size or reduce the number of clusters. An included "d" takes on the same value as that in the other cells in the group. An excluded "d" takes on the opposite value.

We are now in a position to make some comparisons between intuitive design techniques, as introduced earlier in Section 1.4, and more formal methods using algebraic or graphical (map) techniques. Consider the examples at the end of Section 1.4. The intuitive solution to Example 1.1 is shown in Fig. 1.17. From this logic diagram, we developed the Boolean function and table of combinations shown in Table 1.7. Suppose we start out instead with the table of combinations as the initial behavioral description. We may use it to develop the map solution shown in Fig. 1.28(a). Note that the cluster of two squares in the third row (whose product term is AB) is not necessary. The two essential groups, shown encircled, already fully cover the function. The algebraic expression derived from the map is identical to that of the original intuitive solution.

Example 1.2 discussed an eight-input problem not directly tractable using maps. The map for Example 1.3 is drawn in Fig. 1.28(b). It is unique in that no graphical simplification is possible. The resulting algebraic function, which is identical to the canonical form, may be algebraically manipulated, however. It may be factored to produce:

$$\mathbf{f} = (\overline{A3}\,\overline{A2} + A3A2)\,(\overline{A1}A0 + A1\overline{A0}) + (\overline{A3}A2 + A3\overline{A2})\,(\overline{A1}\,\overline{A0} + A1A0),$$

Since the expression $\overline{X}\overline{Y} + XY$ has a value 1 only when X and Y are *equal*, it is the *inverse* of the EXCLUSIVE OR function. That is, it is the EXCLUSIVE NOR function. Using $\oplus$ for EXCLUSIVE OR and $\odot$ for EXCLUSIVE

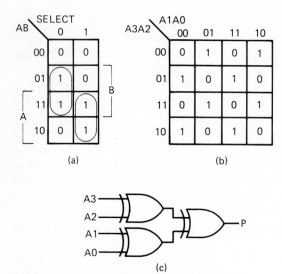

Figure 1.28 Map solutions for Examples 1.1 and 1.3.

NOR, the function above becomes:

$$\mathbf{f} = (A3 \odot A2)\,(A1 \oplus A0) + (A3 \oplus A2)\,(A1 \odot A0),$$

which, knowing that $A \odot B = \overline{A \oplus B}$, may be condensed further to:

$$\mathbf{f} = (A3 \oplus A2) \oplus (A1 \oplus A0),$$

whose logic diagram is shown in Fig. 1.28(c). This solution uses the same gates as that developed intuitively. However, they are structured differently. Both solutions satisfy the original requirements. They are logically equivalent. A different algebraic manipulation of the starting canonical form could have yielded a solution identical to that arrived at earlier. Thus, the intuitive approach—particularly as used by an experienced designer—is usually adequate and often preferable.

PROBLEMS

1.1 Imagine a deck of playing cards containing only the picture cards (jacks, queens, and kings). List all possible three-card sequences that can be drawn from the deck, *disregarding* the suits of the drawn cards. All of your codes will be of length 3 (that is, $N = 3$) and will contain only the symbols J, Q and K (that is, $B = 3$).

1.2 The Morse telegraphy code represents characters by sequences of dots and dashes. List all possible dot–dash ($B = 2$) codes of length 4 ($N = 4$).

1.3   In an opinion survey, respondents are asked to evaluate a list of items by placing each into one of the following categories: excellent, very good, good, fair, bad, and worthless. Define a binary code to be used to encode each response, for computer processing.

1.4   A large clothing store maintains a computer-controlled inventory system. The store has four major departments (men, women, boys, and girls), each stocking 64 styles or types of clothing. Each clothing item comes in eight possible sizes and eight possible colors. Define the format for a minimum-length bit string which describes one item in the inventory.

1.5   A large apartment complex maintains a computer-controlled accounting system. The complex consists of eight buildings, each having 64 floors. Each floor has four corridors, each containing the entrances to eight apartments. Define the format for a minimum-length bit string that identifies one apartment in the complex.

1.6   Write down the octal (base-8) and hexadecimal (base-16) equivalents of the binary number 1011010.

1.7   What is the sum, in base 8, of the octal numbers 265 and 344?

1.8   What is the decimal value of: the binary number 1011011? the octal number 30746? the hexadecimal number 4BD6?

1.9   Write down the hex-character sequence that is the ASCII equivalent of the message "Happy Birthday!". How many bytes does it consume? (The quotes are not part of the character sequence.)

1.10   Several possible wiring patterns for connecting one output terminal to three input terminals are shown in Fig. P1.10. For all practical purposes, would you expect any differences in the behavior of these alternatives? Why?

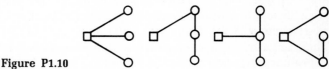

Figure P1.10

1.11   It is desired to transmit a 32-bit code over W wires in T time intervals. Define all possible $W : T$ combinations that may be employed—from purely serial transmission, through all possible composite serial–parallel arrangements, to purely parallel transmission.

1.12   Draw a wiring diagram that realizes an output port C[7 : 0], which is the source of the *constant* hex code A5. Label each of the output terminals with the name of the signal it carries. (Use the constant "1" and "0" signal terminals—which are always available. No gates are needed.)

1.13 Redraw the two signal waveforms A and B, shown in Fig. P1.13, and underneath them draw five waveforms—representing the output signals from two-input AND, NAND, OR, NOR, and EXCLUSIVE OR gates, respectively—assuming that signals A and B are the input signals to each gate.

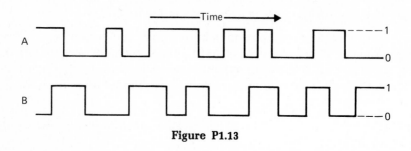

Figure P1.13

1.14 Show that, with proper use of inverters (at the inputs, at the outputs, or possibly at both points), any of the basic gates (AND, NAND, OR, NOR) may be included in a small composite network whose terminal behavior is identical to that of any one of the *other* basic gates.

1.15 Show two ways to convert a two-input NAND gate into an inverter. (Do the same with a two-input NOR.) Intuitively, can you think of any conditions under which one of the two realizations might be preferable to the other?

1.16 Assuming we wish to minimize the number of different gate *types* that are employed, which smallest subsets of the five gate types shown in Fig. 1.6 are sufficient to realize any arbitrary Boolean function? (Such a set is known as a "complete" set. Certainly, AND, OR, and NOT form a complete set. There are others which contain less than three gate types. Use your answers to Problems 1.14 and 1.15 to find them.)

1.17 You are in the process of designing a logic network whose inputs include signals A and B. Signal B comes from a FLIP-FLOP (discussed later), implying that its complement $\bar{B}$ is also accessible for use as an input signal. You need to develop a signal which is the AND of A and B. Unfortunately, AND gates are not available. All of the other basic gates are. Using an inverter and one other gate, which design choices do you have? Which of these do you prefer? Why?

1.18   Use the directions given in Problem 1.13, but employ instead the A and B waveforms shown in Fig. P1.18. Signal A is an arbitrary data signal, while signal B is assumed to be a control signal. Observe how the output signal compares to input signal A.

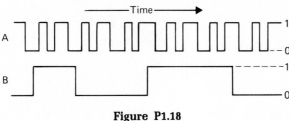

Figure P1.18

1.19   Using any combination of AND, OR, NAND, and NOR, show three alternative three-gate realizations of the function developed in Fig. 1.17(a), assuming that signals SELECT and $\overline{\text{SELECT}}$ are both available. Now assume that the complements of A and B are also available as input signals, and show four more possible three-gate realizations for the same function. (Each has a pair of identical input gates.)

1.20   Prove theorems 10(a) and 11(b), from Table 1.8. Use the classical method which assumes the validity of all lower-numbered theorems.

1.21   Write down a Boolean expression for output signal **f** in the logic diagram in Fig. P1.21.

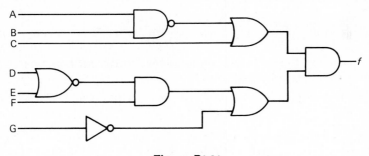

Figure P1.21

1.22   Draw a logic diagram for a network that realizes the Boolean function

$$\mathbf{f} = (ABC + D)\, \overline{EF} + GH\, (\overline{I + J} + K).$$

1.23 Write down a table of combinations for the Boolean function $\mathbf{f} = A\overline{B} + \overline{A}C$.

1.24 Using your knowledge of the elementary theorems of Boolean algebra, write down the simplest equivalents of the following expressions. (See how much progress you can make *without* referring to Table 1.8.)

    a) $\overline{A}B(C + A\overline{B}) + \overline{B}C$;

    b) $\overline{A+B} + \overline{A}\overline{B} + C$;

    c) $AABC + AB\overline{C}$;

    d) $A\overline{B}(C + \overline{D}\overline{E}) + AB\overline{C}D\overline{E}$;

    e) $A(B + \overline{C})D + \overline{B}CD$.

1.25 Draw a single gate that is logically equivalent to the network shown in Fig. P1.25.

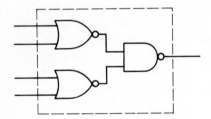

Figure P1.25

1.26 For each of the following, write down an expression for $\bar{\mathbf{f}}$:

    a) $\mathbf{f} = (A\overline{B} + C)\,(\overline{DE} + \overline{F})$;

    b) $\mathbf{f} = A\overline{B} + C\overline{DE} + \overline{F}$;

    c) $\mathbf{f} = (\overline{A}B + C\overline{D})\,(\overline{EF} + \overline{G}(H + \overline{I + J}))$.

1.27 Write down the table of combinations for the network shown in Fig. P1.27. Prove algebraically that it is correct.

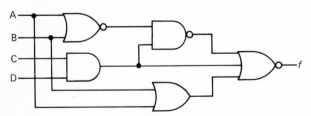

Figure P1.27

1.28 What range of hex values of the code DATA[3 : 0] does the signal Q, in the network shown in Fig. P1.28, detect or distinguish?

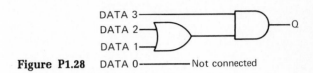

DATA 3 ──────
DATA 2 ──────
DATA 1 ──────   ── Q

Figure P1.28   DATA 0 ──────────── Not connected

1.29 Each of the four-variable maps shown in Fig. P1.29 is assumed labeled as specified in Fig. 1.22(c). It is a map for a function f. In each case, express f as a minimal sum of products and as a minimal product of sums.

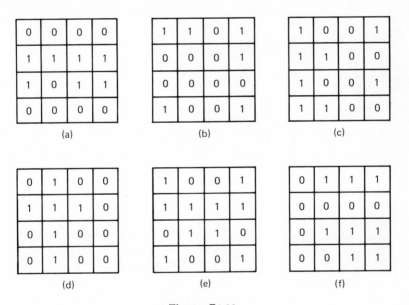

(a)

(b)

(c)

(d)

(e)

(f)

Figure P1.29

2

Data Operations

2.1 ENCODERS, DECODERS, AND CODE CONVERTERS

An electronic keyboard is a very common computer input device. Each of its keys is mechanically coupled to a switch whose electrical output signal is asserted while that key is depressed. The output code generated directly from the keyboard's array of switches is a *one-asserted* code. All of the output signals are quiescent except for, at most, one. (We are ignoring the possibility that two or more keys may be depressed simultaneously. Assume that any special keys, such as SHIFT, are not part of the regular array.) The output signals are called "mutually exclusive" because one assertion precludes any of the others. Note that there are only N different one-asserted codes of length N. The "idle" condition, when no output signals are asserted, is one additional output state.

We wish to transmit the codes for a sequence of key depressions (i.e., for a message) to a computer for storage and later analysis. A typical keyboard contains approximately 55 keys. Clearly, it is inefficient to transmit and store 55 bits per character when six would suffice, since 2^6 (which is 64) bit combinations are possible. (Recall the ASCII character set defined in Table 1.3.)

For this reason, a typical electronic keyboard unit also includes an ENCOD-ER, which converts each key's signal into a compact code uniquely associated with that key.

The process of assigning a code to every possible "object" to be represented is termed "encoding." An ENCODER performs this function electronically. It has an N-bit-wide input port, which takes as input a one-asserted code. Each of the input terminals represents one of the objects to be encoded. It has a K-bit-wide output port, which generates a "built-in" code corresponding to the activated input signal. Every time a specific input is asserted, the same output code appears. Thus, the input code identifies which of the N objects is currently selected, and the output code is the prearranged, internally wired bit string assigned to it. Although the values for N and K are arbitrary, an efficient ENCODER usually has a K value such that 2^K is in the vicinity of N.

An ENCODER is designed using any mechanism that permits directing each input signal only to those output terminals requiring one bit value (e.g., 1) in its assigned code, and not directing it to those output terminals requiring the other bit value (e.g., 0). (Note that, while "directing a signal" implies "wiring," an ENCODER cannot be constructed using wires alone. Recall the discussion in Chapter 1 concerning connected output terminals.) Assuming that a 1 represents assertion, consider, for example, a structure containing K OR gates whose output terminals comprise the K-bit output port. Each gate ORs together only those inputs whose assigned codes have a 1 in its bit position. Since only one input assertion at a time can occur, all OR gate inputs will be 0 except for those connected to the one signal that is currently 1. These gates will deliver a 1 output, while the others will generate a 0, and the proper output code will appear. Observe that the codes assigned to the individual inputs (which represent the "objects" to be encoded) are mechanized in the ENCODER's internal wiring pattern.

An ENCODER is represented two ways in Fig. 2.1. The simplified block diagram in (a) is used once we have all agreed on the detailed definition of the device—on its interface and on its function. Its interface is specified when all input and output signals are enumerated and when any special signal characteristics are explained. Its function is the relationship between its outputs and its inputs. The logic diagram in (b) is an example for $N = 6$ and $K = 3$. The code assigned to each input terminal is indicated along its row. Note that a rearrangement of the connections to the OR gate inputs will alter these assigned codes.

A DECODER performs a function that is the reverse of that of an EN-CODER. It receives a K-bit code, with all 2^K-bit combinations possible, and it outputs a one-asserted code. Normally, it has 2^K output terminals, each corresponding to one of the possible input codes. When a code is applied to the

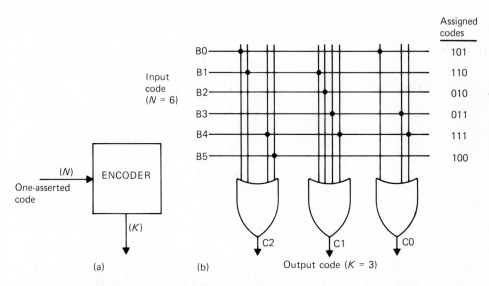

Figure 2.1 Encoder block diagram and sample logic diagram.

input port, the unique output signal associated with it is asserted. Considering the output terminals as numbered, beginning with zero, the input code is the *number* of the output terminal that carries the active signal. Thus, the input code *selects* or *identifies* that output which is asserted. Note that, unlike an ENCODER, a typical DECODER has a well-defined relationship between the width of its input port (K) and the width of its output port (2^K).

Table 2.1 defines the function of a 3-to-8 DECODER (that is, $K = 3$). Note that the asserted output value runs along a *diagonal* of the table. By defini-

Table 2.1 Input-Output Table for a 3-to-8 Decoder

Input Code	Output Code
000	00000001
001	00000010
010	00000100
011	00001000
100	00010000
101	00100000
110	01000000
111	10000000

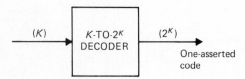

Figure 2.2   Block diagram of typical decoder.

tion, this is a property inherent in every DECODER. Figure 2.2 shows the block diagram of a typical DECODER, which we may proceed to use now that its interface and function have been clearly defined.

As an example of the use of a DECODER, consider the printing of a received message (a serial sequence of encoded characters) by an automatic electric typewriter. Assume that the printer mechanism has one print "hammer" per character. A character is printed when the hammer holding its shaped impression is actuated—causing it to hit the inked ribbon. As discussed earlier, an efficient code uses a minimum number of bits per character. Yet the code required by the array of print hammers is a one-asserted code. A DECODER is used to convert the received code into one that activates only its corresponding print hammer.

There are several approaches to the design of a DECODER. All involve the concept of code recognition and a generalized view of the AND function. A DECODER may be viewed as consisting of 2^K K-bit code recognizers. For example, Fig. 2.3 shows a logic diagram for a 2-to-4 DECODER (that is, $K = 2$). Note that all input signals are immediately inverted so that each input bit is available either directly or in complemented form. A set of 2^K K-input gates is then arranged so that each receives as input a unique combination of the K input variables. That is, each gate implements a unique canonical

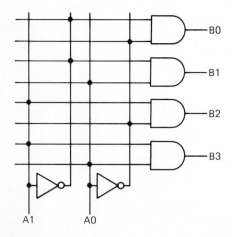

Figure 2.3   2-to-4 decoder logic diagram.

product term, since each of its input terminals is connected either to a direct input variable or to its complement—depending on the code which that gate is designed to recognize. Observe that the numerical index assigned to each output signal is the input code that causes it to be activated.

The complexity, reliability, and cost of a digital device depend not only on the number of gates in it but also on the average number of inputs per gate. (Clearly, the cost of a six-input gate is higher than that of a two-input gate.) Because its internal gate count grows dramatically as K increases, a large DECODER is frequently constructed using smaller internal DECODERs. For example, suppose we derive a DECODER's outputs from a rectangular array of 2^K *two-input* AND gates, as indicated in Fig. 2.4 (for $K = 4$). Each AND gate receives one *row-select* signal and one *column-select* signal. The row- and column-select codes are *themselves* one-asserted codes generated by smaller internal DECODERs. Only the AND gate at the *intersection* of the selected row and the selected column is activated; all of the others are disabled. The K-bit input code has been divided into two (in this case, equal) *fields,* each of which is an input to its own internal DECODER, whose out-

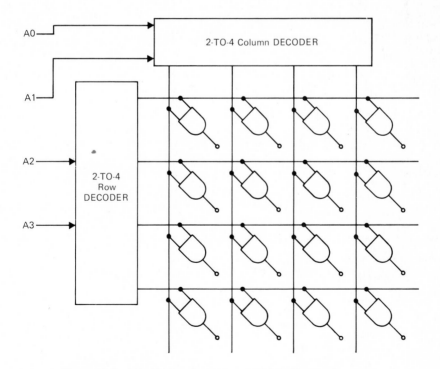

Figure 2.4   4-to-16 decoder using a 4 × 4 output gate array.

puts drive one dimension of the output gate array. In Fig. 2.4, each of the 2-to-4 DECODERs is a duplicate of the structure shown in Fig. 2.3.

Other variations are possible. Several of these utilize another important feature designed into many DECODERs. A DECODER may have an additional input signal, called an ENABLE, whose assertion is required if the device is to operate as described above. If ENABLE = 0, the device is disabled and *all* outputs are forced to be quiescent, no matter what the input code is. Thus, each output signal is *conditional* on the overriding ENABLE signal.

One can easily imagine how any DECODER's design may be modified to include the ENABLE property. Suppose we add one extra input to each output AND gate and tie (connect) all of these added inputs together. This common input is the ENABLE.

As we study other devices, we will encounter numerous examples of the use of a control input signal named ENABLE. Usually, assertion of ENABLE permits a component to function normally. The definition of "disabled" generally depends on the device to which the term is applied. A disabled element usually ignores one or more of its input signals. It may also decouple (via internal TRI-STATE gates) one or more of its output terminals. Since the meaning of "disabled" is not universally defined, you are urged not to use an ENABLE control input to a device unless its function has already been carefully defined.

As another example of the internal design of a DECODER, Fig. 2.5(b) shows the internal network for a 4-to-16 DECODER whose block diagram is

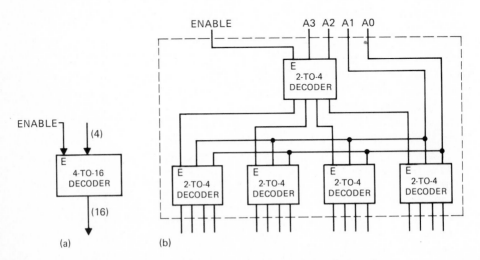

Figure 2.5   4-to-16 decoder using five 2-to-4 sub-decoders.

shown in (a). The device includes an ENABLE input, and it is constructed using five identical 2-to-4 DECODERs, each with its own ENABLE input. The field A[1:0] selects the *same* output terminal in each of the output DE-CODERs. The field A[3:2] selects which of these DECODERs is enabled. Only the enabled DECODER is permitted to have an output assertion. If the overall ENABLE input is 0, the input DECODER is disabled; this in turn disables all of the output DECODERs.

This design approach involves dividing the string of *output* signals into a set of identical fields. The number of bits in each field is a power of two, and so is the number of fields. Each output field is the output port of one internal DECODER. Each of these devices decodes the *same* subset (field) of the input bits. The *remaining* input bits are decoded separately by one additional DECODER whose outputs individually enable the output DECODERs, permitting at most one of them to have an output assertion. Thus, the K input bits are again divided into two fields. This time, one field selects which output DECODER is enabled, while the other selects which of *its* outputs should be asserted.

Note that a sufficiently large DECODER may consist of two or more sub-decoders which *themselves* contain internal DECODER elements. Note also that not all 2^K outputs of a K-input DECODER need be used. For example, a four-bit input code may represent a decimal digit. The most common code of this type is the BCD (Binary Coded Decimal) code in which the bit strings 0000 through 1001 represent the decimal digits 0 through 9 respectively—with the codes 1010 through 1111 unassigned and not used. A DECODER receiving such a code need not have more than the ten appropriate output terminals, since an assertion can never occur at any of the other six. Some economies in design are possible in such "partial" DECODERs.

A CODE CONVERTER has one input port and one output port, both of arbitrary width. For every applied input code, an assigned, wired-in output code is generated. There are no specific restrictions on the input or output values. The device "maps" every input value into an associated output value.

Using this general definition, any combinational circuit (i.e., one described by a table of combinations) may be considered as a CODE CON-VERTER. However, the name is usually reserved for devices having ports of arbitrary width which carry unrestricted code values. For example, consider the problem in which a computer transmits a four-bit Binary-Coded-Decimal digit code to a seven-segment display device for display of that digit. A CODE CONVERTER is required to translate each four-bit code into the corresponding seven-bit pattern for its display, as indicated in Fig. 2.6. Table 2.2 defines the function of this device. Note that six of the 16 possible input codes are unused or unassigned. (As discussed earlier, the BCD code has this property.) Each output bit specifies whether or not its corresponding display

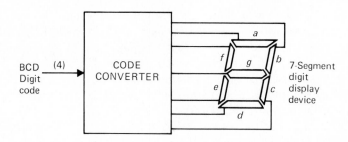

Figure 2.6 Code converter maps BCD digit into its display code.

segment should be illuminated, to define a figure approximating the shape of the input digit. Note also that only ten of the 128 possible output codes are actually used.

CODE CONVERTERs are employed in many other comparable situations—whenever there is a one-to-one correspondence between an input code and an output code, and a device is required to map or translate one into the other. A CODE CONVERTER internally stores a correspondence *table* between its input and output codes. The input code may be considered a number or an "argument," while the output code is some *function* of that argument—i.e., a value associated with it.

An arbitrary CODE CONVERTER normally consists of a DECODER–ENCODER combination, as shown in Fig. 2.7. The K-bit input code is first decoded into a one-asserted code of length 2^K (or, perhaps, less). This code is

Table 2.2 The Function of the
Code Converter in Fig. 2.6

	Input Code	Output Code
		abcdefg
0:	0000	1111110
1:	0001	0110000
2:	0010	1101101
3:	0011	1111001
4:	0100	0110011
5:	0101	1011011
6:	0110	0011111
7:	0111	1110000
8:	1000	1111111
9:	1001	1110011

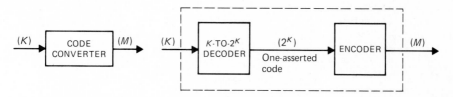

Figure 2.7 Code converter block diagram and typical realization.

then passed into an ENCODER, which assigns a *new* code to the original object. The information stored inside the CODE CONVERTER resides in the wiring pattern of its ENCODER.

2.2 MULTIPLEXERS AND DEMULTIPLEXERS

Codes are transmitted in the form of parallel signals from output ports (called "sources") over interconnecting wires (called "buses") to input ports (called "destinations"). We have already established the fact that a single source may have many destinations, as provided by appropriate wiring. (Recall the bus connection diagram in Fig. 1.5.) Consider now the converse situation, in which a single destination has many possible sources. How are the signals from only one of the potential sources directed to the single destination? How can one select, at electronic speeds, which of the output ports is "connected" to the single input port?

A MULTIPLEXER is a device specifically designed to solve this problem. It has two or more input ports and only one output port. At any instant in time, only *one* of its input ports is effectively "connected to" its output port. We will first explain two alternative approaches to the internal design of a MULTIPLEXER. After doing so, we will define its interface more carefully.

The term "multiplexing" was originally used in electronic communications applications to imply any process whereby two or more signals share the same path. For example, a multiplexing process is used in transmitting numerous telephone voice signals simultaneously over a single, long-distance communications cable. One procedure to permit several signals to share the same path is to divide time into intervals of equal duration. During any one interval, the composite, shared signal is derived from only *one* of the signal sources. It is a "sample" of that signal. If the samples of all of the sources are taken successively at a sufficiently high sampling rate, and if these samples are then merged onto a single composite output path, the individual signals may be reconstructed from the composite, at the receiving end, with negligi-

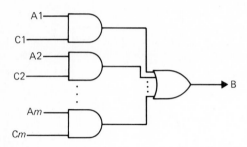

Figure 2.8 AND-OR cluster as a signal steering device.

ble loss in fidelity. The device required to direct any one of the sources to the shared output path is a high-speed, electronic *selection switch* called a MULTIPLEXER. In a computer, each of the signals is restricted to being *digital* in nature (representing, at any instant, either 0 or 1), and each of the paths through the device may carry *several* parallel signals.

Consider the AND-OR cluster shown in Fig. 2.8. Assume that only one of the C signals has a value 1. That is, assume that the code C[m:1] is a *one-asserted* code. The output signal B will be the same as the A input corresponding to the asserted C. (Only one AND gate is enabled. It transmits its A input signal. All of the m inputs to the OR gate will be 0 except for the one carrying the passed A signal.) Thus, any one of the A inputs may be "steered" or directed to the B output by application of the proper one-asserted code to the C input port. (Recall a similar structure in the solution to Example 1.1 in Chapter 1. In that case, m was 2.)

Now consider several such circuits—all identical. Imagine them arranged one behind the other, with corresponding C inputs connected, as indicated in Fig. 2.9. All of the A input terminals form a *matrix* containing k columns and m rows. The A's in a given *row* form a k-bit-wide input port. Suppose we identify the port, consisting of all of the A input terminals in row i, as port Ai. It is also described by the notation Ai[k:1]. There are m such input ports, stacked vertically, and one output port, B[k:1]—all k bits wide. In addition, there is one control input port C[m:1]. The bank of AND gates enabled by the signal Ci permits the signals from input port Ai to pass. If only one Ci is asserted, the code applied to its corresponding Ai input port will appear at output port B. A shorthand notation for Fig. 2.9, originally introduced in Chapter 1, is shown in the upper portion of Fig. 2.10. Each AND gate symbol represents a bank of k AND gates, all sharing a common C control signal. The composite OR gate symbol represents a bank of k m-input OR gates.

To ensure that only *one* of the C control signals is asserted, we derive the C's from the output of a DECODER, as indicated in Fig. 2.10. The input code to the DECODER is the *number* of the A input port that is enabled to the

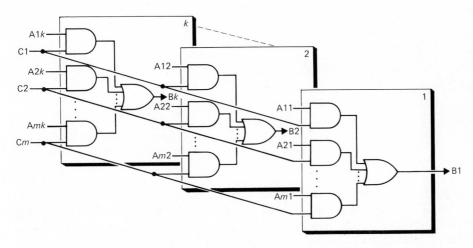

Figure 2.9 A set of identical interconnected AND-OR clusters.

output. If this is a j-bit number, there are 2^j different possible input ports to select from (that is, $m = 2^j$).

This is the most common definition of a MULTIPLEXER: a device with a j-bit input selection control code, 2^j data input ports, and one data output port. All data ports have the same width. The path-select control code defines *which* data input port is effectively connected ("steered") to the output port. All other data input ports are disabled, and their signals are ignored.

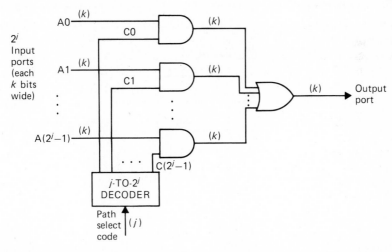

Figure 2.10 Internal network for a $2^j \times k$ multiplexer. [Note: In Fig. 2.9 $m = 2^j$.]

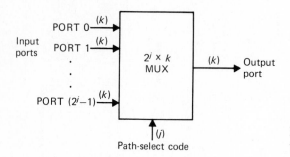

Figure 2.11   Block diagram of the multiplexer of Fig. 2.10.

Figure 2.11 shows the block diagram of such a device. The abbreviation "MUX" is frequently used instead of "MULTIPLEXER." The size of the device depends on the two parameters j and k. The expression "an $M \times N$ MUX" stands for a device with M input ports—all N bits wide. The value of j is implied by the value of M (which is normally a power of two).

While the discussion above describes an AND-OR realization, clearly other implementations, using other gate types or involving negative signal assertions, are also possible. One, in particular, deserves special emphasis. It is shown in Fig. 2.12. As the use of the TRI-STATE gate has grown, this implementation has become preferred. Given the explanation of the AND-OR embodiment, the operation of this structure is clear. For any input path select code, only one TRI-STATE gate bank is enabled—permitting its input port signals to reach the common output bus.

Returning to the communications example that explained how the term "multiplexing" originated, consider the problem of extracting each of the

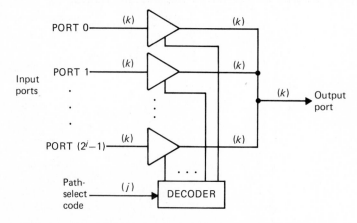

Figure 2.12   Multiplexer designed using TRI-STATE gates.

original signals from the composite. This process is called "demultiplexing." We require another type of electronic selection switch having one input terminal (receiving the shared, composite signal) and as many output terminals as there are signals to reconstruct. Every time the sample for a specific original signal occurs, the switch position should effectively connect the composite signal to its corresponding output terminal. From this viewpoint, a DE-MULTIPLEXER operates as a synchronized signal "distributor," directing each sample in the composite signal to its proper output.

A DECODER having an ENABLE input may be used as a DEMULTI-PLEXER. As explained earlier, the input code to a DECODER selects one of its output terminals. All of the other outputs remain quiescent. The selected output is further conditioned by the ENABLE signal. In fact, the selected output signal will *follow* or *track* all variations in the ENABLE signal. Thus, if an arbitrary data signal is applied to the ENABLE input of a DECODER, the *same* signal will appear at the output terminal selected by the DECOD-ER's input code. Whenever the input code changes, the data input signal is directed to a different output terminal. The input code specifies to *which* output terminal the data signal should be sent.

A general DEMULTIPLEXER block diagram is shown in Fig. 2.13(a). It contains as many DECODERs as there are bits in the parallel transmission path. Note that all of the DECODERs receive the same j-bit path-select code. The device is a true converse of the MULTIPLEXER discussed earlier. It has

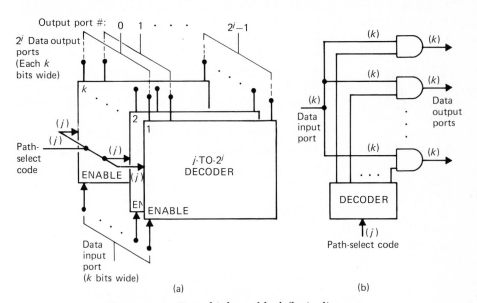

Figure 2.13 Demultiplexer block/logic diagrams.

one data input port (consisting of all of the ENABLE terminals) and 2^j data output ports, all of the same width k. The output port selected by the path-select code is effectively connected to the data input port, so that the data input signals appear there. All of the other output port signals remain quiescent.

A more economical version is given in Fig. 2.13(b). Each possible transmission path contains a bank of gates enabled by one of the outputs from a *single* DECODER. Note that each AND gate bank may be replaced by a bank of THREE-STATE gates.

2.3 INCREMENTERS AND DECREMENTERS

Most of the components that comprise a digital computer transmit and store bit strings intact. They do not modify them in any way. For example, a DE-MULTIPLEXER is fundamentally a path-selecting device. It transmits its data input code intact to one of its output ports.

Any process that generates *new* codes from old ones is termed a "data operation." A device that performs a data operation receives one or more input codes, called *operands* or *arguments*, and generates an output code, called a *result*, which is some logical or arithmetic function of the inputs. The output result is usually different from the input arguments in some way. For example, a CODE CONVERTER performs a data operation. In fact, *any* combinational gate network normally generates new codes from old ones. (The exception is any network concerned strictly with code transmission.)

A *unary* data operation requires only *one* input argument. A *binary* data operation requires *two*. (This use of the term "binary"—meaning "two operands"—should not be confused with its other uses. It is a coincidence that the operands also happen to be represented by "binary" codes.)

Each of the devices to be described here performs a unary data operation. Its design is based on the assumption that the input argument is a positive binary integer. Recall the description of the process of counting in any number system, which was presented in the beginning of Chapter 1, and the previous examples of three- and four-bit binary count sequences. From these, we can develop detailed rules for incrementing and decrementing arbitrary binary numbers.

Whenever a binary digit in any position "advances," it does so by *reversing* its value—whether the counting direction is UP (incrementing) or DOWN (decrementing). While we are counting in *either* direction, the least significant bit always inverts from step to step. During incrementing, a bit in any *other* position advances (is complemented) only if *all* bits to its right were 1.

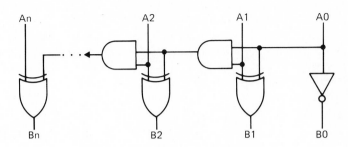

Figure 2.14 Incrementer logic diagram.

Only under these conditions does a carry, generated in the least significant position, propagate all the way up to its position. When decrementing, on the other hand, a bit in any position inverts only when a continuous string of 0's existed to its right, prior to the decrement. Only under these conditions does a "borrow" propagate all the way up to its position. You may verify each of these rules by scanning any of the previously presented binary count sequences, either in the forward (incrementing) or the backward (decrementing) direction. Note the behavior of the individual bits, for either count direction. The least significant bit (in position 0) "toggles" (reverses its value) at every step. The bit in position 1 toggles at every *other* step. That in position 2 toggles at every *fourth* step. And so on. This pattern is characteristic of every binary counting process.

An INCREMENTER mechanizes the "count UP" rules. It has one input port, which receives a binary integer, and one output port, which generates a value one greater than the input value. A common realization is shown in Fig. 2.14. It uses one EXCLUSIVE OR gate per input bit, because a selective inversion operation is implied by the rules specified above. (The exception is in the least significant position, where an INVERTER is used, since this bit always toggles unconditionally.) Note the linked chain of AND gates, starting from the right. The output of any AND is 1 only if all input bits to its right are 1. The iterative structure shown clearly applies to arguments of arbitrary length.

In a dual manner, the design of a DECREMENTER requires detection of a string of input 0's using a chain of OR gates. Since recognition is now indicated by a 0 output, which should cause inversion of the corresponding input bit, an EXCLUSIVE NOR gate is used as the controlled INVERTER, as indicated in Fig. 2.15. The duality between the diagrams in Fig. 2.14 and 2.15 is evident.

Note that each of these realizations has one input value whose corresponding output code is not correct because the permissible *range* of output values has been exceeded. Specifically, applying an all-1's input code to an

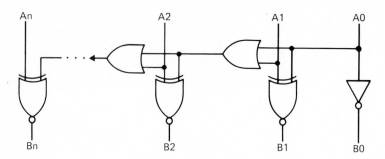

Figure 2.15   Decrementer logic diagram.

INCREMENTER causes an all-0's output code. Similarly, an all-0's input code to a DECREMENTER causes an all-1's output code. As we will see further later, every binary counter exhibits this property: An increment past the maximum possible value "wraps around" to the minimum value, and a decrement past the minimum possible value "wraps around" to the maximum value. Both of these cases indicate *overflow* conditions, because the correct resulting value cannot be represented within the set of output bits available. Neither of the circuits shown is equipped with any provision for detection and indication of this overflow condition. (These features may be added easily, however.) Similar overflow situations will arise in subsequent discussions. In some cases, specific gate structures to detect and indicate an overflow condition will be described.

2.4 ADDERS

All *arithmetic* data operations within a computer utilize one fundamental device—the ADDER—as the central computation element. Consider the addition process in any number system, assuming that there are only two arguments to be added. (You may be guided by your familiarity with the decimal system.) In every digit position, there are two operand digits ("addend" and "augend") and a possible CARRY generated from the adjacent position on the right. These values are used to generate a SUM digit and a possible CARRY to the adjacent position on the left. Note that the value of any CARRY may be considered as either 0 (previously termed the "no-carry" condition) or 1. The following rules apply: The two operand digits and the CARRY IN (coming from the right) are all added. If the result is less than the base of the number system, it is written as the SUM digit, and a CARRY OUT of 0 is generated to the left. Otherwise, the base is subtracted from the result, causing a CARRY OUT of 1 to be generated to the left, and the *new* remaining result is written as the SUM digit. In the rightmost (least significant) digit position, the CARRY IN is always 0. The CARRY OUT from the leftmost (most significant) digit position may be considered as an extra SUM digit.

In the binary (base-2) number system, these rules are simplified to the following equivalent algorithm: Let X be the three-bit code consisting of the two operand bits in this digit position and the CARRY IN bit from the adjacent position on the right. This position's SUM bit is 1 if the number of 1's in X is *odd*, and 0 if the number of 1's in X is *even*. (Note that 0 is an even number.) The CARRY OUT bit is 1 if the number of 1's in X is two or three, and 0 otherwise. The table of combinations in Table 2.3 expresses this rule for all possible operand and CARRY IN values. It defines the required behavior of a device, having three inputs and two outputs, known as a one-bit ADDER.

Table 2.3   One-Bit ADDER
Table of Combinations

A	B	C_{in}	SUM	C_{out}
0	0	0	0	0
0	0	1	1	0
0	1	0	1	0
0	1	1	0	1
1	0	0	1	0
1	0	1	0	1
1	1	0	0	1
1	1	1	1	1

A gate realization of this device requires two circuits—one to generate the SUM bit and the other to develop the CARRY OUT. The problem of designing the SUM network has already been solved. The required circuit is a three-bit odd parity generator, discussed in Example 1.3 of Chapter 1. Thus, the pair of EXCLUSIVE OR gates shown in Fig. 2.16(a) mechanizes the SUM function. The CARRY OUT function is implemented in one of several ways. First, a map solution, as shown in Fig. 2.16(b), yields the circuit shown in (c). Alternatively, we may take advantage of signals already available from the accompanying SUM circuit to slightly simplify the CARRY network. Observe that the signal $A \oplus B$, indicated in Fig. 2.16.(a), when ANDed with C_{in}, "covers" the two starred squares in the $C_{in} = 1$ column of the map in (b). Thus, only the term AB is additionally required to completely cover the CARRY function—giving the alternative network shown in Fig. 2.16(d).

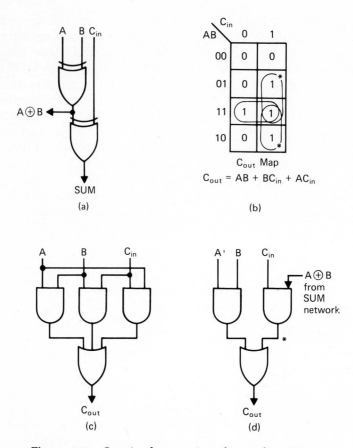

Figure 2.16   Gate implementation of a one-bit ADDER.

Having defined the interface, function, and internal gate structure of a one-bit adder, we may proceed to use it as an indivisible component, whose simplified block diagram is shown in Fig. 2.17(a). In particular, N such elements, interconnected as shown in Fig. 2.17(b), form an N-*bit* parallel ADDER. As you would expect, each C_{out}, from the one-bit ADDER in bit position i, is connected to the C_{in}, of an identical ADDER element in bit position $i + 1$. The N-bit ADDER, whose simplified block diagram is shown in Fig. 2.17(c), accepts two N-bit arguments and a CARRY IN (which may be made a constant 0), and generates an N-bit result and a CARRY OUT (which may be an extra result bit or may indicate an *overflow*, if the result length is limited to that of the operands). A set of M identical N-bit ADDERs may be similarly concatenated, with appropriate CARRY linkage, to form an MN-bit-wide

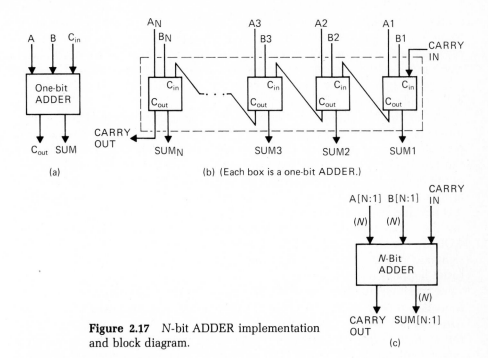

Figure 2.17 N-bit ADDER implementation and block diagram.

parallel ADDER. Clearly, the ADDER performs a binary (two-argument) data operation.

Note that, if the input arguments have a *serial* representation with least significant bit first, a single one-bit ADDER stage may be used to perform an N-bit addition in N time intervals—provided that proper synchronization and storage arrangements are made. Specifically, operand bits must arrive at the ADDER input terminals simultaneously, and means must be provided to connect the ADDER's C_{out} terminal back to its C_{in} terminal via some signal-delaying mechanism (not yet discussed) such that the C_{out} generated at time interval i arrives at the C_{in} terminal during time interval $i + 1$. If these conditions are met, the SUM output terminal will generate a serial representation of the result.

2.5 SIGNED NUMBERS AND SUBTRACTION

An N-bit code may be treated as an unsigned binary integer having a value in the range 0 to $2^N - 1$. Alternatively, it may be interpreted as a signed number, having a 1-bit field called the *sign bit* and an $N - 1$-bit field representing the magnitude of the number. By universal convention, the sign bit is located in the leftmost (most significant) bit position, with a 0 representing a *plus* sign and a 1 representing a *minus* sign. Since positive numbers will have leading 0's, while negative numbers will have leading 1's (shown shortly), this convention permits us to consider the sign bit as an extension of the value field whenever it is convenient.

If the number is positive, the $N - 1$-bit field directly represents its magnitude (a value in the range 0 to $2^{N-1} - 1$). If the number is negative, several possible interpretations for this field are possible. The *two's complement* representation is clearly the most universally accepted. It permits the result of the binary addition of two numbers, each having an arbitrary sign and an arbitrary magnitude, to always appear in the correct encoded form, whether it is positive or negative. That is, if any two arbitrary N-bit operands, *including* their sign bits, are applied to the input ports of a conventional N-bit ADDER, the leftmost output bit will always be the correct result sign, and the rightmost $N - 1$ output bits will already be in two's complement form, if the result happens to be negative.

A positive number, assumed originally expressed in decimal, is represented in binary form by repeatedly finding the largest power of two contained in its remainder, setting a corresponding bit in its accumulating binary representation to 1, and subtracting this value from the remainder to yield a *new* remainder. For example, starting with the value 390, we would find and subtract 2^8 or 256, 2^7 or 128, 2^2 or 4, and 2^1 or 2—giving intermediate remainders of 134, 6, 2, and 0, respectively—to yield 110000110 as the binary equivalent of 390.

The two's complement representation is a special encoded form that is derived from the magnitude of the negative number (which we will call M) by either of the following equivalent rules:

1. Complement all bits in M and then add 1.

2. Copy all rightmost bits in M up to and including the first 1 encountered. Then complement all remaining M bits.

For example, the two's complement of 0110000110 (which represents +390, from the example given above) is 1001111010 (which represents −390). Note that the sign bit may participate in the complementation process.

The second version of the conversion rule above is implemented in the logic network shown in Fig. 2.18. The input port receives a binary number and the output port delivers its two's complement. The OR-gate chain permits the rightmost input 1 to cause all input bits to its left to be inverted.

Table 2.4 indicates the range of representable signed, two's complement numbers of length eight ($N = 8$). Note that the range of values always runs from $+2^K - 1$ to -2^K, where K is the length of the value field (that is, $K =$

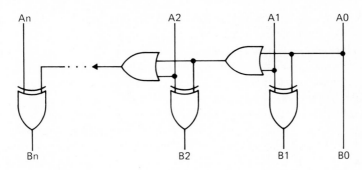

Figure 2.18   Two's complementer logic diagram.

$N - 1$). Observe also that only one code exists for the value zero. This is not true for several other negative-number representation systems in which both +0 and −0 are possible.

By convention, every negative number that participates in an arithmetic operation is assumed to be represented in two's complement form. As pointed out earlier, this form materially facilitates the implementation of binary addition and subtraction using signed numbers. [Note that procedures for converting between representations of numbers as *sequences of characters* (for example, the three-character sequences "+35" or "−63") and their

Table 2.4   Range of 8-Bit Signed
Two's Complement Numbers

Decimal Value	Binary Value	Hexadecimal Value
+127	01111111	7F
+100	01100100	64
+ 10	00001010	0A
+ 5	00000101	05
+ 2	00000010	02
+ 1	00000001	01
0	00000000	00
− 1	11111111	FF
− 2	11111110	FE
− 5	11111011	FB
− 10	11110110	F6
−100	10011100	9C
−127	10000001	81
−128	10000000	80

binary equivalents (00100011 and 11000001) are normally necessary in every computer. We assume that such procedures (typically, in the form of special computer programs) are available.]

We "change the sign" of a number by taking its two's complement. (The sign bit is included in this process. Its value will be automatically reversed. Note that it is *not* sufficient to merely invert the sign bit. "Change the sign" does *not* mean "change the sign bit.") If the number is negative to begin with, the correct positive representation will result. Subtraction is therefore implemented by first changing the sign of the subtrahend and then *adding*.

Table 2.5 enumerates all possible results of the binary addition of two arbitrary, equal-length operands. As stated earlier, the width of the ADDER that is employed matches that of the operands, *including* the sign bit. The final CARRY OUT past the most significant ADDER result bit is discarded. Thus, the result length is the *same* as that of the operands, and the result sign bit is the SUM output of the leftmost ADDER stage. The final CARRY OUT is not totally ignored, however. It may be used to detect when an OVER-FLOW condition exists—when the true result cannot be represented within the range of permissible ADDER output values. This can happen only when the operands have the same sign and when their total magnitude is sufficiently large. From the table entries marked NORMAL RESULT, note that when the operand signs are mixed, two result signs are possible. Any negative result appears in its proper two's complement form. The table entries marked CANNOT OCCUR indicate logically inconsistent conditions. For example, there is no pair of positive operands (with sign bits both 0) which can generate a final carry out of 1. The two entries marked OVERFLOW indicate a result magnitude too large for the number of output bits available.

Table 2.5 Possible Results of Signed Two's Complement Addition

	FINAL CARRY = 0		FINAL CARRY = 1	
RESULT SIGN BIT:	*0*	*1*	*0*	*1*
BOTH OPERANDS POSITIVE	RESULT NORMAL	OVER-FLOW	CANNOT OCCUR	CANNOT OCCUR
MIXED OPERAND SIGNS	CANNOT OCCUR	RESULT NORMAL	RESULT NORMAL	CANNOT OCCUR
BOTH OPERANDS NEGATIVE	CANNOT OCCUR	CANNOT OCCUR	OVER-FLOW	RESULT NORMAL

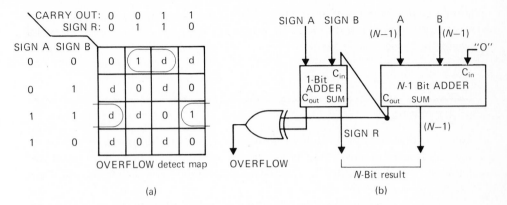

Figure 2.19   N-bit ADDER with OVERFLOW detector.

Problems at the end of this chapter provide arguments that test each of the possible entries in Table 2.5.

Consider what gate network should be used to recognize when an overflow condition exists. Its output signal might be utilized, for example, to indicate that a step in a computation should be retried after the arguments are properly modified. Fig. 2.19(a) defines the requirement for the overflow detector. It expresses the information contained in Table 2.5 in map form. SIGN A, SIGN B, and SIGN R are the sign bits of the two operands and the result, respectively. CARRY OUT is the final carry out. The map shows 1's in the two places where an overflow condition exists. It shows 0's for all normal states, and it shows d's (for "don't care's") for those situations that cannot occur. The solution can be expressed as follows:

$$\text{OVERFLOW} = (\text{SIGN A})\,(\text{SIGN B})\,\overline{(\text{SIGN R})} + \overline{(\text{SIGN A})}\,\overline{(\text{SIGN B})}\,(\text{SIGN R}),$$

which says that an overflow condition exists when the operand signs are the same and yet the result sign does not agree with them. Note that this solution is *independent* of the CARRY OUT signal. Its implementation requires two three-input gates and one two-input gate.

A simpler solution exists, however, if we take into account the logic of the most significant ADDER stage. Recall Table 2.3, which expresses its detailed function. For this stage, the two input bits A and B are the operand signs (SIGN A and SIGN B), the SUM output is the result sign (SIGN R), and the CARRY OUT signal is the discarded final carry discussed above. Note that the two conditions in the logical expression derived above happen to be the *only* cases in Table 2.3 for which CARRY IN *is not equal to* CARRY OUT. Thus, an even simpler overflow detector is realized in one EXCLUSIVE OR gate whose inputs are the CARRY IN and CARRY OUT signals of the leftmost ADDER stage. Fig. 2.19(b) contains a block/logic diagram of an

N-bit ADDER which includes such an overflow detector, assuming the arguments are signed numbers—with negative numbers represented in two's complement form.

2.6 SHIFTERS

Any rearrangement of the bits in an operand is, by definition, a (unary) data operation, since a *new* code is generated from an old one. It is generally classified as a *shift*, and it is normally accomplished exclusively through the use of appropriate wiring.

Consider a device having one input port and one output port—both of the same width—which internally contains only wires. Assume that it also has internal access to the two special "constant-1" and "constant-0" output terminals, defined earlier in Chapter 1. Within these constraints, many different bit-repositioning data operations may be defined.

One of these is a special case, in which the "new" code generated is a *constant*, independent of the input operand. As our studies proceed, we will see numerous examples in which a constant bit string is needed. For example, it may be necessary to increment a variable argument by a fixed amount. An ADDER having this constant as one of its input operands will perform the desired function.

A constant (parallel) code is developed merely by a set of appropriate connections to the constant 1 and 0 reference terminals. For example, Fig. 2.20 shows a wiring pattern that develops the constant hex code "95".

Figure 2.21 contains wiring patterns for six possible realizations of an elementary SHIFTER device, as postulated above. It covers the most common *one-bit* shift operations, assuming ports of width eight. Left shifts are indicated in the top row, right shifts in the bottom row. The input bit in position *i* becomes the output bit in position $i + 1$ (if the shift is left) or $i - 1$

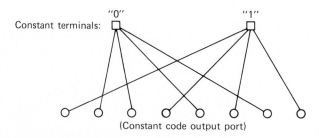

Figure 2.20 Developing the constant code 10010101.

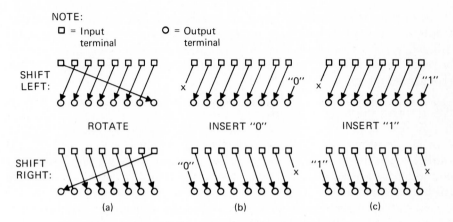

Figure 2.21   Alternative one-bit SHIFTER wiring patterns.

(if the shift is right). Each of the columns in Fig. 2.21 conveys a different scheme for defining the "first" output bit. It may be a constant, as shown in columns (b) and (c), in which case the input bit on the other end (called the "shifted-off" bit) is ignored. Alternatively, the "shift-in" bit may come from some other source. In particular, the shifted-off bit may be inserted in the vacated position, in which case a ROTATE or CIRCULATE or END-AROUND SHIFT is mechanized, as indicated in column (a).

This example demonstrates that there are several possible variations on the SHIFT theme. First, there are two alternative shift *directions* (left and right). Second, the *end conditions* (involving the shifted-in and shifted-off bits) may vary. Third, the *distance* of the shift is also a variable. For example, in Fig. 2.22, (a) shows a *two-bit* ROTATE LEFT, while (b) indicates a shift distance of *four*. The example shown in (b) happens also to implement what is called an EXCHANGE or "SWAP", because the left and right hex digits exchange positions.

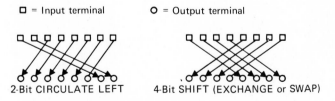

Figure 2.22   Examples of multi-bit shifts using 8-bit operands.

All of the shifts described above are termed *logical* shifts because they manipulate bit patterns without assigning any special interpretations to their individual bits. Another class of shift operations, known as *arithmetic* shifts, are specifically designed by assuming that the participating arguments represent *signed numbers*.

In any number system, a left shift of all of the digits of a positive number (inserting a zero in the rightmost digit position) is equivalent to a *multiplication* of that number by the base of the number system. In particular, a left shift of a positive binary number *doubles* its magnitude. Similarly, a right shift of a positive number (inserting a zero in the leftmost digit position) is equivalent to a *division* of that number by the base of the number system (with the remainder, created by the shifted-off digit, neglected). In particular, a right shift of a positive binary number effectively *halves* its magnitude.

The rules for ARITHMETIC shifts of binary numbers extend the above results to *negative* number representations, while still retaining them if the operands happen to be positive. Assuming that negative numbers are represented in signed two's complement form, the rules for one-bit arithmetic shifts are defined graphically in Fig. 2.23. Note that, for a right arithmetic shift, the shift-in bit is a *copy* of the original sign bit, so that the sign is retained while the magnitude is halved. A left arithmetic shift is identical to a left logical shift with a shift-in bit of 0. This produces the proper result provided that no overflow occurs—i.e., provided that the upper bit in the value field of the original operand is the same as the sign bit. If this is not true, not only will the magnitude of the result not be twice that of the original argument, but the *sign* of the result will also be erroneous. To detect such an overflow condition, we use an EXCLUSIVE OR gate to recognize when the upper two bits of the original operand disagree. This detector is indicated in Fig. 2.23(b).

If negative numbers are represented differently (for example, with a "sign-magnitude" or with a "one's complement" format, both ignored here), slight modifications to the arithmetic shift rules expressed in Fig. 2.23 are necessary.

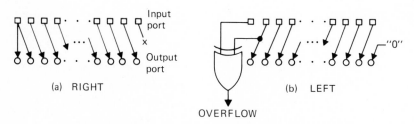

Figure 2.23   One-bit two's complement arithmetic shifts.

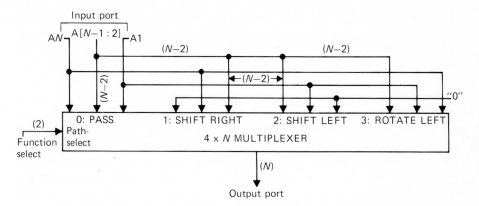

Figure 2.24 Typical shifter realization using a MULTIPLEXER.

A SHIFTER is normally defined as a device having one input port and one output port (both of the same width) that is capable of *more than one* shift operation. It has one additional input port (which we may call the "FUNCTION SELECT" port) whose input control code selects *which* of its shift operations it is to perform. For example, it may be capable of executing any one of four different shift functions (e.g., two arithmetic shifts and two logical shifts) as selected by a two-bit control code applied to its FUNC-TION-SELECT input port. Such a device may be implemented using a MUL-TIPLEXER, each of whose input ports are appropriately wired to the single common input port. The MULTIPLEXER's PATH-SELECT control code now becomes the FUNCTION-SELECT control code of the SHIFTER. Figure 2.24 shows an example of a typical SHIFTER. Please examine carefully how the input ports to the MULTIPLEXER are wired. This SHIFTER is capable of passing the input argument unmodified (if FUNCTION SELECT is 0), exe-cuting either of two one-bit logical shifts (if FUNCTION SELECT is 1 or 2), or rotating the input operand left (if FUNCTION SELECT is 3). Note that the *external* interface of this device has one data input port, one control input port, and one data output port, even though there are four appropriately wired *internal* input ports not "visible" to the "user."

2.7 COMPARATORS

A COMPARATOR receives two input operands, compares them, and gener-ates one or more output signals, each of which indicates whether or not a specific comparison criterion is satisfied. Example 1.2 of Chapter 1 dealt with an elementary COMPARATOR that had a single output signal indicating whether or not its two n-bit input arguments were identical. It contained a bank of n EXCLUSIVE OR gates, each of which tested the equality of a pair of corresponding input bits.

A more sophisticated COMPARATOR provides more than the single output signal that indicates equality. If the operands are not identical, it also conveys information concerning *how* they are unequal. The device is normally designed on the assumption that the input arguments are binary numbers encoded in a specific data format. When the operands are not the same, one or more output signals are available to specify, at least, which has the greater value. We begin by assuming that the input arguments are positive binary integers.

Consider a COMPARATOR having two $n + 1$-bit input operands $A[n:0]$ and $B[n:0]$ and three output terminals labeled "A = B", "A > B", and "A < B". Each output signal is asserted (has a value 1) when the condition specified by its label is true.

The logical equivalent of one EXCLUSIVE OR gate per input bit is still required to determine when the "A = B" output signal should be asserted. In addition, however, a mechanism to compare the relative magnitudes of the operands is also needed. (The device is usually called a *magnitude* COMPARATOR.) We compare the magnitudes by identifying the most significant (leftmost) bit position at which a mismatch between the arguments exists. The operand having a "1" in this position has the larger magnitude.

Most of the logic designs presented in this chapter have had an *iterative* structure, in which a gate pattern in a basic cell is repeated from bit position to bit position. In particular, devices such as the INCREMENTER, the TWO'S COMPLEMENTER, and the ADDER all have an iterative configuration in which information (for example, a CARRY signal) propagates from the least significant end toward the most significant end. A COMPARATOR is also amenable to an iterative cell structure. However, in this case, cell-to-cell information should propagate in the *opposite* direction—from the most significant end toward the least significant end.

More specifically, the cell-to-cell signal requirements are as follows: The cell in bit position i should receive an "EQUAL($i + 1$)" signal from the cell in bit position $i + 1$ (on its left), indicating whether or not all operand bit pairs to its left are identical. A similar signal, "EQUAL(i)", should be generated to its right neighbor. If the operand bits in position i are called Ai and Bi, the two "EQUAL" signals are related as follows:

$$\text{EQUAL}(i) = (\text{EQUAL}(i + 1))(Ai \odot Bi),$$

where $\odot$ represents the EXCLUSIVE NOR operation (that is, $Ai \odot Bi$ is 1 when $Ai = Bi$). On the rightmost end, the signal labeled as "A = B" is the EQUAL(0) signal.

Similarly, a signal named "GREATER" may propagate from left to right indicating that a mismatch, with the A bit being 1, has already been found. The *first* occurrence of a GREATER = 1 condition is caused by the *coincidence* of EQUAL$(i + 1) = 1$ and $Ai\overline{Bi} = 1$, indicating that this is the most significant mismatch with $Ai = 1$. Once this condition occurs, it should cause all GREATER signals to the right to be 1. Thus, we develop the logical relation:

$$\text{GREATER}(i) = (\text{EQUAL}(i + 1))Ai\overline{Bi} + \text{GREATER}(i + 1).$$

The rightmost signal GREATER(0) becomes the signal labeled as "A > B".

Finally, a similar argument may be used to justify the use of a "LESSTHAN" signal, propagating from cell to cell toward the least significant end, and we develop the relation:

$$\text{LESSTHAN}(i) = (\text{EQUAL}(i + 1))\overline{Ai}Bi + \text{LESSTHAN}(i + 1).$$

Again, at the right-hand end, the signal labeled as "A < B" is the LESSTHAN(0) signal.

Note that a LESSTHAN signal is not really required, since the combination of EQUAL = GREATER = 0 *implies* the LESSTHAN condition.

The logic diagram shown in Fig. 2.25 implements the requirements discussed above for a single cell. It includes all three cell-to-cell propagating conditions. The four gates in the top portion of the diagram implement an EXCLUSIVE NOR function. A structure very similar to this one was derived in Chapter 1 in Fig. 1.21(d). The individual gates of the EXCLUSIVE NOR are shown because the signals $Ai\overline{Bi}$ and $\overline{Ai}Bi$ are also required to develop the GREATER(i) and LESSTHAN(i) signals.

In the most-significant-bit position, the five lower gates are not needed. That is, EQUAL$(n) = An \odot Bn$, GREATER$(n) = An\overline{Bn}$, and LESSTHAN$(n) = \overline{An}Bn$.

When the operands are signed two's complement numbers, some modifications to this design are necessary. Clearly, the determination of the EQUAL condition should remain unchanged. However, since the most significant bit position now holds the *sign* bit, some changes are necessary. Specifically, the labels for the GREATER(n) and LESSTHAN(n) signals should be *reversed*, since a 0 (+ sign) now indicates the *greater* quantity, when the signs are not the same. Note that when *both* operands are *negative*, the same criteria for comparison still apply because, at the most-significant-bit pair mismatch, the operand having the 1 bit has the *smaller magnitude*, which gives it the *greater* value.

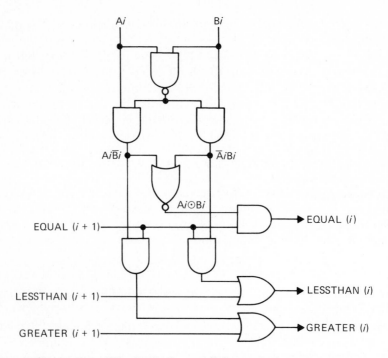

Figure 2.25 "Bit slice" of a parallel magnitude comparator.

2.8 PRIORITY LOGIC

Consider a parallel code of arbitrary length in which each bit corresponds to an independent component. The device associated with each bit may be as elementary as a key on a keyboard or as complex as an entire computer. Assume that assertion of any bit represents the occurrence of some special "event" within its corresponding element. For example, it may represent depression of its corresponding key. More generally, it may represent any form of "request" from its corresponding component.

If the associated devices are *independent*, the "requests" may arrive at arbitrary times. In particular, *more than one* may be asserted simultaneously. (This is true even for a realistic keyboard, in which any two or more keys may be momentarily depressed simultaneously—particularly during high-speed typing.)

Assume that the parallel request code is to be "processed" by a device that can handle only *one* request at a time. Thus, the responding "processor" expects a *one-asserted* input request code. (This "processor" may be as simple as a keyboard encoder, discussed earlier in Section 2.1, or as complex as another computer.) The resolution of conflicting requests—converting a request code with many possible assertions into a one-asserted code whose single assertion corresponds to the requesting device having the *highest priority*—is the function of a priority logic element.

Priority is normally assigned by appropriate wiring. Typically, a priority logic element has an input port whose terminals are *ordered* in priority. For example, the rightmost input terminal may be assigned the highest priority and the leftmost the lowest. The "request" output terminals of the participating devices (one per device) are then connected to the input terminals of the priority logic element (the "conflict resolver") in the order of their assigned priorities.

The iterative structure of a priority logic element resembles that of many of the other components discussed in this chapter. One version of the device has one input port and one output port, both of the same width. The input port receives the request code with many simultaneous assertions possible. The output port generates a one-asserted code by selecting the highest-priority input request. If no input requests exist, the output code contains no assertions. Assume that "1" represents assertion and that the rightmost input terminal has the highest priority.

The device requires one "transmission" gate per bit, which is enabled (passing its input signal to its corresponding output) only if no input assertions exist to its right. The rightmost input assertion should disable all transmissions to its left, forcing all of their outputs to "0". Several alternative realizations are possible. Your first inclination might be toward a structure having one AND gate per bit position. Each gate receives its corresponding input bit and the *complements* of all of the input bits to its right. Thus, the gate in bit position i has $i + 1$ inputs. As the number of input bits grows, this realization (while correct) becomes unwieldy compared to a structure (indicated in Figure 2.26) in which any internal bit position contains the same three elementary gates. Ai and Bi are the corresponding input and output

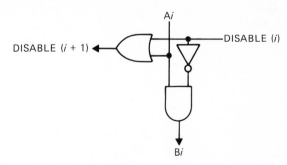

Figure 2.26   Logic for one-bit slice of priority logic element. [Note: In position zero, $B0 = $ DISABLE(1) $ = A0$.]

request bits in position i. The DISABLE signals shown propagate from cell to cell, right to left. Once a DISABLE = 1 condition exists in a given bit position, it forces all DISABLEs to its left to be 1. If DISABLE(i) is 1, Bi is forced to 0, no matter what Ai is. If DISABLE(i) is 0, Bi = Ai. The rightmost Ai = 1 condition causes its DISABLE(i + 1) to be 1. The regularity of this configuration makes it the preferable one.

A PRIORITY ENCODER selects the input assertion of highest priority, as discussed above, and outputs a unique code associated with it. For example, the device may have eight "request" inputs, any subset of which may be asserted, and it may output a three-bit code which is the *number* of the highest-priority input assertion. (An additional output signal is normally available to indicate when *no* input assertions exist.) Such an element may be realized by using the "conflict resolver," shown in Fig. 2.26, followed by a conventional ENCODER which converts each of its one-asserted outputs into the proper assigned code. For a sufficiently small PRIORITY ENCODER, some gate economies may be realized by combining the conflict-resolution and encoding requirements into one design problem. For our purposes, however, such economies are negligible.

2.9 ARITHMETIC-LOGIC UNITS

A parallel bank of identical gates may be used to perform any one of several possible *logical* data operations. The simplest among these is the unary COMPLEMENT function, executed by a bank of INVERTERs. Each bit in the output result is the inverse of its counterpart in the input operand.

Any parallel bank of two-input gates executes a binary (two-argument) logic operation. Each bit in the resulting code is logically derived (via the common gate function) from the two bits in the *corresponding* position in each of the input operands. That is, if Ai and Bi are the input bits in position i, and Ci is the result bit in this position, the relation Ci = f(Ai, Bi), where f stands for the gate name, holds for all i over the lengths of the input arguments.

As explained earlier, we are ignoring the fact that a data operation may be executed by *one* device, if the *n-bit* operands are processed through it *serially* in n time intervals. Unless stated otherwise, parallel operations will always be implied.

Figure 2.27(a) shows a bank of identical arbitrary gates (each box represents one of them), and (b) presents its equivalent shorthand notation. This notation was introduced earlier to describe a structure in which a set of identical gates all shared a single, common input-control signal (recall Fig. 1.11). In Fig. 2.27(b), however, none of the gate inputs are tied together. Rather,

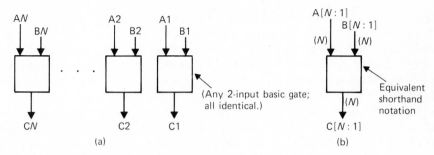

Figure 2.27   Parallel logic functions using banks of gates.

they comprise two identical input ports. The set of gates shown performs any bit-by-bit logic operation, in parallel. The most common functions are AND, OR, and EXCLUSIVE OR. If each of these is followed by the unary COMPLEMENT operation on the resulting code, logic functions such as NAND, NOR, and EXCLUSIVE NOR are accomplished.

The AND operation is most often used to *isolate* a specific field within an arbitrary operand. The argument with which this operand is ANDed is specially constructed as a *mask*, having 1's only in the selected fields' position. For example, the AND of an arbitrary 16-bit variable having a value WXYZ (where W, X, Y, and Z are arbitrary hex digits) with the constant hex mask 00F0 produces the result 00Y0, thus isolating only one of the hex digits in the variable argument.

The OR operation is most often used to *insert* a field into a given position within an argument. This argument is first "prepared" by having the selected field *cleared* (to all zeroes) by a previous AND operation. For example, suppose we wish to replace the digit X in the arbitrary 16-bit variable whose value is WXYZ (all hex digits) with the digit K in the 16-bit operand 0K00 (which may have been derived from a previous AND of an arbitrary value JKLM with the mask 0F00). [*Note:* We are using a notation in which any capital letter *above* F represents an *arbitrary* hex digit, while any character in the range 0–F represents an *explicit* hex digit.] To achieve the required result, we first AND WXYZ with F0FF to yield W0YZ. Then we OR this result with the 0K00 operand to derive the desired WKYZ.

The EXCLUSIVE OR operation is most often used to *compare* two arguments. The result is all zeroes only if the arguments are identical. Alternatively, an EXCLUSIVE OR may be used with a specially constructed "mask" operand to invert only a subset of the bits in an argument while leaving the other bits unchanged. For example, the EXCLUSIVE OR of WXYZ and 0F00 produces WKYZ, where K = F − X. (Recall that K and X are arbitrary hex digits while F is explicit.) In other words, K is the COMPLEMENT of X.

With one exception, each of the devices discussed in this chapter performs a single (unary or binary) data operation. The exception was the

SHIFTER, constructed using a MULTIPLEXER, which was able to execute any one of several shift operations, as selected by an *additional* FUNCTION SELECT input code (which in turn, you will recall, enabled one of the input ports to the MULTIPLEXER). Other devices that are capable of more than one data operation are also realizable. Unquestionably, the most prevalent of these is the ARITHMETIC-LOGIC UNIT or "ALU". Virtually every computer contains at least one ALU. Typically, this device has two equal-width input ports, which receive input operands, and one output port, which delivers the result. Like the SHIFTER, since it has more than one possible function, it requires an *extra* input port whose code specifies *which* operation it is to perform.

As its name implies, an ALU is capable of both arithmetic and logical data operations. Logical operations manipulate bits without regard to their meaning. Examples are functions such as INVERT, AND, OR, EXCLUSIVE OR, and all of the *logical* COMPAREs, SHIFTs and ROTATEs. Arithmetic operations are designed by assuming that the operands represent numbers. Examples are functions such as ADD, SUBTRACT, INCREMENT, DECREMENT, and all of the *arithmetic* COMPAREs, SHIFTs and ROTATEs. The set of operations that an ALU is capable of executing varies from device to device. Typically, an ALU may have a four-bit FUNCTION SELECT input code and may be able to perform any one of up to sixteen different data operations (for example, eight logical functions and eight arithmetic functions).

One possible mechanization of an ALU, which follows the example of the multifunction SHIFTER described earlier, is indicated in Fig. 2.28. The block diagram in (a) conforms to the description of an ALU, as given above. For this example, only eight operations are possible because the FUNCTION SELECT code has a length of three. All operands have a length N. The network in (b) contains several independent units all of which perform different data operations on the *same* arguments *simultaneously*. At any instant, however, only *one* result is selected for output by the MULTIPLEXER. Some of the operations (for example, ADD, AND, etc.) use *both* input operands. Others (e.g., SHIFT, INCREMENT, etc.) are unary operations, which take as input only *one* of the input arguments.

The number of gates in this version of an ALU may become excessive as N increases, and logic economies, achievable by having two or more independent data-operation units *share* the same gate structures, are normally explored. The most profound of these is due to the logical flexibility of the *ADDER*, an element that is fundamental to every ALU.

We have already seen how subtraction may be achieved using an ADDER, if the subtrahend is first converted into its proper complementary form.

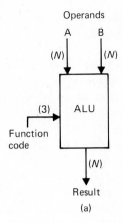

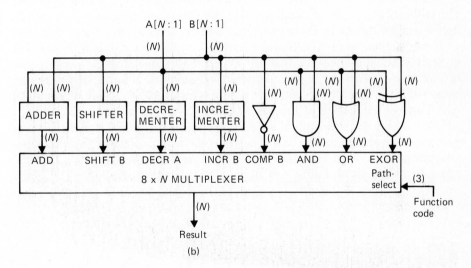

Figure 2.28 ALU block diagram and one possible realization.

While a SUBTRACT operation is not included in the simplified example in Fig. 2.28, it is a function available in most ALUs. With additional modifications, detailed below, an ADDER may also be used to realize functions such as INCREMENT and DECREMENT (which you might have expected), as well as many of the common *logic* functions (which you may not have anticipated). Further, an ADDER, operating in the SUBTRACT mode, may be used to execute a COMPARE function. Before explaining how these operations are implemented, we digress momentarily to discuss the concept of operation *sequences*.

A computer *program* is a planned sequence of operations. A result from one operation is generally *stored* (in a manner to be explained in the next chapter) and subsequently used as an operand in a later operation. Some operations (for example, an N-bit ADD) may be executed by an ALU in one step. Those functions not directly available in the "hardware" of an ALU are normally accomplished by a proper *program* of steps—a *sequence* of those operations that *are* available.

For example, subtraction is still achievable using the ALU of Fig. 2.28 if a proper program of steps is executed. Specifically, the subtrahend may be converted into two's complement form by a COMPLEMENT operation followed by an INCREMENT, both available in the device given. A subsequent ADD completes the SUBTRACT in three steps. As a further example, we will later discuss the hardware realization of a MULTIPLIER. When we do, you will recognize how a computer that does not contain multiply or divide hardware can still be made to execute this operation—as an appropriate *programmed sequence* of ADDS and SHIFTS. Finally, the problem of ADDing or SUBTRACTing operands that are *longer* than those an ALU can process in *one* step (so-called "higher precision" arguments, because they contain more digits) is usually solved using a programmed sequence of separate ADDs and SUBTRACTs of successive *fields* of these operands.

To develop an efficient, ADDER-based ALU, consider first the iterative gate structure shown in Fig. 2.29. There are as many AND and EXCLUSIVE OR gate pairs as there are operand bits. The common control signals X and Y are a two-bit code defining one of four unary data operations which this

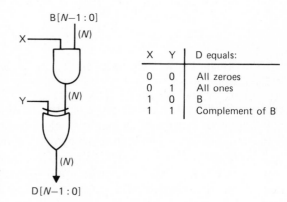

X	Y	D equals:
0	0	All zeroes
0	1	All ones
1	0	B
1	1	Complement of B

Figure 2.29 PASS/
COMPLEMENT/ZEROES/
ONES logic device.

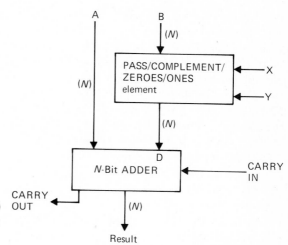

Figure 2.30 Using Fig. 2.29 device in one ADDER input data path.

network can provide: X controls whether or not every B_i is transmitted through its AND gate, and Y controls whether the bit that *is* transmitted is inverted or not. The accompanying table lists the four operations that are available from this device.

Now place this PASS/COMPLEMENT/ZEROES/ONES element in the data path of one of the operands to an ADDER, as indicated in Fig. 2.30, and consider what different data operations are available from this structure, for different values of X, Y, and CARRY IN. Note that the ADDER result for CARRY IN = 1 is always one greater than that when CARRY IN = 0. Observe further that when X = 0, the value of D (the ADDER input on the B side) is either all zeroes or all ones (i.e., a constant, independent of the value of B). Under these conditions, since B is ignored, the system must execute some *unary* data operation on the value of the A argument alone.

If D is all zeroes, the system either PASSes the A operand unmodified (if CARRY IN = 0) or INCREMENTs A (if CARRY IN = 1). If D is all ones (which is the *two's complement representation of* -1; recall Table 2.4), the system either DECREMENTs A (if CARRY IN = 0) or PASSes A (if CARRY IN = 1, which causes an INCREMENT that cancels the DECREMENT). If D is the same as B, the result is either A + B, a conventional N-bit ADD, (if CARRY IN = 0) or A + B + 1, a so-called ADD WITH CARRY (if CARRY IN = 1). [Observe that the "+" sign is used here for ADD, not for OR. In most cases, the meaning of "+" should be clear from the context in which it is used. If this is not the case, two alternative notations will be used and their meanings clarified.] The ADD WITH CARRY operation is used in *multiple-precision* ADDs, in which the operand lengths are a *multiple* of N—the width of the ADDER's input ports. Starting at the least-significant-operand end, the first N-bit pair of argument fields is ADDed with CARRY IN = 0. For all subsequent (more significant) N-bit ADDs, the CARRY OUT from step i (saved or stored by some process not yet explained) becomes the CARRY IN for step $i + 1$. Thus, ADD WITH CARRY is normally used under conditions in which the CARRY IN signal is a *variable* whose value depends on the data being processed. The ADD WITH CARRY makes it possible to ADD two operands of arbitrary length. Finally, if D is the COMPLEMENT of B, the result is either A − B, a conventional N-bit SUBTRACT (if CARRY IN = 1, because the two's complement of B is derived by first *inverting* all of its bits and then *adding* 1), or A − B − 1, a so-called SUBTRACT WITH BORROW (if CARRY IN = 0). Note that a conventional SUBTRACT operation requires a CARRY IN of 1. Like ADD WITH CARRY, the SUBTRACT WITH BORROW operation is used in multiple-precision SUBTRACTs. The first (least significant) N-bit SUBTRACT uses an initial CARRY IN of 1. For all subsequent steps, the CARRY IN bit is the CARRY OUT bit from the previous step. Note the dual interpretation ascribed to an ADDER's stage-to-stage coupling signal. In the ADD mode, it is a CARRY signal, with "1" meaning "carry" and "0" meaning "no carry." In the SUBTRACT mode, it is a BORROW signal, with "0" meaning "borrow" and "1" meaning "no borrow."

We have shown how PASS A or TRANSFER A, ADD, ADD WITH CARRY, SUBTRACT, SUBTRACT WITH BORROW, INCREMENT A, and DECREMENT A are all available from the structure shown in Fig. 2.30. Consider now what further modifications to this network are necessary to permit it to perform conventional parallel *logical* operations, such as AND, OR, and EXCLUSIVE OR.

For each of these functions, the result bit in any position is *independent* of the argument or result bits in any *other* positions. This suggests the necessity of eliminating all stage-to-stage CARRY signals within the ADDER, when parallel logic operations are desired. Imagine, then, adding one AND gate to each one-bit ADDER stage, as indicated in Fig. 2.31(a). If the signal CARRY ENABLE (which is *common* to all N stages) is 1, the ADDER functions normally. If CARRY ENABLE is 0, all internal CARRY input signals are forced to 0. Under these conditions, each one-bit ADDER stage operates as a simple EXCLUSIVE OR gate. (You should verify this fact. Use the table of combinations given in Table 2.3. Consider how the SUM output signal depends on the A and B input signals, under the restriction that $C_{in} = 0$.) How is the behavior of the network in Fig. 2.30 modified by the addition of the extra CARRY ENABLE control signal to the ADDER?

When CARRY ENABLE = 0, the ADDER becomes a bank of N EXCLU-SIVE OR gates which ignores its CARRY IN signal. Consider how the output results depend on arguments A and B for the four possible states of the PASS/COMPLEMENT/ZEROES/ONES device. In the PASS mode, when D = B, the result is the EXCLUSIVE OR of A and B. When D is the inverse of

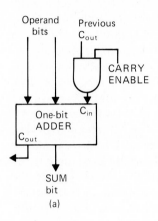

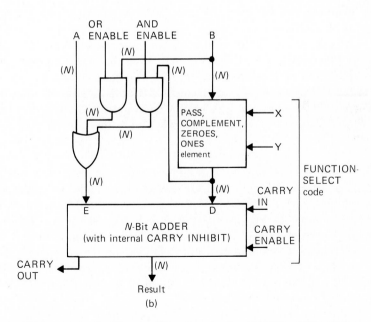

Figure 2.31   Further modifications to the ADDER of Fig. 2.30.

B, the result is the EXCLUSIVE NOR of A and B. (Prove to yourself that A $\oplus$ $\overline{B}$ = A $\odot$ B, where $\odot$ represents the EXCLUSIVE NOR operation.) When D is all zeroes, the network PASSes the A argument, and when D is all ones, the result is the COMPLEMENT of A (since each ADDER stage, now acting as an EXCLUSIVE OR gate, is constrained to operate as an INVERTER). Thus, by adding the CARRY DISABLE feature to the ADDER, we add three parallel logic functions and duplicate one (TRANSMIT A) that was available earlier. If we find means to include functions such as AND and OR, we will develop a truly versatile ALU device.

Having inserted specialized logic elements in the B operand data path to the ADDER and in the CARRY paths that couple its individual stages, it is logical to consider what logic may be inserted into the A data path to make AND and OR operations available. The inserted structure must operate in such a way that it is normally "transparent" to A (that is, it merely PASSes A) except when the AND or OR functions are desired. If this is the case, all of the ALU properties developed above will still remain valid.

Consider, then, the logic network shown in Fig. 2.31(b).[†] Note that the signals named OR ENABLE and AND ENABLE each enable a bank of AND gates that permits an additional argument (either B or D) to be ORed with A in the data path to the E input port of the ADDER. Assume that each of these signals is normally 0 except under specialized conditions. If neither ENABLE signal is asserted, the network operates as it did before, and the E input argument to the ADDER is simply A. Suppose OR ENABLE is asserted only for one of the three conditions under which the network PASSes E. Since E will be the OR of A and B, the result will have that value as well. Finally, suppose AND ENABLE is asserted only for the case where X = Y = 1 (so that D is the COMPLEMENT of B) and CARRY ENABLE = 0 (so that the ADDER operates as a bank of EXCLUSIVE OR gates). The result in this case is $(A + \overline{B}) \oplus \overline{B}$, where "+" here means OR. This is the same as AB, because:

$$(A + \overline{B}) \oplus \overline{B} = (A + \overline{B})B + \overline{A}B\overline{B} = AB.$$

Thus, the AND function now occurs under conditions previously assigned to the EXCLUSIVE NOR function. If OR ENABLE is asserted for the PASS E state for which CARRY ENABLE = X = Y = 0, the final internal ALU control structure shown in Fig. 2.32 is derived. It consists of two simple code recognizers whose outputs are OR ENABLE and AND ENABLE. Table 2.6 summarizes the conditions internal to the device and the functions available from it, for each of the possible control conditions. Observe that the four-bit code consisting of the signals CARRY ENABLE, X, Y, and CARRY IN is the same as this ALU's function-select code.

[†] The inserted gate structure is based on one described in Mano, M., "Digital Logic and Computer Design." Prentice Hall, 1979, pp. 379–381.

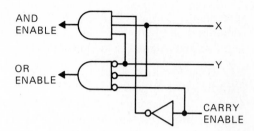

Figure 2.32 Gates that develop
internal AND/OR ENABLE controls.

Table 2.6 Available Functions from the ALU of Fig. 2.31(b)

CARRY ENABLE	X	Y	CARRY IN	Di	Ei	RESULT	FUNCTION NAME
1	0	0	0	0	Ai	A	PASS A
1	0	0	1	0	Ai	A + 1	INCREMENT A
1	0	1	0	1	Ai	A − 1	DECREMENT A
1	0	1	1	1	Ai	A	PASS A
1	1	0	0	Bi	Ai	A + B	ADD
1	1	0	1	Bi	Ai	A + B + 1	ADD WITH CARRY
1	1	1	0	$\overline{B i}$	Ai	A − B − 1	SUBTRACT WITH BORROW
1	1	1	1	$\overline{B i}$	Ai	A − B	SUBTRACT
0	0	0	d	0	A$i \vee$ Bi	A $\vee$ B	LOGICAL OR
0	0	1	d	1	Ai	$\overline{A}$	COMPLEMENT
0	1	0	d	Bi	Ai	A $\oplus$ B	EXCLUSIVE OR
0	1	1	d	$\overline{B i}$	A$i \vee \overline{B i}$	AB	LOGICAL AND

Note: "d" = "Don't Care". CARRY IN may be 0 or 1.
  "+" = Add. "$\vee$" = Logical OR.

PROBLEMS

Note: Unless you are directed otherwise, whenever a problem calls for the design of a component, you are urged to make your design description as concise as possible by utilizing *known* higher-level *inner* components wherever applicable. For example, if a 4 × 3 multiplexer will satisfy all or part of a requirement, you may draw it as a single, appropriately labeled element. There is no need to detail its internal logical structure, unless the problem specifically asks for it. Note, however, that a request for internal detail is sometimes implied. For example, an appropriately labeled encoder box is *not* a sufficient answer to Problem 2.1.

2.1 Draw the logic diagram of an ENCODER having ten inputs, each corresponding to a unique decimal digit, and seven outputs, each tied to a specific segment of a seven-segment digit display, as described in Fig. 2.6. A "1" output causes the corresponding display segment to light. The ENCODER should deliver each of the output codes listed in Table 2.2, in which case an assertion on a single input line creates a display of the corresponding digit.

2.2 The simplest DECODER is a 1-to-2 DECODER. Draw its logic diagram.

2.3 Using only NOR gates (and three inverters), draw the logic diagram of a DECODER that mechanizes Table 2.1.

2.4 Draw the logic/block diagram of a 5-to-32 DECODER that has an ENABLE input. Use four identical 3-to-8 DECODERs, each having its own ENABLE input, plus a minimum of additional logic.

2.5 A jukebox has a control network whose interface is shown in Fig. P2.5. Every disk is assigned a unique binary number. A user selects a recording by setting its binary number into a bank of switches, defining the signals DISK[3:0], and then depressing the PLAY button, which asserts the PLAY signal. This, in turn, asserts the ACTIVATE signal corresponding to the desired record. Design the control network.

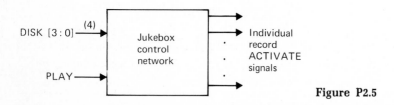

Figure P2.5

2.6 Design a code converter having two two-bit input arguments A[1:0] and B[1:0] and a five-bit output code C[4:0]. It treats all codes as positive integers, and it implements the function $C = A^B$.

2.7 A typical computer contains the control network shown in Fig. P2.7. A pulse emanating from any one of the output terminals of the network causes a specific operation to be performed. The operation code OP[4:0] identifies the operation selected for execution. When the EXECUTE PULSE is asserted, the proper output terminal is simultaneously activated. Design the control network.

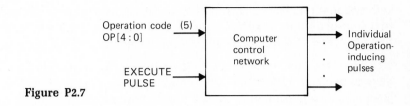

Figure P2.7

2.8 Write down the code for the decimal number 255 in binary and in BCD (binary-coded-decimal).

2.9 Devise an alternative realization for the function described in Fig. 2.29, using a MULTIPLEXER and a minimum of additional logic.

2.10 Each student desk in a special classroom is equipped with a bank of switches. The teacher asks a multiple-choice question, and each student responds by setting the binary number of his or her answer into the switches. The teacher may then view any student's answer by setting the binary number of the student's *desk* into a special bank of switches and then reading the selected answer on a bank of lights. Design the logic of the system. Draw an appropriately labeled diagram.

2.11 Because its number of interface pins (terminals) is limited, an integrated circuit employs an eight-bit output port for *two* purposes. Part of the time this port carries an internally generated data code DATA[7:0]. At other times the same port carries an internally generated "state" code STATE[7:0]. An additional internally generated signal, named SC, has a value "1" when STATE[7:0] is the selected output code. This signal is available, on an extra output pin, to specify to the external devices, *which* code is currently appearing at the output port. Show the logic network, inside the IC, that implements the function described above. The circuit has 17 input terminals: DATA[7:0], STATE[7:0] and SC, and nine output pins: OUTPUT[7:0] and SC.

2.12 The INCREMENTER in Fig. 2.14 provides an erroneous result when the input argument has its maximum value. An $n + 1$-bit code recognizer, which examines either the input argument or the output result, may be employed to deliver an OVERFLOW = 1 output assertion whenever this situation arises. Draw both realizations. However, a simpler, *two-input* gate structure will do the same job. Define its Boolean function.

2.13 A four-bit binary ADDER is shown in Fig. 2.17(c) (assuming N = 4). A BCD (binary-coded-decimal) adder has a similar interface. It receives two four-bit arguments and a CARRY IN and generates a four-bit SUM and a CARRY OUT. However, the rules for its operation are unique because a BCD adder adds two *decimal* digits, producing a decimal digit SUM, while a conventional four-bit ADDER adds two *hex* digits. Design a BCD adder using two four-bit binary ADDERs and a minimum of additional logic. As explained above, it should have nine input terminals and five output terminals.

2.14 Express decimal +80 and −80 in binary, each in eight bits. Similarly, express decimal +270 and −270 in binary, each in twelve bits. Use the two's complement representation for the negative numbers.

2.15 Verify all entries in Table 2.5 by simulating a six-bit ADDER and adding the six-bit binary equivalents of the following pairs of decimal numbers: (a) +15, +14; (b) +15, +25; (c) −25, +15; (d) +25, −15; (e) −25, −15; and (f) −15, −14. Express negative numbers in two's complement form. In each case, note the sign bit of the result and the final CARRY OUT value.

2.16 Design a SHIFTER having a one-byte data input port A[7:0], a one-byte data output port B[7:0], and a two-bit input control code N[1:0]. The B output code is always the A input code rotated right by N bit positions. (Thus, when N = 0, B = A.)

2.17 Design a general-purpose COMPARATOR having two input ports A and B, an input *relation select* code R[2:0], and a single output signal named TRUE. The R code selects a relation r between the magnitudes of A and B, and TRUE = 1 if the selected relation is true (i.e., if ArB is true). Otherwise, TRUE = 0. Values of R from 0 to 5 correspond, respectively, to the following relations: =, <, ≤, >, ≥, and ≠. R values of 6 and 7 are undefined. Use the COMPARATOR, described in Section 2.7, as one component in your network.

2.18 Using logic similar to that illustrated in Fig. 2.26 (show all individual gates), design a priority encoder having a four-bit input code A[3:0] and a two-bit output code N[1:0]. Here N is the subscript or index of the *leftmost* A that is "1". (Note that $N = 0$ may indicate *either* A = 0001 or A = 0000. To eliminate this ambiguity, include an output that is asserted whenever A is *not* zero.)

2.19 Replace the "leftmost 1" detector, in your answer to Problem 2.18, by one (alluded to in Section 2.8) in which the number of inputs, to each A_i transmission gate, varies from stage to stage. While such a structure is usable in this case, note that it becomes unmanageable as the input code widens.

2.20 Design a priority encoder, meeting the requirements described in Problem 2.18, which *minimizes* the total number of gates.

2.21 Given two eight-bit arguments X and Y, whose hex values are AA and C5, respectively. Write down the hex results of each of the following logical operations: AND(X,Y), OR(X,Y), and EXCLUSIVE OR(X,Y).

2.22   Given an arbitrary one-byte (eight-bit) argument, specify a second operand (in hex) and a corresponding logical operation, whose result will be the same as the original operand, but modified in the following way: (a) its sign bit will be set to "1", (b) its middle four bits will be inverted, and (c) its rightmost hex digit will be cleared.

2.23   As suggested near the end of Section 2.9, prove that $A \oplus \overline{B} = A \odot B$. This theorem states that by inverting either *input* signal to an EXCLUSIVE OR gate, we achieve the same result as would have been achieved had we inverted its *output* signal instead.

2.24   Utilizing the circuit in Fig. 1.19, or its equivalent in Fig. 1.28(c), plus a minimum of additional logic, design an odd/even parity generator/checker. (The definition of a "parity bit" was given at the end of Section 1.1 and in Example 1.3.) The network should have five inputs: A[2:0], PARITY IN, and POLARITY, and one output, labeled either as PARITY OUT or as PARITY ERROR, depending on how the network is employed. When it is used as a parity *generator*, PARITY OUT is the *odd* parity of A[2:0], if POLARITY = 0, or the *even* parity of A[2:0], if POLARITY = 1. (You must specify the disposition of the PARITY IN input terminal, in this case.) When the network is used as a parity *checker*, PARITY IN is the received parity bit attached to input code A[2:0], and PARITY ERROR = 1 only if this parity bit is incorrect. POLARITY specifies which parity is being checked ("1" selecting *even*).

Flip-Flops and Registers

3.1 BASIC LATCHES

The curve in Fig. 3.1(a) is the signal-in versus signal-out characteristic of a typical INVERTER. Permissible ranges for its "0" and "1" input signals are indicated, showing that some variations in these levels are tolerable, provided that 0 and 1 are always clearly distinguishable. Note that over either of the input ranges, the output level remains virtually constant. All gates have this ability to "re-quantize" signal levels.

A graphical analysis of the two-INVERTER loop in Fig. 3.1(b) is shown in (c). The "feedback" connection makes the circuit symmetrical. Each gate's input signal is the other's output signal. That is, signal P is the output of INVERTER1 and the input to INVERTER2, while signal Q is the output of INVERTER2 and the input to INVERTER1. Only those points that *simultaneously* satisfy *both* device characteristics are permissible operating points for the circuit. Thus, the *intersections* in (c) are the circuit's "equilibrium" points. The middle point is unstable; even the slightest electrical signal variation (which is always present) causes the circuit to jump to one of the other two *stable* states. You can verify that the circuit has two stable states, one

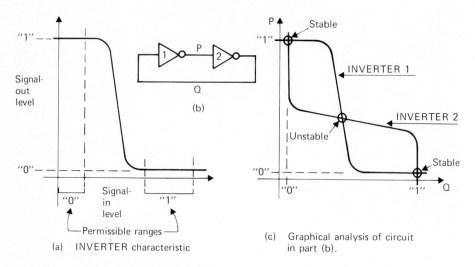

(b)

(a)   INVERTER characteristic

(c)   Graphical analysis of circuit in part (b).

Figure 3.1   Graphical determination of equilibrium points

with Q = 0 and the other with Q = 1, by assuming a value for Q and seeing whether the network is "satisfied" with this value, i.e., whether the assumed value, traced around the loop, generates the same value on return to the starting point. Any consistent set of conditions defines a stable state.

Without information about the network's past history, we can only say that both of its states are equally likely. Once it assumes one state, it remains there *indefinitely* (and Q remains constant) until some externally applied stimulus causes it to switch to its other state.

Such an elementary network, called a FLIP-FLOP, is said to hold or *store* or "remember" a bit. It may be viewed as a cell into which a bit is placed (by some mechanism not yet described). The signal Q represents the *contents* of the cell. The process of *loading* the cell with a bit (to be explained) is termed *writing* into it. The bit in the cell is *read* whenever the signal Q is examined, displayed, or used in some way. The cell retains the bit stored in it (that is, Q remains constant) until a write of the opposite bit takes place, at which time Q makes a transition ("flips" or "flops") to its other level. Reading the stored bit does not alter it. Note that the outputs of the circuit are always complementary (that is, P = $\overline{Q}$). Every FLIP-FLOP normally comes with Q and $\overline{Q}$ output terminals.

The circuits in Fig. 3.2 include input terminals to give externally derived signals control over the state of the FLIP-FLOP. While both input signals are quiescent (i.e., while SET = RESET = 0), each gate acts like one of the IN-VERTERs discussed above, and two stable states are possible. Note that the NAND realization has negative-assertion input signals, which have a high (1)

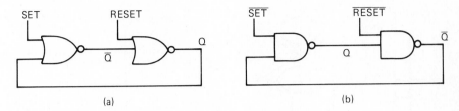

SET   RESET $\overline{\text{SET}}$ $\overline{\text{RESET}}$

                                  Q $\overline{Q}$

        $\overline{Q}$ Q

              (a)   (b)

Figure 3.2   Basic bistable latches

dormant level. If SET is momentarily asserted, Q is forced to 1 and $\overline{Q}$ is forced to 0—no matter what the previous state was. (You should verify this by tracing the signals that would exist around the loop during and after the SET pulse, assuming RESET remains 0.) The FLIP-FLOP is termed *set* by this process. If Q is already 1, no change in it is discernible. Similarly, if RESET is pulsed (while SET remains quiescent), the circuit is reset, forcing Q to 0, no matter what its state was previously.

The network is called a LATCH because it remembers—or "latches" or "locks onto"—the *last* control input assertion. The situation in which SET and RESET are *simultaneously* asserted is normally avoided because the new state is unpredictable if the trailing edges of the SET and RESET pulses are coincident. Note, however, that if one of these pulses lasts longer than the other, the circuit will lock onto *its* corresponding state.

Every FLIP-FLOP is a "sequential" circuit, defined in Section 1.3 as one whose behavior depends not only on its present inputs but also on its past history. To demonstrate this, consider how you would define the present value of output Q, given that the present values of inputs SET and RESET are both 0. The answer is that Q is "whatever it was earlier"—either 0 or 1—depending on the past history of the circuit.

During the discussion (in Chapter 2) concerning ALU operation sequences, the need to save or *store* a result from one operation, so that it may be used as an operand in a subsequent operation, was pointed out. Similarly, most prior references to *serial* operations expressed the need to save output bits at time i for subsequent use as *inputs* at time $i + 1$. The FLIP-FLOP is the basic element used to save or store a single bit.

With the addition of two gates to the basic cell, we derive a network, shown in Fig. 3.3(a), which may be set or reset only in *synchronism* with a control pulse C. The circuit within the dashed outline is the one from Fig. 3.2(a). (Recall that lines that cross are assumed not connected unless a bold dot appears at their intersection.) While C is not asserted (positively), both AND gates are disabled and the signals SET and RESET are both 0, in which case the latch retains its previous state. When a C pulse occurs, both AND gates are enabled, permitting signals S and R to reach the SET and RESET

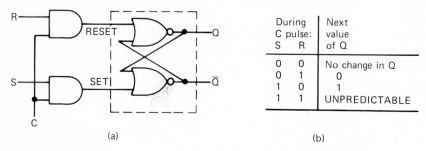

During C pulse: S R	Next value of Q
0 0	No change in Q
0 1	0
1 0	1
1 1	UNPREDICTABLE

(a)   (b)

Figure 3.3   A clocked bistable circuit and its behavior table

terminals. The values of S and R *at that instant* determine the next state of the latch, according to the table in Fig. 3.3(b).

Here is our first example of a circuit that remains in a fixed state until it is activated or stimulated by a control pulse. It may change its state only in coincidence with this signal. The circuit is termed "clocked," and the control pulse is called a *clock pulse*. The signals S and R, which define what the circuit is to do when it is clocked, are called *control levels*. It is assumed that they remain valid over the duration of the C pulse.

By modifying this circuit slightly, we derive the network shown in Fig. 3.4(a). Now, while C = 1, SET = D and RESET = $\overline{D}$. Thus, assuming D remains valid over the duration of the C pulse, whenever C is activated, the FLIP-FLOP *loads* the value of D. That is, Q *becomes* whatever D is at the instant when C is asserted. We say that the circuit "samples" the value of D every time a clock pulse occurs; Q retains this value until a new clock pulse occurs. The behavior table in Fig. 3.4(b) summarizes this simple rule. The circuit is called a "D LATCH."

The character of a LATCH—the fact that it retains or "locks onto" input conditions existing at the *termination* of its activation pulse—implies that it remains responsive over the entire *duration* of this control pulse. For example, in Fig. 3.4(a), while C is 1, if D were to change, Q would follow or

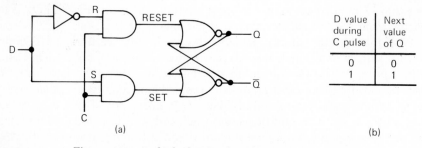

D value during C pulse	Next value of Q
0	0
1	1

(a)   (b)

Figure 3.4   A clocked D latch and its behavior table

"track" D. (Similarly, every other LATCH "tracks" its inputs while it is acti-vated.) The final, latched state of the circuit would depend on the value that D had at the *trailing edge* of the C pulse, no matter what D did over its duration. In typical use, of course, D is guaranteed to remain valid while C is asserted. However, timing conditions may exist (as explained further in the next section) that render a simple LATCH inadequate as a storage element. Under these conditions, an *edge-triggered* storage device is normally used instead.

3.2 EDGE-TRIGGERED FLIP-FLOPS

A computer processes bits that are internally stored in FLIP-FLOPs. Typical-ly, the input signals to any of its logic networks (for example, one of those discussed in Chapter 2) are derived from FLIP-FLOPs. Similarly, any net-work's output signals are normally directed to FLIP-FLOP inputs. In other words, for any arbitrary logic network, it is normally safe to assume that those inputs whose sources are not explicitly shown in the diagram come from the *Q output terminals* of FLIP-FLOPs, and that those outputs whose destinations are not explicitly indicated are connected to the input terminals of still other FLIP-FLOPs.

A clocked FLIP-FLOP may change state only in synchronism with its input clock pulse. This pulse may be viewed as a "command," asking it to come out of its quiescent holding condition and to examine or sample its other inputs—the control levels—to define what its next state should be. Thus, the clock pulse specifies *when* to "do it," while the control levels speci-fy *what* to do at that instant.

Every digital computer contains a control unit which has clock pulse out-puts whose signals are distributed throughout the machine. Each clock pulse activates or "triggers" one or more specific components. The control unit orchestrates all of the micro-operations of the system by generating appropri-ate clock pulse *patterns*, so that the elementary electronic "events" triggered by them occur in the proper sequence. Those events that should happen *simultaneously* are triggered by the *same* clock pulse.

To ensure a predictable, unambiguous next state, a FLIP-FLOP's input control levels (which define its next state) must be *valid* at the instant when it is activated by its clock pulse. In many useful configurations, however, these levels may be derived from sources whose signals may change as a result of the *same* pulse. That is, they may be derived from the Q's of FLIP-FLOPs that are triggered *simultaneously*. In fact, a FLIP-FLOP's control inputs could be a logic function of its *own* state. Simple LATCHes cannot be used in such situations, because the input control levels *themselves* change and become invalid just at the instant when they are being sampled. However, such structures are possible if the sampling instant is made extremely short, using a mechanism known as *edge-triggering*. It takes into account the fact that all gates have some inherent signal delay.

An edge-triggered FLIP-FLOP is activated only during one specific *transition* or edge of its clock pulse. Contrasted with a LATCH, it is *not* activated during the entire interval while its clock pulse is asserted. The device normally consists of two or three appropriately coupled LATCHes (examples are given later), forming a composite network which behaves as a *single* FLIP-FLOP. It is designed to ignore its other inputs at all times except during the extremely short instant while a specific (positive or negative) clock edge is occurring.

Ideally, the edge of a signal takes no time to occur. In reality, an edge occupies a duration of time comparable to the delay of a signal through a typical gate, which is normally measured in "nanoseconds"—billionths of a second. Thus, the sampling instant of an edge-triggered FLIP-FLOP is *so short* that it ends *before* any of the sampled control levels have had a chance to change, *even when* such changes are induced by the *same* clock edge. This is true because a signal change due to a clock edge must be delayed from it in time by *at least one* gate delay. In particular, the fact that an edge-triggered FLIP-FLOP's control inputs may be derived directly from its *own* Q outputs introduces no ambiguity. The signal delay through the FLIP-FLOP itself is sufficient to ensure reliable, predictable operation.

The control input values pertinent to an edge-triggered device are those existing *before* (and hence during) the clock edge of interest. The fact that some of these signals may change *immediately after* the edge occurs is immaterial, since the edge is *over with* by that time, and the device is again ignoring what its control inputs are doing. (Of course, the control inputs must still be valid *at* the clock edge.)

We will henceforth assume that *all clocked devices* (FLIP-FLOPs and any of the more sophisticated elements that contain them) are edge-triggered, unless otherwise specified. Observe that an edge-triggered device does not "care" how *wide* its clock pulse is. It is triggered only during *one* of its edges. In most cases, it will not be necessary to specify which edge is the significant one. When it is necessary, the edge polarity of interest will be defined.

To demonstrate the power of edge-triggering, consider the problem of designing a FLIP-FLOP that always "toggles" (reverses its state) every time it receives a clock pulse. Assume we are restricted to using the D LATCH of Fig. 3.4 or an edge-triggered version of it (whose internal design will be discussed presently). Recall that a D FLIP-FLOP *loads* the value of D (that is, Q becomes what D is) whenever it is clocked.

Using an edge-triggered device, we accomplish the desired result merely by *connecting its $\overline{Q}$ output to its D input.* Just before each clock edge, D is always the inverse of the present value of Q. *This* is the value that is sampled when the edge occurs. It is true that after one or more gate delays (depending on the internal design of the FLIP-FLOP), the value of D will change. However, by this time the edge instant will have passed, and D will have no further effect.

This is the simplest example in which a FLIP-FLOP's control input is a function (in this case, merely the inverse) of its own output.

Consider the same connection ($\overline{Q}$ to D) made using the (non-edge-triggered) D LATCH of Fig. 3.4. Recall that while the clock pulse C is asserted, Q follows or tracks D. Thus, over the entire duration of the C pulse, the circuit will be unstable and Q will *oscillate* between 0 and 1. Every time D changes, Q makes a similar change after two or three gate delays, which, in turn, causes D to change again, and so on. The circuit will marginally operate properly only if the C pulse is made critically narrow (having a width comparable to two or three gate delays)—a very unreliable situation. Note that the edge-triggered version operates reliably *independent* of the clock pulse width.

Having explained the signal timing conditions for which edge-triggering is particularly suited, and having postulated the existence of edge-triggered FLIP-FLOPs, we continue by explaining how such devices may be realized.

Consider the circuit shown in Fig. 3.5. It contains a D latch (recall Fig. 3.4) whose outputs are connected, via a pair of coupling AND gates, to a SET-RESET latch (recall Fig. 3.2). The inner latch is called the "master" latch, the outer latch is called the "slave" latch, and the composite circuit is called a MASTER-SLAVE FLIP-FLOP. Note that the composite device has two input terminals, C and D, and two output terminals, Q and $\overline{Q}$. Its internal signals, such as P and $\overline{P}$, are not "visible" to external components. Assume a positive

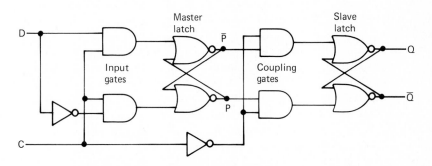

Figure 3.5   Master–slave edge-triggered D FLIP-FLOP

C pulse, with D required to be valid only while either of its *edges* is occurring.

Before the pulse, since C = 0, the input AND gates are disabled. Thus, the master latch ignores D and merely retains its previous state. Since the coupling gates are *enabled*, the slave latch is forced to *copy* the state of the master, in which case Q = P. Consider this the normal, quiescent state of the circuit.

At the leading (positive) edge of the C pulse, the input gates become enabled and, after one gate delay through C's INVERTER, the coupling gates become disabled. Since P and $\bar{P}$ could not have changed yet (because any effect of enabling the input AND gates takes *two* gate delays to reach these terminals), the slave latch—now decoupled—merely *retains* its previous state. It remains decoupled during the entire duration of the C pulse, and the output signals Q and $\bar{Q}$ continue to hold their old quiescent values. They are, so far, impervious to the fact that a C pulse has occurred.

During the duration of the C pulse, the master latch and the internal signals P and $\bar{P}$ *track* any variations in D that might occur. From the external point of view, however, since signals Q and $\bar{Q}$ remain constant, the composite device appears oblivious to these changes.

At the trailing edge of the C pulse, the input gates become disabled again. The master latch locks onto the value that D has at this instant. After one gate delay through C's INVERTER, the coupling AND gates are re-enabled, and the slave latch is forced to copy this last latched state. It is only at this instant, at the *negative* edge of the C pulse, that the output signals Q and $\bar{Q}$ may change, and only if the value of D at that instant disagrees with Q. After the negative C transition completes, the network again ignores D.

From the *external* point of view, the composite circuit is a *negative edge-triggered* D FLIP-FLOP. It appears to ignore D at all times except at the negative C edge, at which instant Q copies the D value.

As a second example of an edge-triggered FLIP-FLOP, consider the circuit in Fig. 3.6(a). It contains three identical SET-RESET latches (recall Fig. 3.2), each receiving negative-assertion input control signals. The signal C is the $\overline{\text{SET}}$ input to each of the two input latches. D is the $\overline{\text{RESET}}$ input to the lower input latch, which also has a *second* $\overline{\text{SET}}$ input in the form of Q1. The upper output of each latch is its Q signal. The Q's of the two input latches, Q1 and Q2, are the $\overline{\text{SET}}$ and $\overline{\text{RESET}}$ inputs, respectively, to the output latch. Note, again, that the composite network has two input terminals, C and D, and two output terminals, Q and $\bar{Q}$, and that internal signals, such as Q1 and Q2, are not visible to external components. Again, assume a positive C pulse, with D required to be valid only during its edges.

Before the pulse, both Q1 and Q2 are held high by the C = 0 condition, so that the output latch merely retains its previous state. Each of the input

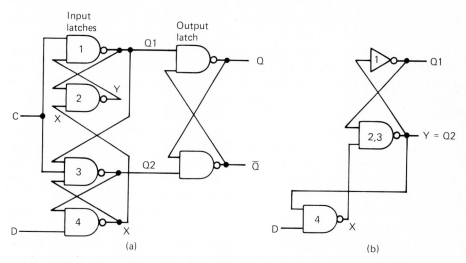

Figure 3.6 Edge-triggered D FLIP-FLOP and equivalent circuit when C = 1

latches operates in an activated, "tracking" mode, with gates 2 and 4 both acting as INVERTERs, tracking changes in D. Thus, while C = 0, X = $\overline{D}$ and Y = D. Note, however, that from the external point of view, the circuit appears to be ignoring D, because Q and $\overline{Q}$ remain constant.

As C rises to 1, the low assertion on the $\overline{SET}$ input to each of the input latches is removed, permitting one of them, whose $\overline{RESET}$ input is *not* asserted, to lock into the *set* state, while the other, whose $\overline{RESET}$ input is still asserted, ends *reset* with its Q at 0. The outcome depends on the value that D has at that instant. If D = 0, the lower input latch ends reset and Q2 falls to 0, while (since X = 1) the upper input latch retains the set state. On the other hand, if D = 1, the lower input latch retains the set state, while (since X = 0) the upper input latch ends reset with Q1 at 0. Thus, at the termination of the positive edge of C, Q1 and Q2 have *complementary* values, with Q2 = D. The output latch, in turn, responds by taking on this value, so Q becomes equal to D.

Once C = 1 (i.e., for the duration of the C pulse), the circuit, excluding the output latch, may be replaced by the equivalent network shown in Fig. 3.6(b). Remember that any NAND or AND input signal, known to be "1", may be ignored while it has that value. (The output signal depends on the *other* input values.) Thus, while C = 1, NAND gate 1 acts as an INVERTER of signal Y. In addition, NAND gates 2 and 3 may now be combined because they are functionally identical, since each has the same pair of inputs: X and Q1. Therefore, while C = 1, Y = Q2. Note the storage loop consisting of the INVERTER and NAND gate "2,3". An analysis of this network reveals that it can lock into one of two possible states, each of which *holds* the initial, complementary values of Q1 and Q2. *Neither* of these states is sensitive to variations in D. If Q2 is low, X is held high via gate 4, no matter what D does, and Q1 remains high. If Q1 is low, Q2 is held high, no matter what X (which is now tracking D) does. Thus, the (complementary) values of Q1 and Q2, established at the positive edge of C, remain in effect over the entire duration of the C pulse. Consequently, Q and $\overline{Q}$ continue to hold the values established at that instant, *independent* of how D changes over the duration of C.

Whenever C returns to 0, Q1 and Q2 return to their quiescent "1" conditions, causing the circuit to again behave as described above for C = 0, in which case Q and $\overline{Q}$ continue to hold their previous values. Thus, from the *external* point of view, the entire network behaves as a *positive edge-triggered* D FLIP-FLOP. Normally, D is ignored and Q and $\overline{Q}$ hold their values, except at the positive edge of C, at which time Q copies the D value.

Many other edge-triggered FLIP-FLOP realizations are possible. Our assumption, that *every* clocked device is edge-triggered (unless stated otherwise), is based on an overwhelming preference for such devices by logic designers.

3.3 FLIP-FLOP VARIATIONS AND STATE SEQUENCES

Figure 3.7 contains typical symbols and behavior tables for the most common types of clocked FLIP-FLOPs. Note the special notation for a CLOCK input terminal (labeled "CK"). Each of these elements is assumed to be an edge-triggered device. The left side of its behavior table specifies all of its possible control input values, assumed valid at the instant of triggering. The right side defines its new Q state, just after triggering. The symbol Q, in the Q_{next} column, represents the value that Q had *before* triggering. Each table in Fig. 3.7 is independent of which CLOCK edge *polarity* actually triggers the FLIP-FLOP. While a specific internal logic network for each element is not given, you may assume that structures closely resembling those described in detail in Section 3.2 are utilized.

The D and the T FLIP-FLOPs each have one input control level, while the SR and the JK devices each have two. Recall that a FLIP-FLOP ignores its control level(s), and holds Q constant, at all times *except* at the instant when the crucial CLOCK edge occurs. The D device has been described earlier. In addition to its being the simplest FLIP-FLOP, it is also clearly the most prevalent. When triggered, it *loads* the value of D at that instant (that is, Q becomes that value). The T device, when triggered, toggles (reverses its state) if T is 1, or maintains its present state if T is 0. Note that an element that toggles on *every* CLOCK pulse, discussed as an example in Section 3.2,

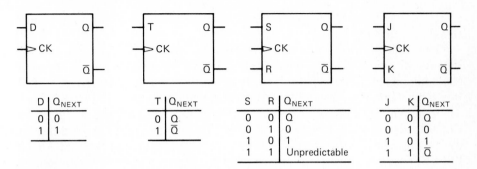

Figure 3.7 FLIP-FLOP symbols and behavior tables. [Note: Q = state before triggering; Q_{NEXT} = state after triggering.]

is equivalent to a T FLIP-FLOP whose T is a *constant 1*. The SR device is an edge-triggered version of the SR LATCH of Fig. 3.3. Observe that its behavior is unpredictable if it is triggered while S = R = 1. The T FLIP-FLOP and the SR FLIP-FLOP descriptions serve as an introduction to the JK device, which combines the properties of *both* elements. That is, input signals J and K have the same purpose as do signals S and R, for all acceptable values of S and R. In addition, the condition J = K = 1 is equivalent to a T = 1 condition for a T FLIP-FLOP. Surpassed in importance only by the D FLIP-FLOP, the JK device is the second most prominent bit cell. In future discussions, you will find it helpful if you have the simple properties of these basic elements committed to memory.

Clearly, all of these devices represent minor variations on a single theme. Numerous other variations are possible. For example, a FLIP-FLOP having an additional CLEAR or PRESET control input may be constructed. Figure 3.8 shows a JK element having both of these features. The assertion of CLEAR causes the device to assume the Q = 0 state. Conversely, a PRESET assertion forces a Q = 1 state. These signals are normally used to *initialize* a bit cell to a predefined state. Their assertion generally *overrides* any clocked commands. The device's response is immediate and is not contingent on the

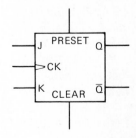

Figure 3.8 Addition of CLEAR and PRESET overriding inputs

occurrence of a CLOCK pulse. Examples to demonstrate the use of these signals are provided later.

The behavioral description of any device must clearly specify its next state under all possible input conditions. It is not uncommon for certain input combinations to define what appear to be *contradictory* commands. The S = R = 1 input condition to an SR FLIP-FLOP (while the critical CLOCK edge is occurring) is an example. As another example, suppose JK = 10 at the CLOCK edge (asking the cell to SET), while CLEAR is also asserted (asking the cell to RESET). As mentioned earlier, for most devices the CLEAR (or PRESET) assertion overrides any clocked command. The behavioral description must include all such control-signal "precedence" information. It must also clearly define all input combinations that should not occur because the results are unpredictable.

A network containing N FLIP-FLOPs has 2^N possible *internal states*. An internal state is defined as a distinguishable internal quiescent condition. Specifically, the internal state of a network is characterized by a *code* consisting of all of the Q's of its FLIP-FLOPs (i.e., the string of bits stored in its internal bit cells). The network *remains* in a state, with all of its Q's holding *constant*, until an externally derived "excitation" or "activation" causes it to make a transition to a new state. Since all of its FLIP-FLOPs are assumed to be clocked devices, this activation normally arrives in the form of an input signal that causes at least one of the internal FLIP-FLOPs to receive a CLOCK edge *trigger*. Normally, *all* of the internal FLIP-FLOPs of one component receive the *same* edge trigger *simultaneously* because all of their CLOCK inputs are connected together. While exceptions exist (for example, when two connected CLOCK inputs are activated by *opposing* edge polarities, or when the CLOCK input of one FLIP-FLOP is derived from the Q output of another), we will henceforth assume that, unless specified otherwise, a SEQUENTIAL component contains one or more *identical* FLIP-FLOPs, all of whose CLOCK inputs are connected together.

In general, the input control levels to a FLIP-FLOP (e.g., signals such as J, K, or D) are logic functions not only of external input variables but also of the Q's of FLIP-FLOPs *within the same network*. In other words, the *next* internal state of a network is generally a function not only of the values of external input signals (measured at the instant when the network is triggered), but also of the network's *present* internal state (the state just before the trigger occurs). Remember that our assumption of edge-triggering permits a FLIP-FLOP's input control level (for example, J) to be derived from a Q that will change as a result of the *same* CLOCK edge. Examples are provided below.

In general, the output signals from a sequential component are logically derived from its internal Q's and from its input signals. Thus, the outputs are a function not only of the inputs but also of the *present internal state*, which, in turn, depends on the past history of the circuit. (Recall that this is how a sequential circuit was originally defined.)

As stated earlier, it is safe to assume that the common CLOCK input pulse to a component is derived from some central control-pulse generator (whose design we will consider later). The other inputs are generally "levels"—signals that are held valid while the CLOCK edges are occurring; these signals are typically derived from the outputs of other similar sequential components. A computer is an aggregate of many FLIP-FLOPs, interconnected via logic gate structures and activated by CLOCK pulse patterns emanating from a central control unit. Between any two successive CLOCK pulses, the *state* of the entire system is defined as the array of bits stored in all of its cells. On every CLOCK pulse the state of the system changes. (The Q's of one or more FLIP-FLOPs are altered.) *A "level" is any signal derived from the Q's of one or more FLIP-FLOPs.* Thus, it may change only when a CLOCK pulse occurs, but it *remains constant between CLOCK pulses.* A *pulse*, on the other hand, is any signal derived from a CLOCK pulse. While it is possible for an output signal of a sequential network to be a *pulse* (because it is derived from the CLOCK input to that network), we will ignore this possibility except when specifically stated otherwise.

We *analyze* a sequential network by enumerating all of its possible internal states and by specifying all of the input signal conditions under which *transitions* between these states are evoked. An analysis also includes a specification of the value of each output signal, for every possible state of the system. While an analysis of a circuit may be conveyed in the form of a narrative description of its expected behavior, it is often convenient to express this information in the form of a state table or a state diagram.

A *state table* lists all possible internal states and their corresponding output signal values. For each (*present*) internal state, it also lists all possible *next* states, which, in turn, depend on the input signal values that may be present when a CLOCK pulse occurs. Such a table provides a complete description of the network's possible behavior. Starting from some *initial* state and given an arbitrary sequence of input codes (each accompanied by the reception of a single CLOCK pulse), we can use the state table to predict how the internal state of the network will sequence and how its outputs will respond.

The simplest sequential circuit consists of a single FLIP-FLOP. The four tables in Fig. 3.7 are the state tables for their corresponding elementary networks. More complex examples are provided below.

All of the information contained in a state table may be provided in a more graphic form known as a *state diagram*. In a state diagram, each internal state is allocated a drawn box or circle (instead of a line in a table).

Information associated with each state (for example, its Q code and its output code) labels its circle in the diagram. Arrows are then drawn *between* the circles to indicate permissible *transitions* between the states. Each path is labeled with the input conditions under which that transition is evoked (when a CLOCK pulse occurs). The state diagram is particularly effective because it provides a better picture of the *flow* between the states.

For the four elementary FLIP-FLOPs whose state tables are given in Fig. 3.7, Fig. 3.9 provides alternative behavioral descriptions in the form of elementary state diagrams.

We analyze a given circuit by developing a detailed description of its behavior, paying particular attention to the relationship between its inputs and its outputs, and, if possible, by *interpreting* this description to generate a concise *rule* that summarizes this behavior. Creating the behavioral description, in the form of a state table or a state diagram, is a well-defined, straightforward process. Recognizing the behavior "pattern" that the network exhibits is sometimes more difficult. To demonstrate the techniques involved, four sample analysis problems are solved below.

■ **Example 3.1** Consider the network shown in Fig. 3.10. Its CLOCK input signal is assumed to be a continuous, periodic train of pulses with a high repetition rate. The network has one other input x and one output z. It contains two FLIP-FLOPs (both receiving the common CLOCK signal), giving the network four possible internal states, each identified by a different Q2Q1 code. Note that the J's and the K's are logic functions not only of x but also of the Q's; thus the *next* state (on reception of a CLOCK pulse) is a function not only of x but also of the *present* state. While the most general output signal is a function of *both* the Q's and the input signals (in which case, for each

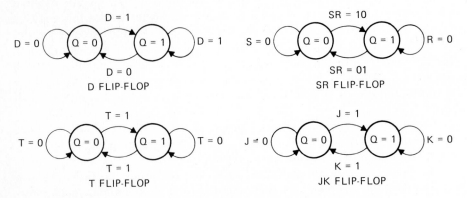

Figure 3.9 State diagrams for the basic FLIP-FLOPs

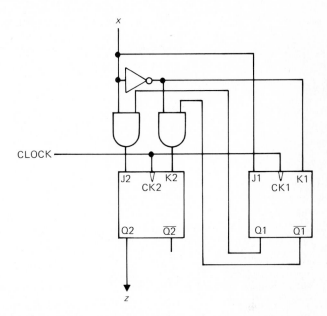

Figure 3.10   Circuit for
analysis Example 3.1

internal state, the output code depends also on the input combination applied), in this circuit z is merely the same as Q2.

A state table or diagram is developed by predicting, for every possible present state and input combination, what the next state (on reception of a CLOCK pulse) will be. Thus we must enumerate all possible combinations of Q2, Q1, and x (in a table or in a map), then find the values of the J's and K's which correspond to them, and then (knowing the rules of behavior of a JK device) specify, for each of the table or map entries, the *new* state of each FLIP-FLOP.

From the network, we see that

$$J2 = xQ1, \quad K2 = \overline{x}\,\overline{Q1}, \quad J1 = x, \quad \text{and} \quad K1 = \overline{x}.$$

We use these relationships to derive the map in Table 3.1. Note that several variables may be plotted simultaneously on the same map, if each square has sufficient room for all of the information. The single map in Table 3.1 is equivalent to four separate maps, each describing the behavior of a single variable. Observe also the typical format of a sequential circuit map. Each row represents a different *present state* of the internal FLIP-FLOPs. Each column represents a different input combination. Thus, each map square or entry corresponds to a different present "condition" or "situation," in which the circuit may find itself, when a CLOCK pulse arrives.

Knowing the properties of a JK FLIP-FLOP, we convert this information into the map in Table 3.2. For every possible present situation, this *state table*

Table 3.1 Plot of the J's and K's
for Circuit in Fig. 3.10

X:		0	1
Present			
Q2	**Q1**		
0	0	0101	0010
0	1	0001	1010
1	1	0001	1010
1	0	0101	0010
		J2K2J1K1	

predicts the *next* state (the new Q's) after a CLOCK pulse. It describes the behavior of the given network. Note that present output information is plotted in a column (labeled "z" here) on the side of the table, if the output variables are functions *only* of the Q's. If the outputs are *also* functions of the *inputs*, this output information must be plotted inside the same map, or on another similarly labeled map. Let us interpret the information contained in Table 3.2 to develop a concise, understandable input-versus-output rule.

The circuit "samples" the value of x every time a CLOCK pulse occurs. Note that, under certain conditions, the next internal state is the *same* as the present one. Many sequential circuits exhibit this property. (On a state diagram, shown later, this is represented by a transition arrow whose destination is the same state as its source.) Note also that, in each x column, the same next state appears in three out of the four cases. The circuit appears to have two "rest" states: 00 (with output 0) and 11 (with output 1). Starting in

Table 3.2 State Table for the
Circuit of Fig. 3.10

X:		0		1		Present
Present						
Q2	**Q1**					**z**
0	0	0	0	0	1	0
0	1	0	0	1	1	0
1	1	1	0	1	1	1
1	0	0	0	1	1	1
			Next			
			Q2Q1			

the 00 state, the circuit remains there for any number of successive $x = 0$ samples. The *first* $x = 1$ sample causes a transition to the 01 state, with no change in the value of output z. A *second* $x = 1$ sample causes a transition to the 11 state, accompanied by a change in z. Note that the circuit moves back to the 00 starting state if a 0 sample follows the first 1 sample. Once in the 11 "rest" state, a dual situation exists. Any number of successive $x = 1$ samples cause no state change. The first $x = 0$ sample moves the circuit to the 10 state, with no change in z. A second 0 sample causes a transition to the 00 state, while a 1 sample restores the 11 rest state.

Having recognized these behavior patterns, we may formulate the following concise rule which describes the network: *z tracks x*—with a delay. That is, while x holds its value (for two or more successive samples), $z = x$. Whenever x changes, z follows on the *second* successive "inverted" sample. This means that a *momentary* change in x, causing at most one isolated inverted sample, results in no output change. It is "ignored."

One example of the use of such a circuit is discussed in detail in Section 3.4 (next), where the same network is *synthesized* from a set of behavioral requirements. From the description given above, we can speculate on the possibility of using this circuit to "filter" all pulses (of either polarity), *narrower* than a specific threshold, out of an arbitrary signal. Such pulses might be "noise spikes" induced by faulty earlier processing.   ∎

■ **Example 3.2**   The circuit in Fig. 3.11 also contains two FLIP-FLOPs (having four possible states) clocked by a common, periodic signal. Note, again, that the D's are functions of the inputs *and* of the Q's. As in the previous example, the outputs happen to be functions only of the Q's. (Generally, they may also be functions of the input variables.) While the network has four input signals, we may simplify the analysis by using only the two input variables T1 and T2, keeping in mind the simple relationships:

$$T1 = T1a + T1b \quad \text{and} \quad T2 = T2a + T2b.$$

As we did before, we proceed by enumerating (in a table or in a map) all present "situations" in which the circuit may find itself and, for each, predicting the next internal state on the occurrence of a CLOCK pulse. All combinations of the variables Q2, Q1, T1, and T2 represent all of the possible present conditions just preceding the arrival of a CLOCK pulse. Since the next state of a D FLIP-FLOP *is* the value of D when it is triggered (i.e., next Q = present D), the map of next states is the plot of the D's as functions of the four variables listed above. Table 3.3 contains this information—a plot of the functions

$$D2 = Q1 \quad \text{and} \quad D1 = \overline{Q2}Q1 + Q1T1 + Q1\overline{T2} + \overline{Q2}T1\overline{T2}.$$

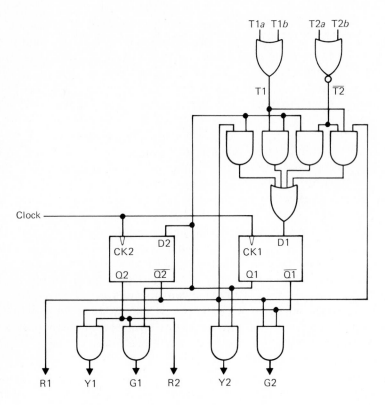

Figure 3.11   Circuit for analysis Example 3.2

As was done in the previous example, the state table is augmented with a listing of the six output variable values for all possible internal states. These are plots of the six elementary functions

$$R1 = \overline{Q2}, \ Y1 = Q2\overline{Q1}, \ G1 = Q2Q1, \ R2 = Q2, \ Y2 = \overline{Q2}Q1, \ \text{and} \ G2 = \overline{Q2}\,\overline{Q1}.$$

Table 3.3 is thus a complete, detailed description of the behavior of the given network.

By examining the state transitions that are possible in the state table, we conclude that this circuit also has two "rest" states: one with Q2Q1 = 00 (having outputs R1 and G2 asserted) and the other with Q2Q1 = 11 (having outputs G1 and R2 asserted). Assuming that 00 is the initial state, the circuit remains there until a CLOCK pulse occurs with T2T1 = 01, at which time a transition to the 01 state occurs (accompanied by a G2 = 0, Y2 = 1 output change). On the very next CLOCK pulse, the circuit moves to the 11 state *unconditionally* (accompanied by another output change). Again, a symmetrical situation now exists. The circuit remains in the 11 state until a T2T1

Table 3.3 State Table for the Circuit of Fig. 3.11

T2T1:	00	01	11	10	R1	Y1	Present G1	R2	Y2	G2
Present Q2 Q1										
0 0	00	01	00	00	1	0	0	0	0	1
0 1	11	11	11	11	1	0	0	0	1	0
1 1	11	11	11	10	0	0	1	1	0	0
1 0	00	00	00	00	0	1	0	1	0	0

Present D2D1
or
Next Q2Q1

sample of 10 occurs, causing a transition to the 10 state (with outputs Y1 and R2 asserted), followed by an unconditional return, on the very next CLOCK pulse, to the 00 state.

This network could serve as an elementary traffic light controller. The output signals individually control the illumination of Red, Yellow, and Green lights in the "1" (North–South) and in the "2" (East–West) directions. The signals T1a, T1b, T2a, and T2b are the *treadle* signals. Each is asserted while a vehicle is positioned at its corresponding threshold to the intersection. Thus, T1 and T2 are North–South and East–West *request* signals, respectively. Each is asserted while traffic flow in its direction is desired. For this application, the CLOCK pulses are assumed to be spaced a few *seconds* apart.

Given this interpretation, the state table merely states that, as long as a request in one direction exists, flow in that direction is permitted. The lights change only when a request in the other direction arrives, *provided* all requests in this direction have been satisfied. Each "warning" state, during which a Yellow light is illuminated, lasts for the time between two successive CLOCK pulses.

Such a controller might be suited to low-traffic intersections. However, a continuous stream of traffic in one direction totally prevents any traffic in the other direction. Worse than that, consider what would happen if a vehicle happened to break down while it was positioned on a treadle!

The problem of *synthesizing* this circuit, given the set of requirements explained above, is treated in Section 3.4 (next). A state *diagram* for this system appears there.   ■

■ **Example 3.3** None of the J's and the K's in the network in Fig. 3.12 are functions of the Q's. For this reason, an analysis of the network does not require the use of a state table. It can be done by inspection. Other than

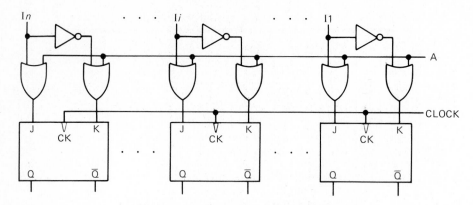

Figure 3.12   Register for analysis Example 3.3

CLOCK, the circuit has one control input A and an input port I[n : 1]. The outputs of the system are the FLIP-FLOP Q's. The string of identical FLIP-FLOPs is called a REGISTER. It *stores* a code, represented by the set of output Q signals. If A = 0, each of the OR gates is transparent to its other input, so that every $Ji = Ii$ and every $Ki = \overline{Ii}$. In this case, the REGISTER *loads* the input I code when a CLOCK pulse occurs (i.e., the Q's *become* the I values). If A = 1, on the other hand, every J = K = 1. (The effects of the I bits are *masked*.) Under these conditions, each FLIP-FLOP toggles when the CLOCK pulse arrives (i.e., all of the Q's are complemented). Note that, for a sufficiently large number of input bits, the construction of a state table becomes unwieldy, and we prefer a behavioral description in narrative form. ∎

∎ **Example 3.4**   The REGISTER in Fig. 3.13 is also easy to analyze without the use of a state table. Its interface resembles that of the circuit in Fig. 3.12. The string of AND-OR clusters, along with the INVERTER, comprise a two-way, n-bit-wide MULTIPLEXER, controlled by the A signal. When A = 0, each $Di = Ii$ and the REGISTER loads the I code on the CLOCK edge. When A = 1, each $Di = Q(i + 1)$ (with $Dn = Q1$) and, on the CLOCK edge, the REGISTER *rotates* its stored contents *right* (i.e., every FLIP-FLOP loads the bit that was its left-neighbor's old contents). Note that by the time the Q's change, the CLOCK edge that *induced* the change no longer exists.   ∎

None of the circuits analyzed above was equipped with any special means to permit establishing a proper *initial state*. Yet the behavior of a sequential circuit clearly depends, in general, on its starting conditions. As our studies proceed, we will come across other examples that will include proper *initialization* provisions.

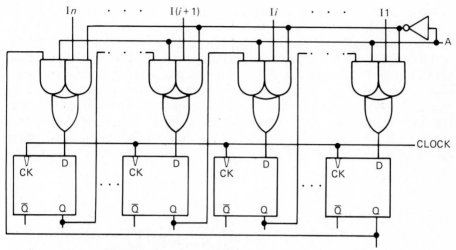

Figure 3.13   Register for analysis Example 3.4

3.4 SYNTHESIS OF SEQUENTIAL CIRCUITS

A digital network design procedure begins with a *specification* of the desired behavior of the as-yet-unknown circuit and ends when its logic diagram is derived. The specification includes a definition of the interface of the device and an unambiguous description of its input-versus-output signal relationship. This description is often in narrative form. Consider, for example, the following word specification:

Design a network having a CLOCK input, an x input, and a z output. Every time a CLOCK pulse occurs, the circuit samples the value of x. It begins operating from an initial state with z = 0. z remains 0 until the 17th x = 1 sample occurs, at which time z becomes 1 and remains 1 until the very next x = 0 sample occurs, at which time the circuit restarts again in its initial state with z = 0.

Every sequential circuit design process begins with an identification of the number of different internal states that the required network must have. A different internal "state" is required for every unique or distinguishable *condition* or *situation* that the circuit may find itself in or must keep track of. Typically, every unique output code requires its own state. For example, each state of the traffic controller in Example 3.2 exhibits a unique output code. However, more than one internal state may correspond to the *same* output code, if the network is required to "remember" more than one different condition or situation. For example, the sample specification given above calls for 18 different states: a unique state for each $x = 1$ count, including the initial state, whose count is 0.

The enumeration of the internal states that are necessary normally accompanies the construction of a state diagram which describes the required circuit's behavior. Each circle in the diagram, representing a unique internal state, is labeled with any convenient notation to denote its purpose. For example, the state diagram for the sample description given above is shown in Fig. 3.14. In this case, each state is labeled with the *count* value which the circuit must keep track of. Note that the output information provided in the specification also labels each state.

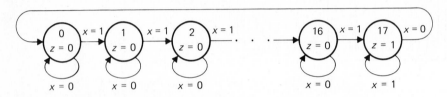

Figure 3.14   State diagram for sample 18-state counter

The paths between the states are labeled with the input conditions that cause them (on a CLOCK assertion). Observe that, for this example, each state has one exit path, for one value of x. The other x value causes no state change. Also, note the "restart" path, from state 17 back to state 0, on the condition $x = 0$.

Once the state diagram for the circuit exists, the "creative" (and, typically, the most difficult) portion of the design procedure has been completed. The remaining steps are well-defined and straightforward. First, the number of required states determines the minimum number of FLIP-FLOPs that may be utilized. For example, at least five FLIP-FLOPs are necessary to mechanize the state diagram in Fig. 3.14, because four FLIP-FLOPs have, at most, 16 different states. (With five devices, a total of 32 states are conceivable. However, a proper design will utilize a subset of only 18 of these.)

Second, a unique *code* must be assigned to each state. This code will be the *contents* of the internal FLIP-FLOPs when the circuit *assumes* that state. The number of possible code assignment choices grows rapidly as the number of states increases. In fact, if the number of states is a power of 2 and if N is the minimum number of necessary FLIP-FLOPs, there are exactly $2^N!$ different possible ways to encode the states. (There are 2^N code choices for the first state. Having made a first choice, there are $2^N - 1$ choices left for the second state, and, in general, there are $2^N - i + 1$ choices left for the ith state. The total number of choices is the *product* of all of these values, giving $2^N!$ possible code assignments.) The resulting network depends, in general, on *which* encoding of the states is chosen. (Some code assignments are equivalent because they generate the same circuit.) If a specific encoding of the states is not suggested by the problem, an arbitrary choice may be made, keeping in mind the rule of thumb that an efficient design often assigns to two "adjacent" states (states between which a transition is possible) codes that differ in only one bit position.

Once the states have been encoded, the original state diagram may be converted into a state table or map in which *specific code values* are used. This table now describes how the Q's of the individual FLIP-FLOPs will behave. Maps for the output variables may now be drawn as well. At this point, the type of FLIP-FLOP to be used must be chosen. It may be suggested by the problem. The D device fits naturally in applications in which bits move intact from one place to another. On the other hand, the JK device is logically more sophisticated because its state table includes more variations. It is more useful in applications requiring some form of bit "computation."

Having chosen the FLIP-FLOP type and knowing the rules for its behavior, we may convert the state table (which specifies how the Q's are expected to behave) into maps for the FLIP-FLOP control levels (the D's, J's, and K's) which will *yield* this behavior. That is, the maps specify how the control levels should behave in order that, when CLOCK pulses arrive, the expected Q sequencing will result. We then derive Boolean functions for the control levels from the maps. Output signal functions are similarly derived. By properly connecting the gate implementations of these functions to the postulated set of FLIP-FLOPs, we construct the required circuit.

In converting the information contained in the state table into a set of maps for the FLIP-FLOP control levels, we continually ask the implicit question: "What must the control level values be to mechanize this required Q transition on the next CLOCK pulse?" Table 3.4 answers this question, for all of the defined control levels and for all possible Q transitions that may be induced by the CLOCK pulse. Note, particularly, that "d's" appear in several

Table 3.4   Required Control Levels for All FLIP-
FLOP Transitions

Required Transition	Necessary Inputs at the Triggering Instant					
	D	T	S	R	J	K
0 to 0	0	0	0	d	0	d
1 to 1	1	0	d	0	d	0
0 to 1	1	1	1	0	d	0
1 to 0	0	1	0	1	1	d
Optional next state	d	d	d	d	d	d

of the table entries. These "don't care" symbols indicate that the value of the corresponding control signal, for *that* required Q transition, is *optional*. It may be 0 or 1. The required transition will occur for *either* value. For example, if the required transition is from Q = 0 to Q = 1, for a JK FLIP-FLOP, it is only necessary that J be 1. If K = 0, the device *sets*. If K = 1, the device *toggles*. In *either* event, the proper final Q state results.

If you are familiar with the detailed properties of the individual FLIP-FLOPs, as given in Fig. 3.7, you may easily derive the information contained in Table 3.4. It is not necessary to memorize it. However, a study of Table 3.4 helps you reinforce your knowledge of the properties of the basic devices. Its use will be demonstrated in the synthesis examples that follow.

■ **Example 3.5**   The signal derived from a typical switch, for example, one of those in a keyboard array, is not as "clean" as you have been led to believe. It usually resembles the waveform x in Fig. 3.15(b). Each time the metallic contacts inside the switch *make* or *break* connection, the signal changes. Since the contacts are not perfect, they normally "bounce" on each single actuation. Waveform x shows the result: several bounces on the switch's depression and a few more on its subsequent release. The time taken before bounces die out, which varies with the quality of the switch, is typically several milliseconds (where 1 millisecond is 10^{-3} second). Since a computer can respond to *submicrosecond* signals (1 microsecond = 10^{-6} second), the single key activation will be treated as a sequence of many. A switch "debouncer" is a circuit that filters out the bounces. One specification for its design is given below.

Design the circuit shown in Fig. 3.15(a), where x is the switch signal—sampled by a train of CLOCK pulses spaced t seconds apart, where 3t is greater than the maximum time it takes for bounces to die out. While x is stable at either level, z = x. On any (bouncing) switch actuation in either direction, z does not change until the *second* successive inverted x sample is detected. An example is indicated in Fig. 3.15(b). The CLOCK pulses shown are much wider than they have to be. The time scale has been modified so that you may distinguish both edges of each pulse. The z waveform is drawn by assuming that the internal devices are *positive* edge-triggered.

The circuit requires four internal states. Two of these are the quiescent, rest states, each corresponding to a stable x signal. Two are the temporary states entered on detection of the *first* inverted x sample. The state diagram in Fig. 3.15(c) describes the behavior of the required circuit. The rest states are named OFF and ON, while the temporary, intermediate states are named PRE-OFF and PRE-ON. All state transitions may occur only on the receipt of a CLOCK pulse. Each is labeled on the diagram with the value of x that causes it. Note that a single, isolated inverted x sample causes a return to the previous rest state.

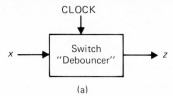

(a)

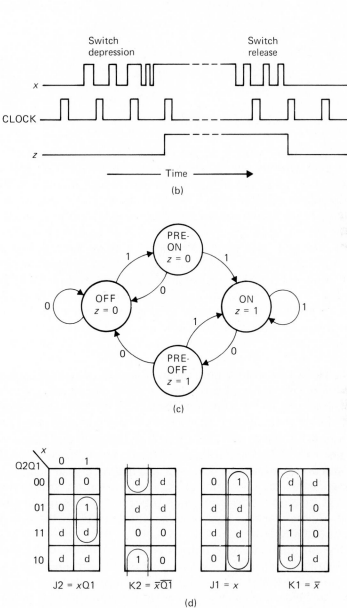

Figure 3.15 Waveforms, state diagram, and maps for Example 3.5

Table 3.5 State Table and FLIP-FLOP Encoding for Example 3.5

Present State	Next State on Clock Edge		Present Output	Binary Assignment	
	x = 0	x = 1	z	Q2	Q1
OFF	OFF	PRE-ON	0	0	0
PRE-ON	OFF	ON	0	0	1
ON	PRE-OFF	ON	1	1	1
PRE-OFF	OFF	ON	1	1	0
	(a)			(b)	

Table 3.5(a) contains the same information as that in the state diagram. Since the circuit exhibits four internal states, two FLIP-FLOPs are required. We now arbitrarily make the binary assignment shown in Table 3.5(b), *defining* which Q codes will correspond to which states. The encoding in (b) may be substituted in (a) to yield the state table (derived earlier via an analysis exercise) shown in Table 3.2. At this point, we choose (again, arbitrarily) to use JK FLIP-FLOPs to realize the network. Knowing the required Q transitions, indicated in Table 3.2, and the J and K values required to *yield* these transitions, indicated in Table 3.4, we derive the maps for the J and K signals shown in Fig. 3.15(d). Note that many of the map entries are filled with "don't care" symbols. We use these to maximize the size of the map clusters found, and thus we derive the functions indicated in the same figure. Their gate implementations result in the logic diagram shown in Fig. 3.10. ∎

■ **Example 3.6** We consider here the synthesis of the traffic controller discussed earlier (from the analytic point of view) in Example 3.2. Its block diagram is shown in Fig. 3.16(a). Recall that the R, Y, and G output signals control the individual traffic lights and that the T signals are the treadle signals. Specifically, T1 and T2 are North–South and East–West traffic requests, respectively. CLOCK pulses are spaced a few seconds apart. Traffic is to be permitted to continue to flow in a given direction as long as a corresponding request exists. The lights change only when no further requests in the permitted direction exist *and* when a request in the *other* direction is received. A Yellow warning light remains illuminated for the time between two adjacent CLOCK pulses.

The state diagram in Fig. 3.16(b) is equivalent to the description given above. The circuit requires four states. Two of these mechanize the normal STOP–GO conditions, and two are required to implement the warning periods, while the lights change. Each state is labeled with the names of the illuminated traffic lights that correspond to it. Thus, for this example, the

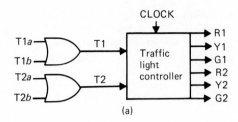

(a)

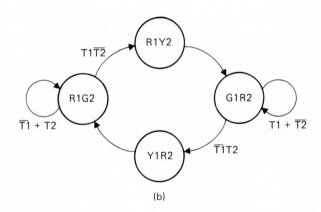

(b)

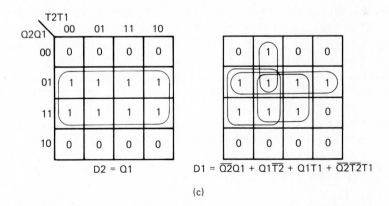

$D2 = Q1$ $D1 = \overline{Q2}Q1 + Q1\overline{T2} + Q1T1 + \overline{Q2}\,\overline{T2}T1$

(c)

Figure 3.16 Block and state diagrams and maps for Example 3.6

Table 3.6 Binary Assignment Chosen for Example 3.6 Problem

Internal State	Assigned Code	
	Q2	Q1
R1G2	0	0
R1Y2	0	1
G1R2	1	1
Y1R2	1	0

name of a state conveniently implies the output condition associated with it. The transitions between the states are labeled with input expressions which, if TRUE (i.e., if they have a value 1), induce them. There is only one T1T2 combination that will cause an exit from a rest state. The other three combinations cause the system to remain in the same state. Note that each intermediate, warning state has an *unlabeled* exit path. This indicates that there is *no condition* associated with it. The transition is *unconditional* (i.e., it will always take place on the very next CLOCK pulse).

Since this network has four states, it may be implemented using two FLIP-FLOPs. We now associate with each state a code that specifies the *contents* of the two FLIP-FLOPs when the network *assumes* that state. Table 3.6 specifies the arbitrary assignment chosen. With this assignment, the information contained in the state diagram may be converted into an equivalent form shown in the state table (Table 3.3) originally derived during the analysis of this circuit, in Example 3.2. Note that output information, originally defined in the state diagram, has also been transcribed to the state table.

We now arbitrarily choose to use D FLIP-FLOPs in the implementation. These devices are particularly convenient because the state table, which specifies the next Q's, *is* the map for the required D values to achieve them (since *next* Q = *present* D). Thus, we derive the maps for the D's shown in Fig. 3.16(c). The Boolean functions for the D's are written beneath their corresponding maps. (The map for D1 is a particularly good example of how clusters of squares may overlap.)

The output information on the right side of Table 3.3 corresponds to six elementary tables of combination whose equivalent functions (only of Q1 and Q2) may be readily derived as:

$$R1 = \overline{Q2}, \quad Y1 = Q2\overline{Q1}, \quad G1 = Q2Q1, \quad R2 = Q2, \quad Y2 = \overline{Q2}Q1, \quad \text{and} \quad G2 = \overline{Q2}\,\overline{Q1}.$$

Finally, the logic diagram in Fig. 3.11 shows gate structures that implement these functions, as well as those just derived for the D's. Note that these gate clusters are properly coupled to the postulated pair of D FLIP-FLOPs. ∎

■ **Example 3.7**   Design a two-bit COUNTER having a CLOCK input and a control input A. It contains two JK FLIP-FLOPs whose Q's are the circuit's outputs. The Q2Q1 state of the system advances (increments) on every CLOCK pulse. While A = 0, the conventional binary count sequence 00, 01, 10, 11, 00, . . . is followed. While A = 1, the sequence is altered to be 00, 01, 11, 10, 00, . . . That is, while A = 1, only one bit change per step is permitted.

Since we are already given the state-sequencing details, we can immediately draw the state table shown in Table 3.7. Using JK FLIP-FLOP rules (Table 3.4), we develop the maps in Fig. 3.17(a) from the transitions specified in the state table. The functions under these maps implement them. Thus, we construct the network shown in Fig. 3.17(b).

Table 3.7   State Table for Example 3.7

A:		0		1	
Present					
Q2	**Q1**				
0	0	0	1	0	1
0	1	1	0	1	1
1	1	0	0	1	0
1	0	1	1	0	0
		Next			
		Q2Q1			

To verify that the circuit shown meets the requirements, let us analyze it, by inspection. When A = 0, J1 = K1 = 1, in which case Q1 reverses on every CLOCK pulse, and J2 = K2 = Q1 (the EXCLUSIVE OR gate passes Q1), in which case Q2 toggles only if Q1 = 1. This fulfills the conventional binary counting requirement. When A = 1,

$$J1 = \overline{Q2}, \quad K1 = Q2, \quad J2 = Q1, \quad \text{and} \quad K2 = \overline{Q1}$$

(the EXCLUSIVE OR acts as an INVERTER), in which case, on every CLOCK edge, FLIP-FLOP2 loads the old Q1 value and FLIP-FLOP1 loads the *inverse* of the old Q2 value. This fulfills the "one-bit-change-per-step" sequencing requirement.   ■

■ **Example 3.8**   A useful exercise, which is actually an elementary synthesis problem, is to devise a circuit, built around *one* FLIP-FLOP type, that behaves as if it were a *different* FLIP-FLOP type. It is instructive because it reinforces your comprehension of the properties of these elements.

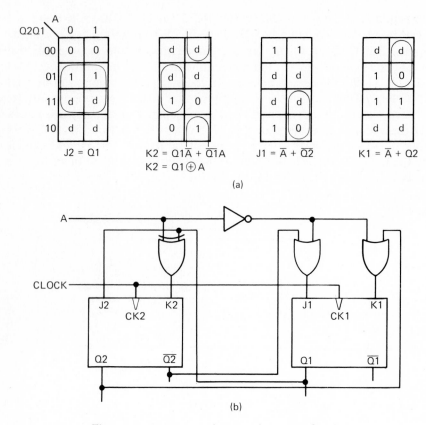

$J2 = Q1$

$K2 = Q1\overline{A} + \overline{Q1}A$
$K2 = Q1 \oplus A$

$J1 = \overline{A} + \overline{Q2}$

$K1 = \overline{A} + Q2$

(a)

(b)

Figure 3.17   Maps and circuit for Example 3.7

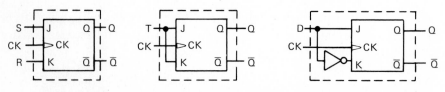

Figure 3.18   Using a *JK* FLIP-FLOP to simulate the other FF types

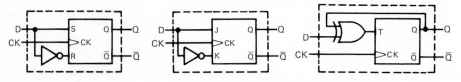

Figure 3.19   Simulating a D device using the other FF types

Virtually all of these problems may be solved "by inspection"—without resorting to the use of maps. We treat a few of them here. Others (including some that require more detailed analysis) are left as exercises at the end of this chapter.

Generally, it is easy to devise a circuit, using a "sophisticated" element, which will behave as a simpler device. It requires more thought to proceed in the other direction. For example, Fig. 3.18 shows how a JK element may be used to simulate either of the other three device types. In two cases, no additional gates are required. Figure 3.19 shows how a D FLIP-FLOP may be simulated by each of the other three device types. Note the EXCLUSIVE OR gate in the realization that employs a T FLIP-FLOP. It is used as a one-bit COMPARATOR. The FLIP-FLOP toggles only when its present state *disagrees* with the value of D. ∎

Table 3.8 contains a summary of the clocked sequential circuit analysis and synthesis procedures that have been discussed here and in Section 3.3.

Table 3.8   Summaries of Clocked Sequential-Circuit Analysis and Synthesis Procedures

Analysis Procedure

1. From the network given, express all FLIP-FLOP control levels and outputs as Boolean functions of the inputs and the *present* Q's.

2. Convert the expressions from step (1) into equivalent maps.

3. Using the proper FLIP-FLOP transition rules, convert the set of control-level maps into a similarly labeled *next* Q map. This is the State Table.

4. Using test input sequences on the *next* Q and output maps, develop a behavior rule for the circuit.

Synthesis Procedure

1. From the behavior rule given, identify all required internal states and draw a state diagram and an equivalent state table. Include output information. (At this point each state is identified by any convenient symbol.)

2. After determining the number of FLIP-FLOPs required, assign a binary code to each state and then encode the information in the state table to produce a *next* Q map and an output map.

3. After selecting a FLIP-FLOP type, convert the *next* Q map into a map of the FLIP-FLOP control levels that will produce that *next* Q behavior.

4. Develop minimal Boolean expressions for the FLIP-FLOP control levels and for the outputs, from their respective maps.

5. Draw the logic diagram of the resulting network.

3.5 REGISTERS AND COUNTERS

A digital computer is composed primarily of REGISTERs. As alluded to in Example 3.3, a REGISTER is a string of one or more identical FLIP-FLOPs. Its length N is the number of FLIP-FLOPs in it. It *stores* (holds, contains, "remembers") a code of length N. Normally, it has an N-bit-wide DATA IN port and an N-bit-wide DATA OUT port. The DATA OUT signals represent the *contents* of the register. They are the Q's of the individual FLIP-FLOPs. (Typically, the complements of the Q's are also available signals.) The output signals remain *constant* (i.e., the data stored remains fixed) until the contents of the register are changed. A register's contents are "read" whenever its output signals are used in any way. Reading a register does not destroy its contents.

The simplest register has one additional input—a single control signal named LOAD. The register normally *ignores* its DATA IN signals until its LOAD control pulse is asserted. On a specific edge of this pulse, the DATA IN bits become the new contents of the register, replacing the old contents. The DATA IN signals must be *valid* at that instant in time only. At all other times the DATA IN signals may change arbitrarily, since they are ignored. Loading a register with a new bit string is termed "writing" into it.

The block diagram of a register, based on the interface defined above, is shown in Fig. 3.20(a). Its internal structure, which should be obvious from the definition given above, is shown in (b). Part (c) of the figure provides a shorthand notation for (b). The device consists of a string of N identical D FLIP-FLOPs, all of whose CLOCK inputs are tied together. The common CLOCK control signal is renamed as LOAD.

The basic definition given in Fig. 3.20 accurately describes an overwhelming majority of the registers encountered in a typical digital system.

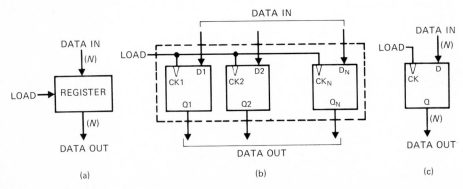

Figure 3.20   Block and logic diagrams of an elementary REGISTER

Each device is used simply as a cell in which a code may be saved or stored indefinitely. (Recall, for example, the need to save the result of one step in a sequence of arithmetic operations, so that it may be used as an operand in a later step—pointed out in the ALU discussion in Section 2.9.) The term LATCH is sometimes used interchangeably with REGISTER to describe this elementary device. Recall, however, that a LATCH does not have the edge-triggered property, which we ordinarily assume. Its DATA IN signals must remain valid over the entire duration of its LOAD pulse.

Numerous additional "features" may be added to the basic register defined above. As we discuss these, you should keep in mind that *code storage* remains as the fundamental purpose of the element. A register may have other control inputs, in addition to the LOAD signal. For example, a common CLEAR input terminal may be included in its design. Assertion of CLEAR causes the contents of the register to become zero. (Recall the discussion, concerning the overriding FLIP-FLOP control input signals CLEAR and PRESET, presented in Section 3.3.) A register may contain internally a bank of N TRI-STATE output gates, all enabled by a common control input signal named (for example) OUTPUT ENABLE. If the register is so equipped, its DATA OUT signals will appear only while OUTPUT ENABLE is asserted. Similarly, a register may have an additional control input named LOAD DIS-ABLE, whose assertion *prevents* the load that would otherwise occur when the common CLOCK pulse arrives. This feature may be mechanized internally using one additional gate, which inhibits transmission of the common CLOCK signal to the individual FLIP-FLOPs, if LOAD DISABLE is active.

The capability of performing *data operations* may be embedded within a register by adding suitable gates to it. On activation of the proper input control signals, the register's contents change. The *new* contents are some (unary) *function* of the *old* contents. The most important internal register data operations are COUNT and SHIFT. A register having incrementing or decrementing capabilities is called a COUNTER. A register that is able to shift its contents is called a SHIFT REGISTER.

When a register has more than one possible function, there are several alternative means by which it may be controlled. On the one hand, each possible function may have its own control input signal (named LOAD, IN-CREMENT, SHIFT RIGHT, etc.) whose assertion initiates it. In this case, the control signals are assumed to be mutually exclusive. (Only one may be asserted at a time.) On the other hand, the register may receive a single CLOCK pulse which causes it to execute the operation specified by *other* control signals—levels assumed valid while the crucial CLOCK edge is occurring. This method is preferable because it separates the control of *when* to "do it" from that of *what* to do. Combinations of these methods are also possible. For example, a register may have a common CLOCK input, a "func-

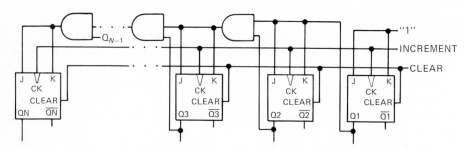

Figure 3.21   An elementary UP COUNTER

tion code" input port, and a separate CLEAR input terminal tied to all of the FLIP-FLOP individual CLEAR terminals.

To introduce the implementation of "more intelligent" registers, consider the logic diagram shown in Fig. 3.21. Its common CLOCK input has been renamed as INCREMENT, to indicate the internal operation that is executed when this signal is asserted. Note that this device has a common CLEAR input, whose function was described earlier. If you compare the gate structure shown in Fig. 3.21 with that of the INCREMENTER in Fig. 2.14, you will note that the AND-gate chain is present, but that the EXCLUSIVE OR gates are missing. The reason for this is that each JK FLIP-FLOP already *has* the capability to selectively invert its contents (i.e., to toggle) based on a control signal value. Observe that, since each $Ji = Ki$, every JK device is acting as a T FLIP-FLOP. The entire structure is a COUNTER whose contents increment every time an INCREMENT pulse is received. To convince yourself that this is true, you need only remember that each FLIP-FLOP toggles only if $J = K = 1$ *just before* the critical CLOCK edge. The fact that this situation may change immediately *after* the edge is immaterial.

A DOWN COUNTER (one which *decrements* on the application of an input control pulse) may be similarly designed merely by replacing each Qi AND-input connection by one to its *complementary* $\overline{Q}i$ terminal. Under these conditions, a bit toggles only if all less significant bits (before arrival of the CLOCK pulse) were *zero*.

Note that the COUNTER in Fig. 3.21 is not easily used as a general-purpose register, because it has no parallel LOADing capability. To place an arbitrary value in it, one must CLEAR it and then INCREMENT it that number of times.

An alternative rule, to specify how an arbitrary bit in an incrementing COUNTER should behave, may be expressed as follows: "Bit i should toggle whenever the bit to its right (bit $i - 1$) makes a 1-to-0 transition. Bit 0 always toggles." You may easily convince yourself that this rule is logically equivalent to those discussed earlier in Section 2.3. It suggests a COUNTER realization containing negative-edge-triggered T FLIP-FLOPs (with each $T = 1$, so that each device *always* toggles), in which each CLOCK input signal comes from the Q of the FLIP-FLOP on its right. The entire system increments whenever the least significant (rightmost) stage receives a negative CLOCK edge.

Such a COUNTER is called a *ripple* COUNTER, because not all of its FLIP-FLOPs are CLOCKed simultaneously. Rather, a CARRY generated in the rightmost position propagates, in a "ripple" effect, up to the first stage making a 0-to-1 transition (at which point the ripple stops). The time to reach the new state depends on the CARRY propagation time (the "distance" of the ripple). The slowest transition is the advance from the 111...111 state to the 000...000 state.

Note that a series of *momentary* states is assumed during a typical INCREMENT. For example, in incrementing from 0111 to 1000, the sequence of momentary states 0110, 0100, and 0000 is assumed before the final state is reached. If, for example, the COUNTER output were directed to a DECODER input port (a common structure), temporary erroneous pulses may appear on those DECODER outputs corresponding to the momentary COUNTER states. It is conceivable that these erroneous signals could cause one or more other FLIP-FLOPs in the system to assume erroneous states. For this reason, we will ignore the ripple COUNTER and will continue to assume *synchronous* devices (in which all FLIP-FLOPs receive the same CLOCK edge simultaneously).

A register having both LOAD and INCREMENT capabilities is shown in Fig. 3.22. The one-bit FUNCTION CODE defines which of two operations will be evoked when CLOCK is asserted. Note that the chain of AND gates, beginning at CARRY IN and ending at CARRY OUT, duplicates the function of similar chains in Figs. 2.14 and 3.21. If the FUNCTION control level is 0, all of the pairs of AND gates directly enabled by it are *disabled*—forcing their outputs to 0—in which case, the DATA IN signals have no effect on the system. Under these conditions, every $Ji = Ki = Ti$, so that the network has the same structure as the COUNTER in Fig. 3.21. Here Ti is the *toggle* command signal to FLIP-FLOP stage i. Since gate x is *enabled*, CARRY IN is permitted to pass. If CARRY IN = 1, the register's contents will INCREMENT on the next CLOCK pulse. If CARRY IN = 0, the register will merely hold its present contents, since all T's will be 0. (Note that the equivalent of CARRY IN, in Fig. 3.21, is a constant "1", causing an INCREMENT on *every* CLOCK pulse.) The signals CARRY IN and CARRY OUT permit this register to be concatenated with other identical units to form a device whose width is a multiple of that of one unit. In such a configuration, every CARRY OUT is connected to the CARRY IN of its left neighbor, and the least significant CARRY IN is made "1".

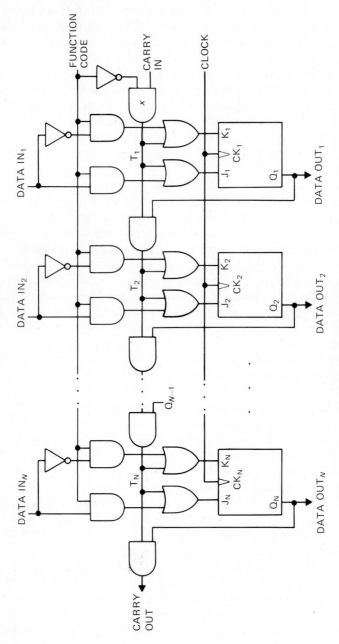

Figure 3.22   Register with INCREMENT and LOAD capabilities

In short, when FUNCTION CODE = 0, the register INCREMENTs on a CLOCK pulse if CARRY IN = 1. When the FUNCTION control level is 1, gate x is *disabled,* causing all of the Ti's to be 0—in which case, each OR gate pair merely passes the pair of signals coming from the AND gate pair above it. These AND gates are now *enabled,* permitting the DATA IN signals and their complements to pass, so that every Ji = DATA IN(i) and every Ki = $\overline{\text{DATA IN}(i)}$. On the occurrence of the CLOCK edge, the register will LOAD the (assumed valid) code applied at the DATA IN port.

It is frequently necessary to devise a COUNTER whose total number of states is *not* a power of two. For example, a "decade" COUNTER has a total number of states that is a power of *ten.* It normally consists of a concatenation of stages, each of which contains four FLIP-FLOPs but has only ten possible states. It is used in decimally oriented applications, such as those in which "events" are counted, with the count displayed as a sequence of *decimal* digits. As another example, a digital watch or clock contains counters that increment every second or every tenth of a second. The natural total number of states for one of its internal counter stages is either 60 (for the seconds or minutes counter), 12 or 24 (for the hours counter), 30 or 31 (for the day-of-the-month counter), and so on.

While one may use the sequential-circuit design techniques described in Section 3.4 to develop a network having an arbitrary number of states, the following simple guidelines are usually sufficient for the design of such COUNTERs: Assume a binary COUNTER having both a parallel LOAD capability and an independent CLEAR. For example, the device in Fig. 3.22 may be used, if it is equipped with an independent CLEAR input. (This may be done by using FLIP-FLOPs having this feature and by connecting their individual CLEAR input terminals together, to yield the common system CLEAR bus.) The total number of states may be reduced, from the maximum of 2^N (where N is the number of internal FLIP-FLOPs), by *detecting* when a specific state is reached and, at this point, *restarting* at some *new* initial state. (The restart value may be chosen as zero.) Using this technique, the system will count, in the conventional manner, up to some prearranged point, where it will be forced to *skip* some states that would ordinarily follow.

Figure 3.23 provides two examples. Starting (a) at count 0, the system increments normally until it advances to the 1010 state, at which point the added detector delivers an output assertion that activates CLEAR and immediately restarts the system at 0. Only ten states (0 though 9) are possible. On an increment from 9, the system momentarily spends an instant (measured in nanoseconds) in state 1010 before it reverts back to 0. This instant is equivalent in duration to the time that a ripple COUNTER spends in one of *its* momentary states, while the CARRY is propagating. In many applications, the momentary erroneous state is tolerable. Note that only two inputs to the

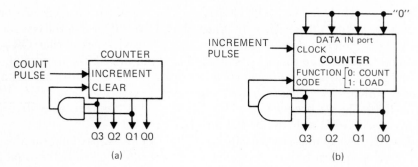

Figure 3.23   Two examples for the realization of a decade COUNTER

AND gate are necessary to detect 1010, because the other 1X1X states will never arise.

The alternative scheme indicated in (b) is preferable because no temporary erroneous state exists. The added detector now recognizes when the count of 9 is reached. (Again, only two AND inputs are required, since the other 1XX1 states will never occur.) The detector's output assertion reverses the FUNCTION CODE signal, causing the device to temporarily exit from the COUNT mode and to enter the LOAD mode. On the *very next* CLOCK pulse, a LOAD of zero restarts the system.

Note that the technique in (b) may be used to restart at *any* constant value. Since the added detector may be wired to detect any arbitrary state, one may devise a COUNTER that counts between any two arbitrary limits (for example, only between states 2 and 7) before restarting. Problems at the end of this chapter explore this issue further.

As indicated in Fig. 3.24, a typical SHIFT REGISTER is a combination of a simple register and a SHIFTER, configured such that the SHIFTER's output code is the register's DATA IN value, while the SHIFTER's input code is the register's present contents. Whenever the register is activated by a LOAD pulse, it *loads a shifted version of its present contents.* Any of the SHIFTERs previously shown in Figs. 2.21 through 2.24 may be utilized.

Figure 3.24 is an important example of a structure that we will encounter many times. It demonstrates the advantage of edge-triggering. The value that is loaded into the register is a function (in this case, a shifted version) of its *own present contents. Immediately after* the LOAD occurs, the register's DATA IN values will *change.* However, since the activating edge is no longer present, these *new* DATA IN values will be ignored. Note that a COUNTER may be implemented using a structure identical to that in Fig. 3.24, if the SHIFTER is replaced by an INCREMENTER or by a DECREMENTER.

A bidirectional SHIFT REGISTER is one that is capable of executing SHIFT operations in either direction. Such a device normally has a FUNC-

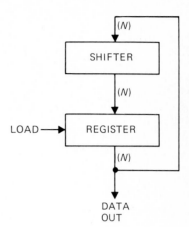

Figure 3.24 The structure of a
typical SHIFT REGISTER

TION CODE input port, which specifies which of several possible SHIFT operations should be executed on the next CLOCK pulse. Typically, one of these function codes is assigned to evoke a parallel LOAD of a new register value (applied to the DATA IN port of the system). Another code is usually allocated to disable *any* operation, in which case the register merely retains its present contents.

Such a SHIFT REGISTER is normally implemented using a MULTI-PLEXER. (Recall the multipurpose SHIFTER design shown in Fig. 2.24.) One of the MULTIPLEXER's input ports receives the external DATA IN code (which is deposited into the register during a parallel LOAD). Another of its ports receives the register's *own* DATA OUT signals (permitting the equivalent of a "no operation," because the register's present contents are merely *rewritten* into it). A simplified example of such a SHIFT REGISTER is shown in Fig. 3.25. On the occurrence of a CLOCK pulse, one of four possible actions is evoked, depending on the two-bit FUNCTION CODE, X. If $X = 0$, the register is *disabled*, since no change in its contents occurs on the CLOCK pulse. (As explained above, in point of fact the present contents of the register are actually *reloaded* internally.) If $X = 1$, the register LOADs the DATA IN code. (Note that the DATA IN port of the system is different from the DATA IN port of the internal register.) If $X = 2$, the present contents of the register are shifted left, and if $X = 3$, they are shifted right. Observe that, for either shift, the *shifted-in* bit is the signal applied to a corresponding, special input terminal. By an appropriate connection, this signal may be made a constant ("0" or "1"), or the shifted-off bit from the other end (if a ROTATE is desired), or a *serial* data signal (to effect a serial-to-parallel conversion). In the latter case, the serial bits are CLOCKed into the register, one bit at a time, until the register is "filled," at which time the serial code is

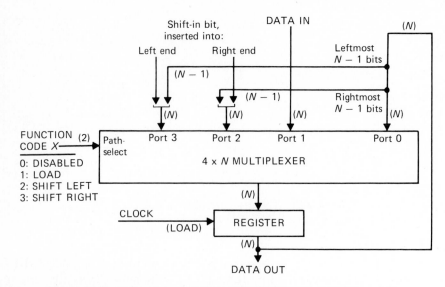

Figure 3.25   Bidirectional SHIFT REGISTER with LOAD capability

available, in parallel, at the DATA OUT port. Clearly, many other SHIFT variations may be added to the basic structure shown in Fig. 3.25.

You are now in a position to appreciate that many possible data operations may be embedded within a register. In the simplest case, you have seen a device, capable of LOADing only, which provides the fundamental function of a register—code storage. On the other extreme, you may envision a device having separate CLOCK, CLEAR, and OUTPUT ENABLE control signals, plus a FUNCTION CODE input port to select from among many possible internal functions, including SHIFTs, ROTATEs, INCREMENTs, DECREMENTs, LOAD, DISABLE, and other unary data operations.

PROBLEMS

3.1   Redraw the waveforms for the signals SET and RESET, shown in Fig. P3.1, and underneath them plot the waveform of Q for the basic LATCH given in Fig. 3.2(a).

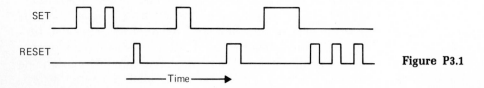

Figure P3.1

3.2 By altering the positions of one or more of the inversion "bubbles" in Fig. 3.2, develop a circuit for a basic LATCH containing one AND gate and one OR gate. Label its inputs and outputs properly.

3.3 Redraw the waveforms given in Fig. P3.3 and underneath them plot the waveform of Q for the clocked D LATCH of Fig. 3.4. [Note that the situation in which D changes while C is asserted (see the last C pulse) does not ordinarily occur.]

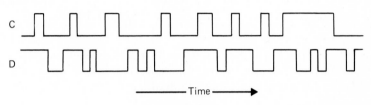

C

D

Time

Figure P3.3

3.4 Imagine a circuit consisting of a single INVERTER whose output terminal is connected directly to its input terminal. Assume that the device exhibits a signal delay, from input signal edge to responding output signal edge, of t seconds but is otherwise ideal. Describe the waveform of the INVERTER's output signal.

3.5 Redraw the signal waveforms given in Problem 3.3 and underneath them plot the Q output waveform for the negative edge-triggered D FLIP-FLOP of Fig. 3.5. (C is the CLOCK input.)

3.6 Redraw the signal waveforms given in Fig. P3.6 and underneath them plot the Q output waveform of a *positive* edge-triggered JK FLIP-FLOP having these signals as inputs.

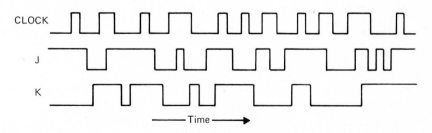

CLOCK

J

K

Time

Figure P3.6

3.7 Assuming that the FLIP-FLOP is edge-triggered, explain the behavior of the circuit in Fig. P3.7.

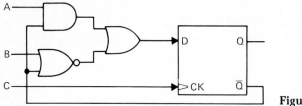

Figure P3.7

3.8 Show how an SR FLIP-FLOP may be realized using a D FLIP-FLOP and a minimum of additional gates. Similarly, realize the SR device using a T FLIP-FLOP plus a minimum of additional logic.

3.9 Show how a T FLIP-FLOP may be realized using either a D FLIP-FLOP or an SR FLIP-FLOP.

3.10 Convert a T FLIP-FLOP into a JK FLIP-FLOP.

3.11 A FLIP-FLOP operates properly only when the electrical power source to which it is connected is active. When power is first turned on, what would you expect its initial state to be? Why? Similarly, when a simple register is first turned on, what would you expect its initial contents to be?

3.12 Using the network given in Fig. P3.12 and assuming real (as opposed to idealized) gates, redraw the waveforms given for D and C and underneath them plot the waveforms for A and B.

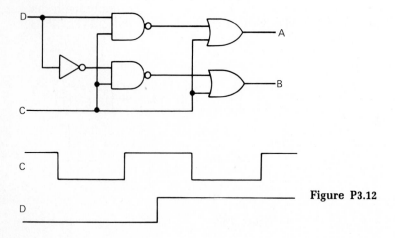

Figure P3.12

3.13 Using your answer to Problem 3.12, explain the behavior of the circuit shown in Fig. P3.13.

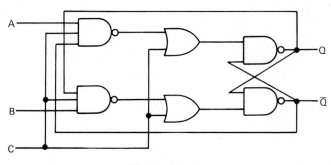

Figure P3.13

3.14 Explain the behavior of the circuit in Fig. P3.14. The CLOCK signal is a train of equally spaced pulses. Operation begins with both FLIP-FLOPs reset.

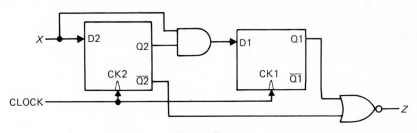

Figure P3.14

3.15 Design a circuit having two inputs X1 and X2 and one output Z. It also has a CLOCK input that receives a train of equally spaced pulses. Whenever a CLOCK pulse occurs, the values of X1 and X2 are sampled. The state of the circuit does not change when both samples have a value 0. Furthermore, simultaneous X1 = 1 and X2 = 1 samples are guaranteed never to occur. Normally, Z = 0. On every *second* successive X1 = 1 sample, following any X2 = 1 sample, Z should become "1". It should remain asserted until a new X1 = 1 or X2 = 1 sample occurs. A properly labeled state diagram should accompany your solution. Use JK FLIP-FLOPs.

3.16 The network shown in Fig. P3.16 contains two negative edge-triggered FLIP-FLOPs, each having overriding PRESET and CLEAR inputs. D1, D0, and A remain valid while pulse P occurs. Explain what the circuit does, on assertion of a P pulse, for the two cases: $A = 0$ and $A = 1$.

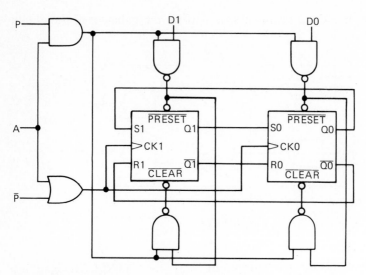

Figure P3.16

3.17 For the network shown in Fig. P3.17: (a) What is the value of the output code DOUT? (b) What happens whenever a P pulse occurs, assuming all other inputs remain valid?

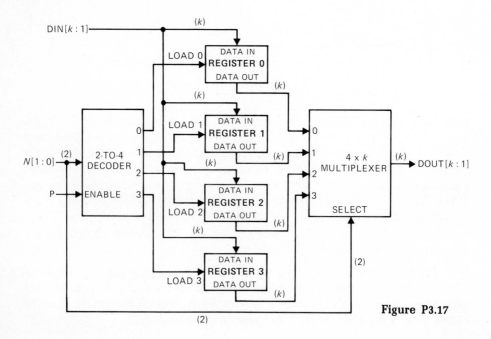

Figure P3.17

3.18 How does the value of Q[2 : 1] (in Fig. P3.18) sequence, on successive CLOCK pulses, for the two cases: $A = 0$ and $A = 1$?

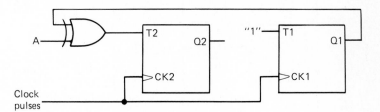

Figure P3.18   Clock pulses

3.19 Design a sequential circuit having an X input, a Z output, and a periodic CLOCK input, which samples X. Here $Z = 1$ if the previous *two or more* X samples were the *same*. Otherwise, $Z = 0$. You may assume any convenient starting state. Use D FLIP-FLOPs.

3.20 The FLIP-FLOPs in Fig. P3.20 are edge-triggered. Explain the function of the network.

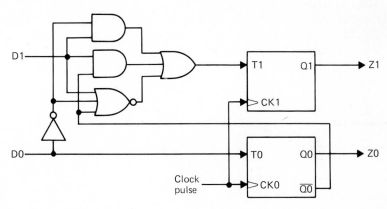

Figure P3.20

3.21 Using two edge-triggered T FLIP-FLOPs and a minimum of additional logic, design a base-3 counter. On successive CLOCK pulses, the counter's Q2Q1 state sequences as follows:

$$00, \quad 01, \quad 10, \quad 00, \quad 01, \quad 10, \quad 00, \quad \dots, \quad \text{etc.}$$

3.22 The network shown in Fig. P3.22 is driven by a continuous train of equal-duration, equally spaced positive pulses. The FLIP-FLOPs are negative edge-triggered. Draw an input pulse waveform containing about 10 to 12 pulses, and underneath it draw the four output waveforms.

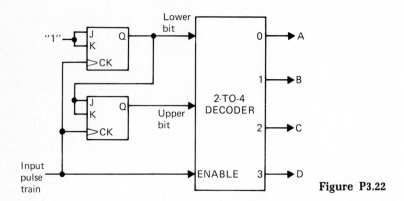

Figure P3.22

3.23 Derive an expression for the number of different binary assignments that encode S states into N bits, assuming that S is *not* a power of 2. (That is, $2^{N-1} < S < 2^N$.) Your answer should reduce to $2^N!$ (as explained in Section 3.4) when $S = 2^N$.

3.24 A four-bit (edge-triggered) register is shown in Fig. P3.24. Three external connections are made from its output terminals to its input terminals. If D_{IN1} is also connected to D_{OUT4}, how will the contents of the register behave when a LOAD pulse occurs? Suppose D_{IN1} were connected instead to the constant "0" signal terminal. On successive LOAD pulses, how will the contents behave now?

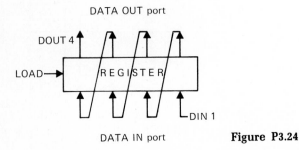

Figure P3.24

3.25 A two-bit (edge-triggered) register with some added external logic is connected as shown in Fig. P3.25. How will the contents of the register behave whenever a LOAD pulse occurs?

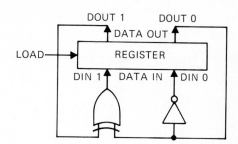

Figure P3.25

3.26 Devise a four-bit counter that counts only between the hex values 3 and C. An increment past C restarts at 3 again. States 0, 1, 2, D, E, and F never occur.

3.27 A register has eight built-in operations. Show how the first control approach described below may be converted into the second. (1) Each operation is induced by its own unique control pulse, requiring eight mutually exclusive control pulse inputs. (2) Four inputs are employed, a CLOCK pulse signal and three control levels which select one of the eight operations. The selected operation is evoked when the CLOCK signal is asserted.

Memories and Register Transfers

4.1 RANDOM-ACCESS MEMORY INTERFACE AND INTERNAL STRUCTURE

A MEMORY is a collection of identical registers, all contained within a single component. The interface to a MEMORY closely resembles that of a register. It has an N-bit-wide DATA IN port and an N-bit-wide DATA OUT port, where N is the length of any one of its internal registers. In its simplest form, it also has an input control signal, called WRITE, whose function is virtually identical to that of the LOAD input signal to a register.

At any instant in time, this interface is "coupled to" or "connected to" *only one* of the internal registers, the one selected by the code applied to an *additional* input port called the ADDRESS port. Each of the internal registers is identified by a unique *number* called its ADDRESS, in the same way that different houses along a street are uniquely labeled. The input ADDRESS code specifies with *which* internal register the rest of the interface is currently communicating. For this reason, an ADDRESS is also called a "pointer." It selects or names or "points to" a single MEMORY location.

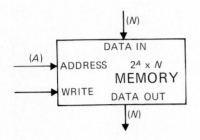

Figure 4.1 Typical MEMORY block diagram

Figure 4.1 contains a block diagram of the MEMORY defined above. If its ADDRESS length is A, the MEMORY contains 2^A registers. Its storage *capacity* (the number of bits it holds—the number of internal FLIP-FLOPs) is $2^A \times N$ bits (where N is the length of each register). For example, a 4096×16 MEMORY contains 4096 registers, each 16 bits long, giving a total capacity of 65536 bits. Its ADDRESS length is 12, because 2^{12} is 4096. Register numbers begin at zero.

At any given instant, only the register selected by the ADDRESS may be *accessed* (read or written). The DATA OUT port carries the contents of that register. The signals applied to the DATA IN port are normally ignored, except when the WRITE signal is asserted, at which time the register selected by the ADDRESS *loads* the DATA IN code, which must be valid at that instant only. All of the *unselected* registers continue to hold their last-written bit patterns.

A MEMORY behaves, at any instant, as if it were a *single* register (the one selected by the ADDRESS). Whenever the ADDRESS changes, a short period of time must elapse (due to the delays through the many internal gates of the device) before the newly addressed register is *accessible* (effectively "connected" to the interface). This time is known as the "access time" for the register. All of the registers in a RANDOM-ACCESS MEMORY (abbreviated as "RAM") have the *same* access time, independent of which register was *previously* addressed. A typical RAM access time is comparable to 10 to 100 gate delays.

Observe that the word "address" is used in the above discussion not only as a noun but also as a verb. You may find it helpful to remember the sentence: "An ADDRESS addresses a unique register in a MEMORY." The term "word" is sometimes used as a substitute for the contents of a MEMORY register. Thus, we may say: "A RAM access consists of the READ or the WRITE of a word."

Viewed as a sequential network, for all practical purposes, a large MEMORY has an infinite number of states. If the bit pattern stored in it disappears when its source of electrical power is removed, it is called a *volatile* MEMORY. Since a typical FLIP-FLOP or REGISTER cannot operate without an electrical power source, it is natural to assume that every RAM is a volatile element. (Magnetic devices are the notable exception.)

When power is first applied to a sequential network, each FLIP-FLOP in it normally assumes an *arbitrary* initial state. It must be "initialized" properly before normal operation may begin. Typically, a common RESET or CLEAR signal is generated (perhaps by a switch actuation) to set up the proper initial state. A system may include a special "power-on RESET" circuit, which automatically generates the initialization signal whenever power is turned on.

The power-on initial state of a volatile RAM is arbitrary. (A programmer terms such a useless, random bit pattern as "garbage".) A RAM is initialized properly by a sequence of one or more WRITEs of bit patterns that have been preplanned by a programmer. Such a sequence is called a MEMORY *load.*

The MEMORY in Fig. 4.1 may be constructed using 2^A identical registers, *one* DECODER and *one* MULTIPLEXER. The DATA IN port of the RAM is wired to *all* of the individual register DATA IN ports, so that all registers receive the *same* DATA IN values. (Recall that a register ignores its DATA IN signals at all times except when it receives a LOAD assertion.) The DECODER is used to direct the WRITE signal to the LOAD input of the selected register. Each register's DATA OUT port is connected to a separate MULTIPLEXER input port. The MULTIPLEXER is used to direct the contents of the selected register to the system's DATA OUT port. Figure 4.2 contains a diagram of this organization.

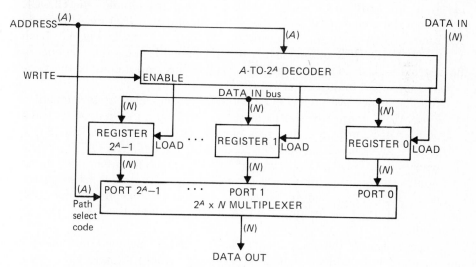

Figure 4.2 One possible RAM internal organization

Note that WRITE is applied to the ENABLE input of the DECODER, while the ADDRESS code is applied to its normal input port. The DECODER is being used as a DEMULTIPLEXER—a "signal distributor." The ADDRESS code specifies *to which* of its outputs the WRITE signal will be directed. Whenever a WRITE pulse occurs, only the register selected by the ADDRESS will receive a LOAD pulse, causing it to load the DATA IN value. The ADDRESS code is also applied to the MULTIPLEXER's *path-select* input port. It enables a path only between the selected register's DATA OUT port and that of the MEMORY.

It is important that you understand the structure in Fig. 4.2 for several reasons. First, it reinforces your comprehension of the functions of the basic REGISTER, DECODER and MULTIPLEXER elements. Second, it explains, in one concise picture, what has been said in the preceding thousand words.

The design in Fig. 4.2 really contains *two* ADDRESS DECODERs. One is embedded inside the MULTIPLEXER. Since an ADDRESS DECODER is a sizeable element (for example, consider the number of gates required in a 12-to-4096 DECODER!), any modification, which permits one DECODER to be shared by the READ and WRITE portions of the network, is a significant improvement. Suppose we use registers having TRI-STATE outputs. Each now has one additional control input, named OUTPUT ENABLE, whose assertion permits transmission of its DATA OUT signals. In addition, let us equip each register with a LOAD ENABLE input, whose assertion is required to evoke a parallel load on reception of a CLOCK pulse. If LOAD ENABLE = 0, the register ignores its CLOCK pulse. (This feature may be mechanized merely by the addition of a single AND gate, which withholds the CLOCK pulse from the common CLOCK bus of the register if LOAD ENABLE = 0.) The same RAM is now realizable by the structure shown in Fig. 4.3. Each ADDRESS DECODER output serves two purposes. It gates the contents of the selected register to the common DATA OUT bus, and it enables the same register to respond to the common WRITE pulse.

Note that, since every OUTPUT ENABLE is connected to its companion LOAD ENABLE, these two signals may be combined and renamed as REGISTER ENABLE, *provided* that it is clearly explained that, if REGISTER ENABLE is not asserted, the register decouples from its DATA OUT port and also ignores its LOAD CLOCK signal. (Some students have a tendency to use an undefined ENABLE input as a general design "cure-all." As discussed earlier, in Section 2.1, good design practice requires that each use of an ENABLE control input be accompanied by a clear specification as to what its effect will be.)

A comparison of the structures in Figs. 4.2 and 4.3 demonstrates that the *partitioning* within a block or logic diagram (i.e., where the internal component interfaces are drawn) directly affects which devices are clearly identifi-

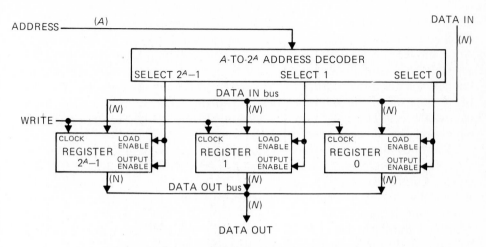

Figure 4.3 Alternative RAM internal organization

able in it. For example, while there is no MULTIPLEXER element shown in Fig. 4.3, it is still present. Its parts have been *redistributed* among the other components shown. It consists of the TRI-STATE gates within the registers, the DATA OUT bus, and the ADDRESS DECODER. For this reason, whenever you examine the logic or circuit diagram of a RAM device, you may not be able to immediately identify the components indicated in the figures above. Logically, however, they are present.

Our implicit assumption of edge-triggering does not apply to a typical RAM element. You will recall (from the discussion in Section 3.2) that an edge-triggered FLIP-FLOP is a complex device consisting of two or three coupled LATCHes. Since a typical RAM element contains an enormous number of FLIP-FLOPs, its total complexity is significantly reduced through the use of the simplest LATCHes. For these reasons, it is necessary that the DATA IN signals to a RAM remain valid over the entire duration of its WRITE pulse. Note that, in addition to having to remain valid *during* a READ or a WRITE access, the *ADDRESS* input signals to a RAM must *have been* valid, *preceding* the access, for a time greater than the *access time* of the system.

4.2 ARRAYS OF MEMORY ELEMENTS

Current semiconductor technology permits a RAM structure, such as that shown in Fig. 4.3, to be fabricated on a minute "chip" of silicon and enclosed inside a small integrated-circuit package. To make it convenient to construct large-capacity memories as iterated arrays of identical chips, one fundamental change to the diagram in Fig. 4.3 is required. Suppose we add an ENABLE input to the ADDRESS DECODER and rename it as "CHIP SELECT" or "CHIP ENABLE." While this signal is asserted, access to any register on the chip (as described earlier) is permitted. On the other hand, if CHIP SELECT is 0, *all* of the internal registers are disabled—in which case, each ignores the WRITE signal, remains decoupled from the DATA OUT bus, and merely retains its last-written contents.

You have already seen several examples in which identical components are concatenated to form "wider" versions of themselves. INCREMENTERs, DECREMENTERs, ADDERs, and COUNTERs of width $M \times N$ may be constructed by linking M identical subunits, each of width N. Techniques for constructing large DECODERs out of identical subDECODERs have been described. Similarly, we now discuss how identical MEMORY elements may be configured to form larger versions of themselves.

The capacity of a MEMORY depends on two parameters: the ADDRESS length A (since the total number of registers is 2^A) and the register length N (the number of bits per register). Assume an unlimited supply of identical MEMORY elements of the type shown in Fig. 4.1. Assume, however, that each device is equipped with the CHIP ENABLE feature introduced above. If CHIP ENABLE = 0, it decouples from its DATA ports, ignores WRITE, and remains dormant, merely continuing to store the bit patterns previously written into it. We consider first configurations of these "$2^A \times N$" components designed to increase one of the capacity parameters (N or A) without changing the other.

■ **Example 4.1** M identical MEMORY elements may be linked side by side to form a composite MEMORY containing the same number of registers as in a single element, but having DATA ports of width $M \times N$. For example, Fig. 4.4 shows four 1024 × 4 devices interconnected to form one 1024 × 16 RAM. (Recall that $1024 = 2^{10}$.) Note that the interface to the *composite* MEMORY still satisfies the requirements defined in Fig. 4.1. Its DATA IN and DATA OUT ports are each 16 bits wide. The entire system has it own "CHIP" ENABLE control input, which is tied to all of the individual CHIP ENABLE input terminals. This makes it possible to use this network as *one* component in an even larger MEMORY. If this structure is the only MEMORY in a system, we may simply connect the *overall* ENABLE input to the constant "1" terminal, so that each chip is *always* enabled. Observe that a single register in the composite MEMORY is actually *distributed* internally among the four components. It consists of a concatenation of four four-bit registers, all positioned at identical locations in their respective elements.

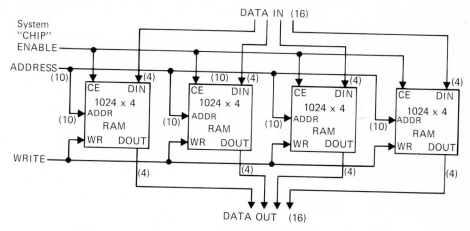

Figure 4.4   1024 × 16 MEMORY using four 1024 × 4 RAM's

This organization is another example of a "bit-slice" structure, in which several identical components are placed side by side, each handling a different field of bits (or "slice") of the entire bit string processed by the composite system.   ∎

■ **Example 4.2**   We may also devise a composite MEMORY whose DATA ports remain as wide as those of one element but whose number of registers is increased. In this case, the ADDRESS length of the composite MEMORY must be larger than that of any of the internal elements. Since every bit added to the length of a code *doubles* the number of possible codes, it is natural to increase the number of registers in factors of *two*. For example, two identical submemories double the number of registers and add one bit to the composite ADDRESS length. Eight submemories multiply the number of registers by eight and add *three* bits to the composite ADDRESS length.

Consider, then, a structure in which the number of identical submemories is a power of two. Neglecting the individual CHIP SELECT terminals for the moment, assume that all of the ports of the internal RAM elements are connected to corresponding internal *buses*. Their names and corresponding widths are as follows: DATA IN (N), DATA OUT (N), ADDRESS (A), and WRITE (1). If all of the CHIP SELECT terminals are gathered together into an input port that receives a *one-asserted* code, only the enabled internal RAM element will pay any attention to the DATA IN, ADDRESS, and WRITE signals and will transmit signals to the DATA OUT bus. That is, READ and WRITE accesses will be permitted only to the enabled chip. We

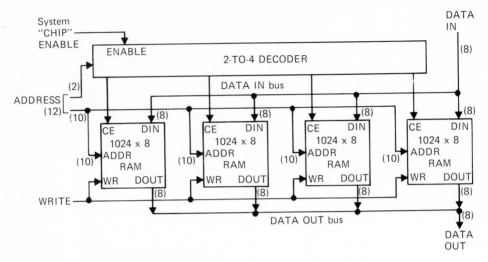

Figure 4.5   4096 × 8 RAM using four 1024 × 8 devices

guarantee that only one subMEMORY at a time will be activated by deriving all of the CHIP SELECT signals from an *additional* DECODER whose inputs are the *extra* ADDRESS bits (those not "bussed" to the individual ADDRESS input ports).

For example, Fig. 4.5 shows a 4096 × 8 RAM consisting of four identical 1024 × 8 register banks and an added 2-to-4 DECODER, which decodes the extra two ADDRESS bits. The ADDRESS length of the composite MEMORY is 12, which is divided into a field of two bits that selects (via the added DECODER) *which* subMEMORY to enable, and a field of ten bits that selects one register *within the selected bank.* Thus, the two-bit field is a "bank number." All disabled components remain dormant.

The interface to the composite system meets the requirements defined originally in Fig. 4.1. Note that the ENABLE input to the added DECODER is the "CHIP" ENABLE for the entire structure, permitting it to be used as an indivisible component in an even larger MEMORY.   ■

■ **Example 4.3**   The techniques described above may be combined to assemble an array of identical elements that comprises a composite MEMORY whose DATA port width is a multiple of that of one element and whose total number of registers is similarly a multiple of that of one element. For example, Fig. 4.6 shows a 4096 × 16 RAM constructed using eight 1024 × 8 devices. Clearly, many other arrays (for example, sixteen 1024 × 4's or four 2048 × 8's) may be assembled to realize the same composite system.   ■

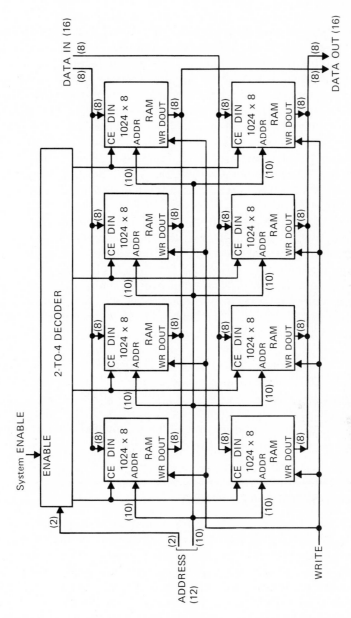

Figure 4.6 4096 × 16 RAM containing eight 1024 × 8 elements

To conserve on the number of "pins" or terminals required for a MEMO-RY element, many RAM devices are designed so that the DATA IN and DATA OUT ports *share the same terminals*. The terminals are *bidirectional*—sometimes acting as inputs (for the WRITE operation) and other times serving as outputs (for the READ operation). You will recall the brief introduction to bidirectional terminals at the end of Section 1.3. (See also Fig. 1.13.) A bidirectional DATA port normally interfaces with a central DATA BUS of a computer system (discussed further later). During a WRITE, it is the responsibility of one of the other components connected to the DATA BUS to gate the information to be written to it. The WRITE signal to the RAM is the indicator that causes it to act as a *destination* for these signals, in which case the bidirectional DATA port acts as an *input* port. During a READ (defined by the fact that WRITE is *not* asserted), the MEMORY serves as a *source* of signals to the DATA BUS, in which case the bidirectional DATA port acts as an *output* port.

In a typical computer system, the MEMORY component (as described above) is only one of *several* devices that interface with the central DATA BUS (the system's "information track"). Under certain conditions, it is desirable to decouple the *entire* MEMORY from the DATA BUS, to permit *other* devices to communicate with each other over its path. All of the MEMORY structures described thus far are always READING (generating DATA OUT signals) when not WRITING. (The condition WRITE = 0 implies READ.) To permit decoupling the MEMORY from a central DATA BUS, many MEM-ORY systems also include a READ control signal, whose assertion permits output data to reach the DATA OUT port. The READ input signal enables a bank of TRI-STATE gates located at the DATA OUT interface. Note that, as a preferable alternative, the overall "CHIP" ENABLE signal to the MEM-ORY may be used to prevent transmission of DATA OUT signals. It need not be held at a constant "1". Rather, it may be *deactivated* when it is necessary to decouple the MEMORY from the BUS.

4.3 MEMORY SPACE PARTITIONING

A MEMORY is an ordered set of registers, numbered from 0 through $2^A - 1$, where A is its ADDRESS length. It is a contiguous string of registers, in which "lower" memory begins with register 0, and "upper" memory ends with the highest-numbered register. It is often convenient, however, to view this one-dimensional array of elements as if it were *partitioned* into smaller submemories. The partitions are not necessarily related in any way to the MEMORY's *physical* structure. They are *logical* partitions, derived by dividing the ADDRESS code into *fields* and giving each field an appropriate interpretation.

Note, for example, that the most significant bit of an ADDRESS identifies whether the selected register resides in the upper or in the lower *half* of the MEMORY. Similarly, the upper *two* ADDRESS bits define in which *quarter* of the MEMORY the selected register is located. Observe further that the least significant ADDRESS bit *also* partitions the MEMORY into two equal parts—the set of odd-numbered registers and the set of even-numbered registers.

Consider an extension of this point of view, in which an A-bit ADDRESS code is divided into two arbitrary fields of length B and C, respectively. For every value in the B-bit field, the C-bit field may take on any one of 2^C values. The B bits may be interpreted as specifying a register BANK number, while the C bits specify a register number *within* that bank. In this case, we are interpreting the MEMORY as subdivided into 2^B banks, each containing 2^C registers, giving a total of $2^B \times 2^C = 2^{B+C} = 2^A$ registers. Thus, if $B = 4$ and $C = 8$, for example, the register whose hexadecimal ADDRESS is 3C7 is also identified as register number C7 within bank number 3.

Figure 4.7 shows a picture of this interpretation. Note that the B-bit bank number selects or "points to" the *base* of a bank of 2^C registers, while the C-bit register number specifies a *displacement* from that base, within the selected bank.

In addition to the name BANK, terms such as BLOCK, SEGMENT, and PAGE are also commonly used as the names of logical subdivisions within a MEMORY. Each such partition occupies a specific ADDRESS *range* or ADDRESS *space*. Although you would rarely carry this concept to such an ex-

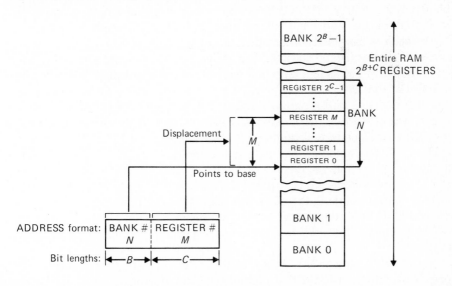

Figure 4.7   MEMORY-partitioning picture

treme, you could imagine an A-bit ADDRESS as subdivided into five fields of lengths B, C, D, E, and F, respectively. Each field specifies the *number* of a selected element contained *within* another selected partition. In this extreme case, you are viewing the MEMORY as consisting of, for example, 2^B segments, each containing 2^C blocks, which each hold 2^D banks, each composed of 2^E pages of 2^F registers each.

A MEMORY is a reservoir of registers. We view it as partitioned in order to *allocate* different subsets of its registers (so-called MEMORY "areas") for different purposes. For example, a MEMORY may contain several computer programs, each assigned a separate MEMORY area. Distinct areas may be allocated also to hold different data patterns. Since an area size is often measured in hundreds or even thousands of registers, it is natural to divide the available space into convenient units—"packages" of registers. While these areas may be delineated by arbitrary ADDRESS limits, they are often conveniently defined as submemories, each containing a number of registers that is a *power of two*.

A typical RAM is commercially available in partitions. As explained in Section 4.2, a large RAM normally consists of an array of interconnected subMEMORY elements. It is often the case that it occupies a physical structure (for example, a printed-circuit board) which is "populated" by the insertion of the individual array elements (the integrated circuits). It is thus possible that a MEMORY may not have its full complement of internal submemories, in which case its physical register set may exist only over a limited ADDRESS range. For example, a computer having modest applications may contain a MEMORY in which only the lower half or quarter (or less) of all of the "addressable" registers is physically present.

In such a case, it is interesting to consider the effect of an erroneous access to a *nonexistent* register. That is, imagine that the ADDRESS presented to the RAM points to a chip that has not yet been installed. If the access is a WRITE, the DATA IN code will not be stored, since all of the existing physical registers will remain disabled. A subsequent READ of the same location will prove that the DATA was never written. If the access is a READ, the DATA OUT code will be the *quiescent value* of the MEMORY's internal DATA OUT bus, since no real data will be gated to it. (Recall the discussion, at the end of Section 1.3, regarding the use of "pull-up" or "pull-down" resistors to define quiescent bus signals.) If, for example, internal pull-up resistors were employed, making the quiescent signal on each bus wire a "1", an erroneous READ of a nonexistent MEMORY register would return a contents of *all ones*, which, of course, is a perfectly respectable value for a real register to have.

Although a typical MEMORY is not equipped with such a feature, it is possible to design a RAM that includes a special error output signal to indicate when a nonexistent MEMORY area is addressed. Such an added facility is discussed in a problem at the end of this chapter.

4.4 READ-ONLY MEMORIES AND PROGRAMMABLE LOGIC ARRAYS

The information stored in a typical computer MEMORY varies as the computer "runs"—as it processes data. Since the stored bit patterns change, the MEMORY must be capable of both reading and writing. There are, however, information patterns a computer needs to access, which remain *fixed*. They are never altered. For example, most computer programs are represented as code sequences that never change. Invariable data patterns—for example, those that define standard messages from a computer to its operator—are also expressed as permanent bit strings. These patterns may be stored in a MEMORY that has no WRITE capability. The stored data is only read. Such a MEMORY is called a READ-ONLY MEMORY (abbreviated as "ROM"). The information stored in it is either built into it at the time it is fabricated or written into it using a special process (explained later) that may be considered as the equivalent of a "refabrication" procedure.

The interface of a ROM need not be as complex as that of a RAM. Since writing will not occur, the WRITE input control signal and the DATA IN input port are both not needed. The device merely has an ADDRESS input port, which receives a code specifying the location of a selected register, and a DATA OUT output port, which delivers the contents of that register. For every input code, there is a fixed, built-in output code. The function of a ROM, as defined here, looks strangely familiar. It is, in fact, *identical* to that of a CODE CONVERTER, discussed earlier in Section 2.1. A READ-ONLY MEMORY, therefore, does not really contain registers. It actually consists of a DECODER-ENCODER combination, as described in Section 2.1. The fact that we *interpret* the input code as the ADDRESS of an internal "register" and the output code as the "contents" of that "register" is merely a convenience for us.

A ROM is the most economical device in which to store a permanent information pattern that must always be accessible at electronic speeds. As we will see later, a typical ROM stores a control program for a computer. By definition, a ROM is a nonvolatile store. The information it holds is always immediately accessible. Figure 4.8 shows the block diagram of a typical ROM. Note that it includes a CHIP ENABLE input. When CHIP ENABLE = 0, the ROM merely decouples its DATA OUT port, using an internal bank of TRI-STATE gates. This permits the ROM element to be used as part of a larger MEMORY, containing other ROM *or* RAM elements. Observe, partic-

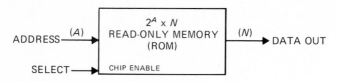

Figure 4.8   READ-ONLY MEMORY (ROM) block diagram

ularly, that a MEMORY may contain a *mixture* of ROM and RAM devices. If this is the case, the MEMORY's DATA IN and WRITE buses bypass the internal ROM elements. Note that, in such an environment, it is conceivable that an erroneous WRITE may be attempted to a MEMORY area containing a ROM. Clearly, by the very nature of a ROM, such an attempt will fail. A subsequent READ of the same location will verify that the original "register" contents have not changed.

Each internal DECODER or ENCODER component of a ROM is normally fabricated as a two-dimensional array, consisting of a set of row wires and a set of column wires, with an electrical coupling element (a transistor or a diode) at each row–column intersection. Any coupling element may be permanently *disabled* (by disconnecting one of its wiring links, for example), in which case it is effectively *removed* from the circuit. A coupling element that has not been disabled remains "active."

To simplify the representation of such arrays, we use the notation shown in Fig. 4.9. Each array is represented by an appropriately labeled matrix of wires. A circle at an intersection indicates the presence of an active electrical coupling element. (Note that it does *not* indicate a direct row–column connection.) Absence of a circle indicates that the corresponding coupling element has been removed or disabled. The network shown is divisible into two coupled arrays. One consists of the leftmost six columns. The other contains the rightmost four columns.

Each array has an interesting dual property—whose electrical explanation is somewhat beyond our present scope. If input signals are applied to its columns, the active coupling elements along any given *row* comprise an AND gate, whose inputs are the corresponding column signals and whose output is the corresponding row wire. On the other hand, if input signals are applied to its rows, the active coupling elements along any given *column* form an OR gate, whose inputs are the corresponding row signals and whose output is the corresponding column wire. Thus, a matrix of M rows and N columns may be utilized either as an array of M AND gates, each having at most N inputs, or as an array of N OR gates, each having at most M inputs. The actual inputs to any composite row-AND gate or column-OR gate correspond *only* to those intersections whose coupling elements have not been

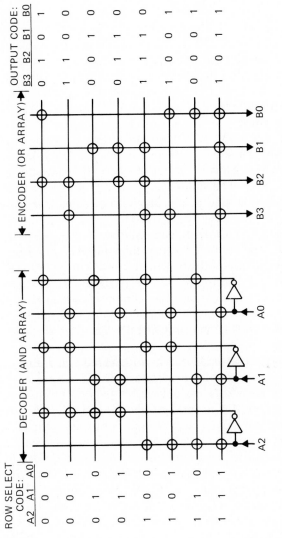

Figure 4.9 AND/OR arrays mechanizing decoder/encoder combination

disabled. The gate ANDs or ORs together only the input signals that correspond to "active" coupling elements.

Thus, the AND ARRAY is distinguished by the fact that its columns carry input signals while its rows are the outputs. Similarly, the *rows* of an OR ARRAY carry the input signals while its *columns* are the outputs.

The AND ARRAY on the left side of Fig. 4.9 mechanizes a 3-to-8 DECODER. The three INVERTERS make available the complements of each of the input signals. Each row is labeled, on the left side of the diagram, with the three-bit input value that activates it. Note that each row implements a different algebraic, canonical-product term of the three input variables. If the number of input variables is N, the AND ARRAY has $2N$ columns and the ROM has 2^N rows.

The structure of AND arrays and OR arrays makes it convenient to mate them in one coupled system, in which the row outputs from an AND ARRAY are connected as the inputs to an OR ARRAY. Both structures may be fabricated simultaneously. The OR ARRAY in Fig. 4.9 is an 8-to-4 ENCODER. The table on the right side of the diagram specifies the output code that is generated, for each possible row activation.

The DECODER-ENCODER combination in Fig. 4.9 is a CODE CONVERTER whose input–output code relationship is defined by combining the two tables on either side of the diagram. It is also a READ-ONLY MEMORY, having eight internal "registers" (whose ADDRESSes are listed on the left), each having the permanent, *wired-in* "contents" indicated in the table on the right. Each row in the matrix corresponds to a different internal "register." For simplicity, the bank of internal TRI-STATE gates at the DATA OUT port is not shown.

The information pattern stored in a ROM may be defined at the time it is manufactured. For example, a standard ROM which converts an input ASCII character code into an output bit pattern for its display (called a "Character Generator") is normally fully defined when it leaves the factory. Alternatively, it is frequently desirable to permit the *user* of a ROM component to tailor its internal bit pattern to a specific application. In this case, the devices used are called *Programmable* ROMs or "PROMs." Typically, the user of a PROM defines or "burns in" its internal information pattern using a special electrical device called a "PROM Programmer." Some PROMs permit only a single initial WRITE process. For example, the Programmer device may destroy selected, microscopic, fusible links to disable corresponding coupling elements. Other PROMs permit reprogramming, when necessary, to insert new information patterns. In all cases, however, the time it takes to program or WRITE a word is several orders of magnitude longer than that necessary to READ it. This time discrepancy (a factor in the range of 10^6) allows us to consider the WRITE process as equivalent to a *refabrication*

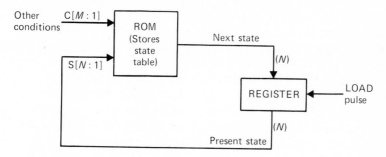

Figure 4.10   Using a ROM to implement an arbitrary state table

procedure. By way of contrast, the READ and WRITE times of a typical RAM are essentially equal.

The network shown in Fig. 4.10 demonstrates one important potential application of a ROM. It may be used to mechanize an arbitrarily complex state table. The contents $S[N:1]$ of the register shown in the diagram define the *present* internal state of a system. Along with other input variables $C[M:1]$ (labeled as "other conditions"), this value is applied as the input code to a ROM, whose corresponding output code defines what the *next* state of the register will be when a LOAD pulse occurs. (The register is assumed to be edge-triggered.) Thus, the next internal state is a function of the present state and of other applied inputs. The pattern stored in the ROM defines this function. It may be *tailored* to conform to any arbitrary state diagram. As we will see later, such a structure may be used to control the internal operation of a computer.

Unfortunately, in many practical situations, the number of ROM inputs makes its required size prohibitive. For example, suppose that the register's length (N) is 6 (giving $2^6 = 64$ possible internal states), and that the number of "other" inputs (M) is 10. This means that the ROM input port has a width of $10 + 6 = 16$. Since a ROM, as defined above, fully decodes its input ADDRESS, the internal AND-OR matrix of the required device must have $2^{16} = 65536$ rows.

Fortunately, in most such situations, a "partial" ROM AND ARRAY is adequate, for two reasons. First, most of the possible input combinations will never occur. For example, suppose that the system shown controls a computer containing an ALU, and that two of the condition input signals represent ALU RESULT IS ZERO and ALU RESULT OVERFLOW indicators, respectively. Clearly, by the very nature of these signals, all codes having *both* asserted simultaneously are ruled out. Second, many state transitions are *independent* of the values of certain condition inputs. For example, the condition of the ALU RESULT normally has no effect on state sequencing while the computer is transmitting a character code to the printer.

Thus, we can envision a ROM-like structure, having an AND ARRAY coupled to an OR ARRAY, in which the code "detectors" in the AND AR-RAY recognize only those input codes *of consequence*. Detectors for input codes that will never occur are not present. Similarly, the detectors that are present are not coupled to those input variables that have *no effect* on what the next state will be. Such a structure is called a PROGRAMMABLE LOG-IC ARRAY (abbreviated as "PLA" or "PAL") because the pattern of active row–column coupling elements is tailorable—not only in the OR ARRAY *but also* in the AND ARRAY.

For example, Table 4.1 contains a hypothetical state table for the structure in Fig. 4.10, assuming $N = 3$ and $M = 4$. It is contrived in order to demonstrate that the PLA required in a specific application may be significantly simpler than a ROM that performs the same function. The left side of the table lists all those present $C[4:1]$, $S[3:1]$ combinations *of consequence*. Each X in the table represents a "don't care" condition. The three-bit output code is independent of its actual value. The table states that, when C4 is 0, the next state depends only on the values of S2 and S1; it is independent of the values of the other four variables. It also states that the signals $C[3:1]$ com-

Table 4.1 Sample State Table Which Generates PLA of Fig. 4.11

					Present			Next	
C4	C3	C2	C1	S3	S2	S1	S3	S2	S1
0	X	X	X	X	0	0	0	0	1
0	X	X	X	X	0	1	0	1	0
0	X	X	X	X	1	0	0	1	1
0	X	X	X	X	1	1	1	0	0
1	0	0	1	0	0	0	1	0	1
1	0	0	1	0	0	1	0	1	0
1	0	0	1	0	1	0	1	1	0
1	0	0	1	0	1	1	0	0	1
1	0	0	1	1	0	0	1	0	1
1	0	0	1	1	0	1	0	1	1
1	0	0	1	1	1	0	1	0	0
1	0	0	1	1	1	1	1	1	1
1	0	1	0	X	X	X	0	0	0
1	1	0	0	X	0	0	1	1	1
1	1	0	0	X	0	1	1	0	0
1	1	0	0	X	1	0	1	0	1
1	1	0	0	X	1	1	1	1	0

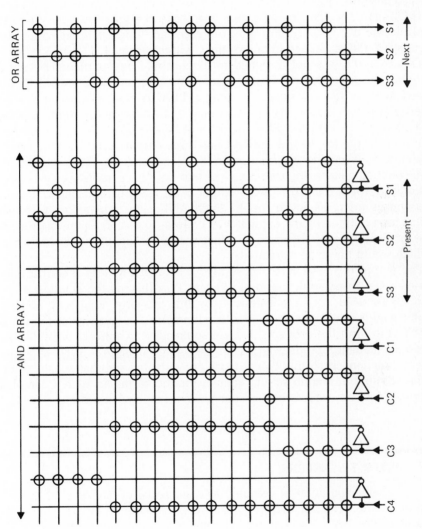

Figure 4.11   PLA replacing ROM in Fig. 4.10—mechanizes Table 4.1

prise a one-asserted code. Combinations other than those indicated will never occur. Note that, while C4 = 1 and C1 = 0, the next state does not depend on the value of S3. Furthermore, when C[4:1] = 1010, the next internal state is independent of its present value. (This C condition may cause a "restart"— in which case the system makes a transition to a standard "initial" or "rest" state.) Observe also that the condition C = 9 and S = 7 causes the system to remain in the S = 7 state. (This may represent an "idle" state, in which the system stays until a change in one of the C values occurs.)

This example was not designed to demonstrate any particularly useful function. (The parenthetical observations above are only incidental.) It was devised to show the advantage of using a PLA. A system whose behavior conforms to the state table in Table 4.1 may be mechanized by replacing the ROM in Fig. 4.10 with the PLA in Fig. 4.11. The PLA's AND ARRAY has seven input variables. Its OR ARRAY has three output variables. The correspondence between the information in Table 4.1 and the PLA's pattern of active coupling elements is evident. Note that the PLA's internal matrix contains only 17 rows. Each row is the output of an AND gate having as few as three and as many as seven inputs. Each AND gate implements a logical product term defined by the explicit 0 or 1 values in its corresponding row in Table 4.1. A ROM with the same interface would contain $2^7 = 128$ rows, most of which would never be activated!

The output of the AND ARRAY of the PLA in Fig. 4.11 is still a one-asserted code. In general, the most efficient PLA (having the smallest number of rows) need not be constrained by this property. Each OR ARRAY output signal is a logical sum-of-products function. The purpose of the AND ARRAY is to form the products that are summed. It is entirely possible that appropriate common product terms can be found, among the various output Boolean functions, such that two or more are activated simultaneously. Finding the absolute minimum set of common product terms, in such a complex multiple-output network, is beyond our present scope of interest.

4.5 REGISTER TRANSFERS

Every computer operation is executed as a sequence of one or more microoperations called *register transfers*. Consider the simple network shown in Fig. 4.12(a). The DATA OUT port of register A is connected to the DATA IN port of register D. (The registers are assumed to have equal lengths.) If LOAD D is asserted, the contents of A will be "transferred" (copied) into D. The contents of A will not be changed by this process. We denote this event by $D \leftarrow A$, which is read as: "The contents of register A are transferred into

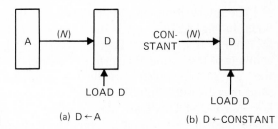

Figure 4.12 Elementary
register transfer examples

(a) D ← A

(b) D ← CONSTANT

register D." A is called the *source* register, and D is called the *destination* register. To simplify the diagrams, input and output ports that are not of immediate interest are not shown. Thus, the DATA IN port of A, the DATA OUT port of D, and the LOAD A control signal are all missing from the drawing.

In Fig. 4.12(b), a *constant* bit string is substituted for the source register. (You will recall one method for constructing a constant, described in Fig. 2.20.) On the appropriate LOAD D edge, the register transfer D ← CONSTANT is executed (where CONSTANT is any arbitrary N-bit code).

In both of the examples above, the value loaded into the destination register was the unaltered contents of a (real or simulated) source register. More generally, this value may be some *function* of the source register's contents. For example, Fig. 4.13(a) shows a structure which executes D ← A + 1 when LOAD D is asserted. This example demonstrates that there may be an *intervening data operation* in the path between the source register and the destination register. The data operation is normally performed by a *combinational* circuit (any of those discussed in Chapter 2, for example). Note that, even though the output signals of the data operator (e.g., the INCREMENTER) always respond immediately to any changes in the contents of the source register, the destination register *ignores* such changes until it receives a LOAD pulse.

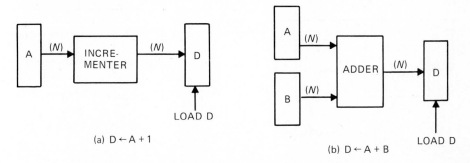

(a) D ← A + 1

(b) D ← A + B

Figure 4.13 Elementary transfers involving data operations

The intervening data operation is not limited to the class of unary functions. In Fig. 4.13(b), when the LOAD D pulse occurs, the register transfer D ← A + B is executed. That is, register D is loaded with the sum of the contents of the A and B registers. This demonstrates that there may be *more than one source register* involved in a single register transfer. Again, a constant may be substituted for either source, in which case transfers such as D ← A + CONSTANT are also possible. You are reminded that *any* data operator (logical or arithmetic, unary or binary) may substitute for its counterpart in the examples above.

Figure 4.14 is a reproduction of Fig. 4.13 with one modification. The data path from source register A is replaced by one from the DATA OUT port of the *destination* register D. Under these conditions, when LOAD D is asserted, what is loaded into D is a function of its *old* contents. Since we are assuming that all registers are edge-triggered, each of these operations is unambiguous. Immediately before the critical LOAD D edge, D's DATA IN port carries a valid set of signals—some function of its *present* contents. This is the value that is loaded when the edge occurs. By the time D's DATA IN signals change (immediately thereafter), the edge instant has passed and D is again ignoring its DATA IN port. Figure 4.14 demonstrates that a destination register *may act as one of its own sources*. Its new value may be a function of its old contents. In the register transfer expressions in Fig. 4.14, the A operand of Fig. 4.13 is replaced by the D operand. The D in each "source expression" (on the right side of the ← symbol) represents its *old* value, before the LOAD pulse occurs. Thus, D ← D + 1 is read as "Increment D." Similarly, in the configuration that executes D ← D + B, D is sometimes called an ACCUMULATOR because every LOAD D assertion causes its value to increase by the amount in B.

In Fig. 4.15(a) the source register is inside a MEMORY. The MEMORY's DATA OUT port connects to the destination register's DATA IN port. (Both are assumed to have the same width. Recall that for simplicity, we are omit-

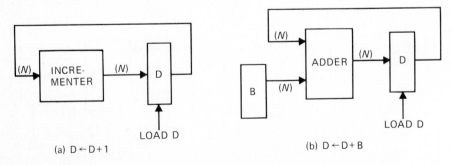

(a) D ← D + 1   (b) D ← D + B

Figure 4.14   Transfers in which destination register is a source

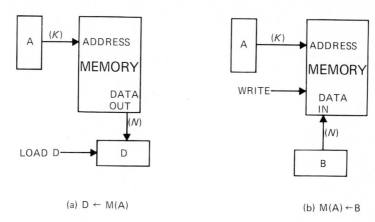

(a) D ← M(A)   (b) M(A) ← B

Figure 4.15   Transfers that involve memory registers

ting all unused ports from the diagrams.) Using this network, when LOAD D is asserted, the register transfer D ← M(A) occurs. The symbol "M" represents the MEMORY element and the parentheses stand for the phrase "as addressed by"—in which case the register transfer expression reads as: "The contents of the MEMORY register addressed by (the contents of) A are transferred to D." Note that register A is *not* the source register. It *points to* the source register. If register A were replaced by a constant, the system might execute, for example, the transfer D ← M(3B7E), which reads as: "The contents of MEMORY location 3B7E are transferred to D." Thus, every MEMORY READ is a register transfer whose source register is located inside a MEMORY.

Similarly, in Fig. 4.15(b), the *destination* register is inside a MEMORY. Register B's DATA OUT port is connected to the MEMORY's DATA IN port. Note that, in this configuration, the MEMORY's *WRITE* pulse must be asserted to effect the register transfer. When it occurs, the transfer M(A) ← B takes place. Again, A is not the destination register. A's value *selects* the destination register. Thus, every MEMORY WRITE is also a register transfer whose destination register is located inside a MEMORY.

Many other variations on the register transfer theme are possible. For example, in Fig. 4.16(a) you see an extreme example involving *two* data operations and *three* source registers. The transfer D ← C op2 (A op1 B) is executed when LOAD D is asserted. Another structure, representative of that found in a typical computer, is shown in Fig. 4.16(b). It includes a MEMORY, $n + 1$ ADDRESS registers and $m + 1$ SOURCE registers (labeled as ADDRESS0, ADDRESS1, . . . , ADDRESSn and SOURCE0, SOURCE1, . . . , SOURCEm, respectively), and two MULTIPLEXERs having PATH SELECT input code values i and j, respectively. On assertion of the MEMORY's WRITE pulse,

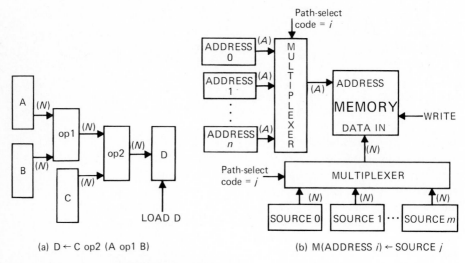

(a) D ← C op2 (A op1 B)   (b) M(ADDRESS i) ← SOURCE j

Figure 4.16   Other register transfer variations

the register transfer M(ADDRESSi) ← SOURCEj is executed. The signals that comprise the i and j values originate from other registers, not shown on the diagram (for simplicity). Note that the specific transfer that is executed depends on which *paths* through the MULTIPLEXERs are enabled. This is not a new idea. Implicit in the use of a MEMORY in a register transfer is the selection of appropriate internal paths within it. The paths are selected by the applied ADDRESS code.

Finally, the network in Fig. 4.10, discussed in the previous section, is another important register transfer configuration. The micro-operation executed, whenever a LOAD pulse occurs, may be written as S ← **f**(S,C), where **f** is the combinational function defined by the ROM/PLA element. The individual Ci signals emanate from an equivalent register, not shown on the diagram. Recall that S, on the right side of the expression above, represents the *old* contents of the control register, *before* the LOAD pulse occurs.

From the various register transfer examples that have been discussed, we may extract a common set of ingredients that generally comprise any register transfer. First, one or more *destination* registers must be *loaded* with new data—implying the assertion of the appropriate LOAD or WRITE control signal(s). Second, a *path* must exist between one or more source registers and the input port of the destination register. Third, an *intervening data operation* may be embedded at one or more points in this path, so that the data loaded into the destination register is generally some *function* of the data in the source register(s).

The examples discussed above have also shown that, first, a *constant* operand may substitute for the contents of any source register. Second, a source or destination register may reside within a MEMORY, in which case, it is selected by the contents of a *pointer* register, applied to the MEMORY's ADDRESS port. (Incidentally, note that the source of a constant may be a READ-ONLY MEMORY, in which case both of the above attributes are combined in one example.) Third, of fundamental importance is the fact that a destination register may act as one of its *own* sources, in which case its *new* contents are some function of its *old* contents.

Most higher-level computer programming languages permit an "assignment" statement of the form VARIABLE = EXPRESSION. The statement executes by computing the value of the expression, using the *current* values of the variables appearing within it, and *assigning* this as the *new* value of the variable named on the left. This variable may also appear *within* the expression, in which case its *old* value is used in the computation of the expression's value. Typically, all variables within a computer program are assigned MEMORY registers. The name of a variable labels its register. It corresponds to the ADDRESS of the register assigned to it. The *contents* of this register are the current *value* of the variable. Thus, an assignment statement such as A = B*(C + D) is actually another notation for a register transfer with intervening data operations. In register-transfer notation, however, we substitute the left arrow for the equals sign because it describes what actually happens much more accurately. The novice programmer who learns about the assignment statement from the register-transfer point of view has little trouble comprehending the meaning of a statement such as A = A + B.

Except for the network shown in Fig. 4.16(b), all of the examples above have utilized direct, simple paths between the source register(s) and the destination register. You should recognize, however, that such paths may follow more complex routes—through MULTIPLEXERs or via BUS structures, for example. If we use a BUS, a path is normally established, first, by the assertion of a control signal that opens a bank of gates, permitting the contents of the source register to be transmitted to the BUS. Then, after the signals on the BUS are valid, the LOAD input control signal to the destination register (whose DATA IN port is connected to the BUS) is asserted to effect the transfer. The notations BUS ← A and D ← BUS may be used to describe the two halves of the register transfer D ← A. Observe, however, that neither, *by itself*, constitutes a register transfer. Only the *combination* does. (Strictly speaking, if only the second control signal LOAD D is asserted, it is most likely that D will load a *constant*—the quiescent value of the BUS when no signals are gated to it.)

In Chapter 3, registers having *built-in* data operations (e.g., COUNTERs and SHIFT REGISTERs) were described. Each of these *internal* micro-operations is also a register transfer. Typically, the source and destination registers are the same register, and the path between them is internal to the device, as is the logic for the built-in data operation. Thus, all internal register functions are valid register *transfers*, satisfying all of the requirements set forth earlier. An appropriate register-transfer expression describes each one. For example, CLEAR C may be written as $C \leftarrow 0$; INCREMENT D is expressed as $D \leftarrow D + 1$; SHIFT A LEFT may be written as $A \leftarrow 2*A$; SET FLIP-FLOP FF is expressed as $FF \leftarrow 1$; and so on.

We are now in a better position to understand why it is generally safe to assume that the signals applied to any unconnected input port on a logic or block diagram are derived from a register not shown on the diagram. Similarly, the signals generated by unconnected output terminals on a logic diagram are probably directed to the DATA IN ports of still other external registers.

4.6 STACKS

A STACK is a special type of MEMORY. It contains an array of identical registers. Its interface, shown in the block diagram in Fig. 4.17, resembles that of a single register even more closely than does that of a RAM. It has DATA IN and DATA OUT ports whose widths match those of the internal registers. In its simplest form, it has an input control signal, called PUSH instead of WRITE, whose function is similar to that of the LOAD input to a register. It has only one additional input control signal, called POP, whose function is explained below.

The internal registers of a STACK are *ordered*, as are the registers in a conventional MEMORY. However, since the device has no ADDRESS input port, no mechanism is provided to permit externally applied signals to explicitly *identify* a unique internal register. Thus, immediate, random access to *any* register is precluded. Instead, the register that is currently accessible

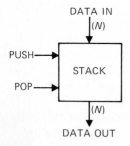

Figure 4.17 Elementary STACK block diagram

(the one coupled to the interface) is *implied* by the way a STACK is organized.

The terms "STACK," "PUSH," and "POP" all originated from the analogy to a spring-loaded stack of plates or trays in a cafeteria. Each item on such a stack corresponds to a *register,* and only the topmost item is the accessible one. Thus, a STACK should be viewed as a physical stack of registers. The currently accessible register in a STACK is called the TOP register.

The rules that govern a STACK's behavior conform to this analogy. On reception of a POP pulse, the register that was *under* the TOP one (called the NEXT-TO-TOP register) becomes the *new* TOP element, and the old TOP register is effectively discarded. A STACK normally ignores its DATA IN signals, except when it receives a PUSH pulse. At that instant, the (assumed valid) input data is written into a *new* internal register, which becomes the new TOP element, while the old TOP element becomes the new NEXT-TO-TOP register. Each register underneath it retains its stored data. It simply moves one step farther away from being immediately accessible. Any data that is PUSHed onto a STACK is assumed retained until it is later POPped from it. From this description, it is clear why a STACK is also called a "Last-In-First-Out" MEMORY.

A register transfer, in which the STACK is the *destination* device, is accomplished by establishing a path between a source register and the STACK's DATA IN port and then asserting the PUSH pulse. A transfer, in which the STACK is the *source* device, requires a path from the STACK's DATA OUT port to the destination register. Its execution requires both a LOAD of the destination register and the assertion of a POP pulse. (The data is "POPped off" the STACK and into the destination register.) This transfer may be accomplished in either of two ways, depending on how the STACK is designed. The STACK's DATA OUT signals may represent the contents of the TOP STACK register, in which case the POP pulse should *follow* the LOAD of the destination register. Alternatively, the DATA OUT signals may represent the contents of the register *just discarded* by a POP pulse (i.e., the *previous* TOP register), in which case the POP should *precede* the LOAD. STACKs are available in both varieties.

Note that the *number* of registers in the STACK described above is *undefined.* As many registers as are necessary (for an arbitrary number of consecutive PUSHes) are assumed available internally. In practice, however, every STACK implementation has a finite number of internal registers. For this reason, a STACK may be equipped with a special, added output signal whose assertion indicates when it is "full." Although most stack implementations do not include such a feature (because the number of internal registers is sufficiently large for all expected uses), it implies an initialization state that is typical of every STACK. A STACK always begins operating in an "empty" condition, in which all of its registers are assumed to contain "garbage"—useless, random bit patterns. If it is equipped with the FULL output signal feature, it must keep track of the number of PUSHes that are not canceled by matching POPs. Observe that when the TOP register is discarded on a POP, it doesn't disappear. Rather, its contents become defined as "garbage," and it is "recycled"—made available for use on a subsequent PUSH. Note also that a POP from an empty STACK is normally just as erroneous as a PUSH onto a full one. For this reason, a STACK implementation may include an additional EMPTY output signal, whose assertion indicates the empty condition.

Before describing possible implementations of a STACK, we briefly discuss one of the reasons why it is considered so important. In the process of executing, a typical computer program frequently needs to temporarily *save* data in MEMORY registers, at one point in a computation, and to *restore* this data for further calculation, at a later point. A SAVE consists of a sequence of MEMORY WRITEs, and its matching RESTORE consists of an equal number of READs. These SAVE–RESTORE pairs are normally *nested*. That is, every SAVE and its companion RESTORE may be separated in time by many other inner SAVE–RESTORE pairs, which may *themselves* be further separated by other pairs (the way parenthesis pairs in an algebraic expression are nested). In such a nested SAVE–RESTORE situation, the most recently saved data is also the information that should be most readily accessible. A STACK is naturally suited to such applications.

While a separate RAM area could be assigned for each different need for temporary registers, it is not necessarily easy to determine specific storage requirements—particularly in a complex system. These requirements may vary with the data being processed or with other unpredictable external conditions. Even when the total need for temporary storage is predictable, such an allocation procedure is inefficient, because only a small fraction of the total area allocated for temporary storage is normally *in use* at any instant. Further, such a scheme forces the programmer to keep careful track of the specific ADDRESSes where data is saved.

Using a STACK, on the other hand, the storage space in use varies dynamically as the computation proceeds. The number of internal STACK registers need only be greater than that required when the maximum number of active saving registers is in use. Concern over ADDRESSes is eliminated. Only the *order* in which the items are PUSHed onto the STACK is important. (They are retrieved in reverse order.)

Detailed examples of specific STACK uses are given later. Consider now how such a device may be constructed. You may initially envision a structure in which a single internal register is permanently coupled to the interface, and in which stored data is physically moved from register to register on every PUSH or POP. Since data has to move in *two* directions (*toward* the

TOP register on a POP and *away* from the TOP register on a PUSH), you may devise a structure in which each register has a two-way MULTIPLEX-ER at its DATA IN port, coupled to the DATA OUT ports of its two neighboring registers. On every STACK operation, each register receives a LOAD pulse. On a PUSH, it LOADS the contents of the register *above* it. On a POP, it LOADS the contents of the register *beneath* it.

An equivalent effect is achieved by using N identical bidirectional shift registers, where N is the width of the STACK's DATA ports. Such a structure is shown in Fig. 4.18. It realizes a STACK whose DATA OUT signals represent the contents of the TOP STACK register. Each shift register has separate SHIFT RIGHT and SHIFT LEFT control input terminals. The *length* of each shift register is equal to the register *capacity* of the STACK. Each of the DATA IN bits is a SHIFT-IN bit to its corresponding shift register. Similarly, the *end* bit stored in each shift register is one of the DATA OUT signals. Note that all SHIFT RIGHT control inputs are tied together and renamed as PUSH. Similarly, all SHIFT LEFT control inputs are connected to a common POP bus. The TOP of the STACK is positioned on the *left* side of the diagram. The SHIFT-IN bits on the right side of the diagram are arbitrary; they are not shown and may be assumed to be zeroes. The BOTTOM of this STACK is an imaginary vertical line that moves right on every PUSH (at which time every shift register shifts its contents right and loads its DATA IN bit) and left on every POP. Note that the interface of this network matches that defined in Fig. 4.17.

A more common realization of a STACK does not employ physical movement of the stored data. Rather, the interface to the STACK, coupling to its TOP register, effectively "moves," with respect to the array of registers, whenever a PUSH or a POP operation takes place. That is, the currently

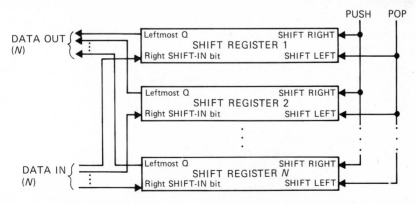

Figure 4.18 STACK implementation using SHIFT registers

accessible register changes, becoming the *neighbor* of the one that was accessible *before* the operation took place. From an alternative point of view, the registers in such a STACK appear to advance past the interface's "window" sequentially—in one direction for PUSH, and in the opposite direction for POP.

A conventional RAM effectively moves its interface over its array of registers. The ADDRESS value *positions* the interface. To move the interface to a neighboring register, the applied ADDRESS value is merely incremented or decremented. Thus, imagine using a RAM to implement a STACK. Connect the ADDRESS input port of the RAM to the DATA OUT port of a bidirectional counter, as shown in Fig. 4.19. The counter is named the "STACK POINTER" (abbreviated as "SP"). A POP pulse causes it to count in one direction, while a PUSH pulse causes it to count in the opposite direction. Note that these directions are *arbitrary*. They affect the direction of growth of the STACK within the RAM. We have two choices: As the STACK grows, either the TOP of the STACK in the RAM can move toward "upper" MEMORY (i.e., toward higher ADDRESSes) or it can move toward lower MEMORY. We have arbitrarily chosen the latter. Thus, a PUSH pulse decrements the STACK POINTER while a POP pulse increments it.

The POP operation is straightforward. The STACK realization shown is designed on the assumption that the STACK POINTER is pointing at the first *available* RAM location. This means that the DATA OUT port carries the contents of the just-discarded register, after a POP. The STACK POINTER is assumed to decrement on the *trailing edge* of the PUSH pulse. Thus, when the PUSH pulse occurs, the DATA IN value is written into the next available RAM register—just "above" (from the *STACK's* viewpoint) the current TOP register. The decrement of the STACK POINTER occurs as the WRITE finishes. Thus, the ADDRESS change occurs after the access has been completed.

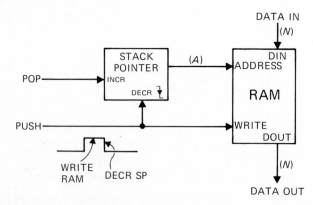

Figure 4.19 STACK implementation with a RAM and a STACK POINTER

Note that, if the STACK POINTER were pointing at the TOP STACK register, the contents of the TOP register would be available for a READ without an accompanying POP. On the other hand, a PUSH would now require decrementing the STACK POINTER *before* the WRITE could take place. Thus, a sequence of *two* control pulses would be required. The first would decrement the STACK POINTER. The second would activate the WRITE. Observe that these pulses must be separated by a time period longer than the *access time* of the RAM, so that the register "above" the TOP one is properly addressed when the WRITE occurs.

Table 4.2 specifies all of the possible micro-operation sequences that constitute a *single* register transfer between a STACK, simulated by using a RAM and a STACK POINTER, and an arbitrary external register, designated as "R". All combinations of three variable conditions are considered. First, the direction of the transfer may be *to* or *from* the STACK. Second, the STACK area in the RAM may grow toward *higher* or *lower* ADDRESSes. Third, the RAM register selected by the STACK POINTER may be the TOP "filled" STACK register or the first-available "empty" register.

Table 4.2   The Micro-Operation Pair That Constitutes a Single Transfer Between a Register R and a STACK in a RAM

STACK POINTER Points to the:	Top Filled		First Available		RAM Cell
TOP of STACK Grows Toward:	**Upper**	**Lower**	**Upper**	**Lower**	**End of MEMORY**
STACK is the *source* **device:**	R←M(SP) SP←SP − 1	R←M(SP) SP←SP + 1	SP←SP − 1 R←M(SP)	SP←SP + 1 R←M(SP)	
STACK is the *destination* **device:**	SP←SP + 1 M(SP)←R	SP←SP − 1 M(SP)←R	M(SP)←R SP←SP + 1	M(SP)←R SP←SP − 1	

Note: R is assumed to be the other register involved in the register transfer with the STACK.

Note that the physical location of the STACK within the RAM is determined by the *initial value* LOADed into the STACK POINTER. While the entire RAM may be exclusively dedicated to simulating a STACK (as assumed in the discussion above), it is much more likely that the RAM is sufficiently large that it may also be used for many other purposes. Under these conditions, a specific RAM area is normally allocated for the STACK, and the STACK POINTER is initialized to point to the *base* of this area. The extent of this area is designed to accommodate the maximum STACK size expected. When a RAM access to a register *outside* of the STACK area is desired, some *other* external register (other than the STACK POINTER) must be used as the ADDRESS source, in which case another path must be established to the RAM's ADDRESS input port. Meanwhile, the STACK POINTER continues to retain its current value.

4.7 CLOCKS, CYCLES, AND CONTROL SIGNALS

An elementary CLOCK PULSE GENERATOR has no input terminals and only one output terminal. It emits a continuous "train" of identical, equally spaced pulses. Each clock pulse is a timing marker—an electronic "tick."

Numerous circuits may be configured to realize such a device. One of these, shown in Fig. 4.20, uses DELAY elements. The output signal of a DELAY element is always a duplicate of its input signal, delayed in time by the device's delay parameter T. That is, every edge in its input waveform appears at its output terminal T seconds later. Assume that the delay through a typical gate is negligible compared to that through either of the DELAY elements shown in Fig. 4.20. The loop consisting of the INVERTER and DELAY element $T1$ comprises an oscillator, which generates a continuous "square" wave whose half-period is $T1$. ANDing this signal with a delayed version of itself (delayed by $T2$) produces a pulse train, having the same period, whose pulses are $T1-T2$ seconds wide (assuming $T1 > T2$). The waveforms shown in Fig. 4.20 fully describe the circuit's behavior.

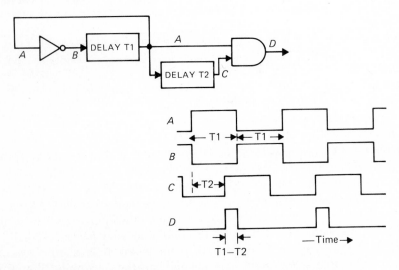

Figure 4.20 CLOCK pulse generator using DELAY elements

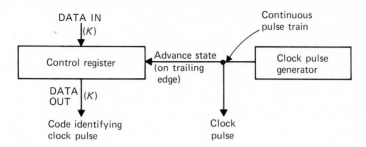

Figure 4.21 Typical clock pulse generator-control register structure

Virtually every digital system (in particular, every computer) is *synchronous* in nature. It contains a CLOCK PULSE GENERATOR, and each of its internal electronic events is executed in synchronism with a specific clock tick. Such a system normally contains a *control register* whose contents change on every pulse. The code stored in this register *identifies* the current clock pulse. It differentiates or distinguishes one tick from another. The structure shown in Fig. 4.21 is typical. Each clock pulse causes the state of the control register to *advance* to a new state. The term "advance" is used to generally represent any means by which the register's contents may be changed. A register normally advances by LOADing, COUNTing, or SHIFTing. Note, particularly, that if the register advances on the *trailing* edge of the clock pulse, its contents will remain valid while the tick is occurring.

A digital TIMER is an elementary example of such a control structure. The control register is a COUNTER whose contents increment or decrement on every clock pulse. A specific event (for example, the activation of an alarm signal) may be automatically triggered at a preset instant of time by using a code recognizer or a COMPARATOR whose output signal is asserted when the counter reaches that predetermined state. In another application, the contents of the counter may be displayed, as in the case of a digital watch or clock. In either instance, the state of the counter, which is measuring elapsed time in clock period units, is different for each clock tick.

More generally, a control register is a concatenation of two or more distinct registers, each holding one *field* of the entire control state. The configuration indicated in Fig. 4.22 is quite common. The clock pulses directly increment the contents of an N-bit counter (the least significant field of the entire control state). On every 2^Nth clock pulse, this counter's contents "wrap around" to restart at zero. At that time, the state of the remaining portion of the control register (which may *itself* contain one or more counters) is permitted to advance to a new state. In such a system, time is divided into control *cycles*, each consisting of exactly 2^N clock periods. The contents of the clock pulse counter identifies a clock pulse *within* a cycle, while the state of the remainder of the control register *identifies the cycle*.

CONTROL REGISTER

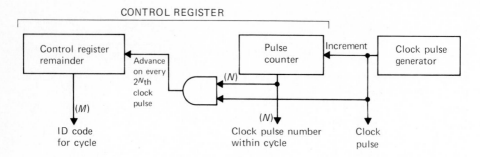

Figure 4.22   Typical network to generate control cycles

It is sometimes convenient to divide each control cycle into a sequence of identical *subcycles*. The contents of the clock pulse counter are regarded as divided into two fields. The upper field identifies the current subcycle, while the lower field is the number of the current clock pulse *within* that subcycle. Note the analogy to dividing a memory address into two fields (discussed in Section 4.3), where the upper field selects a bank of registers, while the lower field identifies one register within that bank.

Thus, a control cycle consists of a repeating pattern of states in some portion of a control register—typically, in a counter. Note that the total number of states in such a pattern (which determines the number of clock pulses within a cycle, or the number of "minor" cycles within each "major" cycle) need *not* be a power of two. Counters having any base may be employed. (The "base" of a counter is the total number of different states it may assume.) For example, Fig. 4.23 shows a chain of counters for a digital watch or clock. Each counter increments on the negative edge of its input signal,

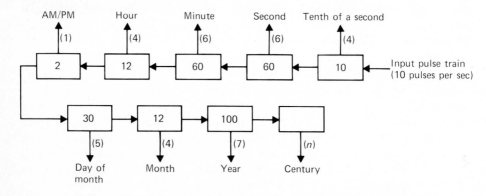

Figure 4.23   Counter/divider chain of a digital watch or clock

which indicates the completion of another *cycle* by its neighbor. Its most significant bit is its output signal, which makes a 1-to-0 transition whenever *it* completes a cycle. Its output port is labeled with its length and with the name of the unit of time it is counting. Its *base* is given inside its symbol. The frequency of its output pulses is its input frequency *divided by* this number. (For simplicity, every month is assumed to have 30 days.) Note that only one stage has a base that is a power of two. This system clearly illustrates the *hierarchy* of cycle sequences within cycles.

In order to define more carefully how control "pulses" and control "levels" are used, we first recapitulate a few key points: A computer is composed primarily of registers, most of which are contained in its main memory. It also contains a central clock pulse generator and a control register. Each of its operations consists of a sequence of one or more register transfers. Every register transfer is executed in synchronism with some clock pulse. Thus, every FLIP-FLOP's Q output signal, *including* any of those from the control register, has a waveform resembling that shown at the bottom of Fig. 4.24. It is plotted using a train of several clock pulses (in the top waveform) as a reference. It is called a *level* because it remains constant over one or more contiguous clock periods. Almost all of the signals within a computer exhibit this behavior. A *control* level is logically derived from the Q's of one or more FLIP-FLOPs, particularly those in the *control* register. A control *pulse*, on the other hand, is asserted only in synchronism with a clock pulse, as indicated by the sample waveform in the middle of Fig. 4.24. We often use the terms "control pulse" and "clock pulse" interchangeably—when the meaning is not ambiguous.

A register transfer normally requires a "preparation" time period, prior to its actual execution, during which control levels define the operation to be executed. For example, control levels are used to define the current function of an ALU, the currently enabled path through a MULTIPLEXER, the currently selected register in a MEMORY, and so on. Once these control levels have been *valid* for a sufficiently long time (an interval known as the "setup" time for the operation), the signal edge that causes execution may occur.

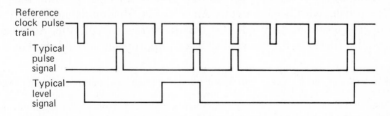

Figure 4.24   Waveforms of typical control pulses and levels

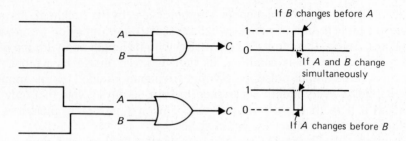

Figure 4.25   Some conditions that may generate "spurious" pulses

In rare cases, it is conceivable that the edge of a control level may be used to trigger a register transfer. Normally, however, control levels are used to *prepare* for the operation (define *what* to do), while a control pulse is used to *evoke* it (cause it to happen).

Two reasons why control levels are rarely used to trigger register transfers are: First, most operations require *valid* control levels while the triggering signal edge occurs. Since a signal is, by definition, *not* valid while it is making a transition, the *same* signal may not be used for both purposes. While a control level may change immediately *after* the triggering edge, it cannot change simultaneously with it. Second, even when the above constraint is not imposed, it is conceivable that a control level signal may contain "spurious" edges if it is derived from two or more changing Q signals whose edges are not coincident. Consider the examples shown in Fig. 4.25. Here A and B are the sample Q signals and C is the sample control level. In both cases, if the Q's change simultaneously, the ideal C stays constant (represented by the dotted portion of the C waveform). However, if one Q edge is delayed with respect to the other, as indicated, the spurious C pulses shown could occur.† Thus, to prevent erroneous operation, a register transfer is normally triggered by a direct clock pulse or by a control pulse derived from it in a simple way. The control levels are used to "prime" the event.

To develop proper control signal patterns, it is necessary to *distinguish* between the different control cycles that may occur and between the different clock pulses within each cycle. An event is "distinguished" when a *signal*, which is asserted *only* when it occurs, is made available. Such signals are normally developed through the use of appropriate decoders. For exam-

---

†The skew in the A and B signal edges may be due to unmatched delays in the gates from which these signals are derived. Using the lower example in Fig. 4.25, suppose $A = XY$ and $B = \overline{X}Z$ and that X makes a negative transition while Y and Z remain 1. The waveforms shown may be due to the fact that the delay through B's AND gate is greater than that through A's AND gate. Such a condition is known as a *hazard*.

ple, Fig. 4.26(a) adds two decoders to the network of Fig. 4.22 to permit every cycle and every clock period within a cycle to have its own output signal. The waveforms generated by the clock-pulse counter's decoder are shown in Fig. 4.26(b), assuming that signal assertions are negative and that the counter has a length N of only two—in which case, the period ID decoder is a 2-to-4 decoder, whose outputs are named PERIOD*i*. All such periodic signal sets, in which assertions are "skewed" in time, from signal to signal, are known as *multiphase* clock sources. Each signal is asserted only while its clock period, within the cycle, is occurring.

As an alternative to using a counter and a decoder, the same signal pattern may be developed directly using the structure shown in Fig. 4.27. In this case, the control register is an "end-around" shift register, initialized with a *one-asserted* code. On every clock pulse, a different one of its Q outputs is asserted. Note that an erroneous counter state transition, using the counter-decoder method, causes only a *temporary* error in the output waveforms. On the other hand, if the code stored in the shift register changes so that it is *no longer* one-asserted, a *permanent* modification to the output waveforms will result.

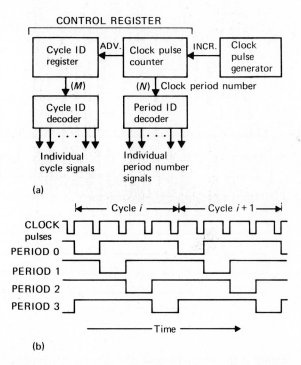

Figure 4.26 Control register decoders and typical multiphase clock

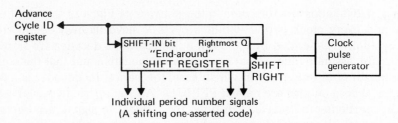

Figure 4.27 Alternative means to achieve waveforms in Fig. 4.26(b)

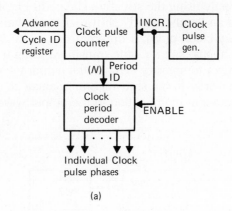

(a)

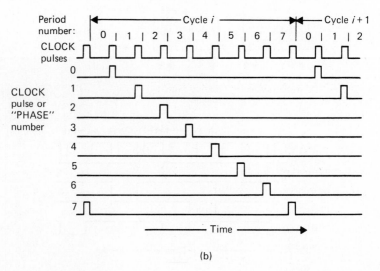

(b)

Figure 4.28 Generation of multiphase clock pulses

To develop individual signals that represent the clock pulses themselves, the decoder arrangement in Fig. 4.26(a) may be modified to that shown in Fig 4.28(a). (Positive signal assertions are now assumed.) By applying the clock signal to the decoder's ENABLE input, we develop output pulses coincident with the individual clock pulses. The value of having the control register advance on the *trailing* clock edge now becomes apparent. Under these conditions, the counter advances while the decoder is disabled, and the waveforms shown in Fig. 4.28(b) result. (In this example, the pulse counter is assumed to have a length N of three.) If the counter were to advance on the *leading* clock edge, the decoder would be *enabled* while the counter's state transition was occurring. Only on a perfect, immediate transition will the waveforms shown be preserved. It is conceivable (in fact, assured, if the counter happens to be a "ripple" counter) that the counter's Q signals will not all change simultaneously—in which case a temporary erroneous decoder output "spike" could be generated.

PROBLEMS

4.1 Define the interface of a 1024-word, 32-bit-per-word RAM.

4.2 Design a component containing eight identical counters. The device has a three-bit COUNTER NUMBER input port, whose value selects one of the counters, an ADVANCE input signal, whose assertion causes the selected counter to increment, and a ZERO output signal, which is asserted only if the contents of the selected counter are zero. Each individual counter has a single INCREMENT input and a single output, named CLEAR, which is asserted when its contents are zero.

4.3 Add a minimum of additional logic to a 16K × 32 RAM to convert it into a 64K × 8 RAM (K = 1024). Treat the 16K × 32 RAM as an indivisible element. To simplify your design, you may assume that all registers inside the memory are *edge-triggered* and that, when WRITE is not asserted, the memory is always reading.

4.4 Construct a 256 × 8 RAM using identical 256 × 4 RAM components.

4.5 Construct a 1024 × 4 ROM using identical 256 × 4 ROM components and a minimum of additional logic. Develop two alternative designs. First, assume that each ROM element has a CHIP ENABLE input signal, which controls its DATA OUT port. Second, omit this assumption; in this case, each DATA OUT port always carries a set of signals.

4.6 Show how a 16K × 16 RAM may be constructed using identical 8K × 4

RAM elements, each of which has a CHIP SELECT or ENABLE input signal (K = 1024). Use a minimum of additional logic.

4.7 A 64-register memory contains registers R0 through R63. (All register numbers are indicated in decimal.) For each of the following specifications, define the required address value. Each address bit should be specified as either 0, 1, or X (for "doesn't matter; may be either 0 or 1").

   a) Register R18.
   b) Any register in the upper half of memory (R32 to R63).
   c) Any even-numbered register (R0, R2, R4, . . .).
   d) The third bank of eight registers (R16 to R23).
   e) The third register in any bank of eight registers (R2, R10, R18, . . .).
   f) Any member of the set of four registers R48 through R51.

4.8 A 4096-word memory is logically divided into 256-word pages. Associated with the memory is a special set of four registers, each of which contains the number of one of the memory's pages. (The means by which the contents of each auxiliary register is controlled need not concern us.) The auxiliary registers are used to permit any register in the memory to be addressed by an externally applied *ten*-bit value, whose upper two bits select one of the auxiliary registers whose contents, in turn, select a page. The lower eight bits of the applied value select one register within the selected page. Define the logic network (which includes the four auxiliary registers) that receives the ten-bit input value and outputs the *address* of the selected memory register.

4.9 Consider a memory constructed as shown in Fig. 4.5. Assume that each 1024 × 8 "chip" position includes an added signal, named MISSING, which has a value 1 only when its corresponding integrated circuit is *not* plugged in. Define the logic that may be added to this memory to develop an error output signal whose assertion indicates that a nonexistent memory cell has been addressed.

4.10 Consider an eight-bit-wide RAM, partially populated (in sequence, starting at address zero) with 1K × 8 chips. Its maximum capacity is 64K words (K = 1024). Explain a strategy that a computer program may use to "size" the memory (i.e., to determine its highest valid address value). The program is able to generate arbitrary addresses and to read, write, and process arbitrary data codes. Where possible, provide specific address and data values in your answer.

4.11 Consider the code converter described in Problem 2.6 as a Read-Only Memory. Divide its array of internal "registers" into sets, where all of the registers in any set have the *same* contents. Specify the number of registers in each set and the contents of each register.

4.12 The network shown in Fig. P4.12 is used as part of a memory-testing device. The counter increments on the trailing edge of each WRITE pulse. The "jumper"element shown contains an arbitrary wiring pattern. For each of the jumper connection patterns shown in (a) through (d), specify the hexadecimal contents of the memory, register by register, beginning with location zero, and assuming that 64 or more WRITE pulses have already been generated.

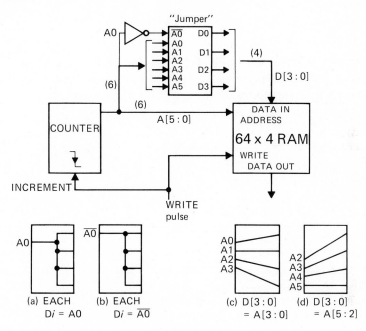

Figure P4.12

4.13 A network contains four identical registers R3, R2, R1, and R0, each resembling the one in Fig. 3.20(a). They communicate with each other, using appropriate logic, via a bus. The network has five input control signals S[1:0], D[1:0], and P. Whenever a pulse P is asserted, the contents of the register selected by the S code is transferred to the register selected by the D code. Draw the network.

4.14 Using the network shown in Fig. P4.14, write down an expression defining what happens whenever a LOAD C pulse occurs.

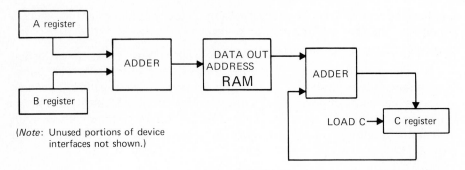

Figure P4.14

4.15   Assume that the RAM in Fig. P4.15 is *edge-triggered*. (You are remind-ed that this is not normally the case.) Write down an expression for the regis-ter transfer that is executed whenever a WRITE pulse occurs.

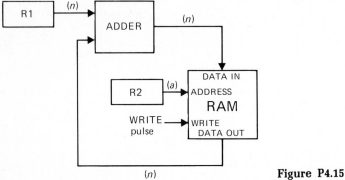

Figure P4.15

4.16   Draw a block/logic diagram for a network, containing three identical registers A, B, and C, which can execute either of the following two register transfers:

$$A \leftarrow A + B \qquad \text{and} \qquad A \leftarrow A + C.$$

(Here "+" means ADD.) Include only those control signals that directly affect the execution of these transfers.

4.17   The network in Fig. P4.17 contains three edge-triggered registers, each of which loads, when it receives a CLOCK pulse, *provided* that its load en-able input signal LDi is 1. Register R2 has an additional overriding CLEAR input. All data paths have the same width N. Construct a table whose col-umns are labeled LD1, LD2, LD3, S1, S2, and CLEAR, and whose rows are labeled a, b, c, and d. Fill in each entry in the table with the value that the signal labeling the column should have such that the transfer(s) listed below will be induced when a CLOCK pulse occurs.

- a) R3 ← R1 + R2;
- b) R1 ← R2,   R2 ← R1;
- c) R3 ← R1 + R2,   R2 ← R3,   R1 ← R3;
- d) R3 ← R1.

Two or more transfers on the same line are executed simultaneously. (*Note*: In the S1 and S2 columns, fill in an X if the value of the signal is immaterial.)

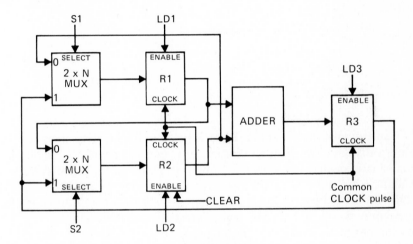

Figure P4.17

4.18   A stack is mechanized using the network shown in Fig. 4.19. Assume a 64-word RAM dedicated for stack use only. The Stack Pointer is initialized with a hex value of 3F. Add appropriate logic to the network to derive STACK FULL and STACK EMPTY signals. Use these signals to prevent erroneous PUSHes and POPs.

4.19   Assume a stack S and as many peripheral registers R1, R2, etc., as needed. (Use them in order, beginning with R1.) For each of the following operations, write down the simplest sequence of register transfers that will implement it. (Use the notation S ← R*i* for a PUSH and R*i* ← S for a POP.)

- a) PUSH a *duplicate* of the TOP stack entry onto the stack.
- b) Swap the TOP stack entry with the NEXT-TO-TOP stack entry.
- c) PUSH a duplicate of the NEXT-TO-TOP stack entry onto the stack.

4.20 In the network shown in Fig. P4.20, pulses P1 and P2 are mutually exclusive. The destination register C normally loads from register A whenever pulse P2 is asserted (because P1 = 0). The network is configured so that a P1 pulse will cause a C ← B transfer. Can you find any fault with this aspect of the design?

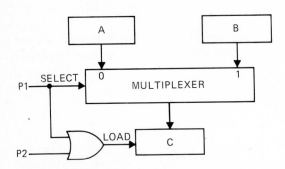

Figure P4.20

4.21 The network shown in Fig. P4.21 is used to display a 32-character message on a display. The display consists of a matrix of 192 × 7 lights. Each character is allocated five adjacent columns (35 spots) for a dot pattern approximating its shape. The display expects only one of its 192 COLUMN SELECT inputs to be asserted at a time. A specific light spot illuminates only if its column signal *and* its row signal are *both* asserted. The 32 × 8 RAM stores the character codes for the current message. The code converter or ROM receives an 11-bit code, representing the current RAM output character, concatenated with its current display column number, which runs between values 0 and 5. The code converter (also known as a "character generator") outputs the proper seven-bit display code for the specified column of the specified character. (Column 5 is always blank—seven zeroes—representing the space between characters.)

At any instant only one of the display columns is illuminated. However, the persistence of the eye is such that, if all of the columns are displayed *in sequence, at a sufficiently high rate,* a stationary message is observed. The clock pulse generator provides a continuous train of pulses P at that rate. Design the network labeled "YOUR LOGIC", which cycles through all of the display characters and all of the columns of each display character, to provide the proper RAM address sequence, the proper character column-number sequence, and the proper column-select signal sequence to the RAM-ROM-display system shown. Assume that all device delays are negligible.

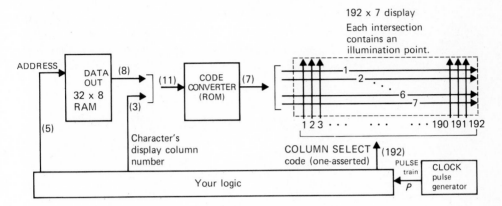

Figure P4.21

4.22 Without employing a third register in your solution, write down a sequence of register transfers that constitutes a *swap* of the contents of two identical registers A and B. You may use any intervening logical data operations that you find convenient.

5

Digital
Systems

The purpose of this chapter is to dissect and examine in detail three relatively complex digital systems. Each demonstrates how many of the elements introduced in the previous chapters are employed. The first example may be considered as "specialized," because it contains some introduction to a few elementary musical concepts. (It is presented first because its *digital* content is the least complicated.) For this reason, some readers may prefer postponing its study so that it follows that of the other examples.

5.1 AUTOMATIC MUSIC ACCOMPANIMENT

The availability of inexpensive digital devices has induced a significant growth in the field of electronic music synthesis. An example of this growth is the development of electronic organs containing circuits that generate sounds simulating *accompanying* instruments. These devices are of interest not only to novice musicians, who are now able to "play" popular songs with little or no musical training, but also to some professionals, who are now able to make a single instrument sound like several. As a first example of an integrated digital system employing many of the elements previously studied, we consider the internal design of a simplified keyboard instrument that contains such an "auto-accompaniment" feature. Before doing so, we must review some musical fundamentals.

A typical signal that represents a single instrumental tone (for example, that extracted from a recording, amplified by an amplifier and applied to a speaker) is complicated. It is described by many different parameters, each of which affects the character of its sound. Only two of these are of immediate interest to us here: its frequency and its waveshape. Every single tone signal is periodic. It consists of a repeating or *cyclic* waveform. The time for one cycle is the *period* of the signal. The *frequency* of the signal is the number of cycles that occur per second, the inverse of the period. The frequency of a signal defines the *pitch* of its sound, its "highness" or "lowness."

All conventional music is constructed by using only twelve different notes (named, for example, C or G). An "octave" is a set of twelve tones, corresponding to these notes, within a given pitch range; they are *adjacent* on a keyboard. All audible tones range over approximately nine octaves, each containing the same twelve note names. A next lower version of a given note (i.e., the same note in the next lower octave) has exactly *half* its frequency. Its next higher version (i.e., the same note in the next higher octave) has exactly *twice* its frequency.

The waveshape of a signal (the "hills" and "valleys" within one of its cycles) defines the *timbre* of its sound: its characteristic quality, once pitch and loudness are disregarded. We distinguish between different musical instruments (sounding the same tone) by the timbre of their sounds. A "square" wave (shown, for example, in Fig. 5.1) has an uninteresting sound, not resembling any conventional instrument. It does, however, have a well-defined *frequency*. One common method used to synthesize a musical tone is to generate a square wave of the proper frequency and then to *shape* it, by passing it through an appropriate electronic "filter," to derive a waveform having the desired timbre. The design of such filters is beyond our present scope. We will limit our attention to generating square waves, having the proper pitches, assuming that appropriate filters may be constructed to tailor them so that they sound like specific musical instruments.

Rhythmically speaking, conventional music is divided into cycles of equal length called "measures." All measures in a typical popular song contain the same number of "beats," normally four. (Every waltz measure, on the other hand, contains three beats.) *Durations* of notes are specified in numbers of beats. Beats are themselves divided into subbeats (typically, two half-beats or four quarter-beats per beat). A sound that begins on a beat that is normally not accented is said to be "syncopated." Much of the rhythmic

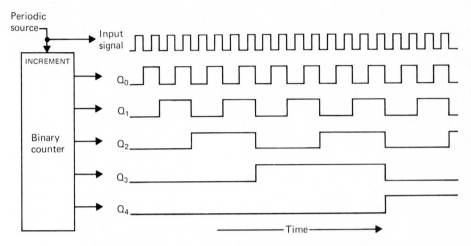

Figure 5.1   Binary counter used as frequency divider

appeal of typical percussion sound can be attributed to its high degree of syncopation.

The sample system discussed below omits consideration of several important aspects of music synthesis, including loudness control, generation of attack and decay "envelopes," simulation of vibrato (regular variations in pitch) and, particularly, insertion of randomness into the synthesized signals. Its digital portion, which is of interest here, chiefly contains counters, banks of gates, and a single Read-Only Memory. Before studying its structure, we briefly review how a counter is used as a frequency *divider*.

It was pointed out in Section 4.7, in conjunction with the digital watch example in Fig. 4.23, that if a counter is driven by a continuous, periodic signal (for example, a pulse train or a square wave), the frequency of its most significant output bit will be its input frequency *divided* by the base of the counter. Figure 5.1 shows a typical binary counter receiving a square wave at its INCREMENT input terminal. (We ignore whether or not the counter has any parallel LOAD capability. The INCREMENT terminal may be a CLOCK input, if the logical structure of the device causes it to increment on every CLOCK pulse.) Note that the frequency of the counter's least significant Q (Q0) is *half* the input frequency, and that the frequency of any other Qi is half of that of its less significant neighbor, $Q(i - 1)$. A frequency *divider* is thus a counter that advances continuously.

Figure 5.2 shows an elementary, but interesting, musical application of such a device. It is assumed that the audio input signal comes from an appropriate microphone, mounted to pick up the sound of a single musical instrument. The function of the Frequency Tracker is to convert the complex audio

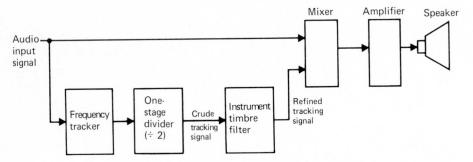

Figure 5.2   "One-octave-below" accompanist network

input waveform (whose pitch continuously varies) into a square wave or pulse train *of the same frequency.* The frequency of the Frequency Tracker's output signal, now digital in nature, is then *halved,* using a one-stage binary counter. The divider's output signal is therefore always *one octave below* that of the performer. It tracks all changes in the original signal. It is called a "crude" tracking signal because it is a square wave, having little musical appeal at this point. The circuit called the INSTRUMENT TIMBRE FILTER is designed to *shape* this waveform into one resembling that of a specific instrument, without changing its frequency. Its output, called a "refined" tracking signal, is then combined with the original in a MIXER. The output signal of any MIXER is always a *superposition* of all of its input signals. This composite output signal is then amplified and passed on to a speaker. The resulting sound retains all the qualities of the original performance. In addition, an *accompanying* "instrumentalist" is heard, playing the identical melody (and tracking all variations in it, no matter how complex) *one octave lower.*

Note that the only digital portion of the network in Fig. 5.2 is the single FLIP-FLOP, operating as a counter. All of the other circuits are analog devices (not within our present scope of interest). We will have occasion to use MIXERs and TIMBRE FILTERs in several places in the system to be described. One simplifying assumption has been made in discussing the network in Fig. 5.2: All considerations regarding tracking *loudness* changes in the input signal have been ignored.

Musical accompaniment is both rhythmic and harmonic in nature. Every measure in a piece of music includes not only a melody note sequence but also an underlying *harmonic* structure, a sequence of one or more "chords." A *chord* is a set of three or more different notes, sounded simultaneously, in support of the sequence of melody notes. The number of possible N-note chords is

$$12 \times 11 \times \cdots \times (12 - N + 1),$$

since there are 12 choices for the first note, 11 for the second, and $12 - (N - 1)$ for the Nth. Of these, only a relatively small number is used in conventional popular songs. Let us limit our attention to the rudimentary "major" and "minor" three-note chords. Each is defined using a simple note selection rule, once the *first* (or "root") note is selected. The two other chord notes, in addition to the root, are called the "third" and the "fifth," respectively. There are two possible thirds (one called the "major third"; the other, the "minor third"). The one chosen distinguishes a major chord from its corresponding minor chord. (The two have distinctly different sound qualities.) Thus, we restrict our attention to a total of 24 (out of the 1320 possible) three-note chords: 12 major chords and 12 minor chords. Under these conditions, a chord is specified by a one-out-of-twelve choice, accompanied by a single bit defining either "major" or "minor."

The most common combination of rhythmic and harmonic instruments, to accompany the performance of a popular song, includes a set of percussive devices (drums), a chord instrument (piano or guitar), and a bass instrument (bass fiddle or bass guitar). In keeping with the simplified chord choices described above, we limit the bass instrument note to either the root or the "fifth" of the current chord.

A piece of music is described by a melody note sequence and a supporting chord sequence, normally encoded on a piece of sheet music. We are concerned with simplifying how this information is delivered to the performing musical instrument, and also with how the intricacy of the resulting sound may be enhanced without making unreasonable demands on the performer. One can imagine a system in which all of the information on the sheet music is encoded and stored in the internal memory of the instrument, which proceeds automatically with the *entire* performance, once certain parameters (such as tempo, style, etc.) are set and a start button is depressed. Under these conditions, the user's participation in the performance is negligible, and the instrument acts as if it were a type of phonograph. (Similarly, one can imagine an automated bowling alley which includes not only automatic pin-setters and score-keepers but also automatic ball-rollers, or a card game played by four bridge-playing computers, each of which can not only shuffle the deck and bid and play the hand, but also complain about its partner's line of play!)

While an intermediate instrument can be designed, in which some information concerning the melodic or harmonic structure of the song being played is internally stored, we choose here to omit this capability and to retain a reasonable degree of participation on the part of the performer. Specifically, the operator's interface to the instrument under discussion is shown in Fig. 5.3.

The MELODY KEYBOARD contains three or four octaves of conventional piano keys, played in the customary manner. While one or more melody

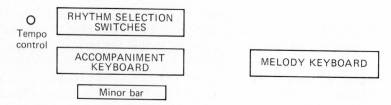

Figure 5.3   Operator interface of elementary accompanying organ

keys are depressed, the instrumental sound generated is internally controlled by a MELODY TIMBRE FILTER. (An organ of this type normally includes a set of "voice" selection switches, not shown in Fig. 5.3, to permit the operator to vary the texture of the produced sound by controlling parameters within the melody timbre filter. We ignore these switches because the internal design of the timbre filter is outside our present purview.) The ACCOMPANIMENT KEYBOARD also contains a set of conventional piano keys. We assume that this keyboard is exactly one octave (12 keys) wide, and that the performer selects one key at a time to define the *root* note of the current chord. The MINOR BAR resembles a typewriter space bar. Whenever it is depressed (by the heel of the performer's left hand), the internal circuits convert the accompaniment chord from "major" to "minor."

Each of the RHYTHM SELECTION SWITCHES is labeled with a specific popular dance rhythm (e.g., "Latin," "fox trot," "waltz," etc.). Only one may be activated at a time, causing the internal circuits to simulate the percussive sounds of several instruments, playing in the selected style and at a tempo controlled by the TEMPO knob. Thus, to operate the instrument, the performer first sets the rhythm style and tempo, causing the proper percussion sounds to be heard. He then operates the keyboards to generate the melody and to control the internal bass and chord accompaniment circuits.

We study the internal design of this instrument by first examining its block diagram, shown in Fig. 5.4. The TONE GENERATOR is the source of all tones in the system. Its square wave outputs are directed to two subsystems: the melody network, in the upper part of the diagram, and the accompaniment network, in the lower portion. The melody network is quite simple in structure. There is a specific tone signal corresponding to each of the N melody keys. The function of the TRANSMISSION GATE BANK is to pass only the selected tones and then to mix them to develop the crude melody signal. This composite signal is refined (shaped) by the melody timbre filter mentioned earlier.

The accompaniment network is controlled by the AUTO-ACCOMPANIMENT CONTROL LOGIC element, which receives all of the operator-controlled accompaniment signals (on the left side of the diagram), and produces

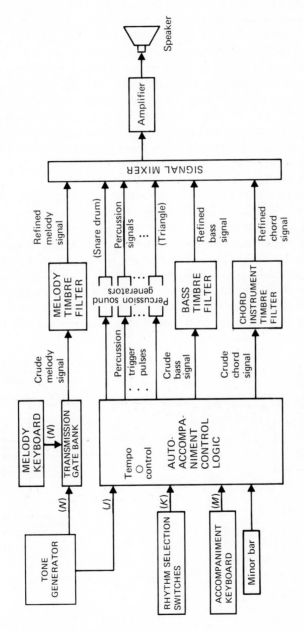

Figure 5.4 Block diagram of elementary accompanying organ

a crude bass tone and a crude chord signal (which is a mixture of three tones), both derived from tone generator outputs. It also generates a set of *trigger pulses*, each of which activates its own PERCUSSIVE SOUND GEN-ERATOR circuit (whose design is also beyond our present scope). When trig-gered, each percussive sound generator produces a signal that mimics the sound of a specific percussion instrument (such as a snare drum, cymbal, or triangle). The bass and chord instrument timbre filters convert the crude bass and chord signals into those whose sounds resemble realistic bass and chord instruments. Finally, all of the individual "instrumental" signals are com-bined in a MIXER, whose composite audio output signal is amplified and passed on to a speaker. (Note that even though volume controls have been omitted for simplicity, they may be imagined positioned at any of several places in the diagram.)

The internal network of the tone generator is shown in Fig. 5.5. It con-tains a central CLOCK OSCILLATOR and numerous counters or frequency dividers. The strategy employed is to develop a set of signals whose frequen-cies closely approximate those of the musical tones in the *highest* audible octave, and then to divide these frequencies by factors of *two* to develop corresponding pitches in any of the lower octaves.

The frequencies of the upper twelve tones must be carefully controlled if they are to sound "in tune" with each other. Rather than employ twelve different oscillators, whose *relative* frequencies must be carefully controlled,

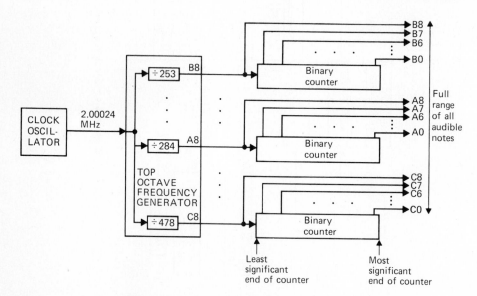

Figure 5.5 Tone generator network

it is preferable to use one central oscillator, whose single frequency is then divided by twelve separate internal *constants*, to produce the twelve different upper tones. To ensure that the pitch of each of these tones is sufficiently close to the "perfect" pitch, knowing that we are restricted to dividing by *integral* constants, it is necessary to make the frequency of the central clock source sufficiently high that twelve integer divisors can be found which each yield a resulting frequency that differs from the ideal by a sufficiently small error. This is how the ideal central clock frequency of 2.00024 MHz (one MHz is 10^6 cycles per second) and the twelve divisor integers in the range between 253 and 478 were derived. Thus, the TOP OCTAVE FREQUENCY GENERATOR contains twelve separate dividers. One is eight bits long (since $253 < 256$) and the others are all nine bits long (since all of the other divisors are less than 512). Each of these counters contains appropriate logic (recall the discussion in Section 3.5) to make its *base* equal to the required divisor.

Each of the top octave signals is given a subscript of "8"—the highest octave number. The corresponding tones in the lowest octave all have a subscript of "0". Note that a conventional binary counter, having at most eight stages, is employed to derive all *lower* versions of each top octave tone. (A simple calculation shows that the frequency of the orchestral tuning tone A4 comes out to be 440.19 cycles per second, instead of the 440 standard.) Since bass tones in this instrument will be derived by a separate circuit (shown later), not all eight stages in each binary counter are absolutely necessary.

It is likely that you have already concluded that the internal structure of the melody transmission gate bank (described earlier) must be that shown in Fig. 5.6. Assuming that you have, we may proceed to examine the most interesting portion of the system, from the digital point of view—the auto-accompaniment logic network. This element is conveniently divided into two parts:

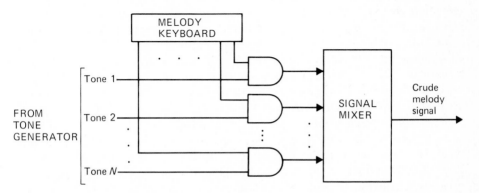

Figure 5.6 Melody transmission gate bank

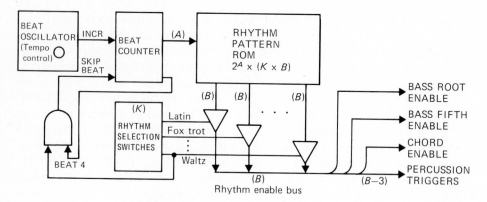

Figure 5.7   Rhythm pattern generator

a rhythm pattern generator and a bass/chord note selector. A block/logic diagram for the rhythm network is shown in Fig. 5.7.

The output of this circuit is a B-bit RHYTHM ENABLE code, each of whose signals activates a specific sound. Of these signals, $B-3$ are the individual percussion triggers, mentioned earlier. The other three signals enable the bass root, bass "fifth," and chord sounds, respectively. Note that these signals have no control over *which* tones are sounded. Rather, they control *when* the sounds will occur. In this way, specific bass and chord rhythm patterns may be developed, consistent with the rhythmic style selected by the operator. Observe that, even though the two bass enable signals are mutually exclusive (only one may be asserted at a time), a *one*-bit selection code is insufficient, because the condition when *both* are off also exists.

The rhythm enable signals are derived from a Read-Only Memory whose input address code is the contents of a BEAT COUNTER. As indicated earlier, time is divided into cycles of equal duration called measures, each containing a fixed number of beats (normally, four). To make sufficiently complex rhythm patterns possible, it is necessary to *identify* all subbeats of interest within a measure. Further, many interesting rhythm patterns extend over more than one measure, before they repeat. In order to keep the required ROM capacity reasonable, we arbitrarily choose to make all rhythm patterns *two* measures long, and to permit identification of all *quarter-beats* within a measure. This means that the length A of the beat counter must be five, divided into an upper one-bit field, which identifies whether this measure is the first or second measure of a pair, and a lower four-bit field, which identifies which *sixteenth* of the current measure is presently occurring. (A more sophisticated system might permit rhythmic patterns to be *four* measures long, and might divide each measure into 32 parts, permitting identification of finer time slots and more intricate rhythm patterns. It would require an increase in the value of A to seven, causing the required ROM capacity to be multiplied by four.)

The rate at which pulses emanate from the BEAT OSCILLATOR (which continuously drives the BEAT COUNTER) is controlled by the TEMPO control knob. The TEMPO knob controls how fast the beat counter advances, which determines how long it takes before the counter "wraps around" and restarts, which occurs on the completion of every other 16-step measure. As the system runs, then, the A-bit ROM address *identifies* the current sixteenth of the current half of a two-measure pattern. Note the analogy to using the contents of a control register to identify a current cycle and a current clock pulse within that cycle, discussed in Section 4.7. In this system, the beat counter is the control register.

The bits that appear at the ROM's output port indicate whether or not certain rhythm instruments should be enabled at this specific point in time, within the repeating two-measure pattern. One of the K RHYTHM SELECTION SWITCHES is activated, which in turn enables one of the TRI-STATE gate banks between the ROM output port and the output bus. Thus, the system is designed so that all K possible rhythm patterns are simultaneously generated, in synchronism, at the ROM output port. Only one is assumed selected. (The selection of two or more is not ruled out, however. If the devices employed permit a "wired-OR" operation, certain interesting effects may be achieved by ORing two or more patterns together.)

The single AND gate shown in Fig. 5.7 demonstrates one technique used to modify the number of beats per measure. Two bits in the beat counter define the current beat number within the current measure. They sequence from 00 to 11 as the beat runs from 1 to 4. The signal named BEAT4 is the AND of these two bits. (It is assumed developed inside the beat counter.) If the WALTZ switch is selected, we wish to convert to three beats per measure. The output signal of the AND gate shown (asserted on "beat 4" of a waltz) is applied to a special input to the beat counter, labeled SKIP BEAT, which causes beat 4 to be skipped. This is accomplished by connecting the SKIP BEAT input to the overriding CLEAR inputs of the two beat-number FLIP-FLOPs, in which case, "beat 4" of a waltz never occurs, because it immediately becomes beat 0. Note that, under these conditions, some ROM locations (i.e., those which would be selected on "beat 4" of a waltz) will never be accessed.

The bass/chord note selection network is shown in Fig. 5.8. In the CHORD NOTE SELECTION MATRIX, a collection of twelve ($M = 12$) tone subsets, out of J tone signals from the tone generator, is selected. The matrix contains J row busses, each carrying a specific tone square wave. Each tone subset contains four ($C = 4$) chord notes: a root, a minor "third," a major

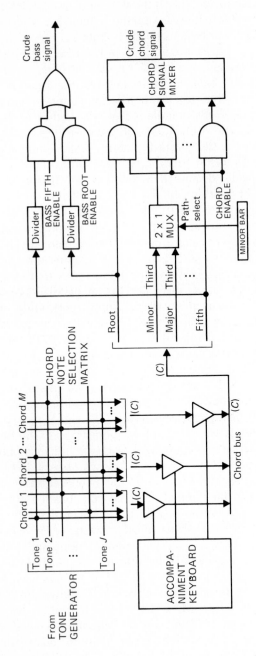

Figure 5.8   Accompaniment bass/chord note selector

"third," and a "fifth"—each selected by a proper connection to one of the rows. Every subset is gated, through a TRI-STATE gate bank, enabled by one of the accompaniment keyboard keys, to a common CHORD BUS. Note that this network is effectively an $M \times C$ MULTIPLEXER, where each of the M input ports carries a unique set of C chord signals, and where the path-select decoder is not required because the code from the keyboard is already in one-asserted form. Variable parameters M and C are used to remind you that a similar structure may be employed in a more sophisticated system, having more chord choices or more notes per chord.

The chord tones on the chord bus are gated to a signal mixer by the CHORD ENABLE signal, which comes from the rhythm network. A chord is heard only while this signal is asserted. Note the elementary multiplexer, which selects one of the "third" signals, based on the state of the minor bar. This idea of selecting some *subset* of the C possible chord notes may be extended, in a more complex system. For example, a set of user-defined signals representing the "KEY" of the piece may be available. The KEY (not to be confused with a keyboard "key") provides information about most likely chord structures. Thus, if C were greater than four, making available additional potential chord notes (for example, the "seventh"), the KEY code could be used to decide which of the "higher" chord tones should be enabled.

Finally, observe the two dividers to develop lower octave versions of the root and "fifth" notes. Each of these signals is also enabled by a separate control signal, from the rhythm network, which defines when it will be heard.

5.2 DIGITAL MULTIPLIER

Consider the multiplication of two N-bit, unsigned arguments X and Y. Each has a value in the range 0 to $2^N - 1$. The product $X \times Y$ has a length of $2N$ bits, because the maximum value in X shifts Y left a distance of N digit positions (inserting zeroes on the right) and then subtracts the original value of Y from this result, which decrements the *upper* N-bit field by only 1, leaving $Y - 1$ there.

We wish to develop a device whose interface is similar to that of an ADDER. It accepts two N-bit input operands and outputs their $2N$-bit product. Following the example of the adder's derivation, we begin by examining the rules by which multiplication is carried out "by hand."

Table 5.1(a) contains such a sample calculation. Since each digit of the multiplier is either 0 or 1, the computation amounts to writing down a copy of the multiplicand, in the correct shifted position, for each occurrence of a

Table 5.1   8×8 Unsigned Multiplication Example

	Multiplicand	10101010
10101010	Multiplier	×10010011
×10010011		

<table>
<tr><td>10101010</td><td>10101010</td></tr>
<tr><td>10101010</td><td>10101010</td></tr>
<tr><td>10101010</td><td>00000000</td></tr>
<tr><td>10101010</td><td>00000000</td></tr>
<tr><td>0110000110011110</td><td>10101010</td></tr>
<tr><td></td><td>00000000</td></tr>
<tr><td></td><td>00000000</td></tr>
<tr><td></td><td>10101010</td></tr>
<tr><td></td><td>0110000110011110</td></tr>
<tr><td>(a)</td><td>(b)</td></tr>
</table>

multiplier digit of 1. A final sum of all of the multiplicand copies yields the product. Table 5.1(b) shows an equivalent computation in which the effect of each 0 multiplier digit is shown explicitly.

Several alternative implementations are suggested by this example. The multiplication process clearly consists of appropriate shifting and adding operations. Since a digital adder accepts only *two* input operands, two or more adders must be employed to add three or more operands simultaneously. For example, the network in Fig. 5.9 contains $N - 1$ N-bit adders and N banks of N AND gates each. Its stage-to-stage wiring pattern implements the necessary operand shifts. At rank i in the array, multiplier bit i determines whether the input argument to adder i is the multiplicand or the constant zero. In the latter case, the adder merely passes the sum that has accumulated up to that point. Note that each adder's C_{in} is 0, and that its least significant output bit is "brought down" as one of the result bits. Its other N outputs (including C_{out}) are applied as an input argument to the next adder stage.

Observe also that the network is fully *combinational*. It includes no internal data storage elements. From the instant when two arguments are first applied at the data input ports, the results appear at the data output port delayed only by the accumulated internal gate delays through the adders. Several alternative combinational array implementations may be similarly configured to realize such a high-speed multiplier. While it delivers its result quickly, it does employ a significant number of internal elements. An alternative design approach repeats the basic set of ADD and SHIFT operations *in time*, rather than in hardware. It includes appropriate storage elements to retain the temporary results between iteration steps, and it demonstrates the well-known time-versus-hardware trade-off, briefly mentioned in Section 1.2.

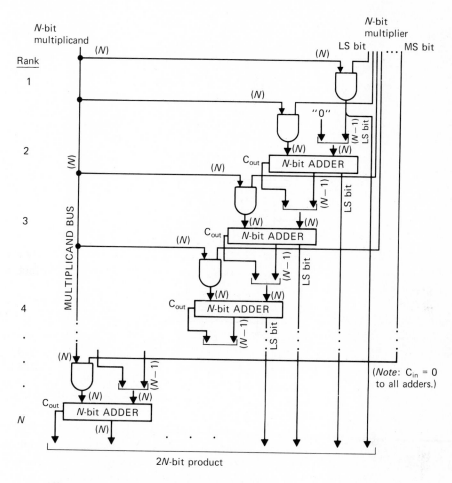

Figure 5.9 Array multiplier network using $N - 1$ N-bit adders

Consider the basic structure shown in Fig. 5.10(a). The 2N-bit-long PAR-TIAL PRODUCT register (abbreviated as "PP"), assumed cleared initially, will contain the accumulating sum from step to step. At the termination of the process, it will contain the result. The MULTIPLICAND register (abbreviated as "MAND"), $2N - 1$ bits long, starts with the N-bit multiplicand in its right half and zeroes in its left half. The 2N-bit adder result (which includes C_{out}) is loaded into the PP register whenever its LOAD pulse is asserted, at which time the register transfer PP ← PP + MAND is executed. Each step in the process includes an examination of the next bit in the multiplier (starting with its least significant bit) and an assertion of LOAD if it is 1. This is fol-

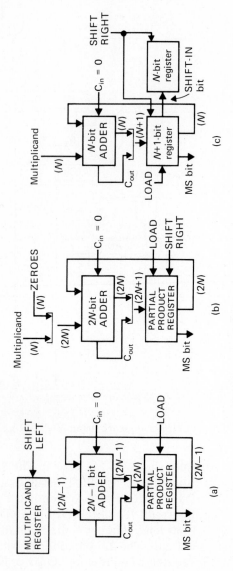

Figure 5.10 Variations on a sequential multiplier

lowed by an unconditional assertion of the LEFT SHIFT signal to the MAND register, causing it to move the multiplicand into a new position (with 0 inserted on the right), in preparation for the next step. You may assume that the multiplier is stored in a MULTIPLIER register (abbreviated as "MIER"), not shown in the diagram. Normally, this register's least significant output signal (its rightmost Q) represents the current multiplier bit, which changes at each step, because the control signal that shifts MAND left is also used to shift MIER right.

In summary, after proper initialization, the multiplication sequence begins with a conditional LOAD of PP (only if the rightmost MIER bit is 1) followed by $N - 1$ steps, each consisting of a left shift of the MAND register, a right shift of the MIER register, and another conditional LOAD of PP based on the new value of the rightmost MIER bit. The MAND register's length is $2N - 1$ to accommodate the original multiplicand after $N - 1$ shifts. The adder's width is tailored to match this value. Note that the leftmost PP bit remains 0 (because the adder's C_{out} remains 0) until the very last step, at which time it may become 1.

Either of two conditions may be employed to terminate the sequence. As implied above, $N - 1$ shifts may be *counted*, with no regard to the value of the multiplier. Alternatively, the state when all *remaining* multiplier bits are zeroes is also a valid end condition. This may be used to cause early termination when the multiplier contains leading zeroes.

Rather than shift the MAND register with respect to the PP register, it may be desirable to keep the multiplicand in a fixed position and to shift the PP register with respect to *it*, as shown in Fig. 5.10(b). The multiplicand is now a fixed N-bit argument, applied to one of the system's input ports. Its value, padded with N zeroes on its right, is applied to one of the adder's input ports. The PP register now has a dual responsibility. Every step consists of a conditional LOAD, based on the current multiplier bit, followed by an unconditional SHIFT *RIGHT*. At the termination of N steps, the process stops, with the rightmost $2N$ bits of the PP register containing the correct result.

Note that this alteration to a uniform sequence of N LOAD/SHIFT *pairs* makes it necessary to increase the PP length by 1, to accommodate the *last* shift. (For all steps preceding the last, the rightmost PP bit remains 0.) The widths of the adder and its multiplicand input argument were both incremented to match the increase in the length of PP.

Since the right half of the $2N$-bit multiplicand argument is *zero*, the right half of the adder and its data path to the right half of the PP register are not needed. Thus, the structure in Fig. 5.10(b) reduces to that in (c). The initial contents of the right half of the PP register are now *arbitrary*, because the right half merely receives shifted-off bits from the left half, and, after N

steps, contains the right half of the product. Consequently, this register may serve a dual purpose. It may be used to initially store the *multiplier* (heretofore, the contents of an "offstage" register). As the multiplier bits shift out at the right end, the product bits shift in at the left end. This leads us to the network in Fig. 5.11(a), in which more of the data paths and necessary control elements are shown.

The left and right halves of the PP register are now labeled as PP.1 and PP.0, respectively. A control counter C, capable of loading the constant N, has been added. The multiplier input port, connected to the DATA IN port of PP.0, is now shown explicitly. So is the dependence of the PP.1 LOAD control signal on the value of the rightmost PP.0 bit. (The AND gate shown permits control signal PULSE1 to pass only if the current multiplier bit is 1.) Several additional control signals are indicated, to permit you to visualize their activation patterns as we review the register transfer flow chart, sometimes called a "*microprogram*," shown in Fig. 5.11(b).

Each line in the sequence defines a micro-operation executed at a separate instant in time. (*Simultaneous* register transfers would appear on the *same* line, separated by semicolons. We begin by ignoring them.) The directed lines are employed chiefly to show alternative paths in the sequence, based on conditions specified within diamond-shaped symbols. Normally, a diamond-shaped symbol has two exit paths, each corresponding to one of the values of a specific *signal* that *represents* the designated condition.

The microprogram in Fig. 5.11(b) begins with three *initialization* steps, corresponding to the following sequence of control-signal assertions:

$$\text{CLEAR PP.1,} \quad \text{LOAD C,} \quad \text{and} \quad \text{LOAD PP.0.}$$

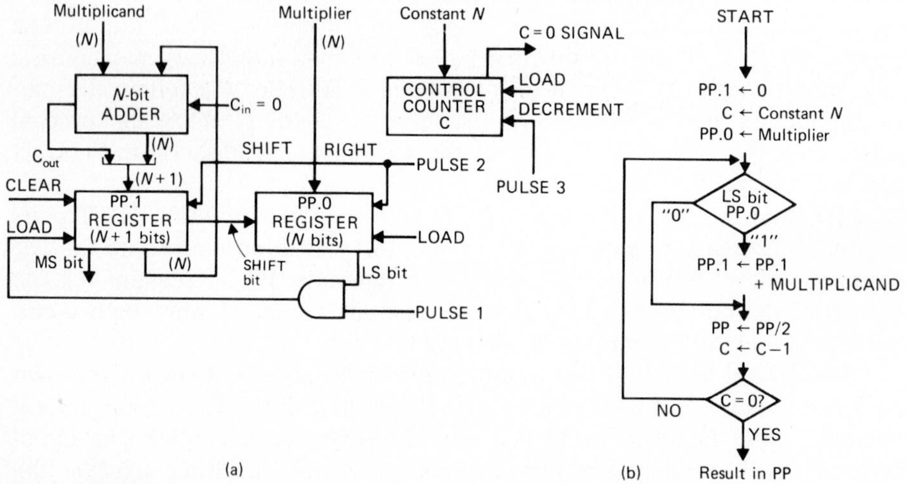

Figure 5.11 Sequential multiplier potential structure and flow chart

While these events are indicated as occurring at different instances, they could have been executed simultaneously, using one common control pulse. The microprogram continues with a repeating *loop* consisting of a sequence of three register transfers. The first of these is conditional on the value of the least significant bit of PP.0. It is skipped if this bit is 0. (The notation "PP/2" represents a right shift of PP.) By examining the logic diagram, you will note that control pulse PULSEi (i = 1, 2, or 3) evokes step i in the loop. Consequently the three-pulse sequence:

PULSE1,   PULSE2,   and   PULSE3

implements one "pass" through the loop. Observe that, while PULSE2 and PULSE3 may be asserted simultaneously, PULSE1 and PULSE2 must be separated in time, because each affects the contents of PP in a different way. The microprogram exits the loop when the $C = 0$ condition is satisfied. This is represented by the assertion of the "$C = 0$" signal presumed developed by a gate internal to the C register.

To make the sequential multiplier operate properly, it is necessary to design a logic network that *generates* the control-signal sequence detailed above. Before doing so, we should examine the interface of the device a bit more carefully.

A combinational version of a multiplier (for example, that shown in Fig. 5.9) has two operand input ports and one product output port. Since it contains no internal storage elements, it has no need for control pulses. The effects of all input signal transitions are transmitted through it immediately. The output results *track* these changes, delayed only by internal signal propagation delays.

A sequential version, on the other hand, requires a source of control pulses. This source may be internal to the device. For example, the "beat oscillator" in Section 5.1 is such an internal pulse source. However, since a multiplier is expected to be only one component in an even larger system (i.e., a computer) which has its *own* central CLOCK, we include in the multiplier's interface an input terminal specifically designated to receive this periodic pulse train.

Since a sequential device performs its function over a span of several successive clock pulses, how do we know when its output results are valid? (We know that the results from a combinational element are valid after a time, measured from the instant when new input operands are first applied, longer than its "worst-case" signal propagation delay. Thus, an *ideal* combinational device, having no internal signal delays, delivers its result instantly.) A sequential device may inform us that its output results are valid by asserting a special output control signal, customarily named "READY". Alternatively, we may treat the device like a combinational element by waiting, from its "starting" instant (defined below) for a specific time (now measured in clock periods) after which its results are known to be valid. Examples of the former method will be given later. We choose here to use the latter approach.

A combinational device intrinsically "restarts" whenever any of its input signals change. How does a sequential element know when to begin its microprogram? We will employ the most common starting method, the assertion of a special input control signal, customarily named START. This event causes the device to reinitialize and begin its function again. Thus, the interface for our sequential multiplier is that shown in Fig. 5.12.

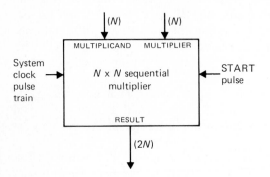

Figure 5.12 Sequential multiplier block diagram

Assume that all internal register elements are triggered by the same clock edge, and that the trailing edge of the START pulse is *not coincident* with this edge. This constraint is necessary to ensure that the *first* synchronous internal event (i.e., one activated by a clock edge) unambiguously occurs *after* the START pulse ends. (Note that this timing restriction is normally automatically satisfied when the device that is the source of the START pulse is *also* clocked by the same central timing pulse train.) There is no restriction on the width of the START pulse. Immediately after it occurs, the system computes the product (taking a specific time period, explained later) and holds it valid, at the output port, until a new START pulse occurs. Details concerning how long the input operands must remain valid during this computation are also given below.

Returning to the multiplier of Fig. 5.11, we may alter its structure slightly to reduce its computation time, by permitting its PULSE1 and PULSE2 register transfers to be executed simultaneously. Consider a modification of the PP.1 register interface so that it has a single CLOCK input terminal plus another input control level, whose value specifies either SHIFT RIGHT or LOAD (on the next CLOCK edge). If this control level is the current multiplier bit, a value of 0 will cause the desired right shift (which now occurs at

PULSE2 time), and a value of 1 will cause the desired load (which now occurs at PULSE1 time). To produce the right shift that *follows* the original load, the data input signals to PP.1 may be reconnected so that the value that is loaded is *already* in its shifted position. Under these conditions, a single "new" LOAD is equivalent to an "old" load–shift combination.

Thus, we derive the modified network shown in Fig. 5.13. The PP.1 input control level X comes directly from the rightmost PP.0 output terminal. The $N + 1$st bit in PP.1 is no longer needed because a shift does not *follow* a load. Note that, to accommodate the change in PP.1's operation, the single source of the shift-in bit to PP.0 had to be replaced by *two* potential sources, one of which is chosen by the value of the current multiplier bit. This function is implemented in the 2×1 MULTIPLEXER shown. Observe also that all *three* registers (PP.1, PP.0, and C) are now triggered by the *same* edge (of a signal named EXECUTE) with no ambiguity in the final outcome.

A completed logic diagram for this sequential multiplier is given in Fig. 5.14. Some of its key control signal waveforms are drawn in Fig. 5.15, and its execution flow chart is shown in Fig. 5.16. The PP.1 and PP.0 registers are now identical components. On a clock edge, each executes either a RIGHT SHIFT or a LOAD, based on the value of its control level X. Each is equipped with an overriding, negative-assertion $\overline{\text{CLEAR}}$ input. The shift-in bit for PP.1 is a constant "0". That for PP.0 is the multiplexer output signal. The PP.1 and PP.0 DATA OUT ports are combined to form the 2N-bit

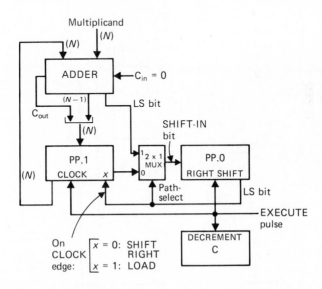

Figure 5.13 Modification of multiplier for parallel operations

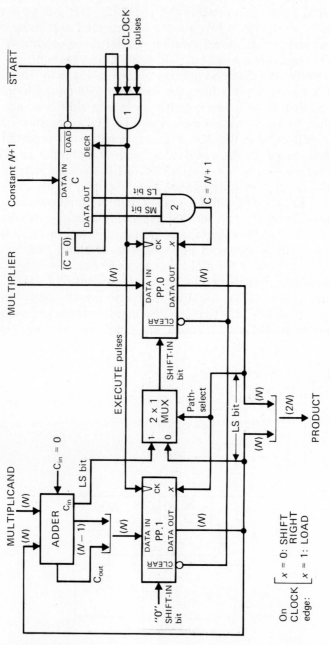

Figure 5.14   Sequential multiplier logic diagram

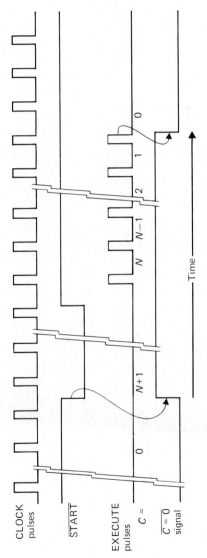

Figure 5.15 Key waveforms for network in Fig. 5.14

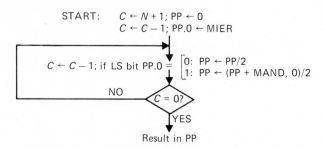

START: $C \leftarrow N + 1$; $PP \leftarrow 0$
$C \leftarrow C - 1$; $PP.0 \leftarrow MIER$

$C \leftarrow C - 1$; if LS bit $PP.0 = \begin{bmatrix} 0: & PP \leftarrow PP/2 \\ 1: & PP \leftarrow (PP + MAND, 0)/2 \end{bmatrix}$

NO

$C = 0?$

YES

Result in PP

Figure 5.16   Microprogram for network in Fig. 5.14

PRODUCT output port. Note that the least significant $PP.0$ output signal is also both the multiplexer PATH SELECT signal and the X control input to $PP.1$. Similarly, the least significant $PP.1$ output is also an input to the multiplexer's "0" input port. The control counter C has an "asynchronous" (independent of its clock input) $\overline{LOAD}$ control, whose negative assertion causes it to load the constant $N + 1$. Its contents decrement whenever it receives a DECREMENT edge. Note that it is equipped with a special output terminal whose negative assertion indicates when its contents are zero.

The system clock pulse train is an input to gate 1. An EXECUTE pulse, coincident with a clock pulse, occurs only if gate 1 is *enabled*. The $\overline{START}$ input pulse is assumed to be a negative-assertion control signal. Whenever it occurs, three *initialization* micro-operations ($C \leftarrow N + 1$, $PP.1 \leftarrow 0$, and $PP.0 \leftarrow 0$) are executed simultaneously. While START is asserted, gate 1 is disabled. The quiescent value for C is *zero*, because, with $\overline{START}$ at its quiescent "1" level, any other value permits clock pulses to pass, decrementing C until it reaches zero, at which time gate 1 is disabled. Gate 2 is designed to recognize when $C = N + 1$. Thus, the X input to $PP.0$ is "1" only while $C = N + 1$, and "0" otherwise. (The inputs to gate 2 were selected under the assumption that N is a power of 2, which is frequently the case. Under these conditions, an AND of the upper and lower bits of C is sufficient to detect $N + 1$. If N is not a power of 2, the inputs to gate 2 must be redefined.)

As we step through the multiplier's operation, you will find it helpful to simultaneously refer to all three relevant Figs. 5.14 through 5.16. The device begins in a quiescent state, ignoring its input operands, with PP containing the results from its *previous* computation. Since $C = 0$, gate 1 is disabled. The external system now applies new argument values to the two operand input ports and holds them valid (for a time interval to be determined). It also asserts the $\overline{START}$ pulse. This clears PP and loads C with $N + 1$, which, in turn, causes the X input to $PP.0$ to have a value "1". Gate 1 *remains disabled* until the termination of the $\overline{START}$ pulse. Thus, while $\overline{START}$ is asserted, EXECUTE pulses are not yet permitted. However, after the trailing edge of

$\overline{START}$, gate 1 is *enabled*, and the input clock pulses are no longer inhibited. On the very *first* EXECUTE pulse, PP.0 loads the multiplier value. PP.1 remains cleared, because its right shift merely shifts in another "0". (This is the only reason why PP.0 was cleared initially, to ensure that the first X value to PP.1 is "0".) Simultaneously, C decrements, giving it the new value N. For all subsequent EXECUTE pulses, C decrements, PP.0 shifts right (because its X remains "0"), and PP.1 either loads or shifts, depending on the current multiplier bit. When C reaches zero, the process stops with gate 1 disabled again and with the result in PP.

We are now in a position to be more specific about the time periods over which the input operands must be held valid. The multiplicand must remain constant for $N + 1$ clock periods from the trailing edge of START. (Note that the results are known to be valid after that time period has elapsed.) The multiplier, on the other hand, needs to remain stable only for *one* clock period from the trailing edge of START.

Observe, particularly, that the system automatically develops a signal that may be used as an *indicator* of the completion of its computation. The "$C = 0$" signal may be renamed as *READY* and added, as an output signal, to the multiplier's interface. With this modification, an external device would not be required to "keep track" of elapsed time from the starting instant.

Observe also that $N + 1$ steps were necessary only because PP.0 was postulated to be identical to PP.1. Had PP.0 been equipped with an asynchronous $\overline{LOAD}$ input terminal, replacing $\overline{CLEAR}$, the assertion of $\overline{START}$ would have completed *all* initialization, and the process could have consumed one less clock period.

The waveforms in Fig. 5.15 were drawn assuming that all registers are triggered on the trailing EXECUTE pulse edge. The S-shaped arrows indicate cause-and-effect relationships. For example, the leading edge of $\overline{START}$ causes C to load, which in turn causes the $\overline{C = 0}$ signal to be deactivated. Similarly, the $N + 1$st EXECUTE pulse decrements C from 1 to 0, which in turn causes $\overline{C = 0}$ to be activated again.

The notation "MAND,0" in Fig. 5.16 represents an equivalent $2N$-bit operand, whose right half is zero.

5.3 VIDEO DISPLAY OF TEXT AND GRAPHICS

We consider here the detailed logic design of a controller that displays computer-generated information on a television screen. In order to do so, we must first review some fundamentals pertaining to black-and-white television signals.

An image on a TV picture tube is generated by a narrow electron beam moving, at very high speed, in a well-defined, constantly repeating, scanning pattern, which covers the entire screen. The beam begins a "pass" over the screen positioned in its upper left-hand corner. It moves, at a constant velocity, in a horizontal line across the screen, until it reaches the right boundary, at which time it instantaneously returns to the left border, at a location just under the previously scanned line. This basic cycle (a left-to-right scan alongside and under the previously scanned line, if one exists, followed by an instantaneous return) repeats continuously until the bottom right-hand corner of the screen is reached. At that instant, the pass culminates in an instantaneous return to the upper left-hand corner, to begin the cycle again. A single pass, called a TV "frame," contains approximately 260 lines and consumes 1/60 of a second. (We are ignoring the fact that two successive passes actually differ slightly, as a consequence of a process called "interlacing.")

While the beam is scanning across the screen, its intensity (the brightness of the tiny spot at which it is currently positioned) is controlled by a VIDEO signal. We limit our attention to video signals that are *digital* in nature. A video signal value of "1" causes the scanning spot to be WHITE, while a "0" causes it to be BLACK. (Grays are not permitted.) An arbitrary black and white picture is "painted" on the screen by using a properly composed video signal, *synchronized* with the scanning pattern. The image is not permanent, however. If it is not redrawn, it disappears after a short time. To achieve a stationary picture, the video signal waveform is continuously repeated, from frame to frame. The 60-frames-per-second rate is sufficiently high that "flicker" in the picture is not discernible.

A TV display controller must supply to a TV monitor or receiver not only a video signal but also *synchronizing* signals to govern the scanning process. In particular, to define a specific picture, the TV display device expects a simultaneous combination of *three* signals: a video signal, a HORIZONTAL SYNC (for "synchronizing") signal, and a VERTICAL SYNC signal. The horizontal sync signal is a periodic train of pulses, each of which induces the TV's beam scanner to begin a new *line*. Similarly, the vertical sync signal is a periodic train of pulses, each of which induces the TV's beam scanner to begin a new *frame*. The display controller's function is to generate these sync signals and, principally, to compose a video signal *synchronized with them* such that the desired picture is produced.

Figure 5.17 pictures the TV scanning process and adds a few more numeric details. The thickness of each scan line is clearly exaggerated. We are assuming a system having exactly 264 lines per frame. Slightly more than one cycle of each sync signal is plotted, for reference, in the dimension that best matches its time scale. Each waveform is meant to convey the fact that the assertion of the sync pulse causes an immediate beam transition to the opposite border. Note that the period of the vertical sync signal is 16.7 millisec-

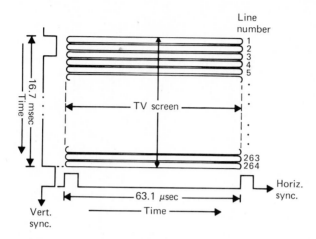

Figure 5.17   Representation of the TV scanning process

onds or 1/60 of a second. Similarly, the horizontal sync period is approximately 63.1 microseconds, meaning that the scanning system draws lines at the rate of 15,840 lines per second.

The sync signal waveforms are shown in more detail in Fig. 5.18. Each horizontal sync pulse is approximately 5 μsec (microseconds) wide. Each vertical sync pulse width is equal to approximately three line-scan times. Note that the position of the vertical sync pulse, relative to the horizontal pulse train, *defines* which horizontal pulse corresponds to line number *one*. A TV display device normally receives this synchronizing information in one COMPOSITE SYNC signal, whose waveform is also drawn in Fig. 5.18. The display element is able to extract both vertical and horizontal synchronizing information from the composite signal, which is simply the EXCLUSIVE OR of the two individual sync signals.

Figure 5.19 presents an example of a video signal, shown relative to the two sync signals. This video signal consists of a burst of pulses. Each pulse begins (at point **a**) 25 μsec after the leading edge of a horizonal sync pulse, and has a width (from point **a** to point **b**) of 25 μsec. The first and last video pulses occur after horizonal pulses *i* and *j*, respectively. The three waveforms continuously repeat, from frame to frame.

The resulting TV display is shown in Fig. 5.20. Here *i* and *j* are assumed to have the values 70 and 170, respectively (meaning that the video signal for one frame contains a burst of exactly 101 pulses). The term "blank," in Fig. 5.20, is synonymous with black. The dashed border indicates that the first and last few lines, as well as the beginnings and endings of all lines, are not normally visible.

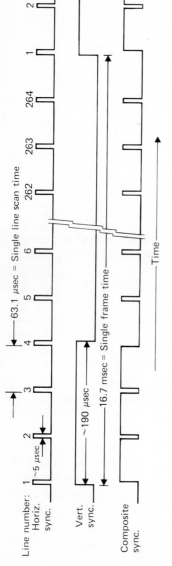

Figure 5.18   Typical TV SYNC signals

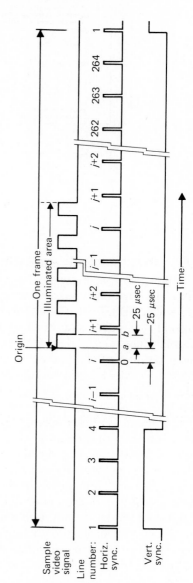

Figure 5.19   Sample VIDEO signal relative to SYNC signals

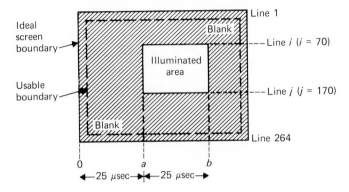

Figure 5.20   Display based on signals in Fig. 5.19

The video waveform in this example was intentionally simplified to permit you to easily visualize its effect. Clearly, a more realistic video signal has an extremely complicated behavior between any pair of adjacent horizontal sync pulses.

Returning to Fig. 5.19, imagine translating one of its waveforms horizontally with respect to the others. Assume that it remains synchronized, but that its timing relationship with respect to the others changes. As the vertical sync signal shifts, the specific horizontal pulse, which is identified as the *first*, changes, in which case the visible pattern moves up or down. Similarly, as the horizontal sync waveform shifts, the left and right *margins* of the visible pattern change, and the picture moves left or right.

Based on the explanations given above, it is likely that you would approach the design of a TV display controller by first devising the sync signal generator, and then, having established the fixed pair of horizontal and vertical reference signals, by developing the network that composes the necessary video signal with respect to them. Consider, instead, the alternative of using the *video* signal as the reference and developing the sync signals subsequently. For example, the waveforms in Fig. 5.19 were drawn assuming the sync signals as the reference. Suppose we erased the sync waveforms and looked only at the video signal. Its natural point of reference is the upper left-hand corner of the *illuminated* portion of the screen. Let us call this area the "window" and its upper left-hand corner, its "origin." (The position of the origin on the video waveform is marked in Fig. 5.19.) The equivalent, "window-based" or "video-based" picture is shown in Fig. 5.21. It is drawn using the *same* video signal, but *beginning* the plot at the origin of the window. The same total area is swept out, but the visible window is always positioned in its upper left-hand corner. We have merely altered our point of reference. The exact position of the visible window on the *physical* screen will depend on the timing of the sync pulses with respect to the video signal.

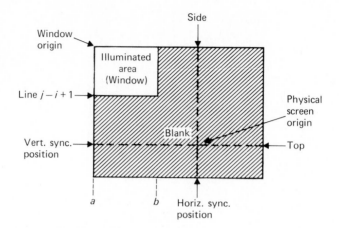

Figure 5.21 "Window-based" equivalent of Fig. 5.20

A specific timing selection, based on the original example in Fig. 5.19, is shown by the two dashed lines in Fig. 5.21. They define where the TV screen borders will be located with respect to the visible window. We will use this window-based viewpoint in the design of our display controller.[†]

The first essential system component is a control register, whose contents *identify* the current beam position on the (window-based) screen. A LINE COUNTER, which has 264 states, is required. Similarly, a DOT COUNTER, which has as many states as there are unique spots in one line (to be determined), is also necessary. The dot counter should be driven at a rate that causes it to "wrap around" and restart every 63.1 μsec. Whenever it does so, the line counter should advance, which will cause it to restart every 16.7 msec, as required.

Assuming that the primary function of the display is the presentation of text messages, the window must be regarded as also consisting of a set of rows, each containing a string of characters. We choose to organize the window into 16 rows of 64 characters each. The shape of each character's symbol will be approximated by a pattern of illuminated dots in a fixed rectangular array. We choose to organize each of the (16 $\times$ 64 = 1024) visible character positions into a 35-dot array, arranged in seven lines of five dots each. We also choose one dot (one-fifth of a character width) as the horizontal space between characters and five lines (five-sevenths of a character height) as the vertical space between character rows. In effect, then, the "subwindow" allocated to each character, *including* its horizontal and vertical spaces, contains

---

[†]Its organization is based on that of the display controller contained in Tandy Corporation's Radio Shack TRS-80 (model I) computer.

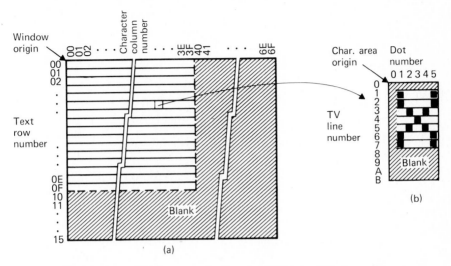

Figure 5.22   Display organization for 16 lines of 64 characters

12 lines of six dots each. (Of course, during text display, those regions allocated for spacing will be blank.)

Figure 5.22 illustrates this organization. Each character *subwindow* is located with a row number and a column number. Furthermore, each dot *within* a character area has its own localized coordinates, a line number and a dot number. All coordinate values are specified as *hexadecimal* numbers. Note that screen space has been allocated for *blank* vertical and horizontal margins around the window area. Specifically, a distance equal to six row heights has been chosen as the *sum* of the top and bottom margin sizes. The exact timing of the vertical sync pulse will determine how this total distance is subdivided. Similarly, a length equal to 48 column widths has been allocated for the sum of the left and right margins. The exact timing of the horizontal sync pulses, relative to the video waveform, will determine how this distance is subdivided. Note that each character's area includes not only the 5 × 7 visible symbol portion but also its vertical and horizontal spaces. (The sample 35-bit dot pattern shown approximates the shape of the character "X".)

The total number of (visible and blanked) rows is 22 (16 + 6). Each row consists of 12 lines, yielding the total of 264 (22 × 12) lines. Similarly, the total number of (visible and blanked) character columns is 112 (64 + 48). Each column contains six dots across, giving a total number of horizontal dot *positions* in a single line of 672 (112 × 6). This number determines a required length of 10 for the dot counter. This length is conveniently divided into an upper seven-bit field, which is a character column number, as shown in the

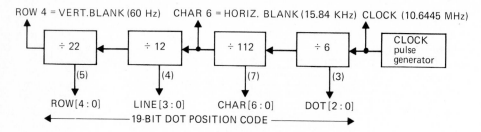

ROW 4 = VERT.BLANK (60 Hz)   CHAR 6 = HORIZ. BLANK (15.84 KHz) CLOCK (10.6445 MHz)

Figure 5.23   Beam position control register

labeling at the top of Fig. 5.22(a), and a lower three-bit field, which is a dot number *within* the selected column, as shown by the labeling at the top of Fig. 5.22(b). Similarly, the line counter must be nine bits long to permit 264 states. It is convenient to divide this length into an upper five-bit field, specifying a text row number, as indicated by the labeling on the left side of Fig. 5.22(a), and a lower four-bit field, which is a TV line number *within* the selected row, as indicated by the labels along the left side of Fig. 5.22(b). This explains how the organization of the BEAM POSITION control register, shown in Fig. 5.23, was derived.

This register is organized as a chain of dividers, in a manner identical to that used for the digital watch of Fig. 4.23. Each counter stage increments on the negative edge of its input signal. Its most significant output bit is the input signal to the next stage. It includes a gate to cause an immediate reset back to state zero when its contents reach the (decimal) base value indicated. Its hexadecimal contents specify the value of a corresponding coordinate in Fig. 5.22.

The system is driven by an internal source of periodic pulses at a 10.6445 MHz rate (1 MHz = 10^6 per second). This number is the line rate of 15.84 KHz (1 KHz = 10^3 per second) multiplied by 672, the number of dot positions per line. The values possible in the four fields of this 19-bit register verify that a frame contains 22 rows, each consisting of 12 lines, each divided into 112 character segments, which each contain six dots. Of the 2^{19} = 524,288 conceivable values in this 19-bit register, only 177,408 = 22 × 12 × 112 × 6 can actually occur. Note that the signal CHAR6, the upper bit of the CHAR[6 : 0] field, is renamed as HORIZ. BLANK because it has a value "1" over that portion of every line that is allocated to the left and right margins. Similarly, the signal ROW4, the upper bit of field ROW[4 : 0], is renamed as VERT. BLANK because it has a value "1" over that set of TV lines allocated to the top and bottom margins. [The hexadecimal coordinates listed in Fig. 5.22(a) imply values for CHAR6 and ROW4.]

Having specified a continuously incrementing control register, whose contents identify a specific screen location, we are in a position to design the network that *decides*, for each dot location, whether or not the corresponding video signal value should be "1" or "0" (i.e., whether the electron beam should be ON or OFF at that point). Note that we can already conclude that if BLANK (defined as the logical OR of HORIZ. BLANK with VERT. BLANK) is "1", VIDEO should be "0".

The second most essential system component is a memory whose contents define what is displayed on the screen. For each possible dot position in the window, the display controller uses data read from this memory to determine a video signal value. The memory is called a VIDEO RAM for that reason. It is also called a "refresh" memory, because the pattern of READs defining one frame's video signal is repeated continuously to keep the image on the screen. (The image is constantly "repainted" or "refreshed.")

Several alternative rules may be adopted to map video RAM bit patterns into display bit patterns. For example, there may be a one-to-one correspondence between RAM bits and display dots, in which case, the required RAM capacity is

$$16 \times 12 \times 64 \times 6 = 192 \times 384 = 73,728 \text{ bits}$$

—the total number of dots in the window area. Such an arrangement would be applicable if the display window's dot pattern were totally arbitrary. This is not the case, however. For a text display, it is more efficient to employ a RAM containing as many registers as there are characters on the screen, with each register containing a code for its corresponding display character. Thus, we choose to use a 1024×8 video RAM, each of whose registers holds the ASCII code (recall Table 1.3) for one display character. (The code occupies the lower seven bits. An application for the eighth bit will develop presently.)

The third most essential system component is a CODE CONVERTER that converts a compact (seven-bit ASCII) character code into a corresponding code ($5 \times 7 = 35$ bits) for its display. Referring to Fig. 5.22(a), note that, as the system runs, the ten-bit combination of ROW[3 : 0] and CHAR[5 : 0] (from the dot position control register) locates a specific character position in the window. (In this region, both ROW4 and CHAR6 are "0".) This ten-bit value, applied as an *address* to the video RAM, selects the corresponding stored character code, which is read and then applied to a ROM, which converts it into a bit pattern for the *display* of that character. Referring to Fig. 5.22(b), observe also that only a *subset* of five of these 35 display bits, as selected by the current LINE[3 : 0] code, is actually *plotted* during a single line scan.

The fourth most essential system component is a SHIFT REGISTER to convert the *parallel* five-bit display code for the current line of the current display character into the *serial* bit stream required by the video signal.

All of the components introduced above are integrated into a display controller system whose logic/block diagram is shown in Fig. 5.24. Observe that all labeled inputs, other than those that are part of the "CPU INTER-FACE", come from the beam position control register of Fig. 5.23. It is the only component not explicitly shown in Fig. 5.24.

At the bottom of the diagram, the individual horizontal and vertical BLANK signals are ORed together to form the overall BLANK signal, introduced earlier. In addition, each of these signals is directed, through a variable delay element, to a pulse generator, which responds to each positive

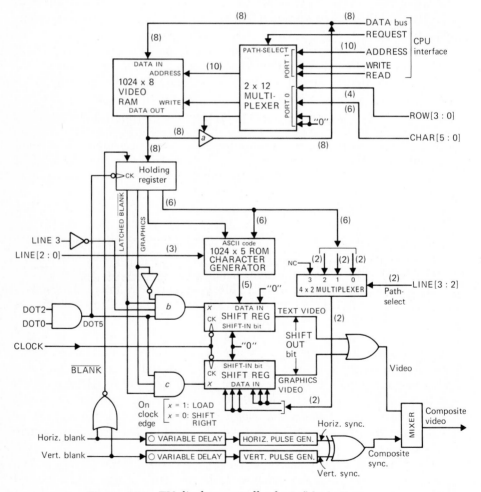

Figure 5.24   TV display controller logic/block diagram

edge by producing a pulse of the proper width. The resulting horizontal and vertical SYNC signals are combined, in an EXCLUSIVE OR gate, to produce COMPOSITE SYNC, which is further combined with the VIDEO signal to form a COMPOSITE VIDEO signal, which is delivered to the TV display monitor. The monitor, in turn, reconstructs the individual SYNC and VIDEO signals from the composite and draws the picture. The horizontal and vertical delays are both adjustable to permit centering the picture in both directions on the screen.

The rest of the system shown produces the VIDEO signal. Consider, first, the 2×12 multiplexer coupled to the video RAM, in the upper part of the diagram. It is controlled by the REQUEST signal, which is part of the CPU interface. The CPU (for "Central Processing Unit") is an external device, whose detailed behavior need not concern us here. The CPU requires access to the video RAM on an intermittent basis, primarily to alter the contents of one or more RAM registers. To directly couple itself to the RAM, it asserts the REQUEST signal. While REQUEST = 1, multiplexer port 1 is enabled, and the RAM's address and WRITE signals are derived from the CPU. In addition, a path between the RAM's DATA OUT port and the bidirectional CPU DATA BUS comes under the control of the CPU's READ signal. (See tri-state gate bank "a".) Thus, the CPU may interject a video RAM READ or WRITE, at any arbitrary instant, merely by asserting its REQUEST signal.

Normally, however, CPU REQUEST = 0, enabling multiplexer port 0, and the RAM address is a concatenation of ROW[3 : 0] and CHAR[5 : 0], as suggested earlier. (This address value remains constant over all of the line segments within any character area on the screen.) In addition, WRITE = 0, so that the RAM operates in a read-only mode, ignoring its DATA IN signals. Further, the path between the RAM's DATA OUT port and the CPU is disabled. Thus, the RAM is decoupled from the CPU. Note that the RAM address advances every time the DOT counter increments from 5 back to 0, and that the same address pattern accompanies the scan of each of the 12 lines in a given row.

All of the system's registers are assumed *negative* edge-triggered. The signal DOT5 (the AND of DOT2 and DOT0) is 1 only while the DOT count is 5. Note that DOT5 is *not* derived from the BEAM POSITION control register, as are DOT2, DOT1, and DOT0. DOT5 is asserted only while the value of DOT[2 : 0] is five. When DOT advances to 0, the negative edge of DOT5 causes the holding register to load the character code coming from the memory, along with an accompanying BLANK condition. Thus, at the instant when the RAM address advances, the holding register loads the contents of the *previous* address. This gives the system the maximum time of 0.56 μsec (six dot times) for the contents of the *new* address to become valid at the RAM DATA OUT port, ready for a *new* load of the holding register.

The combination of the lower seven-bit code stored in the holding register and the three-bit LINE[2 : 0] code is applied, as a ten-bit address, to a 1024×5 ROM, called a CHARACTER GENERATOR. This device contains the display bit patterns for all of the visible characters. It is specifically designed for a line-scanned display in that it outputs only that five-bit display pattern, for the specified character, chosen by the current LINE number. (Recall that, while the video RAM address remains constant over any character's screen area, the LINE code increments from scan to scan.) LINE numbers 1 through 7 produce valid display patterns. For example, LINE 5 of character "X" (whose ASCII code is a hex 58) maps into a binary 01010 output pattern. The ROM is designed so that LINE code 0 always delivers an output of 0, defining one of the five blank lines between character rows. [See Fig. 5.22(b).]

The five-bit ROM output display code is directed, along with a constant 0 bit, to the DATA IN port of a six-bit shift register, which is clocked on every negative edge of the continuously running 10.6 MHz CLOCK. This register is similar to that used in the multiplier of Fig. 5.14. On a clock edge, it shifts right if $X = 0$ and loads if $X = 1$. Its shift-out bit is the current TEXT video bit, which is ORed with the GRAPHICS video bit (presently assumed 0) to develop the VIDEO signal. Its shift-in bit is a constant 0.

AND gate "b" determines the behavior of this register. Assuming that the GRAPHICS signal from the holding register is 0, this gate has three inputs of interest. Assume a sufficient number of shifts, without an intervening load, so that the present contents of the shift register are zero. Then $X = 0$ will cause it to continue shifting 0's in and 0's out, which will keep the display blank. Two logical conditions, LATCHED BLANK = 1 and LINE3 = 1, force $X = 0$. The first causes the display to remain blank *outside* of the window area. The second keeps it blank over the bottom four lines in each row. Thus, a load of the shift register (when $X = 1$) cannot occur unless the beam is positioned *within* the window, on one of the *upper* eight lines of a row. Under these conditions, signal X is the same as signal DOT5, and the sequence of events is clarified by the waveforms shown in Fig. 5.25.

The signal DOT5 is plotted with respect to the CLOCK waveform. A realistic delay is explicitly indicated. Each time slot is labeled with the current contents of the DOT register. Since $X = $ DOT5, the shift register shifts right on every negative CLOCK edge except that between DOT = 5 and DOT = 0. On that edge, $X = 1$ and the register loads its current six-bit DATA IN value. This value then shifts right, on the next five successive CLOCK edges, after which a new load occurs to begin the cycle again. Thus, the TEXT video signal (the register's least significant Q output), during time slot i, is the *same* as bit i of its previously loaded value. The register functions as a parallel-to-

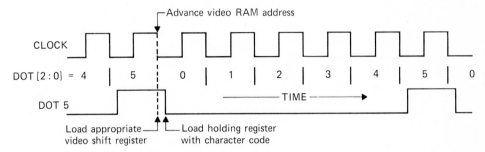

Figure 5.25 Display controller waveforms

serial converter. Note that bit 0 is always 0. This is the one-dot space between characters.

Figure 5.25 also summarizes the three key events that occur, almost simultaneously, each time that DOT advances from 5 back to 0. First, the video
RAM address advances, because CHAR increments. Second, the shift register loads a new value, which will be shifted out during the next six dot time
slots. Third, a new RAM output value is loaded into the holding register.
Note that the serial video output bits, during any six-dot period, are derived
from the contents of the holding register during the *previous* period, which,
in turn, were the contents of the RAM register addressed during the period
before that. This means that the character being plotted on the screen is
always two characters *behind* the one being addressed in the RAM. This is
the reason why the BLANK condition associated with a character is loaded
into the holding register with it.

Throughout the discussion above, it was assumed that the GRAPHICS bit
in the holding register—the upper bit from the RAM—was 0. When it is 1,
the nature of the resulting display is fundamentally altered. First, AND gate
"b" is disabled, forcing TEXT video to be 0. Second, AND gate "c", which
had been disabled (causing GRAPHICS video to be 0), is now enabled. If the
LATCHED BLANK = 1 condition exists, the resulting video signal is again
forced to be 0. However, if the character area is within the window, the
lower shift register duplicates the LOAD/SHIFT behavior just described for
the upper shift register. However, the six-bit value that it loads is *not* derived
from the character generator. Rather, it consists of two triplets of identical
bits. Each triplet has a value equal to one of the output bits from the 4×2
multiplexer. This multiplexer uses LINE[3 : 2] to select one of three two-bit
fields from the lower six bits of the character code.

A LINE[3 : 2] value of 0, 1, or 2 selects the upper, middle, or lower *third*,
respectively, of a row. [See Fig. 5.22(b). A value of 3 cannot occur. That is

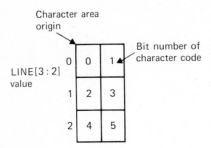

Figure 5.26 Reorganization of character area for graphics

why multiplexer port 3 is not used.] Thus, for the four lines in a given third, the first three dots plotted are determined by one triplet value and the next three are defined by the other. Under these conditions, the character area description is altered to that shown in Fig. 5.26. The illumination of the $4 \times 3 = 12$ dots in one of the subareas shown is controlled by one character bit, whose position is indicated.

Thus, one can use the contents of the RAM to draw *arbitrary* pictures, each of whose "dots" (consisting of a rectangular 4×3 array of original dots) is controlled by a specific RAM bit. The graphics window is therefore divided into 1024 six-"dot" areas, which appear in a contiguous 128×48 array.

In summary, the upper bit in each character (GRAPHICS) *selects* which of the two identical shift registers will be employed to develop the next six video bits. Output from the unselected shift register remains 0. The TEXT shift register delivers the current display code derived from the character generator. The GRAPHICS shift register delivers two three-dot "dashes," directly derived from a pair of bits in the current character.

PROBLEMS

Note: Since each of the digital systems discussed in this chapter is complicated, a detailed understanding of its operation may require rereading part or all of its text description. Most of the problems given below are designed to aid in this process by testing your comprehension of specific operational details. It is likely that when you complete working these problems, you will have a clearer picture of key aspects of each design, at which time, rereading its text description will prove more beneficial.

5.1 Using information given in Fig. 5.5 (and in the portion of the text that supports it), calculate the frequencies of the nine A tones, A8 through A0.

5.2 Assume that the BEAT COUNTER in Fig. 5.7 has a length of five, so that it identifies each sixteenth of a two-measure sequence. Assume also that the first beat in each pair of measures begins at count zero. Specify those hexadecimal BEAT COUNTER values that identify each of the following instants in time:

a) The beginning of every beat, in both measures. (There are four beats per measure.)

b) The third quarter-beat in each beat, in both measures.

c) All possible approximations to the "triplet" (a sequence of *three* subbeats in one beat time) beginning at the second beat of the second measure of a pair.

5.3 What modifications are required to the network in Fig. 5.2 to provide an electronic accompanist that tracks the performing instrument and plays *two* octaves below it?

5.4 How many different notes are needed to define a single elementary "major" chord *and* its corresponding "minor" chord?

5.5 Suppose the Rhythm Pattern ROM in Fig. 5.7 contains only one rhythm pattern (i.e., $K = 1$). The Beat Counter is used as previously described in Problem 5.2 (that is, $A = 5$). Ignoring the bass and chord ENABLE signals, assume that the ROM has four outputs ($B = 4$), which activate, respectively (from left to right), the following four percussion instruments: cymbal, snare drum, bass drum, and triangle. What should the ROM hex contents be (beginning with the contents of memory location zero) if the rhythm pattern requires a cymbal sound on every second and fourth sixteenth of every measure, a snare drum sound on every half-beat *between* beats, a bass drum sound on every beat, and a triangle sound only on beats 3 and 4 of every *second* measure of a pair?

5.6 In the Chord Note Selection Matrix in Fig. 5.8, how many row connections are possible per column?

5.7 Using the Multiplier in Fig. 5.10(a), assuming $N = 4$, specify the hex contents of the Partial Product register after each sequential step in the multiplication of MAND = B and MIER = 6. (The arguments are specified as hex values.)

5.8 Assuming that its length is four, draw the logic, inside the Control Counter C in Fig. 5.11(a), that develops the $C = 0$ control level. (All of the internal FLIP-FLOP Q signals are available as inputs.)

5.9 Repeat Problem 5.7 using instead the network shown in Fig. 5.13.

5.10 Employing the Multiplier of Fig. 5.14, with $N = 8$, list the hexadecimal contents of C, PP.1, and PP.0, after each CLOCK pulse, in the computation of the product of MAND = AA and MIER = 93. (The arguments are specified in hex.)

5.11 Assume you are given four negative-edge-triggered binary counters, of lengths 3, 4, 5, and 7, respectively; each has a negative-assertion overriding CLEAR input. Show how they are connected together, with a minimum of additional logic, to realize the function described in Fig. 5.23.

5.12 In the TV display controller of Figs. 5.22 through 5.24, how much time is allocated to each dot, to each scan-line segment of each character, to each line, to each row of characters, and to each frame? (Include intentionally blanked portions in your answer.)

5.13 For the display controller described in Section 5.3, specify all values of the 19-bit code (the contents of the Beam Position Control Register [Fig. 5.23]) that are *known* to correspond to *blanked* display regions. (Assume that the conventional character display mode is activated.) Each code value should specify 1's or 0's in fields whose values are known to cause a blank display, and X's for bits whose values do not matter.

5.14 With reference to Fig. 5.24, briefly explain why disabling AND gate b (or c) forces the TEXT (or GRAPHICS) video signal to be zero.

5.15 The upper bit (bit 7) in the eight-bit byte from the video RAM (Fig. 5.24) determines how the display will interpret the lower bits. In the GRAPHICS mode, what is the effect of bit 6 (the one just below the GRAPHICS bit)?

5.16 We want to employ a special control signal, named REVERSE (assume it is derived from a user-controlled switch), whose assertion causes the *negative* of the display picture to be produced (i.e., white areas become black and black areas become white). How should the network in Fig. 5.24 be modified to accomplish this?

5.17 Your answer to Problem 5.15 leads you to suspect that, in the GRAPHICS mode, a better use can be found for bit 6 of each RAM output byte. Consider its use to implement an *underline* facility. (An underline may be used as a "cursor." A cursor is a special visible mark on the screen that identifies only one of the displayed characters. The user employs it as a pointer, whose position he can control.) Let us adopt the following rules: When bit 7 is 0, the character is displayed normally. When bit 7 is 1 and bit 6 is 0, the lower six bits are interpreted in the normal graphics display mode. However, when bits 7 and 6 are *both* 1, the lower seven bits still define the character to be displayed, but it appears on the screen *underlined*. Specifically, of the four lines that are normally blanked under it, the *next-to-top* one is illuminated. Note that only characters having ASCII codes in the range 40 to 7F hex may be so underlined. (As Table 1.3 verifies, this covers all of the alphabetic characters.)

What modifications to the network in Fig. 5.24 are necessary to implement this facility? Use a minimum number of added logic elements. You may modify the number of inputs to any existing gates. Your diagram should clearly distinguish between existing and added elements. The sources of all input signals and the destinations of all output signals should be clearly named.

Processors and Programs

6.1 INSTRUCTIONS AND THE FETCH–EXECUTE CYCLE

Every PROCESSOR is equipped with a *repertoire* of operations which it has the capacity to execute. The operation it selects for execution is based on its interpretation of a command code, called an INSTRUCTION. This instruction is part of a *sequence* of instructions, called a PROGRAM, which is stored in a memory to which the processor has access. The processor executes the program, one instruction at a time, by reading the current instruction, interpreting it, executing it, and then proceeding to the next instruction. Since each instruction is available to the processor almost instantaneously, the execution time for an entire program may be very small.

A program is planned by a programmer, using a set of rules based on the instruction repertoire of a specific processor. This set of rules is known as a programming LANGUAGE. (An instruction in a programming language is also called a STATEMENT.) A program written for one processor may be *translated* into an equivalent program for another processor, even though the two machines have entirely different instruction sets. For this reason, a programming language may be based on a *hypothetical* machine, which does

231

not physically exist because it is too difficult or too expensive to build. It is defined strictly because its language is easier to use—more convenient to express programs in. It is called a VIRTUAL machine because it is the one that is "visible" to the programmer. Consequently, the program that a processor executes may have been planned directly for it or may be a translation of a program written for some other (possibly virtual) machine.

The memory containing the program may be a ROM, in which case the program was built into it at the time it was fabricated. Alternatively, the memory may be a volatile RAM, in which case the program must first be made *resident*, using a sequence of memory writes called a program LOAD, before its execution may commence. In subsequent discussions, unless specified otherwise, we will assume that the program already resides in the memory to which the processor has access.

To read an instruction, the processor presents the *address* of the instruction to the memory. This address is the contents of a processor register, commonly known as the PROGRAM COUNTER (abbreviated as "PC"). It is called a counter because it is normally incremented in order to point to the *next* instruction in sequence. (We are assuming, to begin with, that every instruction is one word long—the contents of a single memory register.) The Program Counter keeps the processor's *place* in the program. If each instruction in the program is executed only *once* (an oversimplified assumption), the Program Counter distinguishes those instructions already executed from those which the processor has not yet encountered.

Figure 6.1 shows two alternative sketches used to represent programs in the process of execution. In (a), each horizontal line represents an instruction; part (b) conveys the notion of a program as an instruction "stream." In both cases, the PC *pointer* indicates the processor's current place in the program. Using the elementary program example, in which each instruction is executed only once, the PC pointer merely moves downward as time passes.

The *execution* of an instruction consists of a *sequence* of one or more *register transfers*. Thus, what constitutes execution may vary over a wide range, depending on the definition of the processor and on the specific instruction selected. An instruction may call for an operation as trivial as the

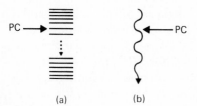

(a)   (b)

Figure 6.1 Sketches that are used to represent programs

setting of a single flip-flop. Conversely, its execution may consist of an arbitrarily complex microprogram, containing any number of micro-operations. Recall the definition of a microprogram, given in conjunction with the multiplier example in Fig. 5.11. A microprogram is itself a *program* of register transfers.

Note that any one of the execution register transfers may itself involve a memory access. (We are assuming a single processor interfaced with a *single* memory.) For this reason, it is necessary to *save* the currently executing instruction code in a special register, so that its contents are available to the processor, for reference, during its entire execution phase. This register is commonly known as an INSTRUCTION REGISTER (abbreviated as "IR").

Thus, as a processor "runs," every instruction's execution is preceded by its "*FETCH*"—which consists of the register transfer sequence:

$$IR \leftarrow M(PC)$$
$$PC \leftarrow PC + 1$$

This sequence "stages" the instruction in the Instruction Register, in preparation for execution, and then points the Program Counter *past* the current instruction, to the *next* one in sequence, in preparation for the FETCH that will follow execution of this instruction. In other words, a processor *runs* by executing a *continuous sequence of FETCH-EXECUTE cycles,* as represented by the elementary flow chart in Fig. 6.2. The FETCH is a *standard* register-transfer sequence, as defined above. The EXECUTE is arbitrarily complex. It depends on the processor's instruction repertoire and on its interpretation of the instruction just fetched.

Note that the execution of an instruction may *alter* the contents of the Program Counter. If it does, a BRANCH or JUMP or SKIP is said to occur, in

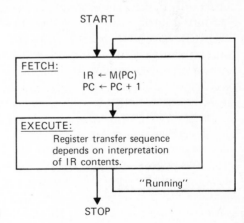

Figure 6.2 The fetch–execute cycle

which case, the next instruction fetched is *not* located immediately after the current one. Uses of such instructions are discussed later.

To tie these ideas together, consider a processor equipped with a RESET button, a START button, and a control flip-flop named RUN. While RUN = 1, the device runs, executing a continuous sequence of FETCH-EXECUTE cycles. A typical program "run" consists of the following sequence of steps: First, the RESET button is depressed, which clears RUN and places the processor in a "dormant" state. Second, if the program is not already resident in the memory, it must be LOADed (by a process we presently ignore). Third, the Program Counter must be *initialized* with the address of the program's *first* instruction. Alternatively, if the Program Counter is always initialized with a constant value (for example, zero), the program must be loaded such that its first instruction resides at the corresponding location. Fourth, the START button is depressed, which *sets* RUN, causing the processor to start running, beginning with a FETCH of the first instruction. (Note that this is the first instruction *executed*. It is not necessarily the instruction located at the lowest program address.) The program then continues to run until a HALT instruction is encountered. The *execution* of the HALT instruction consists of the single register transfer RUN ← 0, which restores the processor to the dormant state and terminates the run.

An instruction, as seen by a processor, is an encoded bit string, each of whose fields has a specific interpretation. While it is possible to write each instruction of a program directly in encoded form (for example, as a string of binary or hexadecimal digits), it is preferable to use a notation in which each command more closely resembles a natural language sentence. (Certainly, for example, it is easier to say "ADD" than it is to remember and write down the *code* for ADD, which might be "11010".) Consequently, a programmer customarily develops a program as a series of statements, each containing an intelligible string of *characters*. This form of a program is known as SOURCE code. Note that it is still *code*, albeit more readable code, and must conform exactly to the rules of a specific programming language. While a hardware processor may be designed to interpret source code directly, it is usually preferable to convert the source program into a form more naturally suited to digital hardware. This code form is known as OBJECT code. Thus, the program that a processor executes is an *object* program.

The conversion or translation from source code to object code, which we may imagine to be accomplished "by hand," is normally performed by a special computer program, an ASSEMBLER or a COMPILER. This program reads the source code and generates *equivalent* object code, in the "machine language" of a specific processor. Note that this translation phase precedes and is *separate* from the program's *execution* process, which was briefly outlined above. Since our interest will be focused on the internal organization of a typical processor, we begin by viewing instructions as it sees them—in object form. Whenever convenient, however, we will employ symbolic equivalents of actual binary or hexadecimal code values.

In addition to the *explicit* information contained in an instruction, over which the programmer has direct control, the execution of each instruction is usually accompanied by *implicit* operations, which are built-in, automatically executed, and *assumed* by the programmer. As a simple example distinguishing "explicit" from "implicit," consider the operation of an automobile turn signal, from the driver's point of view. Its activation requires an explicit command (which happens to be latched, mechanically). Its return to the reset state is implicit. Similarly, a vehicle having a "stick" shift requires explicit commands to shift gears. The same process is implicit in a car equipped with an automatic transmission. In an analogous manner, an ADD instruction for one processor may permit the programmer to explicitly specify, in the instruction, information about where the operands to be added reside and where the computed result should be placed. A different processor may automatically assume that one or both of the operands already reside in specific registers. It may also implicitly place the result in a destination whose selection is not programmer-controllable.

Clearly, the more that is implicit about an instruction's execution, the less has to be explicitly stated *in* the instruction. Thus, the *length* of an instruction is directly related to the freedom that a processor gives to the programmer to explicitly control its execution. A sophisticated processor has a rich repertoire of available commands, each permitting the programmer explicit control over numerous *variations* in its execution. The instructions for an elementary processor are generally short, each having much more implied about its execution. For example, a sophisticated SHIFT instruction might include fields giving the programmer control over the direction, distance, and end conditions of the shift's execution. An elementary shift, on the other hand, might execute by merely shifting *right*, a distance of *one* bit position, with the constant *"0"* shifted in on the left.

Although much of the subsequent discussion will center on fixed-length instructions, you should keep in mind that, by their very nature, instructions should be *variable-length* quantities. (Processors exist having either fixed or variable instruction lengths.) Generally, the information that has to be explicitly stated by the programmer varies with the type of instruction. For example, there is not much more you can add, once you say "halt." On the other hand, an instruction specifying an arithmetic or logical operation may include information about the locations and lengths of the operands, and about pertinent variations on the theme of the operation.

For this reason, the definition of a FETCH, given above, may be expressed in more general terms, for instructions of arbitrary length. Assume that each instruction begins with information that defines its length. For example, an initial two-bit field may indicate one of four different length variations. In addition, assume that the Instruction Register is sufficiently long to accommodate the longest instruction. Under these conditions, a FETCH may be redefined as the following two-step process: First, the current instruction (which begins where the Program Counter is now pointing) is read out of memory and placed in the Instruction Register. This may involve a *sequence* of memory READs. Second, the Program Counter is advanced *past* this instruction, regardless of its length (using the proper number of increments), so that it points at the beginning of the next sequential instruction in memory.

An N-bit field in an instruction selects one of 2^N variations on the sequence of register transfers that constitute execution of that instruction. We proceed by introducing three of the most fundamental of the interpretations ascribed to an instruction field. First, since a processor is equipped with a repertoire of operations that it can execute, an instruction field that *selects* one of these is certainly required. This field is known as an *Operation Code* (abbreviated as "opcode"). An N-bit opcode implies a processor having, at most, 2^N different operation classes. Second, since each instruction's execution consists of register transfers, an important instruction field would give the programmer explicit control over *which* registers participate in the operation selected by the opcode. In particular, since virtually all of the available registers reside in the memory to which the processor has access, an *address* field in the instruction gives the programmer such control. Processors exist whose instruction formats contain one, two, and even three or more address fields. Third, since the execution register transfers may include data operations, another useful instruction field is one that contains a *data value*. It is called an *Immediate* operand field, to distinguish it from an address field, which *points to* data.

With *opcode*, *address*, and *immediate data* fields defined, we are in a position to discuss the logical structure of a specific elementary processor and to demonstrate its programmability.

6.2 SAMPLE PROCESSOR I

A processor contains a set of internal registers, two of which (PC and IR) are almost universal. The number of other registers, and their functions, varies widely. Every processor fetches and executes instructions. The number of instructions, and their formats and detailed execution results, also varies widely. An instruction repertoire generally reflects the internal register set, because registers are most useful when the programmer has explicit *access* to them by means of instructions. A processor interfaces with a memory, which contains both the executing program and registers for data storage. Other characteristics of a processor's interface vary widely as well. Normally, the interface includes at least one port for an external device (other than the memory) with which the processor communicates.

The detailed description of a specific processor is normally supplied in an accompanying manual or data sheet, which defines its interface, its internal register complement, and its entire instruction set. We proceed here to develop such a manual, along with a complete logic description, for an elementary hypothetical machine.

Its interface is illustrated in Fig. 6.3, using a very common system structure. The MEMORY portion of the interface conforms to that introduced in Chapter 4. It is assumed that the memory's DATA OUT port always carries the contents of the addressed register (once its access time has elapsed.) The EXTERNAL DEVICE is any arbitrary element having DATA IN and DATA OUT ports resembling those of the memory. (All DATA ports in the system have the same width N.) The external device receives a signal from the processor, named "STROBE", whose function will be explained later, and it supplies a signal to the processor, named "FLAG", whose value may affect the behavior of the running program. The program is also able to control when the processor accepts data coming from the external device.

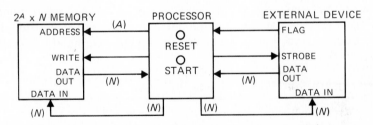

Figure 6.3 Sample processor interface to memory and external device

The processor is equipped with a RESET button and a START button, whose functions were described earlier. Depressing RESET places the processor in a dormant state and *clears* PC. Depressing START causes the system to run. Running continues until a HALT instruction is encountered, at which time the dormant state is reestablished. Note that, for this sample processor, the *first* instruction executed, on a START after a RESET, is the one residing at memory location zero.

This processor has only one programmer-accessible internal register, in addition to PC and IR, named "Y", whose length is N. (Necessary control registers will be defined as they are needed.) Note that, by definition, the

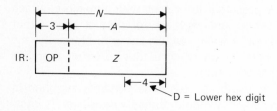

D = Lower hex digit

Figure 6.4 Instruction format for sample processor

length of PC must be A, the memory's address length. Since every instruction is one word long, the IR length must be N.

The format for each instruction is shown in Fig. 6.4. Every N-bit command is divided into a three-bit OP field and an A-bit Z field. Immediately, this format constrains A to be $N - 3$. (You are cautioned not to draw any general conclusions from this relationship. Even though this system's memory has $A < N$, a memory with $A > N$ is just as feasible.) The Z field will be used primarily, though not exclusively, as an address field.

Table 6.1 lists the instruction set for this machine. It specifies, for every possible N-bit instruction value, what the corresponding execution operation is. For this simple processor, each execution consists of only one register transfer. Note that several of the executions (corresponding to OP codes 1, 3, 4, and 5) involve memory accesses, using Z as the address value. The JUMP executes by replacing the PC contents with a new value, as specified in the instruction. JUMPFL jumps *conditionally*: only if the FLAG signal, at the instant of execution, has a value "1". Thus, the external FLAG input may

Table 6.1 Instruction Set for Sample Processor

OP	D = Z[3 : 0]	Name	Execution
0	X	LOADI	$Y \leftarrow Z$ (Load *immediate* data value)
1	X	STORE	$M(Z) \leftarrow Y$
2	X	JUMP	$PC \leftarrow Z$
3	X	LOAD	$Y \leftarrow M(Z)$
4	X	ADD	$Y \leftarrow Y + M(Z)$
5	X	SUB	$Y \leftarrow Y - M(Z)$
6	X	JUMPFL	If FLAG = 1, $PC \leftarrow Z$
7	0	NOOP	No Operation
7	1	STROBE	Generate STROBE pulse
7	2	SKIPNEG	If Y is negative, $PC \leftarrow PC + 1$ (Skip)
7	4	DATAIN	$Y \leftarrow$ External Data
7	8	HALT	Stop running

Notes: D = LS hex digit of Z;   X = "Not applicable."

affect the program's behavior. LOADI executes by replacing the value in Y with the immediate data value in the instruction.

OP code 7 imparts a *new* interpretation to the Z field. The bits of D, the lower hex digit of Z, now individually control four possible operations. (For simplicity, we restrict D to be a one-asserted code, or zero.) The execution for D = 4 transfers the data value coming from the external device into Y. Thus, the program may "read in" data from the external element whenever it wishes to. The STROBE instruction executes by merely asserting the STROBE pulse. It is assumed that this action will cause the external device to respond by loading the value at its DATA IN port, which will always be the value of Y. Thus, the program is also able to control when computed data is "written out." The SKIPNEG instruction executes by skipping the next sequential instruction if the value in Y is negative. (It is assumed that negative values are represented in signed two's complement form.) Note that a skip is merely an *extra* increment of PC, over and above that performed during the fetch phase. The NOOP (for No Operation) is useful for minor program alterations during testing. It permits the programmer either to erase an existing instruction or to leave room for an instruction to be added later. In both cases, instruction deletion or insertion is possible without requiring modification to any of the address values in the other instructions.

The portion of Z above D is ignored for the case OP = 7, demonstrating that a field may be undefined or unused under certain conditions. There are also several instances to show that an instruction's execution may involve *implicit* actions. For example, one of the operands for either ADD or SUB is constrained to be Y. Similarly, the arithmetic result is always deposited in Y, replacing the operand there. The programmer has no control over such implicit operations.

Having defined the interface, internal registers and instruction set for our sample processor, we have specified all of the essential information required for its programmer's manual. Given a mechanism for loading instruction sequences into the memory, a programmer may now develop and run arbitrary programs, without caring about the inner logical structure of the processor. However, since our purpose is to study how such a device is designed, we proceed now to discuss its internal organization.

Once all of the required FETCH and EXECUTE register transfers have been specified, we may begin a processor's design by assembling all of the registers, data operation elements, and interface ports needed to implement these transfers. Figure 6.5 illustrates the result for the present problem. The only new element shown is the ADDER-SUBTRACTOR. It is required to implement execution of the ADD and SUB instructions. The device has a one-bit function control input, which selects between ADD and SUBtract. (For simplicity, we are ignoring all CARRY/BORROW signals.)

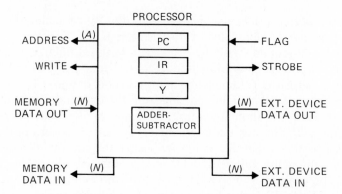

Figure 6.5 Sample machine registers, data operators, and interface

Having assembled the "parts," we may proceed by defining all of the necessary *paths* between them, such that every one of the required register transfers is executable. At this point, the sources of all of the input control signals, whose assertions *evoke* the transfers, are still not known. To implement the system of paths, we have at our disposal wires, busses, tri-state gates, and multiplexers. We must keep in mind that, if a destination input port has more than one source, a multiplexer or its equivalent is required. The present problem demonstrates that it is often convenient to distinguish between *data* paths (N bits wide) and *address* paths (A bits wide).

Figure 6.6 shows the result for our sample processor. The right side of the diagram contains the data paths and the left side the address paths. There is a direct path between Y and the memory's DATA IN port because there is no other source of data to the memory. Had several sources existed, a multiplexer would have been required at that point. Two multiplexers were found necessary. First, since there are four possible sources of input data to Y, a four-way multiplexer is required. One of these input paths is from the IR, to permit implementing the LOADI instruction. (Its OP value of zero conveniently allows Y ← IR to also implement Y ← Z.) The OP codes were assigned to the instructions to permit OP[2 : 1] to select the source of data to Y, as shown. Similarly, OP0 is used to distinguish ADD from SUBtract. Second, the registers named in all "M(reg)" expressions all constitute sources of the memory address. Since there are two, PC and Z, a two-way address multiplexer, whose path-select control level is defined later, is also necessary. Note that a path is required from Z to PC, to implement a JUMP. Observe, in addition, that the PC is equipped with an INCREMENT input signal, whose assertion mechanizes a SKIP or part of a FETCH.

All of the unconnected inputs in Fig. 6.6 represent *control* signals which, when properly asserted, evoke each of the necessary register transfers. The

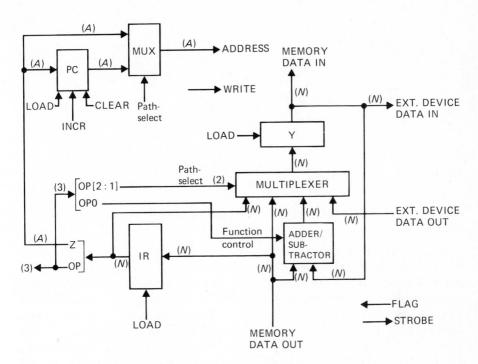

Figure 6.6 Sample processor data and address paths

most formidable part of a processor's design is the development of the logic that generates the proper pattern of control signals. We begin by extracting from the control network that portion which deals with starting, stopping, and cycling.

As alluded to earlier, this processor contains a RUN control flip-flop, whose state defines whether or not it is running. While it is running, a central clock pulse generator provides the basic timing signal. Each clock pulse causes a control register to advance, identifying the next phase of a control cycle. (Recall the discussion in Section 4.7.) In such a simple system as this one, only *two* phases are actually required, one for FETCH and the other for EXECUTE. Thus, a *single* control flip-flop, which toggles on each clock pulse, is sufficient.

The control network shown in Fig. 6.7 implements the required starting, stopping, and cycling behavior. All pulses in the system are assumed positive. The two control flip-flops trigger on negative edges. (It is assumed that all other devices in the system respond to positive edges.) Each button signal is "1" while its button is depressed. To begin with, assertion of RESET clears both flip-flops, and the resulting RUN = 0 condition prevents PULSES from

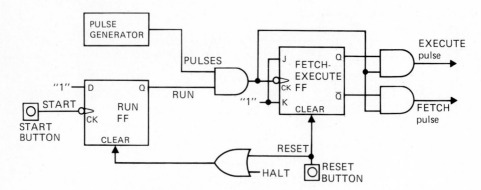

Figure 6.7   Start, stop, and cycling control network

reaching the clock input terminal of the FETCH-EXECUTE flip-flop. FETCH and EXECUTE PULSEs are therefore inhibited, and the system remains dormant. When the START button is depressed, its *release* sets RUN, permitting PULSES to pass. RUN remains set, and each clock pulse activates either a FETCH PULSE or an EXECUTE PULSE, depending on the control flip-flop state, which toggles on each trailing clock pulse edge. Thus, FETCH and EXECUTE pulses *alternate*. The *first* is always a FETCH pulse, because the flip-flop is cleared initially. When the signal HALT is asserted, it clears RUN again and re-inhibits the PULSES signal.

Each FETCH PULSE evokes two micro-operations simultaneously: a LOAD of IR and an INCREMENT of PC. (We are ignoring the situation in which the START button is released *while* a pulse is asserted. It is discussed in a problem.) The EXECUTE PULSE must be *directed* to the proper point in the system, to evoke the transfer that constitutes execution of the current instruction. This leads us to study the OP DECODER portion of the control network, shown in Fig. 6.8.

An opcode decoder asserts the single output selected by the opcode. This signal either directly evokes a corresponding execution operation or enables a *sequence* of such operations. In Fig. 6.8, the 3-to-8 OP DECODER directs the EXECUTE PULSE to one of eight output terminals, as selected by the OP code. Each of the outputs is labeled with its corresponding instruction name. Note that the execute pulse for OP = 7 enables a bank of four AND gates, which each receive one bit of the D code, the lower hex digit of Z. Their outputs (appropriately labeled) are similar execute pulses for the four OP = 7 instructions.

The STORE execute pulse activates a memory WRITE. Five of the execute pulses are ORed together to develop the LOAD Y signal. The input multiplexer to Y ensures that the value that is loaded is the proper one. Note

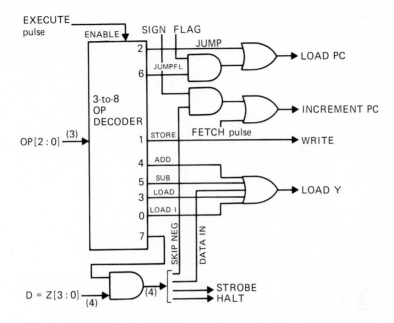

Figure 6.8   OP decode logic for sample processor

that, had the OP codes for LOADI, LOAD, ADD, and SUB corresponded to a cluster of four-squares on the OP map, this logic could have been simplified. (This is discussed further in a problem at the end of this chapter.) However, such an assignment would have spoiled the simplicity of the path-select code to Y's input multiplexer. The solution in Fig. 6.8 was adopted because it has more generality. For example, it is more amenable to alterations in the definitions of specific instructions.

The gate clusters that develop the LOAD PC and INCREMENT PC control signals happen to be similar. Each of these events has one *unconditional* trigger (JUMP or FETCH) and one *conditional* trigger (JUMPFL or SKIP-NEG). In the latter case, the condition control levels, which decide whether or not the event will occur, are FLAG and SIGN, respectively. FLAG is an arbitrary control signal from the external device. SIGN is Y's sign bit.

A completed logic/block diagram is shown in Fig. 6.9. The processor, consisting of all elements excluding the MEMORY and EXTERNAL DEVICE blocks, has an interface conforming to that introduced in Fig. 6.3. We are now in a position to tie together a few remaining loose ends. First, note that the RESET signal is applied as a CLEAR input to the PC, as specified earlier. Second, observe that the path-select control level to the address multiplexer is the FETCH signal. When it is asserted, PC is selected. During the

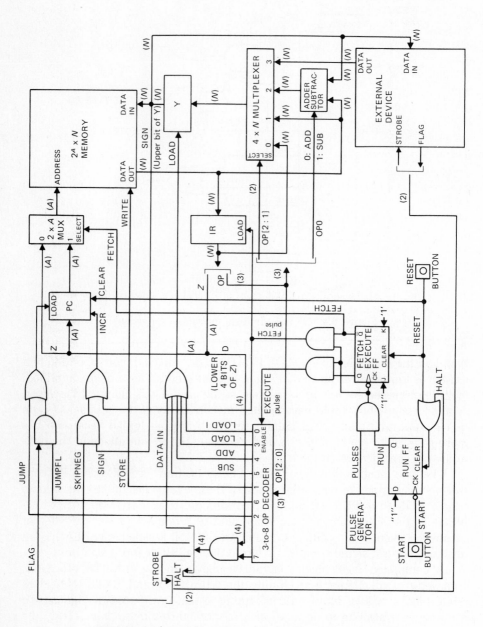

Figure 6.9 Sample processor complete logic diagram

EXECUTE phase, Z is selected. Third, note that the SIGN signal comes from the upper terminal of Y's output port. Finally, observe the HALT, STORE, and LOAD Y signal connections and the FLAG and STROBE direct paths to the external device.

Having specified the instruction set and the logic diagram for this hypothetical processor, we are in a position to make some observations about its operation which apply to processors of much greater complexity. The first relates to how it distinguishes "instructions" from "data."

Normally, there is nothing in a memory word to indicate whether it is an instruction or whether it is data. The distinction is made by the *state* of the processor at the instant when the word is accessed. By definition, any word accessed during a fetch cycle is an instruction, and any word accessed during an execute cycle is data. During a fetch cycle, the processor directs the memory's output to the IR and hence to its *control* network. Here the word is interpreted as a command and then *executed*. During an execute cycle, words are routed between the memory and the data processing network in the processor. Here they are treated as data (numbers, characters, logical variables, etc.).

When a typical program run begins, the memory contains not only the program *but also* initial data values, stored in an area separate from the program. Normally, as the program runs, the contents of the program area remain fixed while the stored data values continually change. Thus, while a program may be embedded in a ROM, a data area normally requires a RAM. (A program LOAD into a RAM consists of a sequence of WRITEs, not only of all of the program's instructions, but also of all of its initial data values.) As a program runs, it receives its data values not only from the data area in memory but also from immediate data values in instructions (for example, using the LOADI instruction) and from external devices (for example, using the DATAIN instruction).

While it is possible to operate on an instruction as if it were data (for example, to increment its address field), such a practice is now extinct for several reasons. First, processors generally offer other means to more conveniently accomplish equivalent results. Second, programs so written may not be stored in ROMs. Finally, such programming "tricks" generally lead to errors that are difficult to isolate and correct. Thus, we will treat the access of a register in a program area, during the *execution* of an instruction, as an error. (A common cause of program failure, for example, is the attempt to store *data* in a *program* area.) Similarly, the *fetch*, and consequent interpretation and execution, of *data* is also an error. (Another common cause of program failure, for example, is a JUMP into a *data* area.)

Our sample processor demonstrates that some instructions [those whose execution descriptions contain "M(Z)"] are "memory reference" instructions, while others are not. In other words, not all instructions require memory access during execution.

As the sample machine runs, its fetch and execute time durations are constant and equal. Note that the period of the central clock source must be greater than the memory's access time. Since the memory address changes at the trailing edge of every clock pulse, this permits the contents of the new address to be valid at the memory's DATA OUT port by the time the *next* clock pulse occurs. In general, a processor need not have constant fetch or execute time durations. For example, if the instruction lengths vary, the fetch time will normally also vary. Similarly, the execution time for an instruction depends, in general, on the *complexity* of the execution. Some executions require no memory accesses. Others require many.

Note that an element within a processor may perform its function even when the operation is not needed or used. For example, the ADDER-SUB-TRACTOR is always generating a new result, which is ignored at all times except during an ADD or SUBtract execution. Similarly, the memory's data output, during the execution of non-memory-reference instructions, such as LOADI or DATAIN, is also ignored.

Observe also that control signals that establish paths or select device functions are generally levels, while control signals that specifically evoke register transfers are generally pulses. (Recall the pertinent discussion in Section 4.7.) Specifically, the multiplexer path-select signals, the ADDER-SUBTRACTOR function-select signal, and the *condition* signals SIGN and FLAG are all levels. The other control signals, such as LOAD Y, INCR PC, WRITE, and HALT, are all pulses. In some cases, it is mandatory that a control signal be a pulse. For example, imagine what would happen if HALT were not a pulse but a *level*, asserted while OP = 7 and D = 8. Once asserted, because a HALT instruction resides in the IR, this signal would *remain* activated, *preventing* the processor from being restarted!

The instruction repertoire listed in Table 6.1 was not selected for its utility. Very few practical programs may be easily developed using it. It was chosen as an elementary, but representative, vehicle. The primary purpose of the sample machine is to explain how a processor operates internally. If you imagine an instruction sequence resident in memory, beginning at location zero, you may depress the hypothetical RESET and START buttons and visualize the pattern of control signal assertions and data transfers as the system runs.

Table 6.2 provides a specific elementary program example. It lists a short routine, in hexadecimal form, which waits for an input FLAG signal assertion and then responds to it by reading in one word from the external device. It is assumed that the FLAG signal is used as a DATA READY indicator, and that its assertion lasts for at least two instruction execution times. The pro-

Table 6.2   Demonstration Program for Sample Processor

Memory Location	OP	Z[7 : 0]	Comments
50	6	52	While FLAG = 0, take next instruction.
			When FLAG = 1, exit this WAIT loop.
51	2	50	JUMP unconditionally back to location 50.
52	7	04	Read in the external data to Y.
53	6	53	While FLAG = 1, loop on this instruction.
			Fall through to next instruction,
			terminating the WAIT, when FLAG = 0.
54	.		Program continues here.
	.		
	.		

gram segment begins at memory location 50. Thus, we are assuming that the *previous* instruction executed either resides at address 4F or is a JUMP to address 50. (Addresses are assumed to be eight bits long, in which case words are 11 bits long.) The first two instructions constitute an elementary *loop*, which waits for the FLAG signal assertion. When it is detected, the program exits to location 52, where the DATAIN response is executed. To prevent the possibility of another later response to the *same* FLAG assertion, the JUMPFL instruction at location 53 waits for FLAG to become "0" again. When it does, the program proceeds to the code that begins at location 54.

6.3 DATA FORMATS

The execution of a program by a processor causes "data" to be processed in some useful or meaningful way. Encoded in the form of bit strings, the data is stored in registers accessed by the processor. Most of these registers reside in the central memory with which the processor interfaces. (This memory also holds the executing program.) Additional registers, in some cases a significant number of them, are contained within the processor itself. We consider here the formats of the most common data types, and how data "processing" is defined. (Note that the term "data" is customarily used for both the singular and the plural forms.)

As explained earlier, data may be placed in registers, *before* a program run, by the programmer, who derives the data from some pertinent original source (for example, from a set of readings in a laboratory experiment). Alternatively, the data may be derived from devices (for example, keyboards or magnetic tape readers) whose output signals are read by the program *during* the run. Note that a set of signals from an external device may be considered as the output of an *equivalent* external source register.

In discussing data and instruction formats, we will envision codes of *arbitrary* lengths, assuming that registers of corresponding lengths are available to store them. Virtually all of the internal registers in a typical computer have the *same* length, known as the "word length" of the machine. The lengths of the codes processed by the machine and its word length are always *compatible*. That is, either a word length is a multiple of a code length, permitting one or more codes to fit into one word, or a code length is a multiple of a word length, permitting several registers to be *concatenated* to accommodate one code. In the former case, a code item is accessed by selecting one *field* from the contents of a single register. In the latter case, a code item, stored in a memory, is accessed as a *sequence* of READs or WRITEs. For example, while an instruction length is normally the same as the word length, instructions that are stored in two, three, four, or more contiguous memory words are quite common. Alternatively, a single word may accommodate two or more instructions if such a format is desirable. Thus, the *boundaries* between instruction or data codes, stored in a memory, and the boundaries between the memory's physical registers do not necessarily correspond on a one-to-one basis. The ensuing discussions will provide some specific examples.

Data codes typically represent *numbers, characters,* and *logical variables*. While a data area in a memory may contain any arbitrary mixture of such data types, it usually contains an *array* of data items, all having the *same* type. Examples of arrays are also given later.

We have already discussed some aspects of numeric data representation—namely, the signed two's complement system for encoding positive and negative integers. At various points, we have also encountered examples of *unsigned* integers (i.e., those which are *implicitly* positive). In particular, an *address* is an unsigned integer. Each of these codes actually represents a sequence of digits, with the least significant on the right and the most significant on the left. The term "integer" arises from the (natural) assumption that the *radix* point is positioned to the right of the least significant digit. A radix point conventionally separates the digits constituting the *integer* portion of a number from those constituting the *fractional* portion.

In point of fact, since no explicit radix point indicator exists, it may be imagined positioned *anywhere* without affecting the sequence of digits that constitute the results of an arithmetic operation using that number as an argument. That is, an arithmetic operation's resulting digit string is *independent* of which radix point positions were assumed for its operands. (Add and subtract operations do require proper *alignment* of their operands. Multiply and divide operations normally require appropriate shifts of the results, to retain the maximum number of significant digits.) Thus, the radix point of a number may be imagined positioned to the left of the most significant digit, in which case the operand is assumed to be a fraction. Alternatively, it may be imagined positioned at any convenient inner point, in which case the operand is assumed to be a mixed number.

Such operands are often called *fixed point* numbers because computations involving them are most convenient when a single, standard radix point position is assumed for all operands. (For example, computations involving operands that represent amounts of money normally implicitly position the radix point so that both "dollars" and "cents" values may be conveniently represented.) Having assumed a fixed radix point, the programmer must still make appropriate allowances for values that do not fit within the permissible numeric range. (For example, a bank program that processes dollars and cents must still provide for daily or quarterly interest rates.) In particular, if the range of a specific variable value, over a program run, is sufficiently wide, the programmer may find it necessary to store, along with its sequence of significant digits, another number specifying its "scaling factor"—the number of leading or trailing zeroes that must be appended to it.

The *floating point* numeric data format carries such a scaling factor along with *every* number, relieving the programmer of the burden of keeping track of whether or not numbers fall within implicit ranges. A floating point number consists of *two* signed numeric fields. One, called the *mantissa*, contains the significant digits of the number. The other, called the *exponent*, specifies its number of leading or trailing zeroes. That is, if M is the mantissa and E is the exponent (each either positive or negative), the value of the number is interpreted to be:

$$M(B^E)$$

where B is a standard *base* value, often 2 or a power of 2. Such a format permits a very wide range of numeric magnitudes, from extremely small values to extremely large values. A floating point numeric format is used in most conventional electronic calculators. They use the familiar "scientific" notation (in which $B = 10$). The floating point representation is mandatory in most complex scientific computations, which normally require a wide numeric range.

Figure 6.10 contains a comparison of three of the most common numeric data formats, all normalized to the same 16-bit word. If the word is an unsigned integer, as shown in (a), a range of values between 0 and +65535 (which is $2^{16} - 1$) is possible. Adjacent expressible numbers are a distance of one apart. The signed, two's-complement representation in (b) retains the same numeric distance between maximum and minimum limits, and the same granularity of expressible values. However, the range of representable

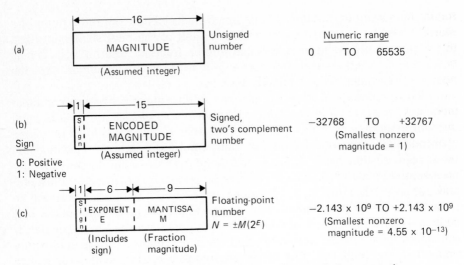

Figure 6.10 Three alternative 16-bit word numeric interpretations

numbers is now balanced around the zero point, running between −32768 (which is −2^{15}) and +32767. (Recall the previous definition of the signed two's complement representation, given in conjunction with Table 2.4.)

A typical 16-bit floating-point format is shown in Fig. 6.10(c). The sign bit on the left represents the sign of the number, not of the exponent. The six-bit exponent field has a range of values between −32 and +31. It is essentially a signed, two's complement number. (It is customary to invert its sign bit for convenience in processing. Under these conditions, it is called an "excess 32" code.) With an implicit base value of *two*, the B^E scale factor, which multiplies the mantissa value, ranges between 2^{-32}, which is 2.328×10^{-10}, and 2^{31}, which is 2.147×10^9. It is also customary to assume that the mantissa is a *magnitude* value, in the form of a *fraction* (with the radix point assumed positioned on its left). Thus, this nine-bit field, also called the "fraction" field, has a range of values between 0 and 0.998 ($1 - 2^{-9}$), in steps of 0.00195 (2^{-9}). Consequently, representable numbers may have magnitudes as small as 4.55×10^{-13} (neglecting zero) and as large as 2.143×10^9. Since the same number of code values (2^{16} points) is now spread over the approximate range between −2 × 10^9 and +2 × 10^9, it is clear that local accuracy (the number of significant digits in a number) has been sacrificed to achieve a very wide representable numeric range. The accuracy is improved by increasing the length of the mantissa field.

Speaking of accuracy, clearly any number has a greater precision when its number of expressible digits is increased. To allow arithmetic computations whose precision is beyond that available in the hardware, most proces-

sor designs include instructions that permit the programmer to employ instruction *sequences* which will process operands whose length is a *multiple*
of that of a machine word. For example, the execution of a typical fixed-
point ADD instruction not only stores the resulting sum in an appropriate
register. It also stores the final carry out in a special CARRY FLIP-FLOP. A
variation on the ADD instruction, usually called ADD WITH CARRY, is also
made available. Its execution is identical to that of a conventional ADD, with
the exception that the *input* carry to the adder is not a constant "0". It is the
contents of the CARRY FLIP-FLOP. Thus, the carry out from one ADD may
be employed as the carry *in* to a subsequent ADD, permitting the programmer to develop a sequence of instructions to perform *multiple-precision*
addition.

The most extensively used data form is the *character* code. The ASCII
code (see Table 1.3), in particular, is the most prominent means for representing alphabetic and numeric symbols. Computer programs ordinarily
process data in the form of character *strings*. Because the eight-bit character
code is so fundamental, the word length of virtually every processor is a
multiple of eight.

As Fig. 6.11 indicates, character strings are customarily stored in memory
in *lines* of variable length. Each line of alphanumeric characters is a data
item available for processing. It may be a business record (for example, a
description of an inventory item), a source statement in a computer program
undergoing translation, or a communications message. A sequence of such

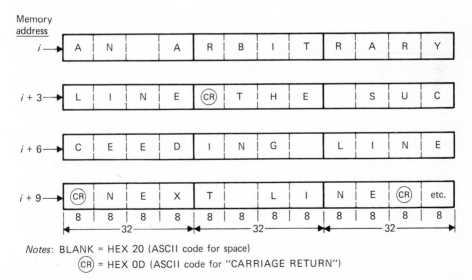

Notes: BLANK = HEX 20 (ASCII code for space)
(CR) = HEX 0D (ASCII code for "CARRIAGE RETURN")

Figure 6.11 8-bit character sequence stored in 32-bit memory words

lines is called a *file*. Typically, a memory area contains all or part of a file, and the lines in it are separated (or "delimited") by one or more special control characters. The example in Fig. 6.11 assumes 32-bit memory words, with lines separated by a single control character, a hex "0D", which is the ASCII code for the "carriage RETURN" character. This is the most natural line terminator, since virtually all character data originates from *keyboards*, each having a RETURN key, whose depression causes the beginning of a new line.

The Binary-Coded-Decimal or BCD code, introduced in Section 2.1 in conjunction with Table 2.2, is also a commonly used character code. An arbitrary decimal number is represented as a sequence of four-bit characters, each standing for one of its decimal digits, as shown in Fig. 6.12. Each BCD pair of characters conveniently fits into one eight-bit character space. The BCD code is employed particularly in calculator-oriented devices. Observe, especially, that an interpretation of a bit string as a BCD number is totally different from its interpretation as a binary integer. For example, the 16-bit code in Fig. 6.12 has a value 5720, if interpreted as a binary number.

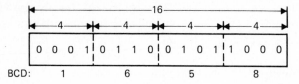

BCD: 1   6   5   8

Figure 6.12   The number 1658, encoded in BCD, in a 16-bit word

The interpretation of a word as a *logical* or Boolean variable really indicates the *absence* of any special, implicit data interpretation built into the hardware. A word is merely treated as what it is, an arbitrary binary code. Given facilities to manipulate and examine the contents of arbitrary fields within it, a programmer is able to define code interpretations that were not conceived by the system's architects. These facilities normally include *logical* instructions that execute AND, OR, EXCLUSIVE OR, and appropriate SHIFT operations. The programmer employs them to process the specially defined data codes.

For example, Fig. 6.13(a) shows a format that may be used by a card-playing program, running on a 24-bit machine. A card value is represented in a six-bit field, containing a two-bit field for its suit and a four-bit field for its value within that suit. (Three value codes are unused.) Each memory data word represents four card values. Alternatively, Fig. 6.13(b) shows a format that may be used by a music-synthesizer program, running on the same machine. Each eight-bit character specifies the pitch and the duration of a musi-

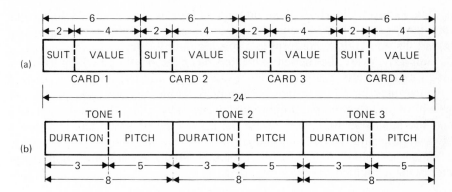

Figure 6.13   Examples of arbitrary data formats for a 24-bit word

cal tone. There are 32 pitches to select from and eight possible durations. Each memory data word contains a three-tone sequence.

The term "data processing" embraces all possible operations on data values. Sometimes the data that is "processed" is not modified in any way. For example, a device that receives data messages, and later transmits them, actually "processes" them without modifying them. Similarly, a program that moves a block of data from one memory area to another actually performs an elementary processing task. A more sophisticated processing function, which still does not involve data modification, is one in which the data is sorted, merged, or re-ordered in some way.

On the other hand, many data operations, particularly those studied in Chapter 2, actually generate new data from old data. As explained there, a typical data "processing" device receives one or more input operands and generates one or more results. It is designed by assuming a specific *data interpretation rule*. For example, the ADDER was defined assuming that the input operands were unsigned binary numbers, with radix points aligned. (The signed, two's complement representation was specifically invented to "fool" an adder into executing a subtraction.) Such a device cannot be expected to add BCD arguments, which have a totally different interpretation rule. (The design of a BCD adder was the subject of Problem 2.13.) Similarly, an arithmetic operation on two *alphabetic* character codes is attempted *only* when it appears desirable to treat the characters momentarily as if they were numbers. Likewise, the design of a floating-point adder is significantly different from that of a fixed-point adder. Typically, for example, a floating-point adder will align the operands, with appropriate mantissa shifts and accompanied exponent adjustments, before executing the add. Furthermore, it may *normalize* the results. (A floating-point number is normalized by shifting its mantissa left, and decrementing its exponent, until the mantissa contains no leading zeroes.) Clearly, a floating-point adder is not designed to accept fixed-point arguments. More generally, any data processing device normally *expects* its operands to conform to a specific data format.

Similarly, every instruction execution has a fixed rule by which its operands (the data) are interpreted. For example, in addition to the fact that a processor may have two or more different ADD instruction types (permitting both fixed and floating-point operands), it may also allow the programmer to vary the *length* of the operands, for the *same* type of ADD. The fact that a "double-precision" ADD expects operands that are twice as long as those for a "single-precision" ADD also demonstrates that *operands must match the operations for which they are intended.*

6.4 PROGRAM FLOW

The value of the Program Counter identifies the current instruction. The current instruction is the one "in control"—the one that defines what the processor will do next. The portion of a program that is in control is the one into which the Program Counter is currently pointing. A program portion "gives up" or "transfers" control when it alters the Program Counter value so that some *other* program portion assumes control. Thus, a jump or branch, which executes by replacing the Program Counter value with a new one, is also called a "transfer of control."

A typical program is divisible into subprogram segments, called "modules" or "routines," each consisting of a sequence of instructions which together have a specific computational function. This function is normally described by a concise sentence or phrase, for example, "print next record." A *flow chart* represents each program portion with a box, containing this functional description and having "entry" and "exit" *directed lines.* The module that is in control defines what subprocess is currently occurring. The paths between the boxes represent the flow of control between the modules. Each directed line is normally labeled with the conditions under which its path is taken. The Program Counter value may be represented on a flow chart by a small arrow—a "spot" of activity—pointing within the currently executing module. A flow chart is thus like the state diagram introduced in Section 3.3. The Program Counter selects the currently active "state," and the behavior of the Program Counter value, plotted over time, describes how the program "flows"—how control is passed between its submodules.

The most fundamental transfer of control is the procedure or subroutine CALL. A CALL is a jump accompanied by a push of the *old* Program Counter value onto a stack. (A processor that includes a CALL instruction in its repertoire must have access to a stack. An example will be discussed later.) Thus, the old PC value is *saved* before it is destroyed. The subroutine, which receives control as the result of the CALL, is a subprogram or module that always *exits* by executing a RETURN instruction, another necessary part of the same repertoire. The RETURN executes by popping the saved address value back into the Program Counter, restoring the value that it had before the CALL was executed. (This is the PC value *after* the CALL was *fetched* but *before* it was executed.) Thus, the *next* instruction executed, after the RETURN occurs, is the one that *follows* the CALL in memory.

In register transfer notation, a CALL execution may be written as:

$$STACK \leftarrow PC$$
$$PC \leftarrow ADDRESS$$

while a RETURN execution may be expressed by:

$$PC \leftarrow STACK$$

where we adopt the simplifying convention that, unless stated otherwise, the term "STACK" as the *destination* of a transfer *implies a push,* and the appearance of the term "STACK" in the *source* expression of a transfer *implies a pop.* (Recall that a push or a pop may itself consist of a pair of transfers, such as those defined in Table 4.2.) The term "ADDRESS" above represents the source of the new PC value, the address of the subroutine's *entry* point. ADDRESS may be a field in the instruction (for example, the Z field for a processor resembling the one described in Section 6.2). On the other hand, it may be the contents of some other register. The choice depends on the detailed definition of the CALL's execution, for the specific processor under discussion.

Note that a CALL actually represents an arbitrarily complex "instruction" that is not available in the repertoire of the processor—i.e., not executable by the hardware in one instruction. It is executed instead by a subroutine, in a sequence of two or more instructions. Thus, every procedure *extends* the set of operations available to the programmer. Its execution is mechanized in "software" rather than in hardware. For example, a program may require frequent use of a PRINT CHARACTER "instruction," whose execution prints the symbol, selected by the code in a specified register, on an attached printer. If this instruction is not available in the hardware, it may be mechanized in a subroutine.

Since a CALL saves the PC value on a stack, CALLs may be *nested.* That is, a procedure may *itself* make CALLs to other procedures, which may themselves make still other CALLs. For example, a PRINT FILE subroutine may make numerous CALLs on a PRINT LINE subroutine which may, in turn, make numerous CALLs on the PRINT CHARACTER subroutine, mentioned above. With return addresses stored on a stack, CALLs and RETURNs may be arbitrarily intermixed, provided that each RETURN properly restores a previously saved PC value. The address restored into the PC, on a specific RETURN, is the one that was pushed on the *most recent* unresolved CALL. The use of a stack permits every CALL to be properly matched by its corresponding RETURN, no matter how intricate the nesting structure between them is.

Figure 6.14 contains an example. It shows a "main program" and six subroutines. The lower-case letters represent the addresses of instructions that immediately follow CALLs. The instruction that is the destination of each CALL or RETURN is indicated with an arrow labeled with a number denoting its order in time. The contents of the STACK, after each transfer, is also shown.

A subroutine is a particularly economical program structure when its function is evoked at *several* different points within the calling program. At each such location, a single CALL instruction serves the purpose of an entire sequence of "in-line" instructions (which constitute the body of the subrou-

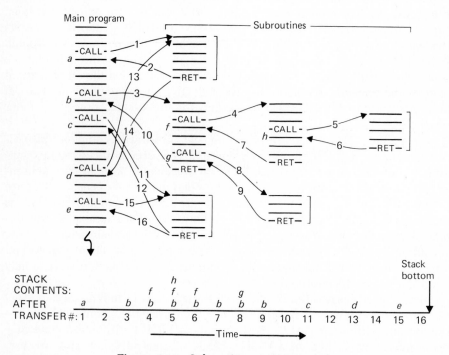

Figure 6.14   Subroutine nesting example

tine). Thus, only one *copy* of the subroutine needs to reside in memory, even though its function is invoked at several points. This conserves on the memory space used by the program.

This might lead you to conclude that it is *not* desirable to extract a program portion and define it as a subroutine unless you expect it to be called more than once. While it is true that the memory space used by the CALL instruction and its matching RETURN would be saved if the routine were placed in-line, and that some execution time would also be saved by not executing the CALL and RETURN linkages, many programmers still prefer to "package" an instruction sequence as a procedure, first, because the organization of the program is usually easier to understand and to document and, second, because the packaged function may later be required in *other* parts of subsequent versions of the same program.

Instruction sequences may be broadly divided into two classes: those which actually *do* data processing, which we will call ACTIONs, and those which control the *flow* of the program between ACTIONs, which we will call CONDITIONALs. An ACTION is an arbitrarily long instruction sequence, having a single entry and a single exit, which may be represented on a flow chart by a separate box containing a concise description of its function. It occupies a well-defined memory area and may be imagined as a "straight-line" instruction stream, during whose execution the PC value increases monotonically. Recognize, however, that it may *itself* contain an arbitrarily complex *internal* flow. For example, it may include CALL instructions that invoke complicated functions whose routines are located elsewhere. Nevertheless, we will treat it as if it were a simple, monotonic instruction sequence.

A CONDITIONAL has a single entry and *two or more* exits. It evaluates one or more functions and then selects one of its exit paths based on this evaluation. A path is selected when a corresponding *condition* or relationship is true. On a flow chart, a CONDITIONAL is often represented by a diamond-shaped symbol identifying the function(s) that it evaluates. Each exit path is labeled with the condition under which it is taken. (Recall that a path is taken when the entry address of its destination is placed in the PC.) Note that a CONDITIONAL also may be arbitrarily complex internally. In particular, its function evaluations may themselves require complicated computations.

Figure 6.15 contains some typical ACTION and CONDITIONAL flowchart symbols and a possible instruction sequence for implementing one of them. Separate symbol shapes are not really required. The fact that an ACTION has *one* exit distinguishes it from a CONDITIONAL, which has *two or more*. Any of the symbols may have an arbitrary number of paths *into* its single entry point. It is entered whenever the PC is given the address of its

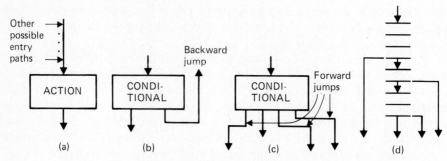

Figure 6.15 Typical ACTION and CONDITIONAL symbols

first instruction. Part (a) shows the notation that is used when multiple entry paths exist. Note that an exit path may either "fall through" to the next sequential instruction or jump forward or backward within the instruction stream. (You are reminded that an arbitrary, two-dimensional flow chart is always mechanized with a *one-dimensional,* linear instruction stream.) In particular, while an ACTION normally exits by falling through, it may also exit with an unconditional forward or backward branch. While most CONDITIONALs have only two exits, part (c) shows one having four, of which three happen to be forward jumps. Its possible implementation in (d) illustrates that an exit may occur on *any* instruction in a sequence, not necessarily the last. (A horizontal line segment, having two exit arrows, represents a single *conditional branch* instruction, which, after execution, leaves the PC with one of two possible values.)

A CONDITIONAL allows the behavior of a program to depend on the data it is processing. While arbitrarily complex program flow diagrams may be configured using CONDITIONALs, the number of flow variations that are actually employed is surprisingly small. The most common ACTION/CONDITIONAL combinations are summarized below.

A program *loop* combines an ACTION and a CONDITIONAL with paths that permit the ACTION to be *repeated.* During each iteration or "pass" through the loop, the ACTION, whose function may vary from pass to pass, is executed once. After each "trip" around the loop (made by the PC), the CONDITIONAL is responsible for deciding either to initiate another pass or to exit the loop. (The CONDITIONAL has two exit paths, one that exits the loop and the other that re-enters the ACTION.) Typically, a CONDITIONAL will compare two functions and select an exit depending on whether or not a specific relation between them is true. For example, it may change the value of an integer and then determine whether or not the integer has yet reached a predetermined limit value.

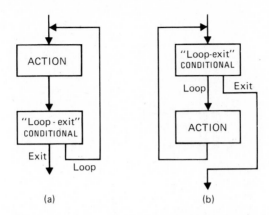

Figure 6.16   Two conventional ACTION–CONDITIONAL loop configurations

Figure 6.16 contains the two conventional ACTION-CONDITIONAL loop configurations. Each is ordinarily preceded by one or more instructions that properly initialize some of the variables used in the body of the loop. (A variable value is the contents of a register.) These loop structures mechanize higher-level language statement sequences that feature key words such as DO, WHILE, FOR, REPEAT, and UNTIL. Note, especially, that loop structures may be *nested*. That is, since an ACTION may contain an arbitrary substructure, it may, in particular, be a loop *itself*. Observe that each of the diagrams in Fig. 6.16 has only one exit and therefore is itself an ACTION.

A CONDITIONAL is also frequently employed to permit a program to decide from among two or more computational alternatives. The most common flow structure is shown in Fig. 6.17(a). Only one pass through it is possible. The conditions existing on entry determine which of the ACTIONs is executed. Part (b) contains an important simplification of part (a), in which ACTION2 does not exist. ACTION1 is *selectively* or *conditionally* executed based on the CONDITIONAL's evaluation. Both of these structures mechanize higher-level language-statement sequences that feature key words such as IF and ELSE. That is, ACTION1 is executed only *if* a specific condition is true. Otherwise (i.e., or *else*), if the condition is false, ACTION2 is executed, if it exists. Observe, again, that each of the diagrams in Fig. 6.17 has only one exit and therefore is itself an ACTION.

Since an ACTION may itself be arbitrarily complex, it may be a loop or another IF structure. In the latter case, a tree-like flow chart, such as that shown in Fig. 6.18(a), may be configured. (Many other variations are possible.) In this example, a function F is evaluated and a set of successive tests is made on its value. Once an "F = Vi" condition is found true, a corresponding ACTIONi is executed. At each level in the flow chart, the ELSE path for one

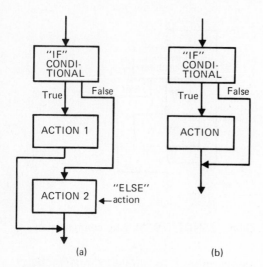

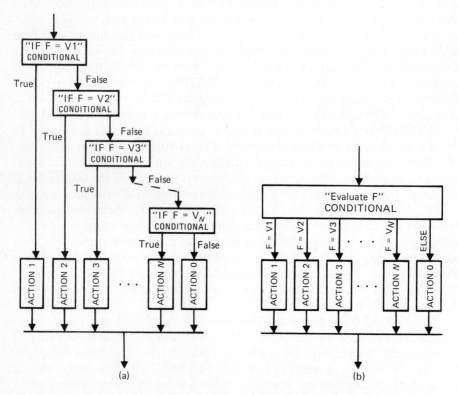

(a)   (b)

Figure 6.17   Two conventional "IF" structures

(a)   (b)

Figure 6.18   A "tree" of IF structures and its equivalent

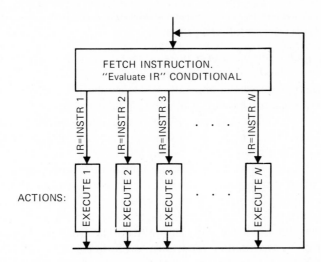

Figure 6.19   Fetch–execute cycle as a variation of Fig. 6.18 (b)

IF structure is itself *another* IF structure. ACTION0 is executed if F is not equal to any of the Vi's. Here is another example of *nesting,* in which an IF structure itself contains another IF structure.

Figure 6.18(b) illustrates an equivalent of part (a), in much simpler form. The single CONDITIONAL at the top, having many exit paths, replaces the network of two-exit-path CONDITIONALs in (a). The flow structure in (b) mechanizes higher-level language statement sequences which feature key words such as CASE. Observe, again, that each of the diagrams in Fig. 6.18 has only one exit and therefore is itself an ACTION.

Note that a variation on this organization, shown in Fig. 6.19, is in fact a more detailed version of the FETCH-EXECUTE cycle flow chart of Fig. 6.2. This demonstrates that a processor, originally defined as implemented in hardware, may be also implemented in *software.* A program, which behaves as if it were a processor, is called an INTERPRETER. If the processor that it simulates also exists physically in hardware, the program is called a SIMU-LATOR of that processor. We will return to discuss how virtual machines are implemented in Chapter 9.

The universal flow structures shown in Figs. 6.16 through 6.18 are easy to remember because they comprise a small set of simple configurations. Yet they are used to implement arbitrarily complex programs, principally be-cause they may be *nested in a hierarchy.* That is, as explained above, each module in a flow chart at one level may itself consist of a network of lower-level subprograms.

6.5 INSTRUCTION TYPES AND FIELDS

A good instruction set permits a programmer to express a desired function concisely, in a compact instruction sequence. Typically, a short program is more efficient than a longer one not only because it occupies less memory space but also because its execution time is shorter. An "ideal" function—which perfectly matches a processor—is one that is expressible in only *one* instruction. Generally, of course, this is not the case, and the function must be *programmed* as a sequence of several instructions.

A "special-purpose" computer is one whose instruction set is specifically tailored to a given application. That is, its instructions were defined with this application in mind. For example, an elementary electronic calculator is specially designed to process numbers, while a "general-purpose" computer may be programmed for a wide variety of applications, from solving equations to searching files. Its instruction repertoire is chosen as the best compromise that permits the entire spectrum of anticipated applications to be easily expressed or programmed. Thus, a computer architect designs an instruction set keeping in mind the operations that typical programmers will require.

A processor has an internal set of registers and an access path to a memory. In addition, it interfaces with one or more external devices, each of which acts *as if it were* a register. An INPUT device (for example, a keyboard) simulates a source register, while an OUTPUT device (for example, a printer) simulates a destination register. [Further details on INPUT/OUTPUT (abbreviated as "I/O") device interfaces and operations are given in Chapter 8.] The execution time of an instruction depends on the number of micro-operations it contains and on their respective durations. The execution time of any single register transfer in turn depends on the *accessibility* of the registers that participate in it. Typically, a *processor* register may be accessed in a time at least an order of magnitude shorter than that required to access a *memory* register. (Recall the definition of memory access time, given in Chapter 4.) Consequently, instructions may be classified according to *where* the registers that participate in them reside. A "register-to-register" operation is one involving only *processor* registers and not requiring any memory accesses. Similarly, a "memory-to-memory" operation is one involving only *memory* registers, while both register types participate in a "register-to-memory" operation.

The execution of an instruction may *move* data, *produce* data, *test* data, or alter program *flow*. While an elementary instruction usually performs only one of these operations, there is nothing to prevent an appropriate combination of two or more functions in one composite instruction, particularly if it is frequently employed in programs. We proceed by enumerating the most common instruction types that belong to each of these functional categories.

A programmer has access to a register and control over its use principally through instructions that permit him to LOAD it with a value from an arbitrary source and to STORE its contents into an arbitrary destination. Thus, every programmer-accessible processor register has corresponding LOAD and STORE instructions in the processor's repertoire. Typically, each of these instructions executes by moving a value between a *memory* register and the designated processor register, in which case it is a "register-to-memory" operation. LOAD and STORE instructions are the most "classical" data movement operations. A LOAD IMMEDIATE instruction executes by moving data from the instruction itself into the designated processor register. An EXCHANGE instruction executes by *swapping* the contents of one or more pairs of registers. Each register that participates in a SWAP is both a source *and* a destination. Instructions that move data between *memory* registers (they are therefore "memory-to-memory" operations) are generally called MOVE instructions. Note that a data MOVE is better termed a COPY, because the contents of the source of the data is normally not altered in the process of execution.

In addition to LOAD, STORE, and MOVE instructions, the execution of INPUT or OUTPUT instructions also results in the movement of data, in this case between I/O devices and system registers. Typically, during a program run, data to be processed is read in via INPUT instructions, and computational results are written out via OUTPUT instructions. Note that a *program load*, in particular, is a data movement function, consisting of a sequence of INPUT operations in which the program being loaded is the *data* being moved. (After the load completes, execution begins when control is transferred to the first instruction of the program just loaded.)

Communications and sorting or merging routines are examples of programs that principally execute data movement operations. In most other applications, a significant amount of data movement is still necessary, to make it more convenient to process the data or to reduce its processing time. For example, arithmetic or logical operations frequently require that the operands reside in specific registers. They usually must be *moved* there. A typical programmer often finds it necessary to copy data before modifying it, to preserve the original data values. In particular, SAVE and companion RESTORE functions, which store and later reconstruct the contents of a set of registers, so that they may be temporarily used for other purposes, are both data-movement functions. Similarly, PUSH and POP instructions, which respectively execute by saving data on a stack and restoring data from it, are also data-movement operations.

In summary, most instruction types that *move* data have operation names like LOAD, STORE, EXCHANGE, SWAP, MOVE, COPY, PUSH, POP, SAVE, RESTORE, INPUT, and OUTPUT.

Instructions that *produce* data are often considered the ones that actually "compute." They generate new data from old data. Each of the data operations discussed in Chapter 2 produces new data, by delivering a result value based on one or two argument values. Such instructions are generally divided into two categories: those that execute *arithmetic* operations and those that execute *logical* operations. Typical operation names for arithmetic instructions include ADD, SUBTRACT, MULTIPLY, DIVIDE, NORMALIZE, INCREMENT, DECREMENT, NEGATE, and ABSOLUTE VALUE. (Recall that the mantissa of a *normalized* floating-point number has no leading zeroes. An ABSOLUTE VALUE instruction executes by negating an operand if it is negative.) Typical operation names for logical instructions include AND, OR, EXCLUSIVE OR, COMPLEMENT, SHIFT, CIRCULATE, ROTATE, SET, RESET, CLEAR, TRANSLATE, and CODE CONVERT. (The latter two instructions permit arbitrary, programmer-selected code conversions.)

An instruction that *tests* data leaves that data unmodified and in place. Its purpose is to return, in a special register, one or more bits called *condition indicators* or *flags,* which represent the results of the test. Since the data being tested constitutes an operand, and since a result is delivered, a TEST instruction may be considered as part of the class of logical instructions. It is used in a CONDITIONAL (defined in Section 6.4) to evaluate the truth or falsity of specific conditions on which subsequent conditional branches will depend.

The most common test command is the COMPARE instruction. Its execution is mechanized using logic similar to that defined in Section 2.7. Normally, two operands are compared, and the comparison results (e.g., EQUAL, GREATER, LESS, etc.) are left in "indicator" or "flag" flip-flops, for subsequent use by conditional jump instructions. A more sophisticated COMPARE, typically named SEARCH, SCAN, or FIND, executes a *sequence* of comparisons. For example, it may search a specific memory area, character by character, until a match to a comparison argument is found. When the match occurs, execution may terminate with the address of the matching character in a special processor "pointer" register. Thus, instructions that *test* data have operation names like COMPARE, TEST, SEARCH, SCAN, and FIND.

An instruction that alters program *flow* does so by modifying the contents of the Program Counter during its execution. Typical operation names for such instructions, already introduced earlier, include BRANCH, JUMP, SKIP, CALL, and RETURN. These instructions come in two varieties: those that alter program flow *unconditionally*—independent of any previous computed results—and those that modify PC *conditionally*—only if specific evaluated conditions are true. A CONDITIONAL uses one or more conditional branches.

The following execution definitions normally apply: A JUMP or BRANCH loads PC with a new value. A SKIP increments PC past the next successive instruction. A CALL is a JUMP preceded by a PUSH of the PC value onto a stack. A RETURN is a POP from this stack into the PC. Note that, if the prerequisite condition is *not* met, a conditional flow-altering instruction normally executes *no* operation. The processor merely proceeds to fetch the next consecutive instruction.

In addition to the instructions listed above, there is a large variety of *miscellaneous control* instructions, whose execution descriptions do not easily fit into any of the above categories. For example, HALT is a control instruction. So is WAIT or HOLD, whose execution is equivalent to a temporary HALT. Many control instructions are concerned with *I/O device* activity. For example, REWIND executes by rewinding a tape drive. SEND STATUS executes by reading a code defining the state of an I/O device. Instructions in this area are the most difficult to categorize because of their variety. We may state generally, however, that any feature, specially built into the hardware of a system, must have associated with it one or more instructions in the processor's repertoire, to give the programmer *control* over its use.

The discussion above demonstrates that an instruction is distinguished primarily by its name, which is an operation *verb* like LOAD or ADD. This name is normally encoded into one of the possible *opcode* field values. Table 6.3 summarizes the most common operation verbs and their usual meanings. We proceed now to consider the other fields that may comprise a typical instruction.

Imagine that you were a processor, about to execute one of the commands listed in Table 6.3, having been given its opcode. What *other* information would you require, to have a precise definition of the register-transfer sequence that is called for? This supplementary information must be supplied to you by one of two means: Either it is explicitly specified to you, in fields of the instruction, by the programmer, or it is implicitly understood by you, because it is already built into your structure. The nature of the information you require varies with the instruction. For example, as stated earlier, very little more has to be said to you once you are told to HALT. On the other hand, most of the other commands in Table 6.3 require further (explicit or implicit) elaboration, to clearly define the operations required. If you consider each of these instructions individually, and list the additional information required for each, and then sort all such requirements into logical groups, you develop a rationale for each of the instruction fields discussed below.

Virtually every instruction needs to *identify* the registers that will participate in its execution. (Those that are already implicitly known need not be

Table 6.3 Typical Instruction Names and Their Usual Meanings

Data Movement Instructions

LOAD	Move word from memory register to processor register.
STORE	Move word from processor register to memory register.
MOVE	COPY word(s) from source register(s) to destination(s).
EXCHANGE	Source and destination registers SWAP contents.
PUSH	Deposit selected register's contents onto stack.
POP	Move top stack item into selected destination register.
SAVE	A sequence of STOREs into a memory area.
RESTORE	A comparable sequence of LOADs from a memory area.
INPUT	Transfer data from an I/O device into system registers.
OUTPUT	Transfer data from system registers to an I/O device.

Instructions that Produce New Data

Arithmetic operations

ADD	Compute the sum of the selected arguments.
SUBTRACT	Compute the difference between the selected arguments.
MULTIPLY	Compute the product of the selected arguments.
DIVIDE	Compute the quotient of the selected arguments.
NORMALIZE	Remove leading zeroes from a floating-point mantissa.
INCREMENT	Add one to the selected operand.
DECREMENT	Subtract one from the selected operand.
NEGATE	Reverse the sign of the selected argument.
ABSOLUTE VALUE	Make the sign of the selected argument positive.

Logical Operations

AND	Form the parallel AND of the selected arguments.
OR	Form the parallel OR of the selected arguments.
EXCLUSIVE OR	Form the parallel EXCLUSIVE OR of the arguments.
COMPLEMENT	Reverse all bits of the selected argument.
SHIFT	Shift the selected argument left or right.
ROTATE	CIRCULATE the selected argument left or right.
SET	Set the selected bit in the selected argument.
RESET	Reset the selected bit in the selected argument.
CLEAR	Change the selected argument's value to all zeroes.
TRANSLATE	CONVERT a given code into a corresponding code.

Data Testing Instructions

COMPARE	Set flags based on the relationship between two codes.
TEST	Set flags based on the value of a specific argument.
SEARCH	SCAN a memory area and FIND a specific character.

Transfers of Control

BRANCH	If the condition is true, PC ← Address (i.e., JUMP).
SKIP	If the condition is true, increment PC.
CALL	A BRANCH preceded by a PUSH of the old PC value.
RETURN	POP the top of the stack into the PC.

Table 6.3 *(continued)*

Miscellaneous Control Instructions

HALT	Stop running.
WAIT	Stop running and HOLD until later resumption.
NO-OP	Execute no operation. Continue with next instruction.
REWIND	Rewind the specified tape unit.
SEND STATUS	Retrieve a code describing an I/O device's state.

named.) The process of identifying a participating register is broadly termed "addressing"—even when that register is not part of a memory. The selection of a branch destination is also an "addressing" issue. Since the number of possible addressing mechanisms is large, treatment of this subject is postponed until the reasons behind some other typical instruction fields are explained. In the meantime, we will make the oversimplifying assumption that all participating registers reside in the system's central memory, and that every instruction includes as many address fields as are necessary to point them out.

An operand is stored in a register because its value generally changes as a computation proceeds. The instructions of a program, on the other hand, normally remain constant as the program computes. (They may be resident in a ROM, for example.) Thus, while a program runs, data values change while instructions remain fixed. This explains why an instruction does not normally contain an operand. Rather, it contains a field that *addresses or selects the register* containing the operand. There are, however, conditions under which it is convenient for an instruction to *itself* contain an operand. Such an operand is called an IMMEDIATE DATA field. An immediate operand is a *constant*. Its source, during instruction execution, is the appropriate field of the Instruction Register. (Recall that the term "immediate operand" was first introduced at the end of Section 6.1.) Let us enumerate some of the conditions under which the use of an immediate operand is preferred.

First, whenever an operand of an arithmetic, logical, or test instruction is a *constant*, it may be an immediate operand. For example, a programmer may wish to increment a variable value by a constant or to compare each character in a sequence of characters to a constant test argument. In both cases, it is usually inefficient to store the constant in a separate register, which is, in turn, *addressed* by the ADD or COMPARE instruction. It is preferable to place the constant directly *in* the instruction, if the processor's repertoire permits it. Second, it is common practice to *initialize* a register by executing an instruction that moves a constant data value into it. This value may reside directly in the instruction that executes the move. In particular, a LOAD IMMEDIATE instruction (like the one described in Section 6.2), which permits initialization of any processor register, is an essential part of every instruction set. Note that a CLEAR instruction is equivalent to a LOAD IMMEDIATE whose operand is zero.

A field in an instruction is often employed to specify the *length* of the participating operand(s). For example, a MOVE instruction may execute by copying a memory area of variable size from one memory location to another. A field in the instruction may specify the *number* of words to be moved. Similarly, an INPUT or an OUTPUT instruction may execute by transferring a variable-length sequence of words between an I/O device and a memory area. A field in the instruction may define the number of words to be transferred. A SEARCH instruction may scan a memory area, whose length is specified in the instruction, for a match to a specified argument. A STORE instruction may execute by storing a *set* of processor registers into a contiguous set of memory registers. A *count* field in the instruction may specify the number of registers to be stored.

A processor may allow the programmer to have control over the lengths of the arguments of arithmetic or logical instructions. For example, multiple-precision ADDs or SUBTRACTs may be permitted. Again, an operand-length field may be employed to specify the level of precision. Note that, if a processor gives the programmer a small number of length choices (for example, between single-precision and double-precision only), different *opcodes* may be employed in lieu of a separate (one- or two-bit) operand-length field. This demonstrates the general rule that, if the number of variations on the theme specified in one instruction field is sufficiently small, a second field, selecting the specific variation, need not be employed. Rather, the variation alternatives may be included as separate choices in the first field, in which case, the second field is actually *embedded* in it. Observe also that an operand-length field (which contains a number) is not itself an operand. It is an attribute or descriptor of an operand.

The value in an N-bit instruction field selects one of 2^N objects. It is the selected object's number or label. The nature of programmer-selectable "objects" varies considerably over the spectrum of processors. Some common interpretations are given below.

An instruction set may include logical operations on individually addressed *bits* in a selected register. Typically, a bit-addressing instruction includes a field that selects *which* bit in that register will be SET, RESET, or TESTed. Thus, an instruction field may contain a bit number.

A processor is normally designed under the assumption that it will interface with several external devices. An INPUT or OUTPUT instruction, whose execution involves one of these elements, generally includes a field to identify *which* one it is. Thus, an instruction field may contain an I/O device identification number.

A processor design may permit transfers of control that are conditional on any one of several possible conditions. For example, a conditional branch may depend on the sign of the last arithmetic result, whether or not the contents of a specific register is zero, whether or not an external signal is asserted, whether or not a carry was generated or an overflow occurred on the last arithmetic operation, the last shifted-off bit, and so on. Consequently, a processor may include in its repertoire one or more general-purpose, conditional branch instructions, each having a field selecting *which* branch condition is the applicable one.

If a processor permits several addressing modes (discussed further in the next section), its instructions may include addressing mode selection fields.

As the examples above indicate, an instruction field is often used to select a variation on the theme specified by another field. For example, it may further clarify the operation selected by the opcode. Thus, a SHIFT instruction may include a field selecting the shift *mode* (i.e., direction, distance, and end conditions). An ADD opcode may have appended to it a modifier field specifying the *type* of add (i.e., binary or decimal, fixed or floating point, normalization and rounding options, degree of precision, etc.).

The examples above also demonstrate that it is common for the value in one field of an instruction to influence how the value in a second field is *interpreted*. For example, the same field may specify the ADD's type, the SHIFT's mode, the BRANCH's condition, the MOVE's count, and the IN-

Table 6.4 Common Instruction Field Names and Their Uses

Field Name	Its Typical Use
OPERATION CODE	Identifies the operation to be executed.
ADDRESS	Locates a memory operand or BRANCH destination.
DISPLACEMENT	A partial address. The distance from a selected base or origin.
OFFSET	A signed, relative-displacement value.
REGISTER SELECT	Identifies a specific processor register.
IMMEDIATE DATA	A constant operand located *in* the instruction.
ADDRESSING MODE	Selects the applicable addressing mode.
LENGTH	Specifies the length of participating operands.
COUNT	Gives an operand length or a repetition count.
BIT SELECT	Locates a specific bit in an operand.
CONDITION SELECT	Identifies the branch condition to be tested.
I/O DEVICE NUMBER	Selects the participating I/O device.
OP VARIATION	Selects a specific variation of the opcode.
GENERAL MODIFIER	Specifies further details on the selection made in another field.

PUT's device number. Note, in particular, that a special value in one field, often called an *escape* value, may *totally redefine* how all of the other fields are interpreted. The opcode value of 7, in the sample processor of Section 6.2, was such an escape value.

Table 6.4 summarizes the most common instruction fields and their typical uses. Several of the items contained in it are explained in the discussion on addressing, which follows.

You are now in a better position to appreciate that the execution time of an instruction depends not only on the fields contained within it but also on the data processed by it. For example, the execution time of an instruction having a length or count field, like MOVE, depends on the count value, while that of a FIND instruction, which searches a memory area for a specific character and terminates whenever a match is found, depends on the data being scanned.

6.6 ADDRESSING MODES

The process by which the registers that participate in an instruction's execution are identified is termed *addressing*. When an instruction "addresses" a register, its execution is directed toward it (i.e., involves it). The registers that are available are those in the main memory and those in the processor. (External devices, whose interfaces resemble those of registers, are also available. We will ignore them momentarily.) In contrast with the elementary machine introduced in Section 6.2, a typical processor contains a considerable number of registers, often organized into a small memory. Regardless of their number, processor registers are generally more important than memory registers, principally because they are more *accessible*. The time to execute a register transfer employing processor registers is substantially smaller than that involving memory registers. For this reason, a typical instruction set maximally utilizes the available processor registers, in order to minimize program execution time. A common programming strategy, for example, is to move operands from memory into processor registers, in preparation for computation sequences involving them, to retain them in the processor while these computations take place, and then to store their resulting values back in memory when access to them is no longer required. For this reason, the small memory, internal to the processor, in which most or all of the processor registers reside, is sometimes called a "scratchpad" memory.

The example in Section 6.2 also gave the erroneous impression that processor registers are divided into two classes: "address" registers, for the address network, and "data" registers, for the data network, since the main memory's address length is generally different from its data length. Regardless of the memory's address/word length ratio, it is normally convenient to make *all* processor registers identical, particularly if they are assembled into a small scratchpad memory. Each register is then called a "general" register, to indicate that it may be employed to store either a data item or a *pointer* to a data item, and to emphasize that computations on addresses are as valid as computations on data. If a memory port width does not match that of a general register, an appropriate, matching *field* of that register (ignoring some of its upper bits, for example) may be extracted and used. Unless otherwise specified, we will henceforth assume that all processor registers have identical lengths.

The number of participating registers that must be (explicitly or implicitly) identified, for each of the instruction types discussed in Section 6.5, is quite small. A data-moving operation normally requires two: a source register and a destination register. A data-producing operation generally requires, at most, three: two operand source registers and one result destination register. A data-testing operation typically requires two registers, containing the arguments that are compared. The flag flip-flops, into which comparison results are stored, constitute a third register. Finally, a branching operation normally develops a single branch address (which is discarded if the branch is not taken). Thus, a typical instruction must explicitly or implicitly identify, at most, three operand registers.

An explicit memory register may be identified with an address in the instruction. An explicit *processor* register is similarly named using an instruction field containing its *register number*, which is effectively an address into the processor's (real or equivalent) "scratchpad" memory. For example, an array of eight processor registers requires a three-bit register number to isolate one of them. Sixteen processor registers call for a four-bit register number. Consequently, an instruction that involves P (three or less) participating registers must explicitly address $P - I$ registers, where I is the number of registers that are already implicitly known. Let us briefly review the most common implicit registers (the ones usually built into the processor's instruction execution procedure), for the various possible values of I.

Assume a conventional "$P = 3$" instruction, having two arguments and one result (for example, an ADD instruction). If $I = 0$, the instruction format permits the programmer to select two arbitrary sources plus an arbitrary destination for the operation. If $I = 1$, the programmer is normally able to specify the two *argument* registers in the instruction, with the understanding that the result's value will *automatically replace* one of them. That is, the result will be stored back into one of the specified argument registers. Alternatively, the hardware may automatically store the result into a special, prearranged or "known" register. A typical $I = 2$ instruction permits the programmer to specify only *one* of the argument registers, with the understanding that the source of the *other* argument is in an already-known register, and with the further understanding that the result will be automatically stored back into this register. For this reason, the implicit register is often called an "accumulator." (You are reminded that any of the above instructions may substitute an *immediate* data item for a pointer to the register that contains the data.)

Finally, an $I = 3$ instruction assumes specific locations for *both* arguments, as well as for the result, without needing *any* operand information from the programmer. Such a machine is normally organized around an operand *stack,* with the understanding that participating operands already reside at the top of the stack, and that computation results will be automatically pushed there. Typically, the two ADD arguments must be the top two stack entries. They are popped as they are used and are replaced with the result value, leaving the stack with one less entry after execution.

Note that any processor that uses implicit registers must provide instructions in its repertoire to give the programmer control over their contents—for example, by permitting him to freely move arguments between the implicit registers and other arbitrary locations. Thus, a typical "$I = 2$" processor has LOAD ACCUMULATOR and STORE ACCUMULATOR instructions. Similarly, a typical "$I = 3$" processor has corresponding PUSH and POP instructions. The programmer employs these commands to prepare for implicit-register operations and to direct their results to proper destinations.

Assuming that explicit registers are identified in instructions with addresses, you may find it helpful to use a common terminology which calls an "$I = 0$" processor a "three-address" machine, an "$I = 1$" processor a "two-address" machine, an "$I = 2$" processor a "one-address" machine, and an "$I = 3$" processor a "zero-address" machine.

The length of an instruction clearly depends on the number of addresses in it. A machine that permits a *variable* instruction length generally allows as many instruction lengths as there are numbers of addresses in them. For example, a processor that permits zero-, one-, and two-address instructions normally recognizes three possible instruction lengths. In this regard, another impression given in Section 6.2, which was not totally accurate, was the idea that an *entire* instruction must be fetched (staged in the Instruction Register) before its execution may begin. When an instruction is longer than one memory word, a processor may use information in the first word to decide whether or not subsequent reads are necessary. The beginning of *execution* may also bear upon this issue. For example, if the second instruction word contains a branch address and the branch condition is *not* met, the second word may be ignored by merely incrementing the Program Counter *past* it, without actually fetching it. Similarly, if the second instruction word is an immediate operand, it may be used directly during execution. That is, its preliminary placement in the Instruction Register may be omitted.

Figure 6.20 contains a set of diagrams describing the most commonly used addressing modes, and Table 6.5 provides the same information in narrative form. When a processor permits a number of addressing modes, its instruction format generally includes a field whose value selects one of them. Alternatively, the opcode value may itself imply the applicable addressing mode. For simplicity, each of the diagrams is drawn after assuming that the entire instruction has been fetched from memory and already resides in the Instruction Register. Most of the examples show how operands are addressed, and only two indicate how branch addresses are developed. Since an address may reference either an instruction or a data item, you should remember that an addressing mechanism may be employed for *either* purpose.

A few of the modes given in Fig. 6.20 were covered earlier. For example, diagram (a) pictures the situation in which an operand resides *in* the instruction. It is an *immediate* operand, addressed by the Program Counter itself. Diagram (b) represents the common mode in which the instruction contains the address of an operand residing in memory. Such an addressing mode, also discussed earlier (for example, in Section 6.2), is termed *direct* addressing. It clearly requires that the instruction length be greater than the memory's address length.

Diagram (c) is the first one that represents the set of processor registers, assembled into the equivalent of a small memory. The instruction contains a *register-number* field, whose value selects one of these registers, whose contents is the addressed operand. This addressing mode, customarily called *register* addressing, was also alluded to earlier. It has the advantage not only of faster execution—because the operand resides in a processor register (not in a memory register)—but also of more efficient use of instruction bits—because a very short instruction field is sufficient to address the operand. The applicability of register-addressing increases either as the instruction length decreases or as the number of addressed operands, for a fixed instruction length, increases.

Diagrams (d) and (e) show two different forms of *indirect* addressing, in which a field in the instruction points not to the operand, but to a *pointer* to the operand. In diagram (d), the address field in the instruction selects a memory register *whose contents* is the operand address (i.e., the address in the instruction is the address *of* an address). Similarly, in diagram (e), the instruction field selects a processor register whose contents, in turn, point to the operand.

Indirect addressing is particularly valuable when a referenced location either varies as a program runs or is not known at the time a program is coded. In both cases, whenever the referenced location becomes known, its address is loaded into the *intermediate* register. Thus, the indirect addressing mechanism permits a program, which references a *varying* location, to itself remain *unmodified*.

Since the register-indirect mode utilizes an intermediate *processor* register, it also has the same speed and instruction-bit usage advantages ascribed earlier to the register-addressing mode. Both indirect modes are our first examples in which the *effective* address—the one that is ultimately applied to the memory's address port, to access the operand—is derived by some intermediate address "computation." The computation, in this case, merely involves the access of an intermediate register. Other forms of address "processing," to derive the ultimate effective address, will be discussed presently.

Note that the indirect addressing mode in diagram (d) employs a memory access *in preparation* for the one to the addressed operand. A processor design may permit an address to be marked as indirect, using a single, appended indirect bit (a one-bit addressing mode field). It may also permit an *intermediate* address to be *itself* marked as indirect. If this is the case, a *chain* of preparatory memory accesses, which continues until a *direct* operand address is finally found, is possible. Observe also that an address value, stored in a processor or memory register, may be itself operated on as if it were data.

A *relative* address is the *sum* of a *base* or *origin* address value and a *displacement* or *offset* from it. The resulting effective address is thus relative to, or *in the vicinity of*, the base value. This form of addressing has numerous applications. It is particularly useful in the execution of relative branches and in the processing of data *arrays*.

As explained in Section 6.4, most program transfers of control, exclusive of CALL and RETURN, are *localized* in the vicinity of the current PC value. For this reason, a relative-jump instruction need not include the full destination address. Rather, a significantly shorter field is sufficient to specify the branch destination, if the current PC value is used as an implicit origin.

Figure 6.20(f) shows two common register transfers that implement relative jumps. The circled "+" represents a binary adder. In diagram (1), the new PC value is the old PC value incremented by an OFFSET. The OFFSET value is assumed represented *in two's complement form*. Its sign bit is extended to develop an adder argument whose width matches that of the PC. (The sign of an argument is "extended" by duplicating it, on the most significant end, as many times as are necessary.) Thus, an $N + 1$ bit OFFSET field permits a forward jump distance of $2^N - 1$ and a backward jump distance of

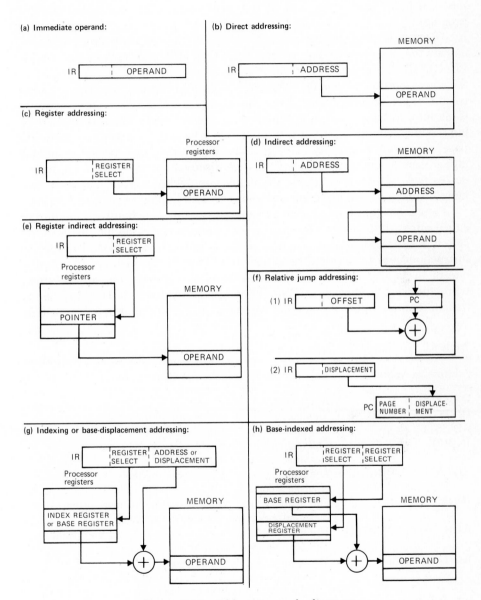

Figure 6.20 Addressing mode diagrams

2^N. Note that the old PC value (the origin for the jump) is already pointing *past* the jump instruction and at the next consecutive instruction in the program.

Diagram (2) in Fig. 6.20(f) shows a simpler jump implementation, not requiring the use of an adder, in which the OFFSET field, now called a DISPLACEMENT field, merely *replaces* the value (having the same length) in the lower portion of the PC. The PC value is interpreted as pointing to a word at a given displacement from the base of a PAGE of memory registers. (This interpretation was first explained in Section 4.3.) Thus, this relative-jump implementation permits a branch to any location within the current PC page, no matter where the PC is pointing within it. While it has the advantage of simple implementation, it has the disadvantage of prohibiting jumps *across page boundaries.* As the PC value approaches a page boundary, the jump *distance* in that direction becomes severely limited.

Figure 6.20(g) shows an important addressing mechanism, commonly called either *indexing* or *base-displacement addressing.* One instruction field selects a processor register, whose contents are added to that of a second instruction field to develop the effective address of the operand. Normally, one of the adder operands is considered as an arbitrary memory address, while the other is viewed as a "small" increment added to it. However, since the addition operation is commutative, *either* adder operand may have either

Table 6.5 Common Addressing Modes and Their Meanings

Addressing Mode	The Operand's Value Is the Contents of:
IMMEDIATE	A field *in* the instruction itself.
DIRECT	The memory location selected by the address.
REGISTER	The specified processor register.
INDIRECT	The memory location addressed by the contents of the location selected by the address.
REGISTER INDIRECT	The memory location addressed by the selected processor register's contents.
INDEXING	The memory location addressed by the sum of the selected index register and the address.
BASE-DISPLACEMENT	The memory location at the given displacement from the value in the selected base register.
BASE-INDEXED	The memory location addressed by the sum of the selected base register's contents and the selected displacement register's contents.
RELATIVE JUMP	PC ← PC + OFFSET, where OFFSET is signed, or PC lower field ← DISPLACEMENT in instruction.

interpretation. The two possible interpretations and their most common applications are explained further below.

A data *vector* is a string of data items, each having a unique *index* (or subscript), normally occupying a set of contiguous memory locations. It is a one-dimensional *array* of data items. All operations on higher-level data arrays (for example, matrices) themselves consist of appropriate sequences of vector operations. A typical vector operation takes the form of a program loop whose *i*th pass processes the *i*th vector element. To permit the code of the loop to remain constant, while it addresses successive vector elements on successive passes, an addressing mode known as *indexing* is normally employed. Each instruction address in the loop, which points to a stepping vector operand, is marked as *indexed*. This causes an index increment, derived from a selected processor register, to be added to it, to develop the effective operand address. The *index value* is the one that changes appropriately for each new loop pass. Indexing is therefore an application in which the processor register contains the ("small") offset on the instruction's address value.

An alternative view of the same addressing mechanism is based on the fact that a typical running program addresses memory locations in *clusters*. Execution of a program loop, for example, requires a clustering of instruction fetches. Similarly, data sets are normally stored in memory *areas*, and while a program processes a data packet, its accesses are localized to that packet's data area. If a pointer to the origin of a memory area is stored in a processor register, a sequence of instructions may reference arbitrary locations in that area by specifying only *displacements* or *offsets* from that base. This significantly reduces the number of address bits required in the instruction. Typically, the programmer will point several processor registers at the origins of those memory areas presently in use. An area is selected using the number of the register that contains its base address. The displacement value in the instruction permits the programmer to retain the flexibility of direct addressing, but only over the selected area's limited address range.

The *base-indexed* addressing mode in Fig. 6.20(h) retains some of the characteristics of indexing or base-displacement addressing and requires fewer instruction bits. The effective memory address of the operand is still the sum of two values, *both* of which are stored in the processor registers selected by fields in the instruction.

To demonstrate a few of the tradeoffs between the various addressing modes introduced above, consider a sample system whose instructions contain 16-bit main memory addresses, 8-bit displacement or offset fields, and 4-bit processor register-select fields. A full 16-bit direct address gives the programmer the freedom to specify any one of 65,536 memory operands. A 4-bit processor-register address limits the number of selectable operands to 16, but dramatically reduces the required instruction length. A 4-bit register-indirect field retains the short instruction length but (indirectly) expands the addressable space back to 2^{16}, because it selects a register *whose contents* are a full 16-bit address. However, since the number of *pointers* is still limited, the number of addressable operands increases only if the pointer *values* can be easily manipulated (i.e., conveniently changed with little instruction-space consumption). The base-displacement mode is a reasonable compromise, which allocates 12 bits to address an operand. It retains some direct-addressing flexibility, because the programmer is free to choose from among 256 operands (in the vicinity of the location pointed to by the selected base register), and it also retains the availability of 16 arbitrary pointers—whose values need not continually fluctuate.

Several other addressing schemes, many of which combine two or more of the modes given in Fig. 6.20, may be defined. For example, a combination of modes (g) and (d), called *indexed-indirect*, is sometimes used. The contents of the memory cell addressed by the adder's output in (g) is not the operand; it is the *address* of the operand. Such an addressing mode is useful, for example, when an intermediate *table or vector of addresses* is accessed in order to, in turn, find a desired operand. Note that, if the order of indexing and indirecting is reversed (i.e., by applying the address in the instruction to the memory first, reading out *another* address value, which is *then* added to the contents of the selected processor register to develop the effective operand address), a totally different operand is accessed.

A composite instruction, whose execution combines two or more operations, is desirable if most programmers find it useful most of the time. For example, since a TEST instruction is invariably followed by a BRANCH conditional on the TEST's results, a combined TEST and BRANCH instruction is customarily found in many instruction sets. Similarly, when a processor register is employed as a pointer, or as an index register, or as a counter, it is invariably incremented or decremented in the process. For example, a routine that processes a character sequence normally accesses the characters in order. The pointer to the current character continually increments. Likewise, a typical loop-ending instruction sequence, which tests a counter's value for zero, usually includes a decrement of that counter (and, possibly, an increment of an index or pointer value). Consequently, many instruction sets include convenient *auto-increment* or *auto-decrement* features. A referenced processor register, normally used as a pointer, counter, or index register, may be automatically advanced before or after its use. Alternatively, its advance may be controlled by a single instruction bit. Thus, an auto-advance operation may be included as part of any addressing mode.

While a processor's scratchpad memory frequently does *not* contain special registers like the Program Counter or the Stack Pointer, some interesting and useful results follow when these special registers *are* included in the programmer-selectable register set, provided that the processor is equipped with appropriate auto-advance facilities. For example, note that a register-indirect addressing mode, which includes an automatic pointer increment after the operand is accessed, is equivalent to an *immediate* operand mode, when the *Program Counter* is the selected pointer register. Similarly, LOAD and STORE instructions, which use the register-indirect addressing mode with appropriate built-in auto-advance, may be made equivalent to POP and PUSH instructions, when the *Stack Pointer* is the selected processor register.

6.7 INSTRUCTION FORMATS

Instruction formats vary widely over the spectrum of processors. They depend on many architectural variables. The most relevant of those that have already been introduced are listed in Table 6.6. Since a design choice for one parameter value affects the viability of the alternatives available for another, the variables are not necessarily listed in the order in which their values are decided.

Figure 6.21 contains a detailed description of a specific instruction format, which we will use as an example. While it is sufficiently comprehensive to cover many of the relevant architectural issues, some of its aspects have

Table 6.6 Some of the Architectural Variables That Affect the Design of a Typical Instruction Format

1. The main memory capacity, which defines its address length.
2. The length of a main memory word.
3. The number of operands that various instructions will be permitted to explicitly address.
4. The number of permissible instruction lengths.
5. The number of memory words per instruction.
6. The number of explicitly addressable processor registers.
7. The number and types of permissible addressing modes.
8. Whether or not auto-advance features are included in them.
9. Whether or not the PC and SP are included in the scratchpad.
10. The number of branch conditions that will be employed.
11. The maximum number of expected I/O devices.
12. The specific operation set that will be made available.

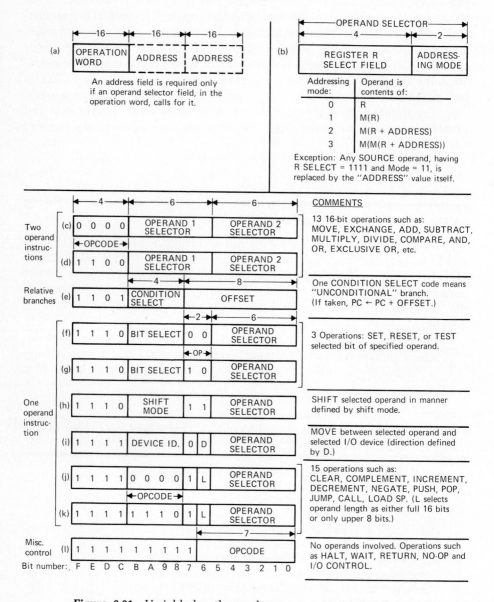

Figure 6.21 Variable-length sample processor instruction format

been intentionally simplified. Each of the parameters listed in Table 6.6 is given a value by the information contained in Fig. 6.21. As we discuss this sample processor, we will concentrate primarily on those questions that bear directly on the structure of its instructions.

The machine has three possible instruction lengths, each a multiple of 16 bits, as indicated in drawing (a). The first instruction word, called the "operation" word, defines the number (zero, one, or two) of additional "address" words that should be appended to it to compose the entire instruction. An operation word may contain zero, one, or two "operand selector" fields, each interpreted using the rules given in diagram (b). Every six-bit operand selector consists of a four-bit processor register number and a two-bit addressing mode selector. This establishes the existence of a 16-register processor scratchpad memory. Its selected register is designated as "R". All of the addressing modes listed in diagram (b) have already been described. The field values of 0, 1, 2, and 3 correspond to the "register," "register-indirect," "indexed," and "indexed-indirect" addressing modes, respectively. Note that an additional 16-bit "address" word is called for only if the upper addressing mode bit is "1".

Observe also that, whenever a *source* operand is selected, having the special combination of mode = 3 and register-select = 15, the added 16-bit "address" word is *itself* substituted for the operand. This is a special mechanism by which an *immediate* data argument is designated. Thus, the highest-numbered processor register is unique in that it cannot normally participate in the "indexed-indirect" addressing mode when the selected operand is a source argument.

All of the possible operation word formats are given in diagrams (c) through (l). The upper hex digit of the operation word is the principal factor governing how it is interpreted. Hex opcode values "0" through "C" designate a family of 13 two-operand instructions, each having two six-bit operand selector fields, as shown in formats (c) and (d). The specific execution details for each of these instructions are not of immediate concern to us here. Some possible two-operand instruction types are suggested in the diagram. You may assume that typical arithmetic or logical instructions execute by implicitly replacing one of the operand values with the computed result.

Hex opcode "D", which designates a relative branch operation, totally redefines how the lower 12 bits of the operation word are interpreted [see diagram (e)]. A four-bit CONDITION SELECT field permits one of 16 different branch conditions to be specified. Some of these may designate "compound" branch conditions (for example, whether or not the last arithmetic result was less than or equal to zero). The eight-bit OFFSET is assumed to be a two's-complement displacement from the present PC value.

Upper hex-digit values of "E" and "F" are "escape" codes, each of which causes a new interpretation for the lower 12 operation word bits. Diagrams (f) through (k) represent the class of one-operand instructions, each having a single operand selector field in its lower six bits. It follows that, at most, one additional 16-bit address word may be called for.

When the upper hex digit is "E", bits 6 and 7 become a local, two-bit opcode and bits 8–B comprise a four-bit operation *modifier* field. Opcodes 0, 1, and 2, respectively, evoke the SET, RESET, and TEST of the operand bit selected by the BIT SELECT value, as indicated in diagrams (f) and (g). An opcode value of 3 causes a SHIFT of the selected operand, with the direction, distance, and end conditions of the shift defined in the SHIFT MODE field. A specific format for the shift mode field in diagram (h) is not given. Its design is left as a problem at the end of this chapter.

When the upper hex digit is "F", the value of bit 7 distinguishes between two possible interpretations. When bit 7 is "0", as shown in diagram (i), an I/O data transfer, between the selected operand register and the device identified by the code in the DEVICE ID. field, is called for. Bit 6, named "D", defines the *direction* of the transfer (i.e., whether the operand register is a source or a destination for the moved word).

When bit 7 is "1" (while the upper hex digit is "F"), the field consisting of bits 8–B is reinterpreted as another local opcode, selecting an operation on the argument isolated by the operand selector field. Hex opcodes "0" through "E" define 15 possible operations, such as those suggested in diagrams (j) and (k). In each of these cases, bit 6, named "L", specifies one of two operand *lengths*. One value of L permits the selected operation on the entire 16-bit operand. The other L value restricts the operation to the upper eight-bit field of the operand, leaving its lower half unchanged.

Note that three of the opcodes are assumed allocated to the functions CALL, JUMP, and LOAD SP. Each of these has a special execution, in which the computed effective address (the one that would normally be used to access the operand) is loaded directly into a designated register. In the first two cases, that register is the Program Counter (preceded by a push of its old value, in the case of CALL). In the last case, it is the Stack Pointer register.

Finally, the highest possible opcode value in field 8–B is used as another "escape" condition. When the upper nine bits of the operation word are all 1's, the lower seven bits are interpreted as a new opcode, for operations requiring no operands. Several suggestions are given in diagram (l).

The example given in Fig. 6.21 does not explain many of the operational details of this hypothetical processor. Yet it is sufficient to demonstrate how a realistic instruction format is put together. Most of the operation classes and field types, discussed in Section 6.5, have been provided for.

The detailed implementation of this processor is clearly much more complicated than that of the elementary sample processor discussed in Section 6.2. For instance, the logic that interprets an operand-selector field and develops the effective operand address is itself a nontrivial subprocessor. Further details on processor logic implementations are given in the next chapter.

PROBLEMS

6.1 Suppose the order of the two register transfers that customarily constitute an instruction FETCH (see Fig. 6.2) were *reversed*. Briefly explain how conventional programs would have to be modified to accommodate this change.

6.2 Name four instruction types whose execution implicitly involves PC. Similarly, name four instruction types whose execution implicitly involves SP. (You should not have to refer to Table 6.3.)

6.3 A computer has two possible instruction lengths. An instruction is either one or two memory words long, as determined by the most significant bit in its opcode field (the leftmost field of the first word; "1" signifies a length of two words). The Instruction Register is two words long. Call its upper half IR.1 and its lower half IR.0. Write down the sequence of register transfers that constitute the FETCH cycle for this machine. Use the notation introduced in Fig. 5.11(b).

6.4 To protect against certain programmer errors, the sample processor of Section 6.2 is modified as follows: An extra bit is added to every word in the main memory. It is used to distinguish an instruction from a data word. (A "1" indicates an instruction.) The machine automatically halts if a data word is fetched or if the execution of a STORE attempts to overwrite an instruction. Add a minimum of logic to the diagram in Fig. 6.9 to implement this feature. You may add extra inputs to any existing gates. Your solution should clearly distinguish between added gates and existing gates. Briefly describe a set of conditions that would lead to the fetch of a data word.

6.5 Referring to the sample processor of Section 6.2, suppose the D digit of an OP = 7 instruction contained two or more 1's. How would it execute?

6.6 The execution of a sample processor STROBE instruction is not strictly defined as a register transfer. Briefly explain the conditions under which STROBE *would* execute a register transfer. Name the participating source and destination registers.

6.7   Make the simplest changes to the network in Fig. 6.9 to convert a SUBtract instruction into an unconditional SKIP instruction.

6.8   In Fig. 6.9, if the START button is released while a pulse from the pulse generator is occurring, how would you expect the system to behave?

6.9   Assuming that the opcode for LOADI remains 0, reassign opcodes to the LOAD, ADD, and SUB instructions (in Table 6.1) to simplify the logic that develops the LOAD Y control pulse (in Fig. 6.9). [Ignore the effect of this reassignment on Y's input multiplexer.] Draw the portion of the logic that is modified, appropriately labeling all signals.

6.10   Referring to Table 6.2 and its supporting discussion, briefly explain why the FLAG assertion duration must be greater than the time to fetch and execute *two* instructions.

6.11   A 32-bit floating-point number is subdivided into an eight-bit exponent field (two's complement representation, including exponent sign), a 23-bit mantissa (a magnitude value in the form of a fraction — i.e., radix point assumed positioned on its left), and a one-bit sign field (the sign of the number). If the number is always normalized (that is, its mantissa field contains no leading zeroes), specify the decimal range of representable numbers. What are the smallest, nonzero representable magnitudes (in decimal)?

6.12   An arbitrary picture is drawn as a sequence of many short line segments, each of which begins where the previous one ends. A specific segment has eight possible directions (each at an angle that is a multiple of 45 degrees) and sixteen possible lengths. It may be visible or invisible. Define a data format that represents a sequence of line segments in a 32-bit word.

6.13   Define an instruction that provides the logical equivalent of a HALT but that does not actually stop the machine.

6.14   It is necessary to insert an instruction into a program whose first instruction resides at memory location zero. All instructions that are positioned *after* the insertion must be moved to the next higher word. What other alterations to the program are necessary?

6.15   As an alternative to altering the contents of all memory locations after an insertion (Problem 6.14), it is desired to achieve the same effect (as if one or more instructions *were* inserted in line) by altering only *one* of the original program's instructions. All of the inserted· instructions (known as a "patch") are located, in sequence, in an unused memory area, external to the program. Briefly explain how this may be done. Use a sketch to clarify your solution.

6.16   The hypothetical program shown in Table P6.16 begins execution at location zero. Using the notation employed at the bottom of Fig. 6.14, define the stack contents after each instruction execution. Specify also the PC value at each point.

Table P6.16

Memory location	Instruction that is its contents
0	CALL 2
1	HALT
2	CALL 4
3	RETURN
4	CALL 7
5	CALL 8
6	RETURN
7	RETURN
8	CALL 10
9	RETURN
10	RETURN

6.17 Briefly explain why a processor register is more accessible than is a memory register.

6.18 Name all of the signals in Fig. 6.9 that you would class as control "levels." (All of the remaining control signals must be control pulses.)

6.19 A machine has the two-address instruction format shown in Fig. P6.19. Its MOVE instruction executes by copying the n-word area beginning at address A into the n-word area beginning at address B. Here n is the contents of the AUX field. Using the notation introduced in Fig. 5.11(b), write down a register-transfer sequence that constitutes execution of the MOVE. (You may postulate any processor registers needed for this process.)

OPCODE	ADDRESS A	ADDRESS B	AUX

Figure P6.19

6.20 For each of the register transfers given below, briefly specify conditions under which it would be executed. (Example of an answer: "During execution of a MULTIPLY instruction.")

a) $PC \leftarrow PC + 1$ b) $PC \leftarrow IR[11:0]$ c) $M(SP) \leftarrow PC$

d) $SP \leftarrow SP + 1$ e) $ACC \leftarrow M(IR[11:0])$ f) $M(SP) \leftarrow ACC$

g) $ACC \leftarrow M(SP)$.

(*Note*: ACC is a processor register known as the "accumulator.")

6.21   The execution time of an instruction may depend on a field (other than the opcode) *in* the instruction or on the data manipulated *by* the instruction. Give an example supporting each variation in this statement.

6.22   A DECREMENT and JUMP instruction executes by decrementing a processor register C and executing a jump, relative to the PC value, if the resulting C contents are not zero. The relative jump employs an instruction address field A, which is interpreted as a signed, two's complement number. Define the execution of this instruction in register-transfer notation and briefly explain one of its uses in a program.

6.23   The address field of a one-address instruction occupies IR[11:0]. Bit IR12 is an *indirect* bit. If it is 1, the address in the instruction is the address *of* an address. Define a register-transfer sequence, positioned between the fetch of the instruction and its execution, which examines the indirect bit and responds properly if it is set. (You may assume that any portion of IR may be loaded, from any convenient source, without disturbing the rest of the register.)

6.24   Your answer to Problem 6.23 provides for one level of indirect addressing. Make the simplest modifications to it to implement *multiple* levels of indirect addressing, in which the memory word obtained via indirect addressing specifies whether or not the address it contains is *itself* the address of still another address.

6.25   The machine described in Problems 6.23 and 6.24 is not equipped with a stack. Instead of a CALL, its instruction set includes a SAVE PC and BRANCH instruction, which executes as follows:

$$M(IR[11:0]) \leftarrow PC; \quad PC \leftarrow IR[11:0] + 1.$$

That is, the return address is saved in memory in the word *preceding* the subroutine's entry point. The machine does not have a RETURN instruction. Define an instruction whose execution will be equivalent to that of a RETURN.

6.26   A one-address machine executes a LOAD D instruction, whose format includes an addressing mode field and an address field, whose value happens to be 5. Memory locations

$$5, 10, 15, 20, 25, \text{ and } 30$$

contain, respectively, the values

$$15, 25, 30, 40, 10, \text{ and } 25.$$

A processor register R, whose contents is 20, is implicitly referenced by all addressing modes. Specify the final contents of the D register, after execution of the instruction, for each of the following addressing modes:

Immediate,   Direct,   Indirect,
Register,   Register Indirect,
Indexed and Indexed-Indirect   (indexing first).

(For convenience, all values are expressed in decimal.)

6.27 Define a format for the SHIFT MODE field in Fig. 6.21(h), which permits shift distances of 1, 2, or 4 bits, in either direction, with shift-in bits being either zero or the values shifted off the other end.

6.28 Define a 16-bit instruction format that permits commands containing either zero, one, two, or three four-bit addresses. The instruction set should include (approximately) as many $i + 1$-address instructions as there are i-address instructions ($i = 0$ to 2).

7

Control
Logic

7.1 SAMPLE PROCESSOR II

To study the alternative approaches to the implementation of control logic, we will use a single, hypothetical processor as a design vehicle. Its organization resembles that of several realistic machines. It provides a useful instruction repertoire and permits a rich set of addressing modes. A few aspects of its internal organization have been intentionally simplified to keep its control logic structure tractable.

A proper understanding of such a nontrivial machine requires attention to a great many details, most of which are presented here. They should be studied slowly and carefully.

The registers and data processing elements of our sample processor are interconnected via a single, bidirectional DATA BUS, as indicated in Fig, 7.1. The system contains a 16-register scratchpad memory m plus four additional registers: IR (the Instruction Register), X and Y (operand registers), and MAR (the "Memory Address Register"). All registers and data paths are 16 bits wide. The Program Counter (PC) and the Stack Pointer (SP) are both contained within the scratchpad. The main memory (M) interface is shown on

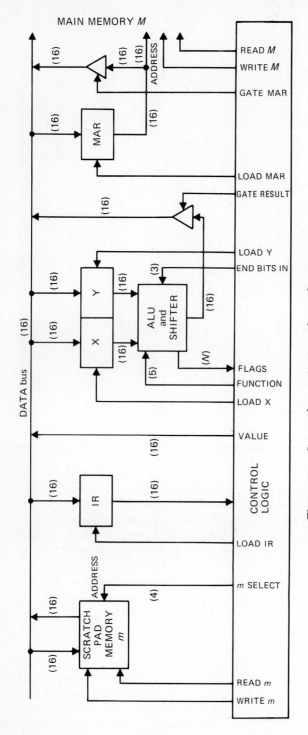

Figure 7.1 Internal organization of sample processor

the right side of the diagram. Note that its address port width happens to match that of its data ports. Observe also that each data path *to* the data bus includes an explicit or implicit tri-state gate bank, enabled by a GATE or READ control signal. Similarly, each path *from* the bus terminates in a destination device having a LOAD or WRITE control input.

Every register transfer in the system will use the central data bus as the path between source and destination registers. The simplicity of this organization leads to its popularity. However, it does limit the speed of the system by permitting only one transfer to be executed at a time. Processors that have two or more common transfer paths, permitting simultaneous or *parallel* transfers, generally operate at a higher speed.

Each general register in the scratchpad memory may be employed to store either data or an address. Thus, many of the possible sources for the main memory address value are not available simultaneously. For this reason, an address multiplexer at the main memory address port is no longer adequate, and a register (MAR) must be employed to hold the current main memory address. Note that a path is also provided from MAR back to the bus, to permit values stored in it to be transferred back into the system.

The 16-bit-wide, all-combinational ALU/SHIFTER contains an arithmetic logic unit (resembling the one derived in Section 2.9) followed by a shifter (resembling the one derived in Section 2.6). These devices share a composite five-bit-wide input FUNCTION code. Thus, the ALU/SHIFTER element performs any one of 32 (2^5) possible data operations and, for simplicity, we assume that a single input bit, FUNCTION4, selects between a set of 16 possible *unary* operations and a set of 16 possible *binary* operations. We further assume that all unary functions use X as the input argument and *ignore* Y. The specific function within a class is chosen by the four-bit code FUNCTION[3:0]. The unary functions include INCREMENT, DECREMENT, all SHIFTs and ROTATEs, COMPLEMENT, CLEAR, and NEGATE. The binary functions include ADDs, SUBTRACTs, AND, OR, EXCLUSIVE OR, PASS X, PASS Y, and possibly combinational MULTIPLY and DIVIDE. Since our objective is the study of alternative control logic implementations, we will ignore the specific operational details connected with each of these functions. Most are implicitly quite clear. We will also ignore the specific function codes assigned to each of them.

The ALU/SHIFTER's delay, for any of its operations, is assumed sufficiently small, compared to the duration of one CPU control cycle, to permit a transfer that changes X or Y, in one cycle, to be immediately followed by a transfer, using a valid ALU/SHIFTER result, in the *next* cycle. In addition to its 16-bit output result, the ALU/SHIFTER delivers an arbitrary number (N) of output FLAG signals. These include CARRY and BORROW OUT, shifted-off bits, and OVERFLOW, SIGN, and RESULT ZERO indicators. These flags are appropriately stored in flip-flops, not shown in the diagram, which may be tested by conditional BRANCH instructions. The three END BITS IN are derived from the stored FLAGS, to permit SHIFTs that shift in previously shifted-off bits, and to allow ADD WITH CARRY or SUBTRACT WITH BORROW operations. The ALU/SHIFTER ignores the end input signals for all functions not requiring their use.

The rest of the processor is contained within the element, labeled as CONTROL LOGIC, whose design is of primary interest here. This device receives the IR contents as an input code and orchestrates the sequencing of operations throughout the system. In addition to controlling the gating of data to the data bus and the loading of data from it, the control element supplies the four-bit mSELECT scratchpad address, a special 16-bit operand VALUE to the bus, when required, and the FUNCTION and END BITS IN codes to the ALU/SHIFTER. In order to further discuss the internal structure of this element, we must first examine the processor's instruction set and permissible addressing modes.

As indicated in Fig. 7.2, four instruction classes are permitted. While most instructions are 16 bits long, some addressing modes will permit the fetch of one additional 16-bit word (as discussed further below). The upper two instruction bits distinguish between the first three instruction classes, and the fourth class may be considered as a special case of the third.

An upper instruction bit of "1" signifies a CALL instruction. Its 16-bit destination address is formed by concatenating the value in a special, program-controlled flip-flop, called H (for "memory HALF"), to the 15-bit AD-DRESS field in the instruction. (Special control instructions, called SET H and RESET H, are available in the repertoire to give the programmer control over the value of H.) In programs that make profuse use of the CALL function, this format is efficient because it consumes the least instruction space to specify an arbitrary location in memory. It is designed by assuming that successive CALL destinations will normally *remain* in one half of the memory or the other, in which case SET H and RESET H instructions need to be evoked rarely.

When the upper instruction bit is "0", the next bit, IR14, distinguishes between two operation classes. A "1" signifies a conditional RELATIVE BRANCH instruction, whose typical operation was explained earlier in Chapter 6. The four-bit CONDITION SELECT field designates one of 16 conditions (for example, whether or not a CARRY was generated on the last ALU operation) to be tested. If the designated condition is found FALSE, no branch occurs and the next consecutive instruction is fetched. If the designated condition is found TRUE, the OFFSET, which is in two's complement

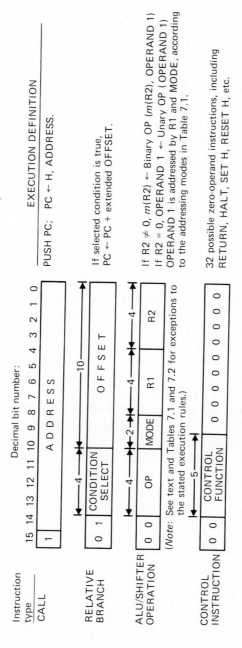

Figure 7.2 Sample processor instruction formats and execution definitions

form, is added to the PC value to define the branch destination. Using a 10-bit OFFSET field, this permits jumps to any destination within −512 to +511 of the current PC value.

We will also ignore the exact assignment of conditions to CONDITION SELECT codes. You may assume that most conditions are derived directly from FLAG indicators or are appropriate logical combinations of them. However, any condition that is represented by a digital signal may be designated. For example, several of the CONDITION SELECT codes may be assigned to test the values of *external* input signals. (Recall the JUMPFL instruction in the repertoire of the sample processor of Section 6.2.)

When IR[15:14] = 0, an operation employing the ALU/SHIFTER is normally called for. The lower 14 bits of the instruction are given a new interpretation. The four-bit R1 and R2 fields contain processor register numbers. The two-bit MODE field selects an addressing mode, and the four-bit OP field selects an ALU/SHIFTER operation.

The MODE bits are used, in conjunction with the R1 value, to select one operand. Typically, $m(R1)$, the contents of the scratchpad register designated by R1 (possibly combined with an additional fetched word), is employed to develop an effective operand address. However, the case R1 = 0 is interpreted as meaning that *no* R1 scratchpad register is involved. This permits the extra word fetched to be itself used unmodified—for example, as a direct address or as an immediate data value. Let us designate as OPERAND1 the argument selected by the MODE and R1 values, regardless of the addressing mode employed.

OPERAND2 is $m(R2)$, the contents of the scratchpad register selected by R2. No special addressing modes are employed to derive OPERAND2. The OP field selects one of the 16 possible *binary* ALU operations, using OPERAND1 and OPERAND2 as arguments, and the results are placed *back* into the R2 scratchpad register, replacing the old OPERAND2. Thus, for most arbitrary R1 and R2 values (including R1 = 0), the instruction's execution may be described by:

$$m(R2) \leftarrow OP(m(R2), OPERAND1),$$

where OP is one of the *binary* ALU operations. Thus, any of the scratchpad registers may act as an "accumulator."

The case R2 = 0 has a special interpretation, similar to that for R1 = 0. It means that *no* R2 scratchpad register is employed, which, in turn, means that no OPERAND2 exists. Consequently, the case R2 = 0 is used to designate a unary operation (as selected by the same OP field) on OPERAND1 alone. In this case, the destination for the result is chosen to be the *same* as the source of the operand, and the instruction's execution, for R2 = 0, may be described by:

$$\text{OPERAND1} \leftarrow \text{OP(OPERAND1)},$$

where OP is one of the *unary* ALU/SHIFTER operations.

The case when both R1 and R2 are zero is normally not particularly special. It is interpreted, using the rules specified above, as a *unary* operation on an operand whose address derivation does *not* involve a scratchpad register. However, as we will verify later when we examine the addressing modes in Table 7.1, the use of two of the addressing modes (those whose lower MODE bit is "0") leads to some illogical consequences—for example, the attempt to replace an immediate operand with the result of a unary operation on its value. For this reason, as Fig. 7.2 indicates, the special case when IR[15:14] = IR[8:0] = 0 is *not* construed as an ALU/SHIFTER operation. Rather, it is interpreted as a CONTROL instruction, requiring no operands. Its opcode is the five-bit field IR[13:9], which permits a maximum of 32 different such operations. Again, we will ignore the detailed assignment of control or "zero-operand" functions to opcodes. Certainly, the list of such instructions will include RETURN, HALT, SET H, RESET H, and NO-OP.

All of the possible addressing modes that may be employed to derive OPERAND1 are listed in Table 7.1. Here "W" represents the *second* instruction word, for those instructions that require it. The table indicates that ALU/SHIFTER instructions that have IR8 = 1 or R1 = MODE = 0 require an *extra* memory access to fetch W. Note that, when R1 is not zero, $m(R1)$ is involved in the derivation of OPERAND1. Specifically, it may be the oper-

Table 7.1 Sample Processor Addressing Modes

R1 = 0?	IR9	IR8	OPERAND1	Addressing Mode	Comments
YES *	0	0	W	IMMEDIATE	*Binary* OP only
YES	0	1	M(W)	DIRECT	
YES *	1	0	M(m(R2))	REGISTER-INDIRECT with AUTO-ADVANCE	*Unary* OP only $m(R2) \leftarrow m(R2) + 1$
YES	1	1	M(M(W))	INDIRECT	
NO	0	0	m(R1)	REGISTER	
NO	0	1	M(m(R1) + W)	INDEXED	
NO	1	0	M(m(R1))	REGISTER-INDIRECT	
NO	1	1	M(M(m(R1) + W))	INDEXED-INDIRECT	

Notes: W = The extra 16-bit word, following the operation word.
      m(R) = The scratchpad memory register addressed by R.
      M(Expr) = The main-memory register addressed by Expr.
      MODE = IR [9:8].
      * = R2 may not also be zero.

and *itself* (register addressing), the address of the operand (register-indirect addressing), or an index value added to W to form either the address of the operand (indexed addressing) or the address of the address of the operand (indexed-indirect addressing). On the other hand, when R1 is zero, $m(R1)$ is not involved in the derivation of OPERAND1. In two of these cases, W is used as the direct operand address (direct addressing) or as the address of the operand address (indirect addressing). In all of these circumstances (those not marked with an * in Table 7.1), the value of R2 determines whether OPERAND1 participates in a unary or in a binary operation, as explained earlier.

Two special cases arise when MODE = IR[9:8] = 0 or 2, while R1 = 0. In the first case (MODE = 0), W is not an address value. Rather, it is the operand *itself*, an immediate data value. This case is special because the operand is a *constant*, known to the programmer. A *unary* data operation on such an operand is excluded for two reasons. First, its result could have been specified to begin with. Second, a write of the result back into the *program area* should not be attempted. Thus, the immediate "addressing mode" is restricted to *binary* operations only (those for which R2 is *not* zero.)

The second special case (MODE = 2) was devised to demonstrate the implementation of an "auto-advance" addressing facility, in which an address value in a register is incremented after the operand to which it points is accessed. Since R1 is already known to be zero, $m(R2)$ is used as the pointer (in this case only) and the operation is constrained to be *unary*, for all values of R2, because only one operand is involved. Again, the case R2 = 0, implying that no R2 register is used, is considered an exception.

Both of the exceptions stated above are indicated in Table 7.1 with the * symbol. The * symbol indicates that the corresponding table entry applies only if R2 is *not* zero. If R2 is zero, then the condition IR15 = IR14 = IR8 = R1 = R2 = 0 exists, which was the code assigned earlier to the class of CONTROL instructions. In other words, a reinterpretation of an ALU/SHIFTER command as a *control* instruction occurs either when a unary operation on an immediate operand is called for or when the auto-advance addressing mode is specified, with R2 = 0.

This information is summarized, from a different point of view, in Table 7.2. The notation, $Zi = 1$ when $Ri = 0$ and $Zi = 0$ when $Ri \neq 0$, is used (i.e., Z stands for "zero"). All possible Z1, Z2, and MODE value combinations are covered. For each, a square in the map specifies the type of ALU/SHIFTER operation called for and the addressing mode that is employed to access OPERAND1. Note the special cases, just explained, corresponding to Z1 = 1 and MODE = 0 or 2.

The discussion above leads us to conclude that $m(0)$, the lowest-numbered processor register, is the only scratchpad register that cannot be direct-

Table 7.2 Operation Types and Applicable OPERAND1 Addressing Modes, for All Combinations of MODE and Z2 Z1 Values

		00	01	11	10
Z2	**Z1**				
0	0	Binary. Register.	Binary. Indexed.	Binary. Indexed-Indirect.	Binary. Register-Indirect.
0	1	Binary. Immediate.	Binary. Direct.	Binary. Indirect.	Unary. Register-Indirect. with Auto-Increment.
1	1	CONTROL INSTRUCTION	Unary. Direct.	Unary. Indirect.	CONTROL INSTRUCTION
1	0	Unary. Register.	Unary. Indexed.	Unary. Indexed-Indirect.	Unary. Register-Indirect.

MODE = IR[9:8] (column header spanning 00, 01, 11, 10)

Note: Z1 = 1 when R1 = 0, and Z2 = 1 when R2 = 0.

ly accessed by the programmer. (Similarly, processor registers X, Y, and MAR are not explicitly addressable.) Our sample processor will use $m(0)$ as the Program Counter. Although there is nothing to prevent a designer from giving the programmer free access to PC as if it were a "normal" general register, most processor organizations continue to permit the programmer to change PC only indirectly, via transfer-of-control instructions.

The CALL instruction's execution includes a PUSH of the old PC value. Assuming that the stack resides in a main memory area, one processor register must be employed as a Stack Pointer. We will choose to make it one of the scratchpad registers, specifically, $m(1)$. Thus, all of the programmer-accessible general registers, $m(1)$ through $m(15)$, have equal standing, except one; $m(1)$ is special because its value is *implicitly* modified when instructions such as CALL and RETURN execute.

To see how this processor's elementary instruction set compares with those of other machines, let us examine the list of typical instruction types given in Table 6.3, to determine which operations are not directly available. First, note that the binary ALU/SHIFTER operation, whose execution merely *passes* OPERAND1, may be renamed as LOAD. Its execution, which is a particular case of the general binary operation, is described by the expression:

$$m(R2) \leftarrow \text{OPERAND1}.$$

Similarly, the binary ALU/SHIFTER operation, whose execution merely passes $m(R2)$, may be made equivalent to a STORE, if the result value is transferred to the *unary* destination, instead of to the customary binary destination. As we will soon see, this special case is easily implemented. Thus, STORE will be the one "binary" operation that will not conform exactly to the register-transfer rule stated earlier.

MOVE, EXCHANGE, SAVE, and RESTORE must be programmed as appropriate LOAD and STORE instruction sequences. Similarly, using the register-indirect addressing mode with R1 = 1, a LOAD (or STORE), accompanied by a suitable INCREMENT or DECREMENT of $m(1)$, is equivalent to a POP (or PUSH).

INPUT and OUTPUT operations are assumed implemented using "memory-mapped" I/O devices. A typical memory-mapped I/O device, explained further in Chapter 8, behaves as if it were a single main-memory register. It responds to a specific address and acts either as a data source or as a data destination. The use of such devices is convenient because INPUT and OUTPUT operations may then be considered as special cases of normal main memory accesses.

With the exception of floating-point and bit-addressing operations, most of the other unary and binary arithmetic and logical functions listed in Table 6.3 are available from a typical ALU/SHIFTER element. Functions such as SEARCH must be programmed. This is true for most processors. While a COMPARE may be mechanized as a special SUBTRACT of one comparand from the other, in which storage of the result is *inhibited*, we choose to omit this variation, for simplicity. Thus, a COMPARE must be programmed as a SUBTRACT followed by a restoration of the argument that is altered. The new FLAG values will reflect the comparison results.

All of the listed transfers of control are available. A SKIP is a special case of a RELATIVE BRANCH. Note that, while a JUMP to *any* arbitrary destination (which is a relatively rare operation) is not directly available, it is easily implemented using a CALL, if the CALL destination *begins* with code that pops the return address off the stack. Finally, since 32 possible control instructions are available, all of those listed in Table 6.3 may be implemented.

Thus, while our sample processor is weak in data-movement facilities, it appears to offer a reasonable set of operations in the other areas.

We proceed by defining, in Fig. 7.3, the few additional logic structures, not shown in Fig. 7.1, that have been implied by the discussions above. They complete the definition of the interface that the control logic system must control.

The network shown in Fig. 7.3 is positioned at the interface between the data network under control (Fig. 7.1) and the control network that regulates it. For this reason, it may be considered as part of *either* system. Note that the input ports at the top of the diagram (FLAGS and IR) and the output ports

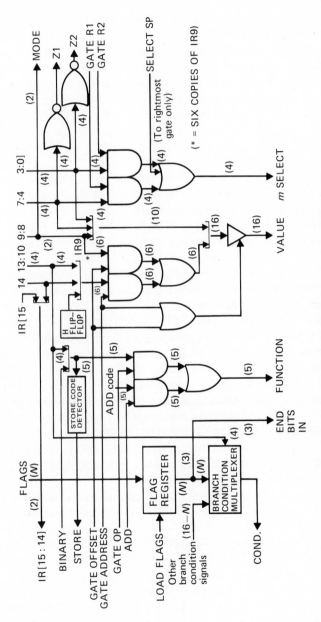

Figure 7.3 Additional logic at the control element's interface

at the bottom of the diagram (END BITS IN, FUNCTION, VALUE, and mSELECT) are the same as those of the control logic element in Fig. 7.1. Thus, this network augments that shown earlier, by explicitly revealing logic that was previously hidden behind the control logic element's interface.

All of the signals on the left and right sides of the diagram are control signals, which will be taken into account when we design the control element. Most of them have been implied by previous descriptions of the sample processor. Observe that the IR input port is subdivided into convenient subports for its fields. Note also that each of the FUNCTION, VALUE, and mSELECT output codes is derived from an AND-OR cluster, which is effectively a multiplexer with a missing decoder. Each data path through it has its own enable signal.

On the right side of the diagram, two four-input NOR gates develop the signals Z1 and Z2, defined earlier. The signals GATE R1, GATE R2, and SELECT SP are mutually exclusive (no more than one asserted at a time). GATE R1 causes mSELECT = R1. GATE R2 causes mSELECT = R2. SELECT SP is an extra input only to the *rightmost* gate in the four-OR-gate bank. Its assertion therefore causes mSELECT = 1, which addresses the Stack Pointer. Finally, in the *absence* of any of these assertions, mSELECT = 0. This means that the Program Counter is addressed whenever *none* of the other scratchpad registers is selected.

The signals GATE OFFSET and GATE ADDRESS are similarly mutually exclusive. The assertion of either opens the tri-state gate bank that permits the VALUE output port to carry a 16-bit value to the data bus. The rightmost 10-bit VALUE field is always IR[9:0]. When GATE OFFSET is asserted, each of the leftmost six VALUE bits is a copy of IR9, in which case, the two's complement OFFSET field, with *sign bit extended*, is directed to the data bus. This EXTENDED OFFSET is a 16-bit number, ranging in value between −512 and +511 (decimal). When GATE ADDRESS is asserted, the leftmost six-bit VALUE field is H concatenated with IR[14:10]. Under these conditions, H,ADDRESS is gated to the data bus. For simplicity, the logic that controls the state of the H flip-flop is not shown.

The data bus also has a "default" or quiescent value, which it assumes when *no* signals are gated to it. We will find it convenient to assume that this value is *zero*.

The mutually exclusive signals GATE OP and ADD similarly control the value of the five-bit FUNCTION code. Assertion of ADD causes the code for ADD (which has not yet been defined) to appear at the FUNCTION output port. Assertion of GATE OP causes a combination of the signal BINARY and the four-bit OP field (in the instruction) to appear at the FUNCTION port. BINARY is the signal that distinguishes between unary and binary ALU/SHIFTER operations. It is essentially $\overline{Z2}$ (slightly modified, as explained later). For convenience, we also assume that a FUNCTION code of zero, which arises when *neither* GATE OP nor ADD is asserted, corresponds to the unary INCREMENT function. That is, INCREMENT is the "default" ALU/SHIFTER function. It is in effect when no others are selected. Both ADD and INCREMENT are needed to mechanize necessary processor operations.

Assertion of the signal LOAD FLAGS causes the FLAG register to load the N FLAG signals from the ALU/SHIFTER. Three of these saved bits (a CARRY/BORROW and two shift-in bits) are directed *back* to the ALU/SHIFTER, as END BITS IN, to be used in those operations that require them. (They are ignored by those operations that don't employ them.) The saved FLAG bits are also directed, along with a set of unspecified signals, labeled as OTHER BRANCH CONDITION SIGNALS, to a 16-to-1 multiplexer, which uses the CONDITION SELECT code (IR[13:10]) to select one of them. The selected condition signal is renamed as COND. It is used to decide whether or not to take a relative branch.

The STORE signal is asserted when the special binary ALU function called STORE is selected. Its use was explained earlier. (A specific five-bit code has not been assigned to the STORE operation.) The two pairs of IR signals, IR[15:14] and MODE = IR[9:8], are needed in the controller, to distinguish between the different instruction classes and between the various addressing modes.

If the diagrams in Figs. 7.1 and 7.3 are combined, the interface that the control element must meet is defined. It contains all of those input control signals, having as yet undefined sources, and all those output "status" signals having as yet undefined destinations. These signals, along with their meanings, are listed in Table 7.3. Each has been discussed earlier. The control element, whose design is the subject of this chapter, has eight input signals, representing the current state or "status" of the processor under control, and 19 output signals, which either gate data to the data bus, cause data on the bus to be loaded, or gate appropriate codes to control input ports.

Table 7.4 is useful for two reasons. First, it contains several shorthand symbols for signals that we will find useful in subsequent discussions. Second, it contains some logical combinations of the nine status signals mentioned above, which may be used to direct the sequencing within the controller. The gates that develop these signals are part of the control element. We will assume their existence without specifically drawing the logic diagram (consisting almost exclusively of appropriate AND gates).

In the table P stands for any one of the Clock Pulses generated by the system's central timing source; C (for Call) is merely short for IR15; B (for Branch) is asserted on a relative branch instruction that should be *taken*; A is asserted on any ALU/SHIFTER operation. Note that A excludes the logical condition that identifies the set of *control* instructions. Each of the Mi signals is one of the outputs of a 2-to-4 decoder whose input is the MODE code.

A review of Table 7.1 will verify that a second 16-bit word W must be

Table 7.3 Sample Processor's Control Interface

I. Control signals TO processor under control:

Signal Name	Action Caused on Assertion

A. Load destination from Data Bus—Control Pulses:

WRITE m	m(R) ← BUS
LOAD IR	IR ← BUS
LOAD X	X ← BUS
LOAD Y	Y ← BUS
LOAD MAR	MAR ← BUS
WRITE M	M(MAR) ← BUS
LOAD FLAGS	FLAG Register ← ALU/SHIFTER FLAGS

B. Gate source to Data Bus—Control Levels:

READ m	BUS ← m(R)
GATE OFFSET	BUS ← EXTENDED OFFSET
GATE ADDRESS	BUS ← H,ADDRESS
GATE RESULT	BUS ← ALU/SHIFTER RESULT
GATE MAR	BUS ← MAR
READ M	BUS ← M(MAR)

C. Gate source to mSELECT or FUNCTION port—Control Levels:

GATE R1	mSELECT = R1
GATE R2	mSELECT = R2
SELECT SP	mSELECT = 1 [m(1) = Stack Pointer]

[Note: Default mSELECT = 0. m(0) = Program Counter.]

GATE OP	FUNCTION = Binary or Unary OP. (OP = IR[13:10])
ADD	FUNCTION = ADD

[Note: Default FUNCTION = 0, selecting Increment.]

D. Other Control Signals:

BINARY	Selects binary ALU/SHIFTER operation.

II. Status signals FROM processor under control:

Signal Name	Meaning
IR[15:14]	Distinguishes major instruction classes.
MODE = IR[9:8]	Selects OPERAND1 addressing mode.
Z1	Asserted when R1 = 0.
Z2	Asserted when R2 = 0.
COND	Represents the selected BRANCH condition. 1 = TRUE (Take the branch). 0 = FALSE.
STORE	Asserted on STORE binary ALU/SHIFTER OP.

Table 7.4 Additional Control Signals Useful in Directing the Flow in a "Hard-wired" Controller

Name	Logic Function	Meaning When Asserted
P		Continuous train of Clock Pulses.
C	IR15	CALL instruction.
B	$\overline{IR15} \cdot IR14 \cdot COND$	Take the relative BRANCH.
*	$\overline{IR15} \cdot IR14 \cdot \overline{COND}$	Branch condition is FALSE.
A	$\overline{IR15} \cdot \overline{IR14}(Z1 + \overline{Z2} + IR8)$	ALU/SHIFTER Operation.
*	$\overline{IR15} \cdot \overline{IR14}(Z1 Z2 \overline{IR8})$	Control Instruction.
M3	$IR9\overline{IR8}$	Indirect Addressing Condition.
M2	$IR9\overline{IR8}$	
M0	$\overline{IR9}IR8$	
W	$IR8 + Z1M0$	Fetch the *second* instruction word.
S	$Z1M2$	The "STEPPING" or Auto-Increment Mode.
U	$Z2M0$	Unary operation on Scratchpad Operand.
BINARY	$\overline{Z2} \cdot \overline{S}$	Selects the binary ALU/SHIFTER OP.

*No name has been assigned to this logical condition.

Note: All signal names listed below A are useful only when A = 1.

fetched whenever the corresponding control signal W, in Table 7.4, is asserted. (The two related uses for the same symbol W will not conflict.) The last three entries in Table 7.4 are best explained with reference to Table 7.2. Assuming that an ALU/SHIFTER instruction has *already* been identified, the two CONTROL INSTRUCTION map entries cannot occur. Therefore, they may be treated as "don't care" combinations. Under these conditions, assertion of the signal S identifies the special, auto-increment addressing mode, explained earlier, in which a unary operation on $M(m(R2))$ is executed. Similarly, the signal U is employed to identify a Unary operation on a register operand. Its application will become clear momentarily. Finally, S is also used to define the accurate version of the control signal BINARY, as consisting of all those $Z2 = 0$ cases *excluding* the one corresponding to $S = 1$.

We are now in a position to consider the micro-operation flow chart which, if implemented, will mechanize the processor that has been defined above. It is shown in Fig. 7.4. Each box in it specifies a single register transfer. You should be able to visualize which of the control signals, listed in Table 7.3, should be asserted, in order to evoke each transfer. The diamond-shaped symbols identify CONDITIONALs, originally defined in Section 6.4. Each has two or more exit paths, each labeled with a logical combination of the status signals which, if true, will cause that path to be taken. The label on the left side of each box is used to uniquely identify it. We will begin by ignoring it.

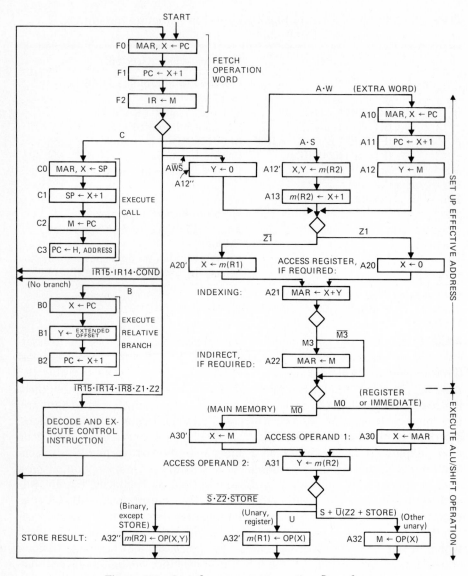

Figure 7.4   Sample processor operation flow chart

Note 1: When STORE=1, transfer A32 should read M ← OP (Y), or more simply M ← Y, because the STORE condition corresponds to the dummy binary ALU operation which merely *passes* Y.)

Note 2: It is *implicit* that transfers A32, A32′ and A32″ are accompanied by the assertion of the LOAD FLAGS control pulse.

You are reminded of the notation: PC = $m(0)$, SP = $m(1)$, and M = M(MAR), which was defined earlier.

The top three transfers implement the FETCH of the operation word. The EXECUTION register-transfer sequences on the left side of the diagram implement all instructions excluding ALU/SHIFTER operations. Note that the CALL's implementation assumes that the stack in main memory grows toward *higher* addresses and that SP points to the first *available* stack register. Since all control instructions are presently undefined, a special box has been allocated for their composite flow chart. For simplicity, its internal structure will be ignored.

The right side of the diagram, entered by one of three paths, all requiring $A = 1$, implements the execution of all ALU/SHIFTER instructions. It includes the application of the proper addressing mode. Note that the $W = 1$ condition causes the fetch of the *second* instruction word, incrementing PC past it in the process. When the Z1 conditional is reached, Y will contain either this extra word, or, if $S = 1$, the old auto-increment pointer value (which has already been advanced), or zero, for all other conditions. The Z1 value then determines whether $m(R1)$ or zero is deposited in X. Therefore, when the M3 conditional is reached, the value in MAR is either W (for the immediate, direct, and indirect modes), $m(R1)$ (for the register and register-indirect modes), $m(R1) + W$ (for all indexed modes), or $m(R2)$ for the one special auto-increment mode.

The condition M3 is now used to determine whether or not the contents of MAR is replaced by the contents of the main memory register that it *points* to. Thus, when the M0 conditional is reached, MAR contains either the final, effective OPERAND1 main-memory address or, for M0 = 1 (which denotes the immediate and register addressing modes), OPERAND1 *itself*. Consequently, when the last conditional is reached, X contains OPERAND1 and Y contains $m(R2)$, *whether or not* a binary operation is called for.

At this point, the control signal BINARY and the four OP bits, IR[13:10], applied to the ALU/SHIFTER's FUNCTION port, determine the proper unary or binary data operation. In the former case, register Y is merely ignored. It remains necessary only to direct the RESULT of this data operation to the proper destination.† For all binary operations, except STORE (explained earlier), the result is directed to $m(R2)$, the normal binary destination. For all unary operations, except that in which OPERAND1 came directly from a scratchpad register, the result *replaces* the old OPERAND1 value

---

†While it is not explicitly shown in Fig. 7.4, it is also necessary to assert the LOAD FLAGS control signal at this point—so that the FLAG bits will reflect the properties of the new ALU/SHIFTER result. (We shall ignore the issue of *inhibiting* this signal's assertion if the ALU/SHIFTER is being used merely to pass data unmodified.)

in main memory. The STORE operation, in which the ALU/SHIFTER merely passes $m(R2)$, is included in this set. Finally, when $U = 1$, the result is directed to $m(R1)$, which is the source of OPERAND1 in the unary, register-addressing case.

Note that all executions terminate with a return to the FETCH sequence.

Given all of the previous descriptions of this sample processor, you should be able to trace through the various paths in the flow chart in Fig. 7.4 and *visualize the machine in operation*, even though specific ALU/SHIFTER FUNCTION codes and CONTROL INSTRUCTION opcodes have not been assigned. If you can, you are ready to proceed. We have now set the stage for all of the subsequent discussions in this chapter. They will be concerned with alternative approaches to the design of a control unit, whose interface contains all of the signals enumerated in Table 7.3. This control unit must develop the proper pattern of control signals to *induce* the behavior described in the flow chart in Fig. 7.4.

7.2 ONE-ASSERTED CONTROL

A control network has as many *states* as there are unique, distinguishable situations that may arise in the processor it regulates. Associated with each control state is a specific register transfer that the control network causes the processor to execute whenever that state is assumed. (More than one register transfer may correspond to the same control state, in which case, all of them are evoked simultaneously.)

Corresponding to each state in a "hardwired" control system is a unique ACTIVATE signal, which is asserted whenever that state is assumed. This signal is *directed*, via appropriate *wiring*, to those control points whose assertions will *induce* the required register transfer. For example, Table 7.3 lists 19 input control points for our sample processor. Consider a control state whose corresponding register transfer is Y ← MAR. If its ACTIVATE signal is directed to the GATE MAR and LOAD Y inputs, the proper transfer will be induced whenever that control state is assumed.

Two typical control-signal waveforms are drawn in Fig. 7.5(a). A control cycle corresponds to the time period between successive clock pulses. (Recall the related discussion in Section 4.7.) Associated with each cycle is a new control state. An arbitrary state sequence J, K, L is indicated, and the ACTIVATE K signal is shown asserted only during state K. Figure 7.5(b) shows a connection of this signal to the control points specified above. Under these conditions, whenever control state K occurs, Y ← MAR will be induced.

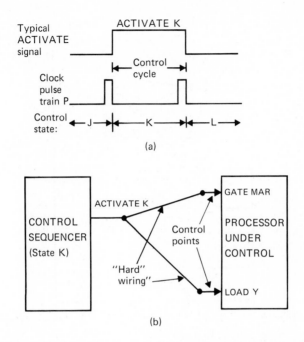

Figure 7.5 A typical ACTIVATE control signal and its use

Normally, a specific control point is activated by *more than one* control state. For example, GATE MAR may be activated also by a second control signal, ACTIVATE M, associated with state M, whose corresponding register transfer is X ← MAR. Consequently, a typical control input is the logical OR of all of the ACTIVATE signals that must induce its assertion. The structure shown in Fig. 7.6 is therefore a more accurate, general description of a hardwired control system.

The control sequencer (which includes a Clock Pulse Generator) is responsible for developing the proper sequence of control states, based on STATUS information which it reads from the network that it is regulating. This state sequence produces a corresponding one-asserted ACTIVATE signal pattern. Each of the input control points of the processor under control receives the logical OR of some subset of all of the ACTIVATE signals. (An ACTIVATE may be directed to any number of control points.) Control *pulse* signals are normally derived from additional gates, enabled only during clock pulse assertions. Thus, what the composite system executes, as it runs, depends not only on the control state sequence but also on the *control wiring pattern* that distributes the ACTIVATE signals among the control points. The

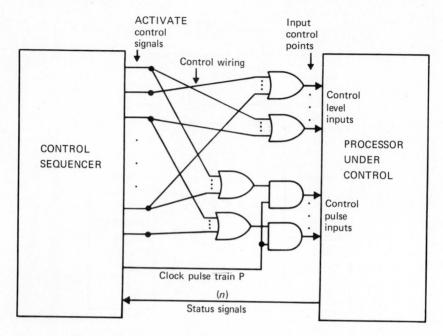

Figure 7.6 General view of a hard-wired control system

system is called "hard-wired" because its behavior is mechanized in a complex, hardware wiring pattern.

Note that each control pulse P always causes *two* events. First, the register transfer, corresponding to the current control state, is activated. Second, the control sequencer is advanced to its *next* control state.

One approach to the design of the control sequencer uses as many identical, edge-triggered D flip-flops as there are control states. All of the flip-flops are clocked simultaneously by the same clock-pulse train P. At any instant in time only *one* flip-flop is set, or activated. Its Q output is the ACTIVATE signal for the control state for which it is set. We will call such an arrangement a "one-asserted" control system.

The logic networks that *interconnect* the flip-flops in a one-asserted control array determine the state sequences that are possible. Figure 7.7 contains some of the most common inter-FF control structures. (The connection of all CLOCK input terminals to the common clock-pulse train P is assumed but not shown; "FF" is used as an abbreviation for "FLIP-FLOP".) Since the control state corresponds to a one-asserted code, only *one* of the control flip-flop D inputs may be "1" whenever the common triggering edge occurs. Assume that this is the case.

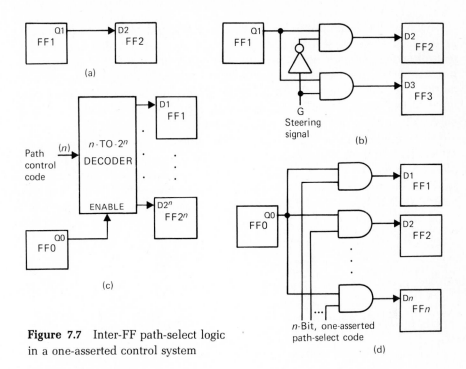

Figure 7.7 Inter-FF path-select logic
in a one-asserted control system

Diagram (a) shows the simplest structure between control elements, in
which FF2 is activated in the cycle that immediately follows that in which
FF1 is set. (Recall that the most elementary form of a shift register uses a
similar arrangement.) Diagram (b) shows a fundamental inter-FF logic structure, in which the next control element activated depends on the value of an
applied control signal G. Assuming FF1 is presently set, the next one activated is either FF2, if $G = 0$, or FF3, if $G = 1$. The interconnecting logic network
is merely a one-bit-wide, two-way *demultiplexer*. It "steers" FF1's activation
in either of two directions, depending on G's value. (Recall that a similar
structure is used in a bidirectional shift register, in which G defines the direction of the shift.)

Diagram (c) shows a logical extension of (b), in which the next FF activated, after FF0, depends on the current value of an n-bit control code. If all
control codes are possible, any one of 2^n activation paths may be selected.
Finally, (d) shows an example in which the applied path-selecting code is
already in one-asserted form. If this is the case, only one inter-FF gate is
required in each possible path. Effectively, only the ENABLE portion of the
decoder in (c) remains. Note that this arrangement is applicable to any number of possible activation paths.

Each of the interconnection networks contained in Fig. 7.7 (except the first) permits one of several *diverging* activation paths to be selected by a control code. Consider now the implementation of a converse structure that permits two or more activation paths, from different FF sources, to *converge* on the same destination FF. An OR gate, which merges together all possible input activations and applies the composite signal to the D input of the destination FF, will accomplish the desired result.

By employing these simple, path-forming logic networks, we may devise arbitrarily complex, one-asserted control structures. Two elementary examples are shown in Fig. 7.8. In part (a), one of two alternative control paths is selected by the value that G has at the instant when FF0 is set. Only one control state exists in the left path, while the right path contains a three-state

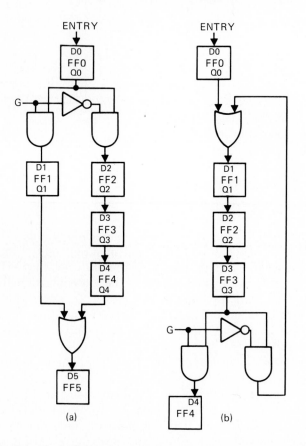

(a)

(b)

Figure 7.8 Typical one-asserted control structures. (The common clock pulse train is assumed but not shown.)

sequence. Note that both paths culminate in the activation of FF5. They merge in the OR gate, as explained earlier. Part (b) shows a three-state sequence configured in the form of a *loop*. Once entered (because Q0 = 1 on a clock assertion), the three-state sequence Q1, Q2, Q3 continues as long as G = 0 at the P edge for which Q3 = 1. As soon as G = 1 under these conditions, FF4 is activated and a loop exit occurs.

A one-asserted control network therefore consists of D flip-flops and two types of interconnecting logic structures. Demultiplexers (or portions of demultiplexers) implement diverging paths, and OR gates implement converging paths. On every clock pulse, a new FF is activated while an old one is deactivated. If you imagine that the single, activated FF is *marked* appropriately, for example with an illuminated pointer, then, every time a P pulse occurs, the light spot moves. The *path* of the light spot, through the network, depends on its connectivity and on the behavior of the path-controlling signals.

Note that an arbitrary one-asserted control network must be *entered* properly (through the activation of one of its input or entry paths). The network remains activated as long as one of its internal FF's is set. It becomes deactivated when the "spot of activation" leaves it, via one of its exit paths.

Observe also that the logic diagram for such a control network resembles a *flow chart*. The flip-flops correspond to boxes in the flow chart, and the paths between them correspond to paths in the flow chart. For example, the networks in Fig. 7.8 resemble common flow chart structures. The fundamental importance of a one-asserted control sequencer is attributable to the fact that *the form of its logic diagram is identical to that of the register-transfer flow chart of the processor it will control*. Consider, for example, the flow chart for our sample processor in Fig. 7.4.

To develop the controller, we assign, to every flow chart box specifying a register transfer, a corresponding control flip-flop. Each diamond-shaped symbol in the flow chart indicates a point at which two or more diverging paths exist. Alternative paths are labeled with *mutually exclusive* conditions (only one may be true at a time). In other words, the set of logic functions labeling competing paths (e.g., Z1 and $\overline{Z1}$) comprise a one-asserted code. Each of these path-labeling functions (for example, $A \cdot W$) is an elementary combination of signals assumed already available, either from the list of eight status signals in Table 7.3 or from the list of additional status signal combinations in Table 7.4. Thus, assuming that every one of the path-labeling functions is *available as a signal*, each of the flow-chart conditionals may be mechanized using one of the inter-FF logic structures shown in (b) and (d) of Fig. 7.7. The most complex of these is the one to implement the conditional located at the exit from the FETCH sequence. Of course, most of the flow paths are implemented using the interconnection shown in Fig. 7.7(a).

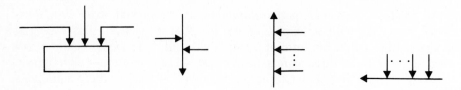

Figure 7.9 Some alternative representations of flow-chart paths that all have the same destination

The flow chart in Fig. 7.4 also contains several points at which two or more paths converge. Typical flow chart representations, for multiple paths that all have the same destination, are shown in Fig. 7.9. As discussed earlier, we mechanize each such converging structure in an OR gate whose output signal is the D input of the destination control flip-flop.

Since the resulting control-sequencer logic diagram directly mirrors the flow chart's structure, the complete network will not be drawn here. (Several parts of it are given as problems at the end of this chapter.) Instead, we will *visualize* its structure merely by examining Fig. 7.4. (The box for the control instructions will be ignored.) Note that the entire system is activated by the assertion of the signal that corresponds to the entry point labeled START. Once activated, one and only one of the boxes is "illuminated" at any instant in time. This spot of activity propagates throughout the network as the processor runs. Observe also that a HALT in such a system is mechanized merely by an exit to a *fictitious* destination, after which the spot of activity disappears (i.e., none of the control flip-flops remains activated).

A one-asserted control sequencer has as many input status signals as are necessary to control all of its *conditional* activation paths. Its outputs are the Q's of all of its flip-flops (each of which is also used internally as the *source* of one or more activation paths). These Q's are the ACTIVATE signals defined earlier. Each must be directed to those control points whose assertions will induce the proper register transfer(s) on the next clock pulse. We assume that processor control inputs that receive *more than one* ACTIVATE signal are already equipped with OR gates to merge them together, and that control *pulse* inputs are already further equipped with AND gates enabled by the common clock pulse P. That is, we assume that the control structure depicted in Fig. 7.6 is applicable.

To complete the present control-unit design, it remains only for us to interconnect the ACTIVATE signals of the control sequencer to the (OR gate inputs of the) proper control points, selected from those listed in Table 7.3. Table 7.5 specifies several of the connections that are required. Others are left as problems at the end of this chapter. Each ACTIVATE signal is named with the identifying symbol that labels its corresponding flow chart box in

Table 7.5   Typical One-asserted Control Sequencer
Connections

Activate Signal Name	Control Wiring Directs It to the Following Destinations
F0	READ m, LOAD MAR, LOAD X
F1	GATE RESULT, WRITE m
F2	READ M, LOAD IR
A20	LOAD X
A21	ADD, GATE RESULT, LOAD MAR
A31	GATE R2, READ m, LOAD Y
A32	GATE OP, GATE RESULT, WRITE M

Fig. 7.4. The wiring pattern defined in Table 7.5 takes into account some implicit or "default" information, explained earlier. Specifically, you will recall that, without the activation of control signals that cause the contrary, mSELECT = 0 (so that PC is addressed), FUNCTION = 0 (so that the ALU acts as an INCREMENTER), and the quiescent value on the data bus is zero. Thus, PC is automatically addressed in cases F0 and F1, while the RESULT is known to be X + 1 in case F1. Similarly, ACTIVATE signal A20 causes X ← 0 because no other data is gated to the bus.

Though a complete logic diagram for the entire sample processor (including its one-asserted control unit) has not been drawn, you now have sufficient information to be able to visualize the flow chart of Fig. 7.4, *implemented in hardware* and in operation. You should be able to specify, clock pulse by clock pulse, all of the micro-events that occur as the processor runs. It is recommended that you take the time to draw this detailed logic diagram. It will tie together information that has been given in several diagrams and tables. It will also help you to isolate those aspects of the design that still remain unclear to you. By attacking the relevant problems at the end of this chapter first, you will be in a better position to construct it.

In the process of developing such a final logic diagram, you will have to devise a proper *starting* mechanism. (Recall the one that was employed in the sample processor in Section 6.2.) You will have to include means to clear all control flip-flops to begin with, to properly initialize the Program Counter, to properly initiate the clock-pulse train, and to properly *inject* the first activation into flip-flop F0, to start the system running. A problem that relates to this issue also appears at the end of this chapter. Note that the default arrangements that exist in the system permit clearing PC merely by asserting the "WRITE m" control signal.

Implicit in this entire discussion is the assumption that the duration of a control cycle (i.e., the period of the clock-pulse train) allows sufficient time to permit all of the specified register transfers to be reliably executed. Specifically, both the scratchpad access time and the longest delay through the ALU/SHIFTER are assumed small, compared to the duration of a control cycle. Since the main-memory access time is *also* assumed less than the duration of a control cycle, these other timing constraints are easily complied with. (As explained in Chapter 4, the main-memory access time is normally long compared to other typical logic delays.) While an efficient control-unit design takes advantage of the discrepancy between memory and logic speeds by executing sequences of logic micro-operations *during* the main-memory access time period (whenever this is possible), we will presently ignore such examples of parallelism in the hardware.

7.3 ENCODED CONTROL STATES

All of the flip-flops in a one-asserted controller constitute a single register whose contents define a control state. When a processor is sufficiently simple, we may prefer to use a one-asserted controller, because its structure is a direct copy of the flow chart that describes that processor's behavior. However, as the complexity of the processor increases, so does the number of control states, and the number of control flip-flops soon becomes excessive.

We may dramatically reduce the number of control flip-flops in such a hardwired controller by *encoding* all of the control states. Consider, for example, an N-bit control register having 2^N control states, whose contents are decoded by an N-to-2^N decoder. Regard it as a replacement for a one-asserted controller containing 2^N flip-flops. The decoder's outputs are the ACTIVATE signals. Such a substitution may be made *provided* that the control state—the contents of the control register—is made to *sequence* properly.

Some aspects of the sequencing of the contents of a control register were discussed in Section 4.7. Certainly, the most common sequencing procedure is to *increment* the register's contents; this causes its decoder's only activated output to shift to a neighboring terminal. A *clear* of the control register also changes the control state. It is frequently employed to reinitialize the control register to a standard, starting state—for example, that corresponding to the start of the instruction FETCH sequence. If the next required state is totally arbitrary, however, the control register must be *loaded* with a proper new value. For example, the loop control structure shown in Fig. 7.8(b) periodically requires that the control code that corresponds to the FF1 = 1 state be loaded into the control register.

Since the state of a sequential circuit also depends on its applied *input* signals, the values stored in the control register need not correspond, on a one-to-one basis, with the ACTIVATE signals. In particular, the same control register state may correspond to several ACTIVATE signals, if intervening logic makes use of the additional input conditions. For example, a single control register state may correspond to a BRANCH instruction's execution. If COND is the branch condition, two separate ACTIVATE signals, BRANCH·COND and BRANCH·$\overline{\text{COND}}$, evoke entirely different operations. Similarly, one control-register state may identify the *i*th execution step for a *set* of instructions. This state may enable a corresponding set of ACTIVATE signals, each of which is uniquely selected by a different opcode.

A general structure for an encoded, hardwired, control sequencer is shown in Fig. 7.10. The control register is divided into two parts: a pulse counter and a cycle ID register. The cycle ID advances to a new value every time the counter begins a new cycle of states. This structure was discussed earlier, in Section 4.7, in conjunction with Fig. 4.26. The processor's Instruction Register is explicitly shown as part of the control sequencer (meaning

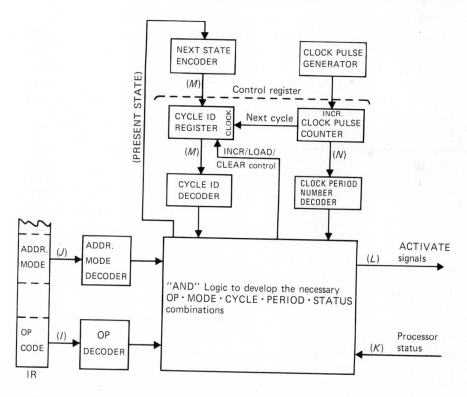

Figure 7.10   General structure of an encoded, hard-wired control sequencer

that any IR bits previously brought over as part of the STATUS signal group are no longer required there). For simplicity, the LOAD IR control signal is not shown. Those IR fields that may affect the micro-operation sequences being executed are usually decoded, as shown. The opcode field is the most important of these. Several others are possible. An addressing mode field is shown as an example.

The central AND logic network receives several different one-asserted codes, representing the type of instruction, the specific variations on its theme, the type of cycle, the specific subperiod within it, and finally, the set of processor STATUS signals (e.g., ALU flags, BRANCH conditions, etc.) that affect the register transfers that are executed. The function of the AND logic network is to develop proper logical *combinations* of these signals—in particular, those that will be used as the ACTIVATE outputs. For example, if a specific register transfer must be induced at time period 3, of cycle 5, during the execution of the COPY instruction, provided that the END status flag is not set, then a gate inside the AND network will develop the ACTIVATE signal COPY$\cdot\overline{\text{END}}\cdot$ID5$\cdot$TP3, which will, in turn, be directed to the proper control points to induce the required transfer.

Note that gates inside the network also develop signals to properly control the *sequencing* of the control register. Since the Clock Pulse Counter continually increments, unconditionally, the cycle ID is the only value whose sequencing needs control. Specifically, a cycle ID input-control code is shown, whose value decides between INCREMENT, CLEAR, or LOAD, when that register is clocked on the next boundary between cycles. For our present purposes, we will assume that INCREMENT is the normal sequencing mechanism, that CLEAR is used at the end of every execution sequence (their lengths vary) to reinitiate the FETCH phase, and that LOAD is used only for special "jumps"—for example, in register transfer loops or conditional sequences, such as those originally described in Fig. 7.8 The NEXT STATE ENCODER, at the top of the diagram, is responsible for developing the proper next state value to be loaded, given one of the unique present-state conditions that causes a cycle ID load.

From the *algebraic* point of view, each of the ACTIVATE signals is an appropriate *product* term, containing a small, selected subset of all of the variables applied as inputs to the AND logic network. Similarly, each of the input-control levels, to the processor under control (see Fig. 7.6), is a *sum of products*. Its expression effectively *lists* all of the conditions under which it should be asserted. For example, the narrative equivalent of the function X = ABCD + EFGH + . . . may be expressed as follows: "The control signal X should be asserted during time period A, of cycle B, while executing instruction C, provided that condition D is true OR during time period E, of cycle F, while executing instruction G, provided that condition H is true OR . . . etc."

Clearly, when a term of the function is *independent* of a specific condition, that variable is *missing* from the term. For example, micro-operations executed during the FETCH phase are normally independent of IR values (specifically, the opcode). Similarly, most register transfers are executed independently of *any* of the processor status signals. Observe also that a typical processor control *pulse* function is expressed algebraically as P·(ABCD + EFGH + ...).

In a sufficiently elementary processor controller, the control register is merely a *step counter*. Assuming it begins *cleared*, the first few steps define the FETCH phase, after which its ensuing states identify the *same* execution steps for *all* instructions. The different opcode values identify separate execution *paths* through the processor's flow chart, and occasionally, a flag indicator value controls whether or not a specific micro-operation is executed. The instruction execution paths generally have *variable* lengths, each terminating with a CLEAR of the control register, to reinitiate the FETCH phase.

The present sample processor belongs to this class of machines. If you examine its flow chart in Fig. 7.4, you will note that the longest path, from initiation of FETCH to termination of EXECUTION, contains between eight and sixteen steps, in which case a four-bit control register should suffice. Following the example in Fig. 7.10, we divide this register into two parts: a two-bit clock-pulse counter and a two-bit cycle ID register. The resulting control structure is shown in Fig. 7.11.

On every clock pulse P, the clock-pulse counter increments. Therefore, the T0 through T3 signal waveforms resemble those of PERIOD0 through

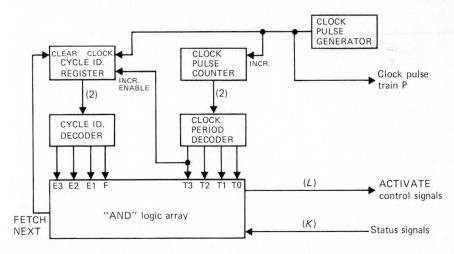

Figure 7.11 Block diagram of an encoded control sequencer for the sample processor

PERIOD3, shown in Fig. 4.26(b). (Using positive assertions, each $Ti = \overline{PERIODi}$.) The cycle ID register is permitted to increment on each clock pulse for which T3 = 1. Its overriding CLEAR input signal, renamed as FETCH NEXT, is derived from the AND logic array. The cycle ID value selects which of signals E0 through E3 is asserted. (E0 is renamed as "F", for our convenience.) The K input STATUS signals are assumed to be those listed in Table 7.3 (part II) and Table 7.4. Note that they include decoded versions of the pertinent IR fields (i.e., the opcode, IR[15:14], and the addressing mode field, IR[9:8]).

Each of the ACTIVATE output signals corresponds to a unique control state, the AND of an appropriate Ei, Tj, STATUS signal combination, whose assertion evokes one of the register transfers in Fig. 7.4. In other words, each of the sample processor's register transfers is *assigned* a unique control state. Many different assignments are possible. We will find it convenient to assign the F cycle to the FETCH phase, the E1 cycle to the first EXECUTE phase, and the E2 and E3 cycles to the second and third EXECUTE phases, respectively, if additional EXECUTE phases are needed. Note that some control states (i.e., some of the EiTj combinations) may remain *unassigned*. When an unassigned control state occurs, *none* of the ACTIVATE signals is asserted, in which case, *nothing* is executed. (All of the processor registers, with the exception of the control register, merely retain their current contents.)

The labels adjoining the boxes in Fig. 7.4 indicate the specific control-state assignment that was chosen. Label "Fi" is an abbreviation for time period Ti within the FETCH cycle. It corresponds to the assertion of the AND function $F \cdot Ti$. Similarly, label "Ci" (or "Bi") represents time period Ti within the EXECUTION cycle of the Call (or Branch) instruction. It corresponds to the assertion of the AND function $C \cdot E1 \cdot Ti$ (or $B \cdot E1 \cdot Ti$), where C (or B) is a signal defined earlier in Table 7.4. Similarly, label "Aij" is an abbreviation for time period Tj within EXECUTION cycle Ei of an ALU/SHIFTER instruction. It corresponds to the assertion of the AND function $A \cdot Ei \cdot Tj$, where A is a signal also defined earlier in Table 7.4. The primes in some of the labels indicate alternative executions, for the same AEiTj combination. Their ACTIVATE signals include *additional* STATUS conditions which are ANDed in. For example, the register transfer labeled as A20 is induced by ACTIVATE signal AE2T0Z1, while that labeled as A20' is induced by ACTIVATE signal $AE2T0\overline{Z1}$.

Thus, each label in the flow chart in Fig. 7.4 implies the algebraic product term for its ACTIVATE signal. A list of all such terms would define the required internal structure of the AND logic array in Fig. 7.11. However, recall from Fig. 7.6 that the ACTIVATE signals are appropriately ORed together to form the direct control inputs to the processor. Thus, by writing

Table 7.6   Equations Defining Sample Machine Encoded Controller

WRITE m = P[FT1 + CE1T1 + CE1T3 + BE1T2 + AWE1T1 + ASE1T3 + AUE3T2 + AVE3T2)

LOAD IR = PFT2

LOAD X = P[FT0 + CE1T0 + BE1T0 + AWE1T0 + ASE1T2 + AE2T0 + AE3T0)

LOAD Y = P[BE1T1 + AE1T2 + AE3T1)

LOAD MAR = P[FT0 + CE1T0 + AWE1T0 + AE2T1 + AM3E2T2)

WRITE M = P(CE1T2 + ASE3T2 + A$\overline{\text{U}}$[Z2 + STORE]E3T2)

LOAD FLAGS = PAE3T2

FETCH NEXT = P(CE1T3 + BE1T3)

READ m = FT0 + CE1T0 + CE1T2 + BE1T0 + AWE1T0 + ASE1T2 + A$\overline{\text{Z}}$1E2T0 + AE3T1

GATE OFFSET = BE1T1

GATE ADDRESS = CE1T3

GATE RESULT = FT1 + CE1T1 + BE1T2 + AWE1T1 + ASE1T3 + AE2T1 + AE3T2

GATE MAR = AM0E3T0

READ M = FT2 + AWE1T2 + AM3E2T2 + A$\overline{\text{M}}$0E3T0

GATE R1 = A$\overline{\text{Z}}$1E2T0 + AUE3T2

GATE R2 = ASE1T2 + ASE1T3 + AE3T1 + AVE3T2

SELECT SP = CE1T0 + CE1T1

GATE OP = AE3T2

ADD = BE1T2 + AE2T1

Note: V = $\overline{\text{SZ2STORE}}$

down all of the sum-of-products functions that correspond to the latter signals, we specify *not only* the AND logic required to develop the ACTIVATE signals *but also* the control-wiring pattern necessary to distribute the ACTIVATEs among the control points. The entire list of such control functions, for our sample processor, is given in Table 7.6. Note that each of the control input signals, listed in Table 7.3, is defined with an appropriate sum of product terms, each containing a proper combination of the E_i, T_j, and STATUS variables. (The expression for the variable BINARY was already given in Table 7.4.) The product terms define the internal structure of the AND logic array in Fig. 7.11, while the sums define the control-wiring pattern between the ACTIVATE terminals and the control points.

The equations, as written, are not in the simplest form. Several modifications may be made to minimize the complexity of the control-logic network. Most important, commonly used product terms (for example, all of the E_iT_j combinations, AW, AS, etc.) may be developed *first* and then wired to the inputs of those gates requiring them. In addition, some factoring within the equations may further simplify the system's logic. However, the controller description, as given in Table 7.6, is sufficient to permit you to visualize the entire system in operation.

Note the expression for the signal FETCH NEXT. It reinitiates the FETCH phase immediately after the first EXECUTE cycle of any instruction not requiring use of the E2 and E3 cycles. Had it been omitted, the system would still have operated correctly. However, the execution time of all CALL and BRANCH instructions would have tripled. That is, E2 and E3 cycles, during which *nothing* was executed, would have occurred.

The issue of *starting* correctly has been ignored in the equations. You may assume that the processor's RESET button clears the control register and asserts the WRITE m signal (which will clear PC). Further, you may assume that the central Clock Pulse Generator is inhibited until the START button is depressed.

Observe that we continue to make the assumption that the main memory's access time is less than the time between two adjacent clock pulses.

7.4 MICROPROGRAMMING

The character of a processor whose control unit is hardwired is determined largely by a complex control-wiring pattern. At any instant, the processor's present state—principally the contents of its control register—selects which register transfers are executed. Two control-sequencing mechanisms have been discussed. The next state of a one-asserted controller is determined by an activation path—one of the branches in the processor's control flow chart. Its selection is usually influenced by one or more status signals. The next state of an encoded controller results from an increment or a load of its control register. (A clear is equivalent to a load of all zeroes.)

In short, a control register's value *selects* the register transfers that are executed and *sequences* either by incrementing or by branching. (A load is equivalent to a branch.) Thus, a control register behaves as if it were an "inner" program counter. It selects, not an instruction, but a *microinstruction*—an elementary operation that is only one component in a larger sequence of operations. Since an instruction's execution is itself a *program* of micro-operations, we may define the planning and organizing of register-transfer sequences as *microprogramming*.

This analogy suggests that the character of a processor may be defined by the contents of an inner control *memory*, which holds all of the microprograms, and that the control register may be employed to *point to* the current microinstruction. Under these conditions, the control register may be renamed as the "micro-Program Counter" and abbreviated as "μPC". Such a control organization is not only possible; it is *preferable* in many cases. It replaces a complex control-wiring pattern with a *bit* pattern stored in an inner Control Memory (which may be abbreviated as "CM"). This memory is normally realized in *Read-Only* form. In-line sequences of microinstructions are addressed, in order, by an incrementing μPC. Branches in the processor's flow chart, normally conditional on one or more status signals, correspond to conditional loads of new μPC values.

Since each microinstruction is a word accessed from the Control Memory, it may be designated as $CM(\mu PC)$. It selects which control signals are asserted, and these, in turn, define which register transfers are executed. To begin with, let us assume that each microinstruction contains as many bits as there are control signals, with a "1" specifying assertion. Such a microinstruction may activate any pattern of control signals and thus may induce any arbitrary set of *parallel* register transfers. It is called a "horizontal" microinstruction because all of the transfers that it evokes may be written down horizontally, indicating that they are all executed *concurrently*.

Since the number of control signals is usually large, a more likely microinstruction format organizes all of the control signals into sets whose assertions are normally mutually exclusive (i.e., at most one, in a set, is asserted at a time). These sets are then *encoded* into corresponding microinstruction *fields*. Under these conditions, it is no longer possible for a single microinstruction to induce a totally arbitrary control-signal pattern. Each is now called a "vertical" microinstruction, because the sequences of register transfers that are evoked (usually one per microinstruction) are written down vertically, indicating that they are executed in *time sequence*.

Before discussing typical microcodes, we proceed by explaining how FETCH-EXECUTE behavior is normally accomplished in a microprogrammed control network. The Control Memory is divided into separate areas, each containing a distinct *microroutine*. There is one FETCH microroutine, and there are as many EXECUTE microroutines as there are corresponding instructions in the processor's repertoire. While a microroutine executes, the μPC pointer points within it.

The FETCH microroutine is responsible for staging the instruction in the Instruction Register and advancing PC (which is *distinct* from μPC) past it. It may also compute one or more effective addresses, based on addressing-mode information contained in the just-FETCHed instruction. The FETCH microroutine exits with a multi-way conditional branch, based on the opcode value. Normally, this is achieved in a *single* register transfer, which *loads* a field of bits based on the opcode (i.e., possibly the opcode itself or some appropriate function of it) directly into a portion of the μPC, such that μPC ends pointing at the first microinstruction of the microroutine for the EXECUTION of the just-FETCHed instruction. This microroutine later exits with a branch back to the beginning of the FETCH microroutine, which begins the cycle over again.

A vertical microinstruction's *format* resembles that of a conventional instruction. However, its responsibility is limited to one (or both) of only *two* functions: First, it may define a register transfer to be executed. Typically, this requires that it include fields identifying the source register, the destination register, and the intervening data operation. Second, it may specify a conditional branch to another location in the Control Memory. Typically, this requires that it include fields identifying the branch condition to be tested (normally, one of the processor status signals) and the branch destination. With these two functions, we may implement arbitrary register-transfer flow charts (and, hence, arbitrary processors).

The use of two separate microinstruction formats, called, for example, TRANSFER and JUMP, consumes the least Control Memory space. However, it also results in a slower processor, because JUMP microinstructions must be separately accessed. A controller having a single microinstruction format, which *includes* the branch fields, permits *every* microinstruction to specify both functions. It is less efficient, because both are not always required simultaneously, in which case, some fields in the necessarily longer microinstructions sometimes go unused. However, it does result in a faster processor, because branches are executed with little time penalty.

Figure 7.12 shows the block diagram of a typical microprogrammed control unit. It is assumed that the processor under control contains an array of registers that communicate with each other via one or more central data buses. Their GATE and LOAD control inputs are assumed separately accessible.

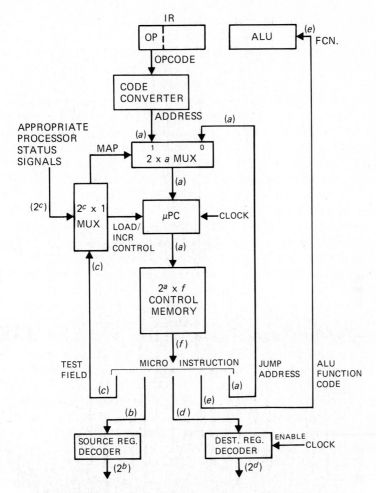

Figure 7.12 Typical microprogrammed control system

Only one of these registers, IR, is shown in the diagram. The others include PC, SP, MAR, the main memory M, and an arbitrary number of additional registers. The system also includes an ALU, shown in the diagram without its data paths. We assume that the ALU is properly positioned to permit all data transfers to pass through it.

The a-bit-wide μPC either loads or increments, whenever it receives a clock-pulse edge, based on the value of one control signal, selected by a multiplexer, from a set of 2^c processor status signals. The μPC value, which starts pointing at the first microinstruction of the FETCH microroutine, selects the current f-bit microinstruction, which is assumed to contain five fields. Three of these define the current register transfer by selecting a source register, a destination register, and an intervening ALU function. The outputs of the SOURCE DECODER connect to the individual source register GATE control inputs. Similarly, the outputs of the DESTINATION DECODER connect to the individual destination register LOAD control inputs. Note that they are all enabled by the system clock pulse. A field in the microinstruction also specifies the ALU function code. The two other fields define a conditional jump, executed by every microinstruction. A TEST field selects one of the status signals, whose current value defines whether or not μPC will load on the next clock pulse. When it loads, it normally loads the jump address value—also part of the same microinstruction.

Two of the inputs to the TEST multiplexer are *constants* ("1" and "0") to permit any microinstruction to jump *unconditionally* or to totally disable the jump mechanism when it is not needed. The code converter at the top of the diagram maps the opcode into the address of the first microinstruction of its *execution* microroutine. This value is loaded into μPC at the *exit* from the FETCH sequence, using a mechanism that employs the special signal named MAP. Let us assume that *one* of the c-bit TEST codes, detected inside the TEST multiplexer, activates the MAP signal and simultaneously asserts the LOAD option to μPC. Only under these conditions will the μPC load the code converter's output address value. This special jump microinstruction, having the MAP test code, is found in the control memory only at the FETCH routine's exit point.

Note that a "μIR" is not required, in this realization, because the Control Memory, addressed only by the μPC, always outputs the current microinstruction. However, a more sophisticated system, in which the execution of one microinstruction is *overlapped* with the fetch of the *next* one, *does* require a μIR to hold the presently executing command.

To undertake the development of a microprogrammed controller for our sample processor, consider once more its control interface, defined in Table 7.3, in light of the model just discussed. The signals listed in categories A and B clearly correspond to those normally selected by microinstruction DESTINATION and SOURCE fields, respectively. The signals in category C naturally divide into two classes—those that define the scratchpad address source and those that select the ALU/SHIFTER function. Consequently, to specify *all* of these aspects of a register transfer, we must designate *four* microinstruction fields, having the possible assignments listed in Table 7.7. This table provides the same information as originally given in Table 7.3, in slightly different form.

Since the number of possible destination registers is nearly eight, a three-bit field permits selecting one of them. Similarly, another three-bit field is

Table 7.7 Symbolic Assignments to Microinstruction Fields

Name	Comment

1. ALU/SHIFTER Functions (2 bits):

INCR
ADD
OP   Function = That specified in instruction
Unassigned

2. Scratchpad Memory Address Values (2 bits):

0	"PC" implies $m(0)$
1	"SP" implies $m(1)$
R1	In instruction
R2	In instruction

3. Sources of Data to BUS (3 bits):

m	Scratchpad memory
M	Main memory
MAR	
RESULT	From ALU/SHIFTER
OFFSET	In Branch instruction
ADDRESS	In Call instruction
NONE	To permit BUS to carry quiescent zero
Unassigned	

4. Destination Registers (3 bits):

m	Scratchpad memory
M	Main memory
X	
Y	
MAR	
IR	
FLAGS	
Unassigned	

5. Conditional Jump Test Conditions (4 bits):

MAP	Load μPC with encoded address based on IR[15:14]
NONE	Take the jump *unconditionally*
COND	The Branch instruction's condition
$\overline{\text{IR8Z1Z2}}$	Defines a Control instruction
W	
S	
Z1	
M3	
M0	
U	
V	$\overline{\text{SZ2STORE}}$

Five codes unassigned

allocated to allow selecting one of the possible sources of data to the bus. Two bits are adequate to specify one of the four possible scratchpad address sources. Note that, since an instruction field *always* has a value, the "default" condition must be included as one of the options in the assignment list. This is the reason why two bits are also required to specify one of the ALU/ SHIFTER function code sources. Thus, it appears that a ten-bit code is sufficient to specify any one of the register transfers defined for our sample processor.

By examining the conditionals shown in the flow chart in Fig. 7.4, we identify most of the sequencing conditions listed in Table 7.7. The first of these, symbolically named "MAP", corresponds to part of the multi-way branch that immediately follows the FETCH sequence. The second, symbolically named "NONE", is included as a *constant* condition, whose selection will always cause its microjump to be taken. Each of the others corresponds to a signal that was defined earlier—either in Table 7.3 or in Table 7.4. (Signal V happens to be a convenient logical combination, originally used in Table 7.6.) For simplicity, we will assume that each of the condition signals listed in Table 7.7 is available for testing. (The first two will correspond to constant "1" conditions.)

The list of 11 TEST conditions means that a four-bit field is required to encode them. Assuming that our controller will have separate TRANSFER and JUMP microinstructions, with ten bits allocated to each, we have six bits left to locate the JUMP's destination. If this code is the full address of the destination microinstruction, the capacity of the Control Memory must be 2^6 or 64 words. Under these conditions, μPC must be six bits long. Thus, we develop the microinstruction format defined in Fig. 7.13.

Each microinstruction must be 11 bits long, to permit one bit to specify either a TRANSFER or a conditional JUMP. This format leads us to adopt the logic/block diagram shown in Fig. 7.14, a particular version of the general case shown in Fig. 7.12, as our present microprogrammed controller.

The ADDRESS ENCODER at the top of the diagram outputs one of three possible six-bit addresses, as selected by the IR[15 : 14] value. They are the

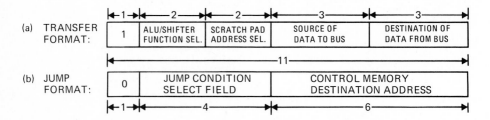

Figure 7.13 Sample processor microinstruction formats

entry points of the microroutines in the Control Memory that execute the CALL, BRANCH, and ALU/CONTROL instructions, respectively. The μPC, which either loads or increments on every clock pulse, as decided by the value of a single control signal, selects an 11-bit microinstruction in the Control ROM. Each of the four TRANSFER instruction fields has its own decoder, whose outputs individually connect to the control points listed. (Those outputs, which correspond to *unassigned* codes, remain disconnected.) The

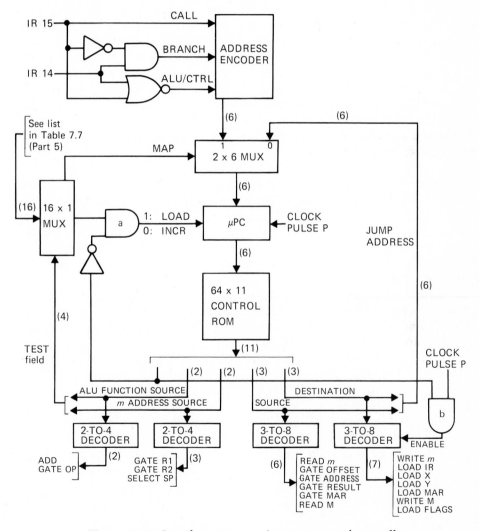

Figure 7.14   Sample processor microprogrammed controller

four-bit JUMP CONDITION SELECT field is directed to the 16×1 multiplexer, which permits only one of the jump CONDITION signals to pass. Two of these, corresponding to the four-bit codes assigned to the MAP and NONE symbols in Table 7.7, are constant 1's. The six-bit jump destination address field is directed to one of the 2×6 multiplexer ports.

The upper microinstruction bit enables one of the two AND gates, labeled "a" and "b". A TRANSFER microinstruction enables AND gate B, which permits clock pulse P to enable the destination decoder, in which case a register transfer is induced when P occurs. Under these conditions, μPC will increment only, because gate a is disabled. A JUMP microinstruction disables all transfers and permits the selected condition to decide whether or not μPC will load on the next clock pulse. If it does load, the loaded value is normally the address field in the microinstruction (i.e., signal MAP is usually 0). However, one of the TEST field values (which selects one of the constant "1" inputs to the condition selector) asserts MAP, which causes the appropriate entry address to be loaded into μPC.

Having defined the required microinstruction formats and their corresponding controller's hardware structure, we may proceed by assigning specific microinstruction field values to all of the items listed in Table 7.7. It then remains for us to write the microroutines (to be stored in the Control Memory) that will induce the behavior described in the flow chart in Fig. 7.4. (We assume, once again, that PC and μPC will be properly initialized to begin with. In particular, μPC must begin pointing at the first microinstruction of the FETCH microroutine.)

Since the assignment of codes to the "objects" listed in Table 7.7 is totally arbitrary, we may bypass this step and, for clarity, write the microprograms using the objects themselves. That is, each microinstruction will be written as the symbolic equivalent of an 11-bit word, stored in one of the locations in the Control Memory. Similarly, we will find it convenient to assign to each microinstruction, not a specific address value locating where it will be stored, but a symbolic address, which will later be assigned an actual six-bit number.

The microprogram listed in Table 7.8 employs such a symbolic notation. It implements the flow chart in Fig. 7.4. Each line in it represents one microinstruction—the contents of one Control Memory word. A microinstruction may be labeled, in the left-hand column, with a convenient symbol that represents its address. Specific six-bit address values may be assigned to these symbols using a counting procedure, starting with 0 for the symbol FETCH. Thus, the symbol CALL, for example, will be assigned the address value 5. The values assigned to the symbols CALL, BRANCH, and ALU/CTRL are those which the ADDRESS ENCODER in Fig. 7.14 generates.

Within the body of the table, each line has one of two formats, corresponding to the two permissible 11-bit microinstruction formats illustrated in Fig. 7.13. Any line beginning with a "J" is a conditional jump microinstruction. It obeys the jump format, shown in the heading. (The J represents an upper microinstruction bit of 0.) Each J is followed by a symbol representing the condition to be tested and by a symbol representing the jump destination—the address of the next microinstruction taken if the signal, corresponding to the specified condition, has a value "1".

Any line that doesn't begin with a J is a transfer microinstruction. It obeys the transfer format, shown in the heading, which requires that four items, corresponding to the four fields in Fig. 7.13(a), be specified. These fields are not all independent. In particular, if an "m" does not appear in either of the SOURCE or DESTINATION columns, the value in the mADDRESS column is of no consequence. In other words, the scratchpad address value doesn't matter if the scratchpad is not used. Similarly, the ALU/SHIFTER FUNCTION select code is of no consequence unless the symbol RESULT appears in the SOURCE column. In other words, it doesn't matter what the ALU/SHIFTER is doing if its output value is ignored.

Each transfer microinstruction is conveniently labeled, in the right-hand column, with the identifier that labels its corresponding box in the flow chart in Fig. 7.4. Thus, any line having an entry in the ID column *cannot* begin with a J.

All of the symbols used in the body of the microprogram come from the list in Table 7.7. Thus, whenever codes are assigned to the objects in Table 7.7, binary equivalents of all of the symbolic microinstructions may be *assembled*. A typical microprogram is normally written in a symbolic form, similar to that shown in Table 7.8. A special computer program, known as an ASSEMBLER, then assigns to all of the symbols in the microprogram corresponding code values.

The omission of a symbolic entry merely indicates that *any* value may be specified for it. It doesn't matter, because the value is ignored. It is a "don't care" entry.

The FETCH sequence exits with the special J MAP microinstruction, whose TEST field value causes the MAP signal to be asserted. The address field in this microinstruction is ignored, because the address comes instead from the ADDRESS ENCODER. Note that each execution routine exits with a J NONE FETCH microinstruction, which unconditionally returns to Control Memory location 0. Observe also that those register transfers specifying *two* destinations in the flow chart require *two* separate microinstructions, because only one destination at a time may be specified.

The microprogram contains 50 microinstructions, leaving 14 available to

Table 7.8 Symbolic Microprogram for Sample Processor

Symbolic Control Memory Address	J	ALU FCN	TEST	\[Symbolic Contents of that Address\] m ADDR	SRC REG	LOC	DEST REG	ID ←(jump format) ←(transfer format)
FETCH	J			PC	m		X	F0
		INCR		PC	m		MAR	F0
				PC	RESULT		m	F1
					M		IR	F2
CALL	J		MAP	SP	m		X	C0
		INCR		SP	m		MAR	C0
				SP	RESULT		m	C1
				PC	m		M	C2
				PC	ADDRESS		m	C3
BRANCH	J		NONE			FETCH		B0
	J		COND			FETCH		B1
		ADD		PC	m		X	B2
					OFFSET		Y	
					RESULT		m	
ALU/CTRL	J		NONE	PC	RESULT	FETCH	Y	A12''
	J		IR8Z1Z2			CONTROL		
	J		W		NONE	EXTRA		
	J		S			AUTOINCR		
AUTOINCR	J		NONE	R2	m		X	A12'
		INCR		R2	m	XVALUE	Y	A12'
	J		NONE	R2	RESULT	XVALUE	m	A13

Label	[	op	const	reg	src	dest	goto	Addr
EXTRA	[			PC	m	X		A10
	[	INCR		PC	m	MAR		A10
	[			PC	RESULT	m		A11
	[				M	Y	CLEAR	A12
XVALUE	[		Z1	R1	m	X		A20'
CLEAR	[		NONE		NONE		INDEX	A20
INDEX	[	ADD	$\overline{M3}$		RESULT	X		A21
	[				M	MAR		A22
OPERAND1	[		M0		M		OPERAND1	A30'
	[				MAR		IMMEDIATE	A30
OPERAND2	[		NONE	R2	m		OPERAND2	A31
IMMEDIATE	[	OP	U			X		
	[		V			Y		
						FLAGS		
BINARY	[	OP	NONE	R2	RESULT	M	BINARY	A32
UNARY	[	OP	NONE	R1	RESULT	m	FETCH	A32''
CONTROL	[	OP	NONE		RESULT	m	FETCH	A32'

Note: V = $\overline{SZ2STORE}$

implement CONTROL instructions, beginning at the end of the table. The first microinstruction of the ALU/CTRL sequence exits to symbolic address CONTROL if the proper conditions exist.

You are urged to take the time to step through this microprogram to verify that it indeed fulfills the behavior specified in Fig. 7.4. With its coded equivalent stored in the Control ROM in Fig. 7.14, we have still another logic network that will perform the control function for our sample processor.

The use of a microprogrammed controller is preferred, in most processor designs, because its complexity is confined to one component—its Control Memory. The complex wiring pattern of a hardwired controller has been replaced by a stored bit pattern. Modifications in the processor's behavior may be produced by alterations to this bit pattern. No other hardware changes are necessary. This permits the entire character of a machine to be changed by replacing one Control ROM with another. In fact, a computer that includes a *writable* control store allows its user to tailor its instruction set to the application at hand.

A major disadvantage of a microprogrammed controller is its limited execution speed. Normally, each microinstruction may specify only *one* register transfer to be executed and may select only *one* elementary branch condition to be tested. Functions that may be accomplished *in parallel,* using a hardwired controller, must be executed *serially* in a microprogrammed system. For example, in a hardwired system, a single ACTIVATE signal may be routed to an arbitrary number of control points, inducing an arbitrary number of parallel transfers. Similarly, a *compound* logical branch condition may be developed using one or more appropriately wired gates, permitting the *next* transfer to be determined immediately. In a microprogrammed controller, on the other hand, a large number of *elementary* branch condition signals is available for testing, and two or more successive conditional tests may have to be executed before the next transfer is decided. For example, if status signals $IR8$, $Z1$, and $Z2$ were available only for testing separately (which is a more likely situation) in the sample controller just discussed, the compound condition $\overline{IR8}Z1Z2$ would have required a sequence of *three* tests.

Note that the number of microinstructions contained in a control store depends on the complexity of the processor's instruction repertoire and on the execution flexibility available in one microinstruction (which increases as its length increases). There is no reason why this number should be a power of two. For example, the implementation described above, as far as it is defined, requires 50 microinstructions. After all of the control instructions are included, this number may easily surpass 64. Thus, the Control ROM required is rarely *fully populated,* and a typical microprogrammed control unit employs, not a ROM, but a PLA instead. As explained in Section 4.4, a PLA is equivalent to a partially occupied ROM.

PROBLEMS

7.1 Which sample processor scratchpad registers have a special significance? Why?

7.2 Which binary ALU/SHIFTER operation does not conform to the rules stated in Fig. 7.2? Briefly explain why this exception was included.

7.3 Which instructions cause the output port VALUE, in Fig. 7.1, to be activated? For each one, specify the source of the code that is gated to the data bus.

7.4 Design a one-asserted control sequencer that implements that portion of the flow chart, in Fig. 7.4, consisting of the FETCH of the operation word, the six-way branch to the proper EXECUTE sequence, and the CALL and BRANCH instruction executions. (Ignore the Control Instruction path.) Show all necessary gates and flip-flops and, in particular, show *all* paths that can cause activation of flip-flop F0. Specifically show a means to activate flip-flop F0 on the *first* clock pulse immediately following the trailing edge of a START signal (from a start button). Properly label all inputs and outputs in your diagram.

7.5 Design a one-asserted control sequencer that corresponds to that portion of the flow chart in Fig. 7.4 that implements all ALU/SHIFTER operations. Your network should have three inputs (derived from corresponding outputs in the solution to Problem 7.4) and three outputs (which connect to three corresponding inputs in the solution to Problem 7.4). Label all inputs and outputs properly.

7.6 Complete the control wiring list begun in Table 7.5.

7.7 Your answer to Problem 7.4 does not include a path for control instructions. If the machine were implemented using your solution, what would it do after fetching any one of them?

7.8 The network shown in Fig. P7.8 is used to generate a complex pattern of pulses as defined by a sequence of count values read from a paper tape. While READY is asserted, the current paper-tape character code is valid at the reader's output port. Whenever the reader receives an ADVANCE pulse, it drops READY and moves the tape to the next consecutive character, at which time it raises READY again. The START element generates a single pulse whenever the start button is depressed, at which time the following sequence of events is initiated: The first tape character defines the *number of pulse bursts* to be generated, and each subsequent character specifies the *number of pulses within one burst*. Each output burst is a train of CLOCK pulses. Note that two adjacent pulse bursts are separated by the time it takes to read the next paper tape character. Design the element, labeled "your control sequencer," to achieve the desired behavior.

Note: Counter LOADS or DECREMENTS on a CLOCK pulse only if properly ENABLED.

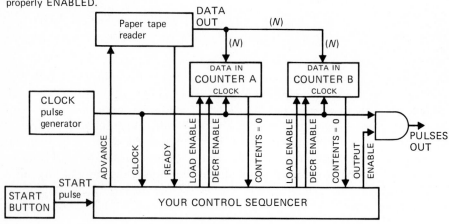

Figure P7.8

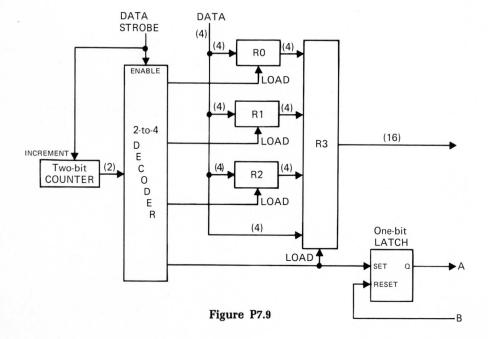

Figure P7.9

7.9 Assume that the counter in the network shown in Fig. P7.9 is cleared to begin with. The DATA STROBE is a pulse that is asserted while the DATA code value is valid. What is the most likely function of this network? Why is it necessary that the counter increment on the *trailing* edge of the STROBE pulse? Briefly explain the advantage of including the R3 register. What are the most likely functions of the A and B signals?

7.10 Some of the devices, paths, and control signals for an elementary processor are shown in Fig. P7.10. The system includes registers PC, SP, IR, and ACC. SP points to the first available stack location, and the stack grows toward *lower* addresses. Each input control signal is labeled with the action that its assertion evokes. First, based on the operations listed below, identify which of the registers named in the diagram correspond to those named above. Then write down, for each of the functions listed below, *which* of the control signals shown must be asserted, and in what *order* they must be activated. Use the signal names that appear in the diagram.

  a) The fetch of an instruction;
  b) The execution of a LOAD ACCUMULATOR instruction;

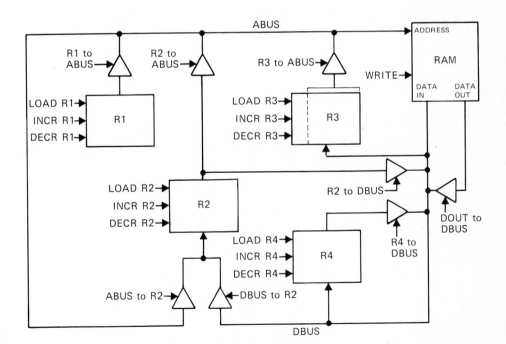

Figure P7.10

c) The execution of a PUSH ACCUMULATOR instruction;

d) The execution of a CALL instruction;

e) The execution of a RETURN instruction.

7.11 Define a *rule* that converts the information found in Table 7.5 (as extended by your answer to Problem 7.6) into the set of equations listed in Table 7.6. (*Note:* Your rule must incorporate some information from Fig. 7.4.)

7.12 Using the elementary processor shown in Fig. P7.12, plot typical waveforms, for control signals 1 through 8, that will induce the FETCH and EXECUTION of the following instructions:

a) ADD: B ← B + M(Q) (where "+" is selected by the F field);

b) STORE: M(Q) ← B.

Use positive assertion waveforms and carefully distinguish between control pulses and control levels.

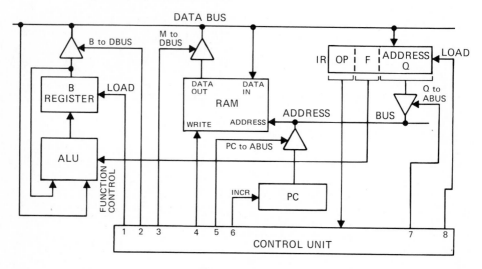

Figure P7.12

7.13 What registers, paths, gates, and control inputs must be added to the diagram in Fig. P7.12 to implement the following instructions?

a) BRANCH to address Q if the condition selected by F is true;

b) CALL to address Q;

c) RETURN.

7.14 Design a processor by interconnecting only the components shown in Fig. P7.14. No other components are required. The machine has a single accumulator ACC and a 32 × 8 RAM. Its eight-bit instruction length is divided

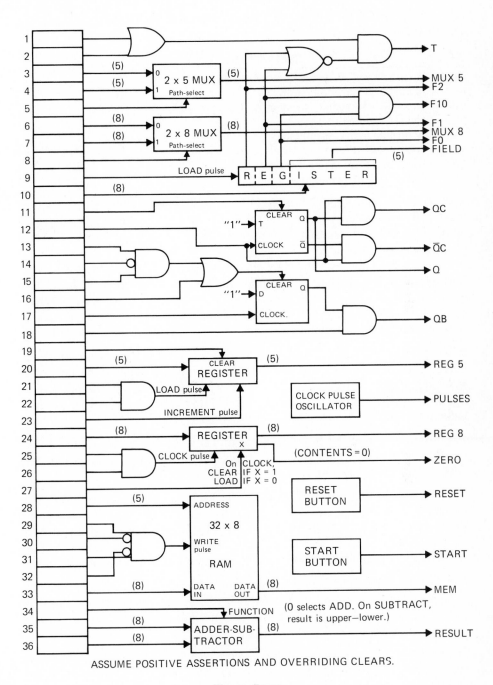

ASSUME POSITIVE ASSERTIONS AND OVERRIDING CLEARS.

Figure P7.14

into a three-bit OP field and a five-bit address field A. The instruction set is given below:

OP	EXECUTION
000	Branch to A if ACC = 0. Otherwise, take next instruction.
001	Branch to A unconditionally.
010	Store ACC at memory location A.
011	Halt. (A ignored.)
100	Add M(A) to the Accumulator.
101	Subtract M(A) from the Accumulator.
110	Load ACC from memory location A.
111	Clear ACC. (A ignored.)

The machine has a RESET button and a START button. The first instruction is fetched from memory location zero. The program is assumed already loaded in the RAM. Assume that all edge-triggered operations are evoked on the trailing control pulse edge.

Outputs are shown on the right side of the diagram and inputs on the left. You define how the system is interconnected by filling in each input slot with the *name* of the output port to which it is connected. Use only the names that appear in the output column. Do not invent your own. (Treat this as a "closed book" problem.)

7.15 In Figs. 7.12 and 7.14, the multiplexer controlled by the microinstruction's TEST field is not quite conventional. Briefly explain the origin of the MAP signal. In Fig. 7.14, when MAP = 1, what is the value of the other multiplexer output signal? Are there any other TEST codes for which this output value (of the signal directed to AND gate a) is guaranteed? If so, name them.

7.16 Assuming that the microprogram in Table 7.8 begins at Control ROM location zero, specify the possible output code values (in hex) of the ADDRESS ENCODER in Fig. 7.14.

7.17 Assuming that the microprogram in Table 7.8 begins at location zero, specify the sequence of μPC values (in hex) as the sample processor FETCHES and EXECUTES an ALU/SHIFTER instruction whose R1 and R2 fields are both nonzero and whose IR[9 : 8] field has a value of three. (Assume that its OP field does *not* select the special STORE function.)

7.18 Write a symbolic microroutine, similar to the one in Table 7.8, that implements the execution of the MOVE instruction described in Problem 6.19. Assume that the only microinstructions that are available for use are those listed below:

1. TRANSFER   SOURCEREG   DESTREG
2. INCR   REG

3. DECR   REG

4. JUMP   TESTREG   JUMPDEST

Each of your microinstructions should begin with TRANSFER, INCR, DECR, or JUMP. An appropriate register name should be substituted for any occurrence of a microinstruction field whose name contains "REG". An appropriate symbolic Control Memory address should be substituted for the occurrence of JUMPDEST in any JUMP microinstruction. This instruction branches to the destination specified if the contents of the register named in the TESTREG field is not zero. Name any new processor registers you will need. The A, B, and AUX fields of the IR, each of which may be selected as a source register, are already defined. Make any convenient assumptions about the lengths of the registers involved.

7.19 Assuming that we employ the encoded controller described by the set of equations in Table 7.6, what will be the execution time of a relative BRANCH instruction whose selected CONDition is *not* met? How can the equations in Table 7.6 be modified to reduce this time interval?

8

Interrupts and Input/Output Systems

8.1 INTERRUPTS

The word "interruption" generally implies the unexpected suspension of one activity, caused by the initiation of some other activity. Typically, the interrupted activity resumes later, when the interfering action completes.

The running of a computer program is a process that may be interrupted in precisely this sense. The interrupting activity is the running of some *other* program. The instant of interruption is generally not predictable, and the interrupted program normally resumes its activity later, when the interrupting program terminates, and computes the *same results* as would have been calculated had the interruption never taken place.

Consider, for example, a computation that is momentarily interrupted by an alarm condition, requiring immediate attention. The interrupting program, which responds to this condition, takes an appropriate action (for example, effectively removing the cause of the alarm), after which the original computation resumes.

This suggests that a typical program interruption consists of the following ingredients: First, *two* programs must be simultaneously resident in memory—the "main" program, whose computation may be interrupted, and the interrupt *response* program, also called an interrupt "handler," which runs when the interrupt condition arises. The implication that the interrupt response program is short as compared to the main program is normally true. Second, a means for detecting the interrupt condition must exist. Typically, an *external signal*, whose assertion "requests" an interrupt, is available. Note that the programmer of the main program cannot predict when, or if, this signal will be activated. Third, assuming that the interrupt handler has been designed to provide the proper response to the interrupt condition (in the event that it develops), the proper *linkage* must be established—*to* the interrupt-response routine from the main program whenever the interrupt condition arises, and back to the main program when the interrupt handler completes its action.

A main program may be designed to periodically test the external interrupt request signal and to transfer control to the response routine whenever its assertion is detected. There are several disadvantages to this approach, however. First, the speed of response to the request is limited; it depends on the frequency with which the tests are made. Second, the main program's computation speed may be significantly reduced by the intermittent tests. Third, the designer of the main program has to consciously take into account the fact that an external request may develop.

Each of these disadvantages is eliminated when a hardware interrupt facility, normally incorporated into every processor's design, is employed. Such a feature provides immediate response, permits the main program to operate at full speed, and includes a linkage mechanism, to and from the interrupt-response routine, which is *transparent* to the main program. By way of analogy, consider a hotel clerk, busy with a task in the back office, who also has to attend to the occasional arrival of a customer at the front desk. Rather than take the time to periodically check the front desk, he installs an attention-getting bell.

We may begin by defining an INTERRUPT as a transfer of control to an interrupt-response routine, from any point within a main program. It is activated by the assertion of an external signal, at some random instant in time, and executed by special hardware built into the processor. It is understood, first, that the interrupt handler is specifically tailored to provide the proper response to the interrupt request and, second, that the interrupted program will resume its computation properly, after the interrupt routine completes (i.e., after the interrupt request has been "serviced," "processed," or "honored"). To mechanize such a facility, we must devise a logic structure that responds to the request signal, first by preserving the *state* of the main program, so that it may be resumed properly, and second by transferring control to the entry point of the response routine.

Consider, for example, a modification to the conventional FETCH-EXE-CUTE cycle of a processor, as indicated by the flow chart in Fig. 8.1(a). While INTERRUPT REQUEST = 0, the system behaves normally. If INTER-RUPT REQUEST = 1, at the onset of a FETCH, a special register-transfer sequence, called "*taking* the interrupt," is automatically executed by the hardware. This simple sequence preserves the current PC value on a stack and then jumps to a prearranged, constant location, symbolically named LOC. Saving the PC value is the *least* that must be done to preserve the state of the interrupted program. It is assumed that the interrupt-response routine already resides in memory, such that its first instruction is located at address LOC. After the interrupt is taken, normal FETCH-EXECUTE behavior re-sumes. The program now running, however, is the interrupt handler. (We are assuming that the INTERRUPT REQUEST signal remains asserted only until its activation has been detected.)

Note that the special TAKE INTERRUPT sequence is equivalent to the execution of a CALL instruction, to a specific location where the interrupt handler is assumed resident. For this reason, it is useful to regard an inter-rupt as a *CALL induced by an external signal*. Of course, this "CALL" does not appear in the main program. The instant at which it occurs is not known to the programmer. It may be termed an "involuntary" CALL because it is not consciously planned to be executed at a specific point in the main pro-gram, as is a conventional CALL instruction. This suggests that the mecha-nism by which an interrupt-response routine should *exit*, after it has com-pleted its task, is by way of the RETURN instruction. This will permit the main program to resume properly. The interrupt is termed "transparent" to the main program because the main program is not "aware" that an interrupt has taken place.

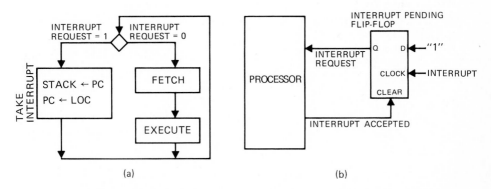

Figure 8.1 Elementary interrupt flow and typical interface

Without the existence of a specific signal indicating that the processor is *taking* an interrupt, the assumption that INTERRUPT REQUEST "knows" that it must deactivate at the proper instant is not realistic. Normally, a processor supplies such an "INTERRUPT ACCEPTED" signal at its interface. Figure 8.1(b) shows how this signal is usually employed. The assertion of INTERRUPT sets the INTERRUPT REQUEST flip-flop. When the processor responds, the assertion of INTERRUPT ACCEPTED resets this flip-flop. Such an interface structure is useful for two reasons. First, it prevents the interrupt service routine from being *itself* "interrupted." Second, it remembers the fact that an interrupt request is *pending,* for as long as it takes for the processor to respond. Since this response occurs at the termination of execution of the current instruction, before the fetch of the next one, the response to the interrupt request may not be immediate if the current instruction is one whose execution time is exceptionally long. The flip-flop ensures that the request is not forgotten.

A typical interrupt system is not designed *expecting* that INTERRUPT REQUEST will be deactivated immediately upon its acceptance. A more realistic arrangement is shown in Fig. 8.2. The processor now includes a special control flip-flop, named INTERRUPT ENABLE (abbreviated as "IE"), which must be SET to permit taking the interrupt. Note that the hardware's interrupt sequence now includes an automatic IE $\leftarrow$ 0 transfer, which ensures that the interrupt service program will not itself be interrupted. As a result of this modification, however, the response routine may no longer return to the main program with a simple RETURN instruction. Rather, a special RETURN FROM INTERRUPT instruction, now included in the processor's repertoire, must be evoked instead. Its execution is virtually identical to that of RETURN, but it also includes an IE $\leftarrow$ 1 transfer, which re-enables *further* interrupts.

Once an IE control flip-flop exists, consider the addition of SET IE and RESET IE control instructions to the processor's command repertoire. Given access to these instructions, a program has *control over its own interruptibi-*

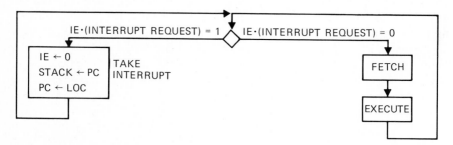

Figure 8.2 Taking the interrupt enable FLIP-FLOP into account

lity. For example, it may declare itself uninterruptible over a particularly crucial segment of code, which has severe real-time execution constraints. Conversely, in a more sophisticated system having several possible interrupt-request sources (and corresponding service routines), an interrupt-response routine may declare itself interruptible for certain "higher-priority" interrupts (discussed further later). Note that now the INTERRUPT PENDING flip-flop, introduced in Fig. 8.1(b), becomes even more applicable, because an interrupt request may *remain* pending for quite some time, if the running program is currently uninterruptible.

Preserving the *state* of the interrupted program, so that, on resumption, it will compute the *same* results as would have been calculated had the interrupt never taken place, requires more than just saving the PC value. The contents of *every* register whose value may affect the outcome of the computation must be preserved as well. Certainly, the contents of all memory areas used by the interrupted program must remain intact. Similarly, its processor registers, including all flag and indicator flip-flops, must also remain unaltered. (The contents of *temporary* registers—for example, the Instruction Register—whose values cannot affect the future of the computation, need not be preserved.) Since the interrupt-response routine is an arbitrary program, which *also* uses the processor registers, their values must be saved *before* they are modified. These saved values are then *restored*, just before the interrupted program is resumed. (We are assuming here that only one set of processor registers exists.)

As pointed out originally in Section 4.6, a stack is a convenient place on which to save a set of register values. If it is located in the main memory, the process of saving all key registers generally involves a sequence of memory accesses. Similarly, the restoration of these saved values requires an equal number of memory READs. As we will see later, a stack is a particularly important register-saving device when interrupt *nesting* is permitted—i.e., when an interrupt routine may *itself* be interrupted.

A processor may contain two or more *duplicate* register sets, only one of which is actively in use at any instant. They are present specifically to permit an *immediate* change of running program, not accompanied by time-consuming SAVE and RESTORE operations. A single collection of processor registers (which includes its *own* PC) is known as a PROGRAM STATE, even though the actual state of a program includes the contents of memory registers, as well. When two or more register sets exist, taking an interrupt constitutes merely changing a register set *selection code*, which may be as short as one bit in length. The old PROGRAM STATE is preserved because its registers are not used until it is re-established later. Under these conditions, an interrupt may be redefined as a *switch to an alternative PROGRAM STATE, induced by an external signal.*

In this regard, consider, for example, a processor having two identical register sets. The one currently in use is selected by a special control flip-flop. Assume that two distinct programs, of equal standing, are resident in the memory. Each of the PC's points within its corresponding program. As the system runs, suppose we have the power to change the state of the control flip-flop at any arbitrary instant in time (between instructions). Observe that each of these changes constitutes a *suspension* of the running program and a *resumption* of the suspended or "waiting" program. We may "throw this switch" as often as we like. In the end, the calculated results will be the same as those computed by uninterrupted runs of the same programs.

Unless otherwise specified, we will assume a *single* set of processor registers, in which case, SAVE and companion RESTORE operations must accompany each INTERRUPT and matching RESUME.

SAVE and RESTORE operations may be carried out either by hardware or by software. If the processor's interrupt capability is limited to that shown in Fig. 8.2, the interrupt-response program is left responsible for preserving the values of all of the registers that it will alter. Usually, such an interrupt handler is organized as shown in Fig. 8.3. (A simple, monotonic instruction sequence is assumed.) Before the specific response action begins, a sequence of instructions *saves* all key register values. After the specific response action terminates, the routine *restores* these saved register values before exiting with a RETURN FROM INTERRUPT instruction.

Note that the execution of a RETURN FROM INTERRUPT instruction essentially *undoes* all those operations performed by hardware when the interrupt was *taken* in the first place. A more sophisticated processor may include some or all of the register-saving operations within the TAKE INTERRUPT sequence. Generally, whatever is *saved* by the hardware, when an interrupt is taken, is *restored* by the hardware when the matching RETURN FROM INTERRUPT is executed. SAVE and RESTORE functions are examples of combined hardware–software tasks. Whatever is not *implicitly* executed by the hardware must be *explicitly* executed by instruction sequences.

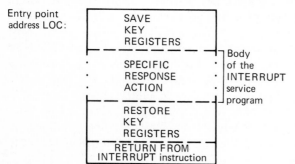

Figure 8.3 Typical interrupt handler organization

Hardware operations are faster than comparable software operations for many reasons. First, hardware register-transfer sequences may be tailored to specific functions; for example, certain micro-operations may be executed in parallel. Second, even when an instruction sequence matches a hardware register-transfer sequence on a one-to-one basis, the speed of the software sequence is reduced by at least the time taken to *fetch and interpret* each of the instructions.

In summary, an INTERRUPT, as we have defined it thus far, is a suspension of the running program (accompanied by a preservation of its state) and an initiation of a suitable response program, induced by an external signal. If permitted by an INTERRUPT ENABLE flip-flop, it is executed as a special register-transfer sequence, inserted *between* instructions.

A computer system may have *two or more* distinct INTERRUPT signal sources, each requiring a unique response. Under these conditions, as many different interrupt-response routines must be available (assumed all simultaneously resident in separate areas of the main memory) as there are interrupt sources. Each interrupt handler provides a response tailored to its cause for activation. For example, the response to an alarm signal may take action to eliminate the cause for the alarm condition. On the other hand, the response to the depression of a key on a keyboard may momentarily suspend the running program only for the time it takes to store the code for that key in a special message area in the memory.

When multiple interrupt sources exist, several new design issues arise. First, in addition to preserving the state of the interrupted program, the processor must now *identify* the interrupt source, so that it may initiate the proper response routine; the process of mapping an interrupt source to its own service program is known as interrupt *vectoring*. Second, since two or more interrupt requests may develop *simultaneously*, the processor must include a mechanism to resolve conflicting requests. (We are restricting our attention to a single processor system, in which only one program may run at a time.) Some type of *priority* rule must be adopted. Third, if several interrupt sources exist, what should be done when an interrupt request occurs while another is being serviced? May an interrupt handler program *itself* be interrupted?

There are numerous answers to these questions. For our purposes, we will concentrate on a single logic implementation, typical of that adopted in several systems, as an example of a solution. Other relevant alternatives will be pointed out as they arise.

Our sample system has an INTERRUPT ENABLE flip-flop whose state may be controlled by the program. Execution of an ENABLE INTERRUPTS instruction sets IE, and execution of a DISABLE INTERRUPTS instruction resets IE. The processor has a single, composite INTERRUPT REQUEST

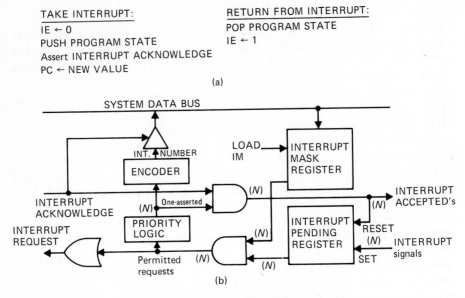

TAKE INTERRUPT:

IE ← 0
PUSH PROGRAM STATE
Assert INTERRUPT ACKNOWLEDGE
PC ← NEW VALUE

RETURN FROM INTERRUPT:

POP PROGRAM STATE
IE ← 1

(a)

(b)

Figure 8.4 A typical multiple-interrupt system

input signal. If it is asserted at the onset of a fetch, while IE = 1, the hardware executes the TAKE INTERRUPT sequence, defined in Fig. 8.4(a). After disabling further interrupts, *all* of the key processor registers (known as the PROGRAM STATE) are automatically pushed onto the system's stack. An output response pulse, named INTERRUPT ACKNOWLEDGE, is asserted, and a new value (whose derivation is explained later) is placed into the PC. Whenever the processor executes the RETURN FROM INTERRUPT instruction, it pops all of the key processor registers and re-enables interrupts. Note that the order in which the processor registers are restored is the reverse of that in which they were saved earlier.

The assumed hardware system, exclusive of that which executes the operations described in Fig. 8.4(a), is shown in Fig. 8.4(b). We imagine N independent external devices, on the right side of the diagram. Each has its own INTERRUPT output signal. If it requires a signal, indicating that its last request is being processed, it also has an INTERRUPT ACCEPTED input terminal. When its request is honored, the interrupt response routine that belongs to it is activated.

The INTERRUPT PENDING register contains N duplicates of the flip-flop (discussed earlier) shown in Fig. 8.1(b). Since the response to an interrupt request may be delayed indefinitely, it is remembered in its own "pending" flip-flop, which is reset when the request is finally "serviced."

The N-bit INTERRUPT MASK register provides the running program with the ability to control its interruptibility to each of the interrupt sources *individually*. Each MASK bit is a unique interrupt enable bit for its corresponding interrupt request. The INTERRUPT MASK register is loaded with a new value whenever a LOAD MASK instruction (also assumed part of the processor's repertoire) is executed, which asserts the LOAD IM control signal shown. Thus, the running program has control over the value in the INTERRUPT MASK register.

The MASK and PENDING register values are ANDed together to form an N-bit code, called PERMITTED REQUESTS, whose assertions define those pending interrupt requests that are currently enabled (i.e., not masked). The overall INTERRUPT REQUEST input to the processor is asserted if *any* permitted request exists.

Since only one of the interrupt handlers may run at a time, when two or more permitted requests exist a priority network is required to *select* only one of them. The PRIORITY LOGIC element shown is a duplicate of that described in Section 2.8 in conjunction with Fig. 2.26. It passes only the *rightmost* request. Since all of its other outputs are zero, its output code is labeled as "one-asserted". A priority logic element is employed in most situations in which only one of a set of competing requests must be chosen.

The ENCODER shown generates a unique INTERRUPT ID NUMBER for each possible input assertion. Typically, this number is the position number or index of the asserted input bit. (That is, the rightmost assertion will cause an output value of 1, while the leftmost assertion will cause an output value of N.) The combination of the PRIORITY LOGIC element with the ENCODER is commonly known as a *priority encoder*. Thus, the priority encoder selects, from all of the permitted interrupt requests, the one with the highest priority, and generates the *identifying* code that corresponds to it.

Note that the INTERRUPT ACKNOWLEDGE pulse is properly gated so that it resets the PENDING flip-flop (and asserts the INTERRUPT ACCEPTED reply) corresponding to that interrupt request that has been selected for service. The identifying code for this request, called INT. NUMBER, is simultaneously gated to the data bus. It is loaded into a destination (discussed further below) not shown on the diagram.

The problem of "vectoring" an interrupt to its proper handler program has several possible solutions. Consider, for example, a system in which all possible interrupts are initially directed to the *same* response routine. This program, commonly known as an interrupt *analyzer,* is responsible for determining the cause of the interrupt (perhaps by "interrogating" the external devices via appropriate I/O instructions) and subsequently transferring control to the proper handler. The flow chart shown in Fig. 8.5 describes such an organization. When it is used, the symbolic address NEW VALUE, in Fig.

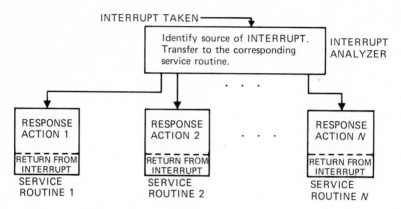

Figure 8.5   Interrupt vectoring via software

8.4(a), is the entry point of the analyzer routine. (NEW VALUE thus has the same purpose as had the symbol LOC, used earlier.)

If the hardware implementation shown in Fig. 8.4(b) is employed, the destination for INT. NUMBER is generally a register that is *accessible* to the interrupt-analyzer program. Under these conditions, the information necessary to determine which interrupt was taken is available without the need for further interrogation of the external devices.

Since the time taken by the interrupt-analyzer program to activate the proper response routine may not be tolerable, a faster vectoring mechanism may be achieved if the *hardware* calculates the proper entry address directly, during its TAKE INTERRUPT sequence. For example, if the INT. NUMBER value is used as an *index*, added to a known base address of a table in memory pre-arranged to contain the entry addresses of all of the response routines, a single memory access will fetch the proper value to be loaded into PC. Figure 8.6 depicts this scheme. When it is employed, the transfer PC ← NEW VALUE, in Fig. 8.4(a), is better described by

$$PC \leftarrow M(\text{TABLE BASE} + \text{INT. NUMBER}).$$

The base address TABLE BASE may be a constant or it may be the contents of still another programmer-accessible register. In the latter case, the programmer generally has available a "SET TABLE BASE" instruction whose execution alters this value. With this facility, the location of the table (of interrupt-service routine starting addresses) may be varied to suit the programmer.

In summary, when several interrupt sources exist, a priority encoder normally *selects and identifies* one of the activated sources. The ID code it generates is mapped into an address (usually by table lookup, either by software

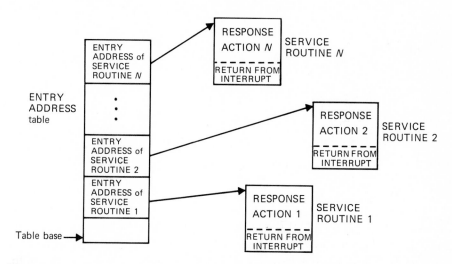

Figure 8.6   Interrupt vectoring via hardware PC ← M (Table base + Int. number)

or by hardware) which is the entry point of the corresponding service program.

A sufficiently simple interrupt system may not permit a response program to be *itself* interrupted. Pending interrupt requests are merely serviced in priority order and, as soon as one handler program exits, the next unmasked request is allowed to be serviced. However, since an interrupt is effectively a special CALL induced by an external signal, there is nothing to prevent interrupts from being *nested*. If a system like that described in Fig. 8.4 is employed, each interrupt merely pushes the PROGRAM STATE of the routine being interrupted onto the stack. When the interrupting routine exits, this state is re-established.

Any handler program may redefine its interruptibility, using a LOAD MASK instruction. After doing so, it may issue the ENABLE INTERRUPTS instruction to allow the possibility of its own interruption. Such a sophisticated system permits classes of interrupt priorities, in which a service routine at one priority level is interruptible only by higher-priority interrupts. Generally, the highest-priority interrupt in such a system is the most "catastrophic" situation—for example, a power failure, requiring attention that cannot be postponed. Note that, when nested interrupts are permitted and when each program has control over its own interruptibility, the INTERRUPT MASK register must be *part* of a PROGRAM STATE. If it is, an interrupt response routine that is itself interrupted may be later resumed with the same interruptibility it had earlier.

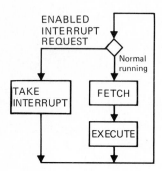

Figure 8.7   Interrupt flow summary

The general behavior of any processor's interrupt facility is recapitulated in Fig. 8.7. While the system runs normally, it executes a continuous sequence of FETCH-EXECUTE cycles, each of which contains an arbitrarily complex register-transfer sequence. (Alternative control-logic implementations were discussed in Chapter 7.) When an enabled interrupt request is present at the end of any EXECUTE cycle, the beginning of the next FETCH is *delayed* only for the time it takes for the hardware to execute the special TAKE INTERRUPT sequence. This "hiccup" may contain any number of register transfers, possibly as few as only one or two. Once its detailed behavior is included in the processor's flow chart (recall Fig. 7.4), its control is implemented using the same techniques previously described in Chapter 7. Specifically, one or more control states must exist that *identify* the TAKE INTERRUPT sequence. They induce the register transfers that comprise it. In addition, the set of condition or status signals whose values direct the *flow* of hardware operations must include signals like INTERRUPT REQUEST and INTERRUPT ENABLE.

The number of circumstances that interrupt request signals may represent is considerable. An interrupt signal is a fundamental mechanism by which an external device gets the "attention" of the processor. It generally indicates the occurrence of an external *asynchronous* event (taking place at an instant independent of the processor's central time clock). Two examples have already been discussed.

The number of "alarm" conditions and the responses they evoke vary widely. An impending power failure may require the appropriate storage of the state of the system, so that any computation already completed will not have to be repeated when power is restored. The response to a signal indicating, for example, that the level of liquid in a container has reached a predetermined threshold may be to close a valve to restrict the flow of that liquid.

There are a wide variety of interpretations that may be given to interrupt signals from external I/O devices. Normally, an I/O interrupt indicates the *completion* of a task previously assigned to the interrupting device. The interrupt handler may respond by processing some accompanying data before issuing *another* task to the same device. An I/O interrupt may indicate an abnormal condition. For example, an interrupt from a printer, indicating that it has run out of paper, may receive a response that temporarily terminates printer activity and informs the computer operator with an appropriate message.

An elapsed time clock or "timer" is an external device that uses the interrupt mechanism. It contains a *counter* that may be loaded by program (via the execution of a SET TIMER instruction, for example). The counter continuously advances, at a rate not necessarily synchronized with the processor's clock. It generates an interrupt when it reaches a predetermined count—typically, zero. A program uses the timer to accurately measure specific time intervals. The program's initialization of the timer value is equivalent to the setting of an electronic alarm clock. The occurrence of the timer's interrupt indicates that the specified time period has elapsed. The response this interrupt receives depends on how the program is using the timer. A traffic-light controller program, for example, may respond by altering the traffic-light pattern that it is generating.

The impression you have been given, that an interrupt may be initiated only by an external device, is not entirely accurate. While the interrupt concept is best introduced by employing external sources, as a matter of fact an interrupt may also be caused by an *internal* event that is *synchronous* with the running of the system. Specifically, a processor may be designed to generate an internal interrupt whenever it detects an *exception* condition, which indicates a program or data inconsistency or error. Such a machine is particularly useful because it is able to inform its user of program or data "bugs" that it has detected.

For example, suppose an instruction field has an undefined or unused value. Such a circumstance virtually always indicates an erroneous condition. Specifically, the interrupt generated by an undefined opcode value is called an opcode "trap." Similarly, an instruction's address value may be in error. It may point to a nonexistent memory area (recall the related discussion in Section 4.3) or to an area, generally termed "protected," to which the program is not permitted access. The attempt to write into a read-only area is also normally an error. Various internal "addressing error" interrupts may be generated in each of these cases. Similarly, faulty data conditions may arise. An arithmetic *overflow* is an example. The existence of an overflow interrupt relieves the programmer of the need to consciously check for the overflow condition after each arithmetic operation in which it might be generated.

Thus, an internal interrupt frequently indicates a fault in the running process. While the response routine may be able to "recover" from the error (for example, by rescaling the operands when an overflow has occurred), it is often necessary to suspend the running program permanently, in order to permit the error to be corrected. In such a case, of course, an orderly resumption of the interrupted main program does not take place. This is an elementary example demonstrating that an interrupt response or analyzer program may include some *supervisory* functions (which decide, for example, not to resume the interrupted routine if certain error conditions arise).

Using the interrupt definition given above, a programmer cannot predict exactly *when* or *if* an interrupt will occur. The body of an interruptible program is written without conscious concern for the interrupt; its occurrence will be "transparent" to the program. However, the evolution of the use of the interrupt mechanism has resulted in conditions under which it is advantageous for a programmer to include (in a program) instructions that are *known* to cause an interrupt. There are several reasons for this development. First, since an interrupt is equivalent to a CALL on a corresponding service routine, a "software-induced" interrupt may be preferable to a CALL, if more functions are implicitly executed by it. For example, if the processor's interrupt facility includes an extensive SAVE-RESTORE capability, a single interrupt-generating instruction may replace a CALL followed by an entire sequence of STORE or PUSH instructions. Second, as we will see further in the next chapter, the hardware of a typical computer system is normally augmented by a resident supervisory or "executive" program, which provides services, via software, that are not directly available from the hardware. An interrupt-analyzer program, as described above, may be considered as a kernel of a supervisor program. Given the existence of such a resident supervisor, it may be desirable for a running program to CALL on the services it provides. By issuing an interrupt-generating instruction (which includes a field whose value identifies the service desired), the CALL may be made without knowing exactly *where* the service program resides.

The idea of an intentionally coded interrupt first arose when the opcode trap was employed to augment the instruction repertoire of a processor. The supervisor program, on reception of an opcode trap, would use the "erroneous" opcode value to select a response routine whose execution would provide an advanced function not available in the hardware. This idea has since evolved, so that the repertoires of several existing processors now include a special instruction, called SOFTWARE INTERRUPT or SUPERVISOR CALL, whose execution merely *causes* an interrupt, with the value in one field of the instruction available to the responding program.

8.2 INPUT/OUTPUT DEVICES AND INTERFACES

A conventional I/O device reads from or writes to an information storage *medium* using one or more *heads*. Typically, it employs an electromechanical drive system to physically position or move the medium with respect to the heads, or to move the heads over the medium. A wide variety of peripheral devices exhibit characteristics that either directly match this model or may be interpreted in such a way that they agree with it.

For example, virtually all secondary memory elements, which provide mass storage for program libraries and data files, utilize *magnetic surface recording*. Each employs a magnetic coating on a surface as the information-bearing medium. The geometry of the surface characterizes the device. Magnetic disk and tape systems are the most common; magnetic drum and card systems are scarce, by comparison. Each device is capable of storing a large quantity of data, at a very low cost per bit. Since access to this data requires mechanical motion, the speed of such an element is several orders of magnitude lower than that of a conventional electronic memory.

A magnetic head reads or writes a magnetization pattern along a *track* in the information-bearing surface. A single track holds a long, *serial* bit string. The magnetic surface normally holds many parallel tracks, accessed by using either a single head or a *bank* of heads operating in parallel. If the heads are movable, an access normally begins with a "seek" operation, during which the heads are positioned properly over the selected tracks. The magnetic surface rotates past the heads at high speed, and each access includes a wait time until the desired track segment reaches the heads. Typically, the total access time is measured in tens of milliseconds, while the bit rate along a track (which depends on the speed of the moving surface with respect to the heads) may be as high as 10^6 bits per second. Since information is stored serially, such a memory is termed "sequentially addressed." The access time is *not* independent of the location of the stored data. To make the most of the relatively long time spent locating information, a typical secondary memory access transfers a *block* of many words to or from the system's main memory.

Paper is, of course, a very important information-storage medium. A *printer* is a computer output device which writes on paper using one or more print "heads." The visible symbol of a character may be created by any one of several methods, including impact through an inked ribbon, local heating of a temperature-sensitive paper, and use of a controlled ink jet. Typically, the paper moves vertically, line by line, while the head moves horizontally, along a line of the paper. A *plotter* also contains one or more print heads coupled with a more flexible drive system to permit creating arbitrary graphical images. A head may contain a conventional pen with its own ink supply, or a means to deposit an electrical charge pattern on the paper, which is later "developed" to form a visible image. A typical drive system moves the head over the paper surface, under computer control. The paper surface may remain flat or it may also move, with respect to the head(s). For example, it may be wrapped around the surface of a rotatable drum.

Computer input devices that *read* marks on paper are also widespread. Optical readers sense light and dark patterns. Magnetic ink readers sense character sequences (for example, on bank checks) that were printed with a special ink. Mark-sense readers detect marks made with special pencils. Each of these devices needs a means to "sense" a localized surface area, using one or more specially designed *read heads,* and a means to transport the paper medium with respect to these heads.

A hole in a paper surface remains as one of the most common bit marks. The writing head is a *punch.* A typical read head either detects a hole optically, by sensing whether or not light can pass through it, or electrically, by sensing whether or not an electrical contact can be made through it. The most common punched-paper medium is, of course, the punched card. However, punched paper tape has also seen extensive use. Each reader (input device) or punch (output device) requires a mechanical drive system, which normally moves the medium past the heads, whose positions remain fixed.

In addition to elements employing magnetic and paper information-storage media, which clearly fit the description given earlier, the characteristics of several other I/O devices may be interpreted as conforming to the same model. For example, a visual display screen is an output device containing a stationary, information-bearing surface on the inside of the face of a display tube. This surface is covered with a *phosphor* coating, which illuminates only at those points struck by an internal, computer-controlled electron beam. The light spot persists for only a short time; it must be "refreshed" (rewritten) to remain illuminated. The beam is thus the *head,* moving at an extremely high speed over the fixed, information-bearing surface. Clearly, no electromechanical drive system is employed. Similarly, the "heads" of an input keyboard may be considered as the fingers that move over it. The information-bearing surface may be real (for example, a sheet which the typist is reading and entering into the computer system), or it may be considered as "virtual" (when the typist is generating information extemporaneously). Note that an external data *communications* element (for example, a telephone data set) may be considered as an *intermediary* between the actual, remote I/O device and the local computer.

The characterization given above is not universally applicable. In particular, an external device that has little or no information-storage capability (for example, a computer-controlled machine) cannot be expected to contain an information-bearing medium or associated read/write "heads." If the external device is another (possibly special-purpose) computer, it may include an information-storage medium in the form of some internal memory, but the heads and mechanical drive system are clearly not present.

Each of the I/O elements introduced above is itself a complex system, many of whose design problems are beyond our present scope. The purpose of the discussion was to convey sufficient information about the characteristics of a typical I/O device so that aspects of its *interface* may be better understood. We proceed now to consider these issues.

Figure 8.8 illustrates the structure of a typical I/O device. The *instrument* contains all of its fundamental operational elements. For example, if the device conforms to the model introduced earlier, the instrument contains the information-storage medium, the read and write heads, the electromechanical drive system, and their immediate, analog control circuits. The *controller* provides the proper digital interface to the rest of the system. It performs all of the functions necessary to match the properties of the instrument with those of the system with which it interfaces. For example, it may contain "buffer" registers for temporary, intermediate data storage. It may contain logic to resolve timing differences between the instrument and the system. It may provide appropriate code recognition, decoding, and encoding functions. It may also perform signal-processing operations, such as digital-to-analog, analog-to-digital, serial-to-parallel and parallel-to-serial conversions.

As shown in Fig. 8.8, a typical controller interface includes a DATA IN port, a DATA OUT port, and one or more data-transfer *control* signals, which regulate the use of these ports. In this sense, the interface resembles that of a register. While a means to *enable* the device may be included as part of the control port, the interface very often includes a separate device *address* input port. The controller responds only when it recognizes its own identifying code at the address port. Note that the two data ports may be combined into a single, bidirectional data port.

Figure 8.9 shows a typical configuration of several I/O devices, coupled to a single bidirectional data bus. The code appearing on the device address lines enables one of the devices. When activated by the proper control-signal pattern, it responds either by gating data to the bus or by loading data from it. All control signals are shown coupled to a single control bus, which interfaces with the processor. The number of control signals, their meanings, and their directions vary. Examples of their use will be given throughout this chapter.

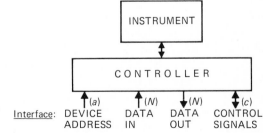

Figure 8.8 Typical I/O device structure

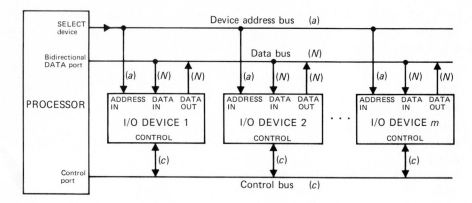

Figure 8.9   Typical I/O bus configuration

The information that crosses a typical DATA port may be classified either as *data* or as *control* information. Data is meant to be (temporarily or permanently) stored. When it passes across the I/O interface, its *form* of storage may change. Note that a block of input data, read from an external device and written into main memory, may actually be a *program*, to be executed later. From the I/O interface's point of view, the subsequent treatment of a data block is irrelevant. Its task is merely to faithfully transmit the data, no matter how it is later interpreted.

A control code, which crosses the I/O interface, has several possible uses. It may be a *command*, which actuates a special I/O control operation. For example, a control code from a processor may cause a tape drive to rewind or a printer to advance to a new page. The control word may be a *status* code, describing the state of the I/O device. It is normally employed to determine when data transfers are permitted and when exception conditions arise. For example, one status bit may specify whether or not an I/O device is ready to send or receive a new unit of data. Another status bit may indicate whether or not an "end-of-medium" (e.g., end of tape, out of paper, etc.) condition exists. The control word may be a data *attribute* code, describing some aspect of the data. For example, the first word of a data block is often used to specify the *length* of the block.

By convention, the words INPUT and OUTPUT imply data-flow directions with respect to the central processing unit. Thus, an INPUT device supplies data via its DATA OUT port, while an OUTPUT device receives data at its DATA IN port. Note that a DATA IN port also receives control information, while a DATA OUT port also supplies status information.

Since the source and destination devices of a typical I/O data transfer have independent timing systems, the most important function of data-transfer control signals is to properly *synchronize* the transmission of data units between them. We proceed now to discuss two of the most common data-transfer control mechanisms.

8.3 DATA TRANSFER CONTROL

Consider the transfer of a single word of data (typically, part of a sequence of transfers) from a source device, along a common data bus, to a destination device. (The term "device" is used here in its most general sense. It may represent a processor, a memory, or an arbitrary peripheral.) Either of the communicating elements may *initiate* the transfer, by asserting an appropriate control signal. Let us name the initiating device the "master" and the responding device the "slave." We begin by assuming that both elements are already aware of the *direction* of the transfer, so that each is ready to act appropriately, either as a source or as a destination.

Numerous control-signal protocols may be adopted to effect the transfer. For example, Fig. 8.10 illustrates an arrangement in which the master element implicitly assumes that the slave is *always ready* to properly respond, immediately, to its control-signal assertion. Under these conditions, only one control signal, which we may name TRANSMIT, is necessary. If the master is the source device [Fig. 8.10(a)], it places the unit of data on the bus and asserts TRANSMIT to cause the slave to load it. Note that TRANSMIT is not asserted until the data on the bus is known to be valid, and that the data is held valid, on the bus, until its reception by the destination device is assured. If the master is the destination device [Fig. 8.10(b)], its assertion of TRANS-MIT causes the slave to gate the data onto the bus. After waiting long enough

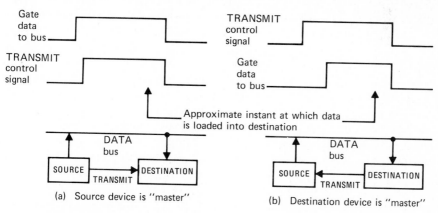

Figure 8.10 Data transfer using a single TRANSMIT control signal

to ensure that the received data is valid, the master loads it, before deactivating TRANSMIT. Note that the *meaning* of TRANSMIT to each device depends on the direction of the transfer. Observe also that the slave has nothing to say during either transaction.

In a more general data-communications situation, one device cannot assume that another device is always ready to respond immediately to its control-signal assertion. For example, suppose that the master is a processor, and that it asserts TRANSMIT every time it executes an I/O instruction. If the slave is an electromechanical device (e.g., a magnetic-tape unit), there is no guarantee that an arbitrary burst of TRANSFER assertions from the processor will always be accommodated by the slave. Conversely, even if the *slow*-er device were designated as the initiator of each data transfer, it is always conceivable that the state of the (albeit faster) responding unit will be such that it will not be able to accommodate the TRANSFER request immediately. For example, it may be momentarily "busy," executing some internal register-transfer sequence, at the instant of the TRANSFER request. For these reasons, a much more general control-signal protocol employs a second control signal, from the slave device, to indicate *when* a response occurs. It is applicable independent of the speeds of the communicating elements, and it operates properly whether or not the responding device is temporarily busy. Its use is illustrated in Fig. 8.11.

A more sophisticated bus structure, resembling the one shown in Fig. 8.9, has been postulated. Imagine that the control bus carries a code defining the *type* of transfer taking place. For our present purposes, we may assume a one-bit code, identifying only the transfer's *direction*. (Other bits may be employed to specify other aspects of the transfer—for example, the data unit *width*.) The initiating device begins by selecting the slave device, via the address bus, and by simultaneously specifying, on the control bus, the type of transfer desired. The transfer itself is effected by the proper interaction of two accompanying control signals, named REQUEST (from master to slave) and ACKNOWLEDGE (from slave to master). Note that four successive events, corresponding to the edges of the REQUEST and ACKNOWLEDGE assertions, are labeled [1] through [4], in both waveform sets. These points are referenced in the explanations given below.

If the master is the source device [Fig. 8.11(a)], it places the proper address, control, and data values on their respective buses and, when they are known to be valid, asserts REQUEST [1]. The addressed device responds, at an arbitrary time later, by loading the data value and asserting ACKNOWLEDGE [2]. The master later replies to the receipt of ACKNOWLEDGE, by disabling all paths to the buses and withdrawing the REQUEST assertion [3]. Finally, the slave detects this action and, in turn, responds by deasserting ACKNOWLEDGE [4], to complete the transaction.

If the master is the receiving device [Fig. 8.11(b)], after similarly placing proper values on the address and control buses, it asserts REQUEST [1], asking that the addressed device *send* it the next data item. The slave responds, at an arbitrary time later, by placing the requested data item on the data bus and asserting ACKNOWLEDGE [2]. When the master later loads this data value, it indicates that it has accepted the data by deasserting REQUEST [3]. Finally, the slave detects this action and withdraws ACKNOWLEDGE [4], to complete the transaction.

This type of control-signal interaction is sometimes called "handshaking." Note that, again, the *meanings* of REQUEST and ACKNOWLEDGE depend on the direction of the transfer. The comments, written alongside their waveforms, are logical interpretations. Observe also that the leading and trailing edges of REQUEST, in Fig. 8.11(b), convey distinctly different messages.

The REQUEST and ACKNOWLEDGE wires in Fig. 8.11 (like the TRANSMIT wires in Fig. 8.10) actually show the equivalent of signal paths normally developed via control buses. While an element may have as many data-transfer control terminals as there are devices with which it communi-

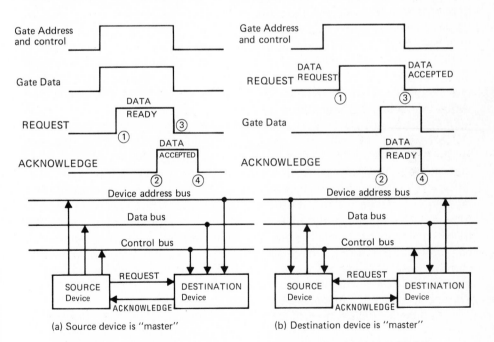

Figure 8.11 Data transfer model using a REQUEST-ACKNOWLEDGE control signal pair

cates, a much more efficient and flexible structure is illustrated in Fig. 8.12.[†] The DEVICE ADDRESS, DATA, and CONTROL buses have the same functions previously attributed to them. The REQUEST and ACKNOWLEDGE buses are considered as extensions of the CONTROL bus signal group.

At any given instant, at most two devices, one a master and the other a slave, may use the common bus. All other devices remain decoupled from it. If the system has one *permanent* master (for example, the processor), all REQUEST and ACKNOWLEDGE terminals are unidirectional. When *any* device may act either as a master or as a slave, a much more flexible communications network exists, and these control terminals must be bidirectional. However, since only one data transfer may take place at a time, conflicts may arise when two or more independent devices simultaneously wish to initiate a transmission.

Whenever there is contention for the use of any system "resource" (in this case, its collection of data-communication paths), a *priority* rule must be adopted to resolve conflicts. (Recall the use of the priority encoder to resolve interrupt conflicts, in Fig. 8.4.) The scheme illustrated in Fig. 8.12 implements a priority rule for bus requests. It may be employed as well to resolve conflicting interrupt requests. Two additional bus lines, BUS REQUEST and BUS BUSY, further extend the CONTROL bus signal group. A set of BUS GRANT signals, which propagate between adjacent devices, is also added. BUS BUSY is asserted while any device is using the bus. The BUS REQUEST bus is designed to deliver the "wired-OR" of all of the individual bus-request signals, in which case BUS REQUEST is asserted when any device requests use of the bus system. [This is one of the few examples in which the "wired-OR" function is an essential property. Any bus that carries the OR of two or more "request" signals (for example, an INTERRUPT REQUEST bus) is generally designed in this fashion.] If BUS REQUEST = 1 (while BUS BUSY = 0), the processor relinquishes control of the bus (at its discretion) by asserting BUS GRANT1. DEVICEi is designed to assert BUS GRANT($i + 1$) only if it receives a BUS GRANTi = 1 and it does *not* have a bus request pending. Thus, the BUS GRANT signal propagates to the *leftmost* device having an unsatisfied bus request. This device asserts BUS BUSY and proceeds to use the bus. While BUS BUSY is asserted, one device has control of the bus and the bus-grant priority system is disabled. When the current use of the bus completes, BUS BUSY is dropped and, if further requests exist, a new arbitration cycle may be initiated by the processor. Such a priority structure is sometimes called a "daisy chain" network.

The above discussion verifies that the number of CONTROL bus signals

---

[†] The organization of this system of buses is based on that of the UNIBUS, employed in Digital Equipment Corporation's PDP/11 family of computers.

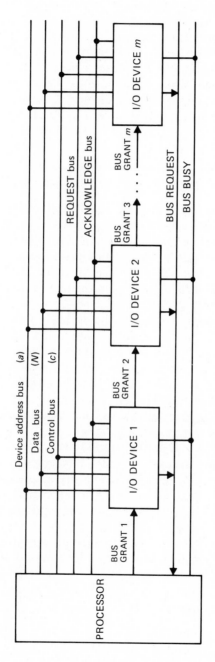

Figure 8.12 General purpose bus system—based on the PDP/11 UNIBUS. (Paths without arrowheads are bidirectional.)

and their meanings vary widely from system to system. In a network like that shown in Fig. 8.12, several additional control signals are normally found in the CONTROL bus group. For example, an INTERRUPT bus, which wire-OR's together all interrupt requests, is customary. So is a GENERAL RESET bus, which is activated whenever the processor is reset (perhaps by the depression of its RESET button). This permits a general reset of the processor to simultaneously reinitialize all peripheral elements. Other additions to the CONTROL bus group will be introduced later.

8.4 PROGRAM-CONTROLLED AND MEMORY-MAPPED I/O

The execution of a typical I/O instruction results in the transfer of data between one or more system registers and a specific I/O device. (You are reminded that, under special conditions, a data word may convey not real data, but control information. That is, it may be interpreted as a command, a data attribute, or a status indicator.) The most conspicuous differences between processors are found in their implementations of I/O functions. We begin by discussing the most elementary of these.

Based on the information you have already been given in Sections 6.2 and 6.5, you can define several possible formats for an I/O instruction. Remember that those aspects of its execution that are not implicitly understood must be explicitly specified. Three conceivable formats are shown in Fig. 8.13. Each has an opcode field, two of whose values represent INPUT and OUTPUT, respectively. Assuming that the number of possible peripheral elements is greater than one, each instruction also has a DEVICE NUMBER field, which selects one of the external devices.

The system register that will participate in the data transfer is implicit in format (a). Typically, it is a special processor data register, often known as the "accumulator." Format (b) includes a memory-address field, giving the programmer the freedom to explicitly select one out of many possible participating system registers. In both of these cases, we envision the execution of the instruction as consisting of a single transfer of a word, in the proper direction, between the selected device and the appropriate register. A more versatile instruction executes by transferring a *block* of words, beginning at a

      (a)   (b)   (c)

Figure 8.13   Three possible I/O instruction formats

specified address. Under these conditions, format (c) is applicable. It permits the programmer to specify the block length.

Figure 8.14 illustrates the implementation of a pair of elementary I/O ports, designed to match instructions like those introduced in Fig. 8.13. The network shown may be considered either as the "front end" of a specific I/O device, or as the logic just inside the processor's I/O interface. A single system data bus is assumed. A code recognizer, assigned to each I/O element, enables its proper response. The control signals IN and OUT are derived from the opcode decoder inside the processor. Each is asserted only during the execution of its corresponding I/O instruction. The device connected to the output port normally requires the destination buffer register shown. This register loads the data value on the bus, coming from the appropriate system source register, at the proper instant. We assume that control pulse P does not occur until this data is known to be valid. The IN signal gates the data, at the input port of the selected device, to the data bus.

Thus, assuming single word transfers, each of the I/O instructions above typically executes as follows:

OUTPUT: Selected output port ← R

INPUT: R ← Selected input port,

where R is the appropriate system register, and where the output port includes a buffer register to hold the data.

Every time an I/O instruction is executed, a unit of data is transferred between the selected I/O device and the appropriate system register. Note that the interface is designed on the assumption that the attached external

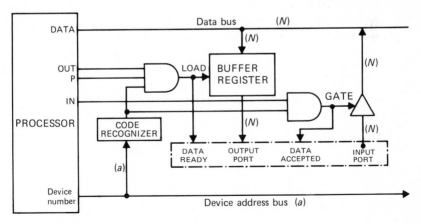

Figure 8.14   Structure of a typical elementary I/O port

elements are always ready to send or receive new data units whenever I/O instructions are executed. It is the responsibility of the program *not* to issue an I/O instruction unless the addressed device is known to be ready to respond to it. Typically, the program may wait some minimum time between transfers to the same device, or it may explicitly interrogate the device (via an INPUT instruction, for example) to ascertain its status, before issuing an I/O instruction to it.

While *all* types of I/O functions are controlled by program, this specific implementation—in which each unit of data transferred is explicitly initiated by the program and takes place during the execution of a corresponding instruction—is known as "program-controlled" I/O, primarily to distinguish it from other forms of I/O execution, to be discussed.

Note that the control signals DATA READY and DATA ACCEPTED, which accompany the I/O port data signals, *notify* the attached I/O devices of the arrival or acceptance of new data units. An output device uses the DATA READY signal as the indication that it must dispose of a new data item. Similarly, an input device uses DATA ACCEPTED as an indication that it should send the next data item to the input port.

Figure 8.15 shows two control flip-flops, which may be employed by output and input devices, respectively, to develop DEVICE READY status signals. We assume that DEVICE READY is one bit in the status code of the I/O device and that its value is available to the running program, by some presently undefined means. Its assertion indicates that the program may issue a new I/O instruction to the device.

In Fig. 8.15(a), the DATA READY pulse resets the flip-flop, causing DEVICE READY to be dropped. The circuit remains in this condition until the attached output device disposes of the new data item, at which time it asserts DATA RECEIVED, which sets the control flip-flop, reasserting DEVICE READY, to indicate readiness for a new data unit. In Fig. 8.15(b), DATA ACCEPTED also resets the control flip-flop, causing DEVICE READY to drop. When the input device has a new data item valid, at the input port, it asserts SEND DATA, which sets the control flip-flop, reasserting DEVICE READY, to indicate that a new data unit has been placed at the input port.

The above interaction, between DATA READY and DATA RECEIVED,

(a) Output control   (b) Input control

Figure 8.15 Status control FLIP-FLOPs matching Fig. 8.14 interface

illustrates the classic use of a buffer register. It is "filled" by a source device, in synchronism with its clock (clock pulse P), and it is "emptied" (figuratively speaking) by the destination device, in synchronism with *its* clock (not shown).

In summary, I/O activity is called *program-controlled* when each data-unit transfer is explicitly initiated by an instruction whose execution directly accomplishes it.

The operation of the circuit in Fig. 8.14 demonstrates that, as far as the I/O interface is concerned, an output device behaves as if it were a destination register, while an input device behaves as if it were a source register. Observe that this "equivalent" register is uniquely selected by a DEVICE ADDRESS code.

Keeping these points in mind, consider the following experiment: In Fig. 8.14, disconnect the DEVICE ADDRESS bus from its present signal source and connect it instead to the processor's MEMORY ADDRESS port. (Assume, for convenience, that the width of the port matches that of the bus.) In addition, disconnect the wire to the IN signal source and connect it instead to the memory's READ signal. Finally, replace the OUT and P inputs to the buffer register's control AND gate by a single connection to the memory WRITE control signal. Further, assume that the address value that *enables* this I/O device corresponds to a *nonexistent* (or permanently disabled) memory register. (Recall the discussion concerning not-yet-installed memory elements, given in Section 4.3.) Assuming that the I/O device is sufficiently fast to respond to all "accesses" to it, do you see that it will appear, to the running program, as the equivalent of a single memory register?

When such an arrangement is employed, the I/O device is termed *memory-mapped*. Every read access to its equivalent memory register will induce an INPUT operation, and every write access to the same register will induce an OUTPUT operation. Observe that, if all I/O devices are memory-mapped, the need for explicit I/O instructions, such as those described in Fig. 8.13, disappears. All accesses to the fictitious memory registers that represent I/O devices will automatically call for *implied* I/O operations. Hence, a processor having a memory-mapped I/O implementation need not have any instruction opcodes specifically allocated to I/O functions. (Recall that a memory-mapped I/O system was assumed during the description of the sample processor in Section 7.1.)

Actually, the width of a typical DEVICE ADDRESS bus is very small compared to that of the main-memory address, and only a few of the lowest bits of the latter are needed as a source for the former, in which case, only a small portion of the memory's addressable space (e.g., a small "page" of registers) need be allocated to I/O devices. A typical organization is illustrated in Fig. 8.16. A 16-bit memory address and an 8-bit device address are as-

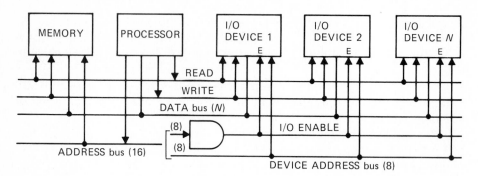

Figure 8.16 Typical system organization employing memory-mapped I/O

sumed, giving the possibility of as many as 256 I/O devices. The AND gate shown detects when the upper half of the memory address is a hex "FF". Whenever it is, the I/O system is enabled via the assertion of I/O ENABLE. Thus, only the uppermost 256 of all of the 65536 possible memory registers may not be normally addressed. Note that the signals WRITE and READ propagate to all devices.

Each of the I/O organizations shown in Figs. 8.9, 8.12, and 8.14 is drawn with the main memory interface omitted, for simplicity. In each case, the main memory module may be imagined as situated to the left of the processor, sharing the system's central data bus, but with its own independent AD-DRESS, READ, and WRITE interface. In contrast to this organization, in which memory and I/O systems are independently addressed, the example in Fig. 8.16 illustrates an organization where the two systems totally share the same addressing interface.

Another common arrangement, shown in Fig. 8.17, is a compromise between the two described above. The I/O and memory systems share the same data and address buses, but have independent READ and WRITE (or

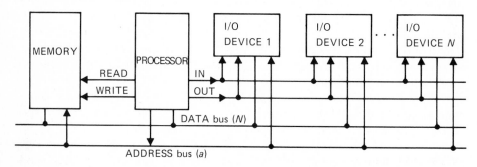

Figure 8.17 Sharing of the address bus by memory and I/O systems

IN and OUT) control signals. The processor in such a system has explicit INPUT and OUTPUT instructions in its repertoire. Their executions activate the corresponding IN and OUT control signals. However, the DEVICE NUMBER field in these instructions emanates from the processor's memory-address port (directed there via an internal multiplexer) to select the addressed device. Such operation is acceptable provided that it is not necessary to *simultaneously* address a register in the memory. Thus, if the system register, which communicates with the selected I/O device, is in the *processor*, the memory-address bus may be shared for the two purposes indicated (that is, the address bus is available if the memory is not used during the execution of I/O instructions).

The use of a memory-mapped I/O system simplifies a programmer's task by permitting I/O devices to be accessed as if they were memory registers. Some economies in hardware implementation are also realizable. There are, however, some disadvantages. Since I/O operations are indistinguishable from conventional memory operations, they are harder to isolate in programs. In addition, addressing errors may convert conventional memory operations into I/O operations, and vice versa. Some address space is also sacrificed when a memory-mapped I/O organization is employed.

8.5 INTERRUPT-DRIVEN I/O AND DIRECT MEMORY ACCESS

A typical I/O process entails a complex sequence of events. It usually begins with a set of one or more control operations, which *prepare* for the data transfer. These may include special electromechanical actions. For example, it may be necessary to position a disk head properly, using a "seek" operation, or to start a tape drive in motion. The initiation phase also may include the setting up of special registers that will govern the data-transfer phase. For example, if the I/O device is capable of more than one data-transfer mode, the proper mode must be established. Similarly, the initialization of a word counter—defining the size of the data block to be transferred, and an address register—locating its origin in memory, are also usually included.

Once the initiation phase has been completed, the main part of the process takes place. It normally consists of a sequence of data transfers between the selected I/O device and a specific memory area. A termination phase may follow. For example, a disk head, which was in contact with the magnetic surface, may be released, or a tape drive may be stopped.

Since the maximum rate at which a typical peripheral device can absorb or generate data is significantly lower than that of the main memory, each data-unit transfer is normally *device-initiated,* not processor-initiated; that is, every memory access, which is part of the data-transfer sequence, occurs in response to a REQUEST control signal from the peripheral. Depending on the direction of the data transfer, the assertion of REQUEST, by the device, signifies one of the following messages:

1. "I am ready for you to send me another unit of data."
2. "Here is another unit of data for you to dispose of."

The request is "honored" when the proper memory access takes place.

If an external device is electromechanical in nature, the execution time of an I/O operation in which it participates is normally measured in tens or hundreds of milliseconds. In contrast, the execution time of a typical non-I/O instruction is measured in microseconds. Thus, a program having any reasonable amount of I/O activity, which does nothing while its I/O operations are in progress, will spend virtually all of its time executing I/O instructions. We proceed now to consider how means may be devised to permit continued program execution *while* time-consuming I/O operations are in progress. Under what conditions is it possible for I/O operations and other computations to take place *concurrently*, and how is such parallelism implemented?

Consider a data block transfer that is executed as a sequence of device-initiated word transfers. Assume that any two successive word transfers are separated by a relatively long time period. For example, suppose they occur 50 milliseconds apart, on the average. The external device may be a data communications element, receiving data at a slow rate. It may be a paper-tape punch, or a printer, which must execute some mechanical motion, of the medium or of the head, before it can accept the next character. It may be a keyboard, which generates data only as fast as its typist can type.

Assume that this I/O operation and the program we wish to run concurrently with it are *independent* processes. That is, assume that the program has no need to access the I/O data area while the data-transfer sequence is taking place. As we will see later, the I/O operation need not *belong* to the program that is running in parallel with it. It may not have been initiated by that program, but rather by some *other* program. However, even if the I/O process *was* initiated by the concurrent program, the assumption of independence is still satisfied if the running program's computation does not involve the I/O area. For example, a program may be designed to process data in one memory area (A) while a second, distinct memory area (B) is taking part in an I/O operation. When this activity completes, the roles of these areas may be reversed, permitting the program to use area B for computation while area A takes part in a newly initiated I/O process.

Given conditions under which parallelism is feasible, we proceed to discuss two possible arrangements that implement it. First, suppose that the I/O device's data transfer REQUEST signal is used as an INTERRUPT signal,

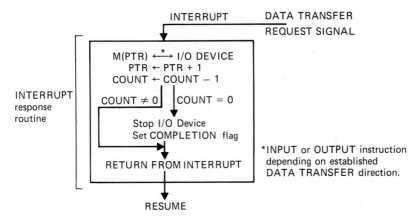

Figure 8.18   A typical interrupt-driven I/O data transfer

whose corresponding interrupt-response routine includes an I/O instruction, whose execution transfers the next data item. Such an organization is illustrated in Fig. 8.18. It depicts only the interrupt-response process. We assume that the main program, which is not shown, has previously issued appropriate I/O control instructions to activate the I/O device, and that its present computation is independent of the I/O area.

Note that the entry path to the response routine simplifies what may be a complex process. It begins with the assertion of the REQUEST signal. Only after the processor has taken the interrupt, saved the main program state, and vectored to the proper interrupt handler (based on an identification of the interrupt source) does the routine indicated begin to run. Its function is quite simple. It issues the I/O instruction that transfers the next data item and then advances a pointer past it. The data item is denoted by M(PTR), and PTR is the pointer (assumed originally initialized by the main program). Following the data transfer, the response routine decrements a count value, representing the number of words left to transfer (which was also initialized by the main program), and tests to see whether or not it has reached zero. If it has, the handler deactivates the I/O device with a special control instruction and sets a status indicator, which the main program may later test, to see if the I/O process has completed. Finally, the response routine returns, to permit the main program to resume.

The elapsed time, from interruption to resumption, depends, of course, on the speed of the processor and on the hardware facilities it offers. An estimate in the vicinity of 50–100 microseconds is not unreasonable. Thus, if requests arrive, on the average, every 50 milliseconds, the time taken to service them uses a negligible portion (one thousandth) of the computation time available.

Such an *interrupt-driven* I/O process is particularly useful when the I/O data rate is sufficiently low. The available time for concurrent computation decreases as the frequency of requests increases. To accommodate high data-rate devices and still permit parallel computation, it is necessary to give the I/O elements *direct* access to the memory. When this is done, it is no longer necessary to use the processor's interrupt facility and a special response program to service each data request. Rather, their functions are incorporated into the hardware of the I/O controller, significantly reducing the time required to service each data request. We proceed, then, to study a typical Direct Memory Access (or DMA) system, which is able to accommodate external devices of much higher speed while still permitting I/O–compute simultaneity.

Consider any instruction whose execution time is inordinately long compared to that of the average instruction in a processor's repertoire. While an I/O instruction is the principal example meeting this criterion, others that may be applicable include an instruction that MOVEs an extremely large data block from one region in memory to another, or an instruction that DELAYs (merely waits) a relatively long period of time. If special hardware were available to execute such an instruction *in parallel* with the processing of others, an entire subprogram of the others might be processed while it is executing. Such an arrangement is workable if the parallel instruction sequence does not assume *completion* of the time-consuming operation. That is, the two parallel processes must be independent.

To implement this proposal, let us redefine the lengthy operation as a process that is only *initiated* by the execution of a conventional processor instruction. The initiating program immediately proceeds with the *next* instruction in sequence, without waiting for the initiated process to complete. All subsequent instructions, assumed independent of the initiated process, are therefore executed in parallel with it. If this is the case, how is the running program made aware of the *completion* of the lengthy process? The answer is that an *interrupt* proclaims this event.

The execution of such a parallel process may be conveniently divided into the following three phases:

Initiation: When sufficient information is made available to the parallel execution element to permit it to carry on independently. The program effectively says to it: "Do this operation and call me when you're done."

Execution: When the register transfers that comprise the main body of the process are performed. (This is the time-consuming portion.)

Termination: When a processor interrupt signal is generated, marking the end of execution.

An elapsed-time clock or timer, introduced in Section 8.1, is a good example of a device that conforms to this model. While it is possible for a program to wait for a specific time interval (doing nothing else) either by executing a DELAY instruction, if one is available in the repertoire, or by simulating such a DELAY with a loop of dummy NOOP instructions (just to waste sufficient time), a program that employs a timer for this purpose may proceed with *other* computations while the time interval is elapsing. The SET TIMER instruction initializes the timer. It effectively says to the timer: "Call me when this amount of time has elapsed." Thus, the function of the timer's termination interrupt is identical to that of the alarm in an alarm clock.

A Direct Memory Access (abbreviated as "DMA") facility is implemented by equipping an I/O controller with sufficient control hardware so that it can carry out a data-transfer operation independently, while the processor continues to run. The controller is initiated by the execution of a START I/O instruction, which assigns to it appropriate data-transfer parameters, including the transfer direction and the location and size of the I/O area in memory. Thus, the hardware required by a DMA controller, to execute the data-transfer sequence, normally includes a pointer register, selecting the next data item in memory, and a counter, specifying the length of the remaining data block. The device also needs a direct access path to the memory, normally provided via a common data bus. During the execution of the I/O operation, in the DMA mode, the controller makes the appropriate number of direct memory accesses, while the processor continues to run. It keeps track of the process by updating its address and count values, until the operation completes, at which time it generates an *I/O termination* interrupt, informing the program of this fact.

Note that, while a timer may run totally independently of the processor, a typical I/O data transfer cannot, because conflicts arise when the processor and the I/O controller both require access to the main memory simultaneously. Again, some priority rule must be adopted. Since the memory-access request rate of the I/O controller is typically very small compared to that of the processor, the priority rule that is normally adopted is to honor the I/O request immediately, whenever it occurs.

To temporarily prevent it from making a conflicting memory access, the processor is equipped with a special input-control signal, called DMA REQUEST or HOLD. Assertion of this signal by the I/O controller causes the processor to decouple from the memory-access buses and to "freeze" in its present state (i.e., to stop running for the duration of the HOLD assertion). As soon as HOLD is withdrawn, the processor continues to run. Since its state was not disturbed during the hold, it proceeds to compute the same results as would have been calculated had the hold never occurred.

Figure 8.19 illustrates the structure of a typical DMA controller and its interface to a processor. We assume that the INPUT INSTRUMENT is already prepared to send data. While ACTIVATED, it periodically delivers a new data item and asserts DATA READY. The input process begins with the execution of a START I/O instruction, which asserts the START I/O pulse, after having placed the initial COUNT and ADDRESS values, found in the instruction, on the data bus. This pulse initializes the COUNT and ADDRESS registers and sets the ACTIVATE (or "BUSY") flip-flop, which signals the input instrument to send data at its own natural rate. Whenever a new data item arrives, its accompanying DATA READY pulse loads it into the DATA BUFFER register and sets DMA REQUEST.

At the beginning of the very next memory cycle, the processor freezes its state and decouples from the buses (at the top of the diagram), no matter what it is presently doing. It indicates that it has done so by asserting DMA ACKNOWLEDGE. This signal gates the DATA and ADDRESS values to their respective buses. It also activates a circuit that generates a WRITE pulse, after waiting for a time greater than the memory's access time. This pulse causes the proper I/O data transfer to take place. It also resets DMA REQUEST.

The processor, in turn, responds by dropping DMA ACKNOWLEDGE and proceeding with its computation. The trailing edge of DMA ACKNOWLEDGE advances COUNT and ADDRESS to their new values, in preparation for another similar sequence. Note, however, that when COUNT reaches zero, the assertion of the COUNT = 0 signal deactivates the input instrument and sets INTERRUPT REQUEST, signifying completion of the data-transfer process. The processor's response to the interrupt asserts INTERRUPT ACKNOWLEDGE, which causes INTERRUPT REQUEST to drop.

Every time a DMA word transfer occurs, a memory cycle is said to have been "stolen" by the I/O controller. Note that such a momentary interruption may occur at the beginning of *any* processor cycle, whether the machine is in the midst of fetching or executing an instruction. Whenever it happens, the execution time of the current instruction is increased by the duration of one cycle (which is extremely short, generally in the vicinity of a microsecond). When we compare this time to the typical execution time for an interrupt-driven data transfer (Fig. 8.18), a dramatic reduction is evident. Yet both processes achieve exactly the same function. This reduction permits much higher I/O data rates, in the simultaneous I/O–compute mode, before interference with the running program becomes noticeable. (*Interference* is generally defined as the fraction of the total computation time available that is used to service concurrent I/O data-transfer requests. It is usually expressed as a percentage value. For example, if one out of every hundred memory cycles is stolen, an interference level of one percent exists.)

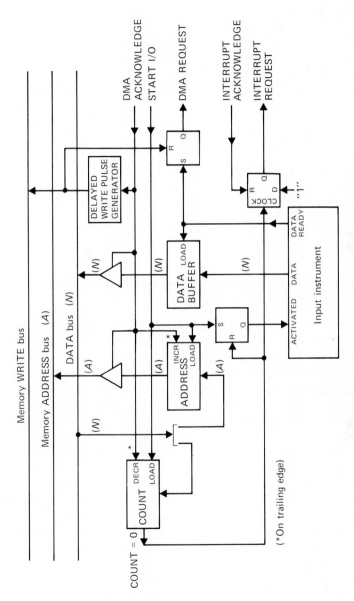

Figure 8.19 Typical DMA controller structure

It is important to clearly distinguish between the momentary "interruption" of a program, for DMA servicing, and a full-program interrupt, as it was explained in Section 8.1. A DMA cycle may occur at the beginning of any processor cycle. It is exactly one cycle long, and the state of the interrupted program is preserved by a simple freeze, because the DMA servicing function does not require use of any of the program's registers. A program interrupt, on the other hand, is a much more profound interruption. It is normally accompanied by a complex SAVE–RESTORE operation. It may occur only between instructions and its duration is unpredictable.

It is instructive to note that a form of DMA activity was actually first introduced during the explanation of the operation of the video display in Section 5.3 (see Fig. 5.24). In that system, the memory (the video RAM) was normally accessed on a regular basis by the *I/O device*, to refresh the display. The CPU required only intermittent access to it, to modify the picture. To gain access, the CPU asserted the CPU REQUEST signal, which gave it the momentary access it required. Observe that, in this case, the *processor* is the interrupting device.

8.6 I/O PROCESSORS

Several new design issues arise when we wish to permit many external devices to *simultaneously* execute I/O data-transfer operations in the DMA mode. First, a priority network is required to resolve conflicting memory access requests from competing I/O controllers. Second, it is conceivable that the composite I/O data rate, when several high-speed I/O devices are simultaneously active, may either raise the interference level to an intolerable degree (in which case, the main program is rarely permitted to run), or, worse, result in lost data during peak I/O servicing demand periods, because some I/O requests were not honored within their maximum response time limits. Third, the program's management of numerous simultaneous I/O activities becomes complicated. For example, it is more likely that the program will have to guard against issuing an I/O instruction to an *already busy* device. Fourth, rather than duplicate the same hardware control structures in each of the I/O controllers, it may be desirable to concentrate all of these networks into one *central* controller which, in turn, communicates with an array of I/O devices configured around it.

An I/O processor is sometimes defined as a "super" I/O controller, which manages an array of devices clustered around it. The configuration shown in Fig. 8.20 is typical. Each I/O processor is situated between the main system data bus and a family of peripherals. Each of its devices com-

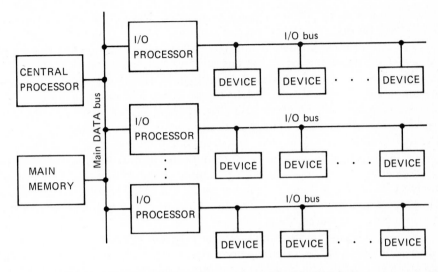

Figure 8.20   A system configuration employing I/O processors

municates with it via a local I/O bus, whose internal organization resembles that illustrated in Fig. 8.9. An I/O processor is sometimes also called a "channel," because all transmissions between its devices and the main memory pass through it.

There is a more fundamental property of such a device that accords it the right to call itself a processor. Consider the nature of a typical I/O process. It is a complex *sequence* (or "chain") of events. Its preparation phase alone may involve a complicated sequence of steps, including status testing, electromechanical action, control-register initialization, and even preliminary data transfer. (For example, once a proper disk track has been found, it may be necessary to read record "header" information, written on the track, in order to locate a desired sector.) The data-transfer phase of an I/O process may consist of a sequence of separate block transfers—possibly because the memory blocks are noncontiguous. The termination phase may itself include a sequence of control steps.

Given that I/O instructions come in sequences, it appears inefficient to duplicate the complicated procedures accompanying the termination interrupt of one I/O instruction, only to go on to initiate the *next* one. A preferable implementation assembles all of the I/O instructions of a process sequentially in memory, as an I/O *program.* The initiating START I/O instruction then passes, to the addressed I/O processor, only the *location* of the I/O program in memory. Once activated, the I/O processor proceeds to *execute* this program independently, fetching and executing each I/O instruction in turn, while the main processor continues to run. Only on completion of the entire program does a termination interrupt occur.

Note that the I/O processor must contain its own "Program Counter" and the means to determine when the current I/O instruction has completed, so that the next one may be fetched. Additionally, the I/O program must include a means to identify the *last* I/O instruction. Its execution induces the termination interrupt. Observe also that, if the I/O processor has its own Program Counter, it has the capability to execute *branches*. Indeed, the instruction repertoire of a typical I/O processor includes a small number of branch or skip instructions to accommodate the typical I/O process, which includes some conditional steps (e.g., simple loops and noncontiguous sequences). Thus, when a main program issues a START I/O instruction to an I/O processor, it is effectively saying to it: "Do this *program* of operations and call me when you're done."

When a computer system employs an I/O processor, we must distinguish between *two* classes of I/O instructions: those in the repertoire of the master processor and those which the I/O processor understands. To make this distinction clear, the instructions in the I/O processor's repertoire are sometimes renamed as "command words." The master processor needs very few I/O commands in its repertoire, because all of the detailed operations of an I/O process are expressed in the I/O program that the I/O processor interprets. Fundamentally, the main processor needs a START I/O instruction, which assigns an I/O program to an I/O processor, a TEST I/O instruction, which permits the CPU to determine the current status of any I/O device, and a HALT I/O instruction, which permits the main program to stop an I/O operation at any time.

A possible format for these instructions is illustrated in Fig. 8.21. The opcode selects one of the three functions listed above. The DEVICE ADDRESS field selects an I/O processor and identifies a specific device attached to it. The MEMORY ADDRESS field is used by the START I/O instruction, to point to the first instruction of the I/O program. Alternatively, this address field may be omitted, if the I/O program's starting address is determined *implicitly*. For example, each I/O processor may be assigned a special memory register whose contents *point* to the I/O program. If this is the case, the main program must ensure a proper pointer value there before issuing the START I/O.

OP CODE	DEVICE ADDRESS	MEMORY ADDRESS

Figure 8.21 Possible format for a main processor I/O instruction

OP CODE	MODE	MEMORY ADDRESS	COUNT

Figure 8.22   Possible format for an I/O processor command

A typical format for an I/O processor command is shown in Fig. 8.22. The MEMORY ADDRESS and COUNT fields normally identify the participating I/O data area in memory. The MEMORY ADDRESS field points to its base, while the COUNT field defines its extent (the number of words in it). The essential commands to which opcodes are normally assigned include READ (or INPUT), WRITE (or OUTPUT), SENSE STATUS, JUMP, CONTROL OPERATION, and STOP. The first two execute by transferring, in the DMA mode, a block of words between the addressed I/O device and the designated I/O area. SENSE STATUS executes by retrieving from the I/O device a code defining its present state. JUMP permits alteration of the flow of the I/O program based on this status information. CONTROL OPERATION permits the I/O program to evoke an arbitrary control action (such as REWIND, PAPER ADVANCE, etc.) in the addressed I/O device. Finally, STOP terminates the I/O program.

The MODE field permits additional flag values, which may be employed to further modify the opcode specification. Numerous other opcode assignments may be made. For example, READ BACKWARD is an applicable operation for a magnetic tape unit which permits its stored data to be read while the tape drive motion is reversed. Note that a DEVICE ID code is not included in this sample format, because it was already specified in the START I/O instruction that initiated the I/O program. Thus, we are assuming that all of the commands in an I/O program are directed to the device named in its START I/O instruction.

An I/O processor may be designed to manage the devices that are assigned to it in any of several ways. Assuming that its devices are capable of high data-transfer rates (for example, assuming they are magnetic disk units), it may be necessary to allow only one device to be active at a time. The system may not be able to accommodate two or more intermixed DMA request sequences, either because the composite I/O data rate may be too high or because the worst-case servicing delays may exceed a tolerable threshold, causing data to be lost. Under these conditions, the I/O processor is designed to remain "busy," incapable of accepting a new START I/O command, while its current I/O program is in progress.

Alternatively, all of the devices attached to one I/O processor may be relatively low-speed I/O components (for example, keyboards, printers, card readers, etc.). In this case, even if all were operating simultaneously, the composite data rate would still be sufficiently low. To permit *several* I/O processes to be active simultaneously, the I/O processor must be more complex. It must have the capability of *multiplexing* a number of separate data streams onto one composite data stream. Typically, it maintains a separate small register set for each of its devices. This set contains, at least, a buffer register for a unit of data, some status flip-flops, and the I/O Program Counter for the corresponding device. Since it receives data-transfer service requests from several sources, each request must be accompanied by the identifying code of the requesting device.

Not all of the instructions in the I/O program for a typical high-speed element call for the transfer of data. For example, most of the preparatory steps, before data transfer actually begins, are time-consuming control operations. Ideally, they should not prevent *other* high-speed data transfers from taking place. A more sophisticated I/O processor, then, improves data throughput by permitting two or more high-speed-data-transfer I/O programs to be simultaneously active. It maintains the restriction, however, that only one data transfer may be accommodated at a time. Thus, while one disk is executing a seek operation, another may be transmitting data.

8.7 ASYNCHRONOUS SERIAL CHARACTER TRANSMISSION

Consider a data-transmission interface containing only a single, *serial* signal in each transfer direction. The telephone network is the most common example of a system employing such an interface. Assume that each signal conveys an *asynchronous* stream of characters. That is, the time interval separating two adjacent characters is not predictable. For example, the character stream that is generated by a keyboard is asynchronous. The signal protocol that we study below was developed to accommodate terminals (employing keyboards) that used the telephone network as the data-transmission medium. It is now employed by virtually every low-data-rate computer terminal device (containing some appropriate keyboard/printer/display combination). Most of its electrical characteristics are spelled out in an Electronic Industries Association standard (identified as RS232–C).

To begin with, let us assign, to one of the two possible signal levels, the responsibility for representing the quiescent IDLE condition, which exists *between* character transmission. This implies that the very first signal transition, to the *other* signal level, must indicate the beginning of a character transmission. All bits in the serial character code are allotted equal-duration time slots. By convention, the least significant bit is transmitted first. Since every transmitted data bit may be "1" or "0", the signal value immediately after the character's leading edge cannot represent the *first* data bit, because its value is already fixed. Consequently, the very first time slot is assigned to indicate the start of transmission. It conveys what is called a "start bit," whose value is always the inverse of the idle level.

Once the last (most significant) data bit has been transmitted, the signal returns to the idle level unconditionally. It must *remain* there for a specific minimum time period, before another character may be generated. This interval permits the receiving device to recover from the just-completed transmission. It ensures that the receiver is ready to accept another character. The minimum terminating idle period is normally either one or two time slots long. Each of these time slots conveys what is called a "stop bit", whose value is always at the idle level.

The number of data bits, between the start bit and the first stop bit, is a known constant. While various conventions have been used, virtually all present systems transmit an eight-bit character. Note that the time taken to transmit each character is either 10 or 11 time slots long. Effectively, the serial data code is preceded by one constant start bit and followed by one or two constant stop bits, of the opposite value.

Figure 8.23 shows an example of the transmission of a single hex "39" character. It assumes a high idle level and two stop bits. Note that a signal edge occurs only when a next bit is the inverse of a persent one. Observe also that the eight-data-bit character transmission consumes 11 bit times, when the fixed "bracket bits" are included.

Transmission takes place at the maximum character rate when the last stop bit of one character is immediately followed by the start bit of the next character. Note that the rate of transmission of actual data bits is somewhat lower than that calculated with the bracket bits included. The latter rate is called the *baud* rate. For example, at 10 characters per second, with two stop bits per character, each time slot is 9.09 milliseconds long. Actual data is transmitted at 80 bits per second, which corresponds (with two stop bits) to 110 "baud." At 30 characters per second, with one stop bit per character, each time slot is 3.33 milliseconds long. Actual data is transmitted at 240 bits per second, which corresponds (with one stop bit) to 300 "baud."

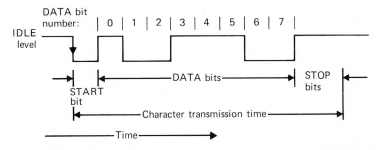

Figure 8.23   Asynchronous serial representation of a hex 39 code

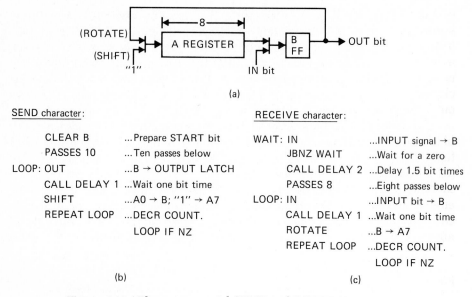

(a)

SEND character:

	CLEAR B	...Prepare START bit
	PASSES 10	...Ten passes below
LOOP:	OUT	...B → OUTPUT LATCH
	CALL DELAY 1	...Wait one bit time
	SHIFT	...A0 → B; "1" → A7
	REPEAT LOOP	...DECR COUNT.
		LOOP IF NZ

RECEIVE character:

	WAIT: IN	...INPUT signal → B
	JBNZ WAIT	...Wait for a zero
	CALL DELAY 2	...Delay 1.5 bit times
	PASSES 8	...Eight passes below
LOOP:	IN	...INPUT bit → B
	CALL DELAY 1	...Wait one bit time
	ROTATE	...B → A7
	REPEAT LOOP	...DECR COUNT.
		LOOP IF NZ

(b)   (c)

Figure 8.24   Elementary serial SEND and RECEIVE routines

Figure 8.24 illustrates two typical routines that might be used to send or to receive a single character. The executing processor is assumed to contain the network shown in part (a). An eight-bit data register A either holds the character to be sent or will hold the character received. The symbols shown at the inputs to A and to its companion B FLIP-FLOP are meant to represent two-way, one-bit-wide multiplexers; B always receives A's shifted-off bit during the execution of a SHIFT or ROTATE instruction. (The shift direction is assumed to be right, as shown.) On a SHIFT, A's shifted-in bit is a constant "1". On a ROTATE, it is the previous value of B. For simplicity, we assume that execution of an IN instruction transfers the current value of the input signal, labeled as IN BIT, into B. Similarly, an OUT instruction executes by transferring the contents of B, labeled as OUT BIT, to an output latch, not shown in the diagram.

We also assume that the processor executes a "PASSES" instruction by loading a special counter with the immediate value specified in the instruction. Further, we assume that "REPEAT" executes by decrementing that counter's value and branching to the address specified if the count has not yet reached zero. REPEAT "falls through" to the next consecutive instruction when the counter value reaches zero. We assume as well that the execution times of all instructions are negligible compared to the duration of one serial time slot.

The routines in parts (b) and (c) are written in an assembly language (i.e., using symbolic equivalents of opcodes and addresses). Each explanatory comment is indicated with a leading "...". The SEND routine begins by resetting B and initializing the counter to 10. Each pass through the four-instruction loop first outputs the value of B, then calls a subroutine that merely delays for one time slot, and then shifts A right. An output idle level of "1" is assumed to have been already established, in which case, the initial clear of B defines the proper start bit. Since 1's are shifted in, the last bit sent out is the stop bit (only one is employed).

The RECEIVE routine begins by waiting for the leading edge of the start bit. JBNZ executes by jumping to the address specified if B is not zero. It falls through when B = 0, indicating the beginning of the start bit. The next call (to address DELAY2, not DELAY1) causes a delay of 1.5 bit times, to permit sampling the input signal in the *middle* of each time slot. Before the loop is entered, the counter is initialized for eight passes, each of which loads the current input bit into B, waits for one time slot and then shifts it into A. After eight passes, the input character has been assembled in A.

PROBLEMS

8.1 Briefly explain the difference, in general, between the execution of a subroutine RETURN and the execution of an interrupt handler RETURN FROM INTERRUPT.

8.2 A processor has an interrupt facility whose behavior is described in Fig. 8.2. Rather than include a RETURN FROM INTERRUPT instruction in its repertoire, its designer recommends that each interrupt handler exit with the pair of instructions: SET IE; RETURN (where the latter is the conventional subroutine return). Briefly explain conditions under which this scheme will prove inadequate.

8.3 It is desired to implement the interrupt facility, described in Fig. 8.2, in the sample processor of Chapter 7. Draw all of the necessary modifications to the flow chart in Fig. 7.4. Assume that the interrupt response entry point is at a fixed address (called LOC in Fig. 8.2). Name the hardware elements (devices, paths, etc.) that must be added to the system, exclusive of those required to control the sequencing of the process.

8.4 We wish to enhance the system derived as a solution to Problem 8.3 as follows: Whenever an interrupt is taken, the four-bit interrupt-identifying code that accompanies it, ID[3:0], determines one of 16 possible interrupt-response entry addresses, each at the beginning of a separate 16-word block in the lowest-numbered 256-word memory page. How should your solution to Problem 8.3 be modified to implement this enhancement?

8.5 Assuming that the sample processor of Chapter 7 is equipped with the interrupt mechanism of Fig. 8.2, which registers should the interrupt-response routine (organized as indicated in Fig. 8.3) save (and later restore) to give it the freedom to freely use all of the processor registers? In this connection, are there any instructions (exclusive of RETURN FROM INTERRUPT), presently *not* in the machine's repertoire, that should be added as control instructions? If so, explain why.

8.6 Briefly summarize how a programmer may control the interruptibility of his program.

8.7 Using the interrupt hardware system in Fig. 8.4, if an *unmasked* interrupt request is pending, while a higher-priority response routine is executing, at what instant is its interrupt taken? If a *masked* interrupt request is pending while the main program is running, at what instant is its interrupt taken?

8.8 Draw the block/logic diagram of an elementary elapsed time clock or timer, assuming that it is initialized from a central data bus. Briefly specify under what conditions each of its input or output control signals is asserted. How can the equivalent of a software interrupt instruction be realized by employing such a timer? Explain any assumptions you make with respect to the rate at which the timer advances, in arriving at your answer.

8.9 Briefly explain how the opcode trap may be used to extend the instruction repertoire of a machine.

8.10 For each of the cases shown in Fig. 8.10, write down a short message that the assertion of TRANSMIT represents.

8.11 Using the "daisy chain" priority arrangement illustrated in Fig. 8.12, draw the logic internal to each I/O device, which implements its contribution to the daisy chain. Have you seen this structure before? If so, where?

8.12 The I/O element shown in Fig. P8.12 interfaces with a central data bus in either of two ways. Using the orientation shown in (a), with MODE = 1, it

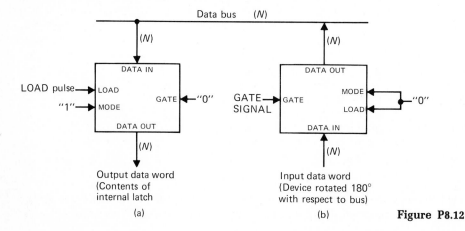

Figure **P8.12**

acts as an *output latch*, loading the data on the bus whenever it receives a LOAD pulse. Conversely, using the orientation shown in (b), with MODE = 0, it acts as an *input gate*, passing the input data word to the bus whenever it receives a GATE signal assertion. Draw the internal logic of the element. Utilize the D latch of Fig. 3.4 and any other necessary devices.

8.13   For each of the cases shown in Fig. 8.15, write down a short message which the assertion of DEVICE READY represents.

8.14   A keyboard consisting of a bank of 16 switches is to be used as a memory-mapped input device. Each key has a single output that is asserted while that key is depressed. The system has a 16-bit central data bus; and the CPU supplies a 12-bit address A[11:0], plus READ and WRITE control signals, to the memory. Whenever the CPU addresses location 7777 (octal), it reads the status of the keyboard. (Assume that the memory register at location 7777 has been permanently disabled.) Draw the logic network that interfaces the keyboard to the rest of the system.

8.15   What is a typical ratio between the time it takes to "service" a single data-transfer request employing an *interrupt-driven* I/O process, and the time for the same function employing a Direct Memory Access mode?

8.16   Consider the transfer of a block of data between an I/O device and an area of memory. The amount of "attention" that a running program has to pay to this process may vary considerably from system to system. For each of the following, briefly define the most likely hardware/software arrangement that is involved:

   a) The program is fully occupied with controlling the data-transfer process.
   b) The program is only intermittently occupied with the data-transfer process. It has time to perform other duties while the data is being transferred.
   c) The program is totally free of the burden of controlling the data-transfer process.

8.17   A timer and a DMA controller both operate concurrently with a running program. Briefly point out their operational similarities. With regard to independence from CPU operations, how do they differ?

8.18   An I/O processor executes an I/O program. How is its initial PC value determined? When its execution completes, how does the I/O processor inform the CPU of this?

8.19   Using the conventions employed in Fig. 8.23, draw signal waveforms representing the ASCII characters "@" and SPACE. Briefly explain why a receiver having inadequate timing accuracy may confuse the two characters.

9

The Hardware/ Software Interface

9.1 SUPERVISORY SOFTWARE

The software component that most directly extends the facilities available from the hardware of a computer is known as a Supervisor program. A Supervisor is also called a "monitor," an "executive," and an "operating system." Typically, it is permanently resident in a portion of the main memory sometimes known as "shaded" memory, to indicate that it is a special area that is inaccessible to other programs. A Supervisor is a collection of routines designed to supply universal "services," of which the operator and all other programs avail themselves.

Figure 9.1 illustrates the typical use of a Supervisor. After power is first turned on (and also after any subsequent general reset of the equipment), control is transferred to the Supervisor, which remains in control at all times except when it, in turn, transfers control to start the running of an application program (also called a "job" or a "task"). When the application program completes its computation, it exits with a transfer of control *back* to the Supervisor. Note that a HALT instruction is *never* executed. When the Supervisor has nothing better to do, it merely "idles"—executing a continuous sequence of NO-OP instructions.

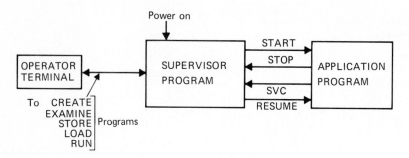

Figure 9.1 An elementary supervisor interface

The Supervisor program communicates with the computer operator via a *terminal*, typically in the form of a keyboard and a display. It reads input messages from the operator by executing INPUT instructions directed to the keyboard. It displays output messages by issuing OUTPUT instructions directed to the display.

The most rudimentary Supervisor contains a small set of utility routines that provide elementary means to create, examine, load, store, and run programs. (A "utility" is a routine written to make the existing hardware or software components easier to use.) For example, to create programs, a utility is needed to read characters from the keyboard and deposit corresponding code elements into proper memory locations. A companion utility, which permits the contents of any selected portion of memory to be displayed (either to verify code just entered or to examine the effects of a just-completed computation), is also essential. Once a substantial body of code has been entered, a facility is needed to record it, so that it need not be manually re-entered later. Thus, another utility program, which copies a specified memory area onto an I/O medium, is necessary. A companion utility, which reads a previously recorded block from the I/O medium and loads it back into memory, must also exist. Finally, an elementary Supervisor routine, which reads an address value from the operator and transfers control to that point, to initiate execution of the application program, is needed as well.

Thus, the most elementary Supervisor provides convenient means to manually read and write memory, to manually initiate data-block transfers between memory and the I/O medium, and to manually start a program run. In other words, it provides the simplest environment that permits developing and running programs. Its sophistication may be greatly enhanced in any of several directions. It may be designed, for example, to accept *calls* for specialized functions from the running application program. Many of the Supervisor routines that are called are designed to facilitate I/O operations. Since a single call may invoke a complex I/O sequence, the application programmer's burden, in the coding of any I/O process, is significantly reduced. This is illustrated in Fig. 9.1, which shows a path, labeled "SVC" (for Supervisor Call), from the running task to the Supervisor, and a matching return, labeled RESUME. The call is often mechanized via the system's interrupt facility. That is, the call generates a software interrupt, at which time the state of the task is preserved. The interrupt-response routine, in the Supervisor, performs the desired service, and the resumption is accompanied by a restoration of the saved state.

A Supervisor may be designed to load, and then transfer control to, any one of several utility routines stored on an external I/O medium, whenever the function provided by that routine is called for. Such utility routines are part of a system program *library*, which normally resides on a prerecorded disk that is accessible to the Supervisor. The library contains a collection of programs, each designed to make an aspect of application-program development or execution more convenient and more efficient. A brief summary of some of the key components in a typical system library is given later.

Historically, Supervisors developed as collections of universally employed subroutines, each of which further extended the repertoire of operations that the bare hardware provided. Extensions in the computational direction were rare. A square-root routine, for example, was not deemed sufficiently universal to deserve permanent residence in the memory. Rather, it was loaded with the application program, whenever it was needed. Most of the resident Supervisor subroutines enhanced operations in two general directions. First, they materially simplified the I/O interface as seen by the application programmer (this is discussed in greater detail later). An interrupt-analyzer routine, for example, which identifies the source of an interrupt and vectors to the proper interrupt handler, is a good candidate for inclusion in a Supervisor. Second, they promoted the efficient *utilization* of the equipment. A modern description of a Supervisor defines it as a component that manages all of the "resources" in a system, where a "resource" is any commonly used hardware or software component. For example, a Supervisor may include a Memory Allocation routine, which keeps track of the utilization of memory space. Whenever an application program needs memory space for temporary use, it makes a request (a call) to the Allocator, and receives, in response, the address of an assigned area. When it finishes using this area, it issues another call to the Allocator, releasing it.

A computer with a resident Supervisor program is thus a *virtual* machine, having all of the facilities of the host hardware, significantly enhanced by all of the Supervisory functions available. A "virtual" machine is the one that is *effectively seen* by the programmer. It may be treated as if it were realized totally in hardware, even though its actual realization is a combination of hardware and software. Observe that a Supervisor has a function, at the "macroinstruction" level, that is distinctly similar to that of a microprogram at the microinstruction level.

A Supervisor may be designed to permit several different tasks to appear to be running simultaneously, on the same processor. The tasks are all resident in separate areas of the main memory, at the same time. Each is in a state of partial completion. At any instant, at most one task is actually running on the processor. All of the others are temporarily suspended. Whenever a running task issues an I/O instruction, it is suspended until its I/O process completes. During this time, *another* task may run on the processor until *it* issues an I/O command. Thus, a task may be "dispatched" to run on the processor if it is *not* awaiting completion of an I/O operation.

Such a system makes very efficient use of the processor and of memory. Ideally, the processor is always busy with useful computation, and every area of the memory is potentially active. Further, each task programmer is assured that every instruction that *follows* an I/O operation is never executed until that I/O process completes. Such an execution arrangement is known as a *multiprogramming* environment. An example of one is discussed below.

The possible states of a resident task are indicated in the state diagram in Fig. 9.2. A task may leave the RUNNING state either by completing its computation (a path that is further clarified below) or by issuing an I/O command. In the latter case, its computation is temporarily suspended, pending completion of the I/O process. During this time, the task is placed (by the Supervisor) in a WAITING state. When the I/O completes, the Supervisor promotes the task to a READY state, where it must compete with *other* READY tasks for "scheduling," before it may run again on the processor. Should conditions arise in which *all* tasks are found WAITING, the Supervisor idles, waiting for one of the I/O's to complete.

The structure of the Supervisor is illustrated by the simplified flow chart in Fig. 9.3. The currently running task is represented by the block at the bottom of the diagram. It has four exit paths. Two of these represent external,

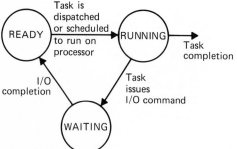

Figure 9.2 States of a task in a simple multiprogramming system

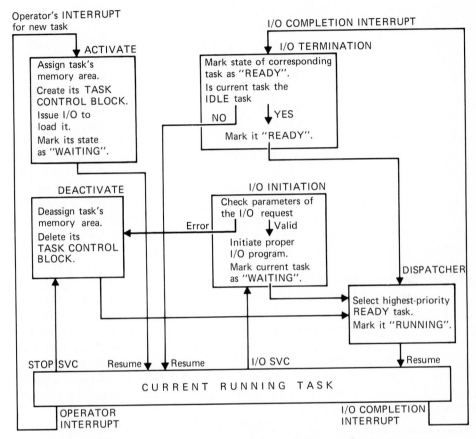

Figure 9.3 Supervisor structure in simple multiprogramming system

asynchronous events (I/O completion and operator action) that cause interrupts. Each of the other two represent internal, synchronous events—the execution of Supervisor Call instructions within the program. A Supervisor Call
may either initiate an I/O process or terminate the computation. An I/O SVC
is assumed accompanied by sufficient information to define the desired I/O
operation. The execution of either SVC generates an *internal*, "software"
interrupt.

Each interrupt, whether external or internal, is accompanied by the preservation of the state of the interrupted task (a procedure not explicitly shown
in the diagram) and the initiation of a corresponding response routine in the
Supervisor. The hardware to resolve simultaneous interrupt requests, to remember pended requests, and to vector to the proper response routine, is

implied but not shown in the diagram. While the Supervisor is in control, further interrupts are assumed *disabled*.

Each of the three entry paths into the current running task (labeled RE-SUME) corresponds to the execution of a RETURN FROM INTERRUPT instruction, which restores the saved program state and re-enables further interrupts.

Each resident task is assigned a small, auxiliary memory block, called a TASK CONTROL BLOCK, by the Supervisor. The data stored in a task's control block is governed by the Supervisor. It includes, at least, a priority code associated with the task, its current state code (representing either RUNNING, READY, or WAITING), a definition of the memory area assigned it, the processor register values (including PC) that were saved on its last suspension, and the identity of the I/O device specified in its last I/O SVC. Note that a stack is not employed to save the program state of the interrupted task, in this realization. Rather, the task's state is saved in its own task control block. Since the Supervisor is uninterruptible, use of a stack is not mandatory. To be consistent with this implementation, we will assume that the RETURN FROM INTERRUPT instruction executes by restoring the processor registers from the task control block selected by the Supervisor.

The Supervisor also keeps track of all available memory space, by a process not indicated in the diagram. Each new task is assigned space from this pool. Conversely, when a task completes its computation, its memory space is returned to the pool. We also assume that all of the addresses in a task are specified *relative* to the PC value, so that each task will run properly no matter which memory area has been assigned to it. That is, all tasks are assumed to be *relocatable*.

In summary, our sample Supervisor consists of the five routines indicated in Fig. 9.3. It also controls sufficient data space to hold all of the task control blocks of the currently active tasks. In addition, the Supervisor may find it convenient to store separate data tables—defining, for example, the memory areas that have been allocated, the tasks that are currently WAITING, and the tasks that are currently READY—even though this information is already recorded in the task control blocks. The table listing all of the currently READY tasks is known as a READY LIST.

The system incorporates one special, permanently resident *dummy* task, known as the IDLE TASK. When given control, the idle task merely executes a continuous loop of NO-OP instructions. Since it never issues an I/O, it is *always* READY (whenever it is not already running). It has the lowest priority.

Each of the Supervisor modules in Fig. 9.3 is labeled with a convenient name. The Dispatcher is the only module that is not directly entered as the result of an interrupt. Its function is to scan the READY LIST, choose the highest-priority READY task, and mark its state as RUNNING. Finally, before exiting with a RETURN FROM INTERRUPT instruction, which causes task resumption, the Dispatcher ensures that the program state that will be restored will come from the control block of the just-chosen task. Thus, the task it selects is the one that is resumed.

Whenever any task issues a STOP SVC, indicating completion of its computation, the Supervisor responds by returning its memory area to the available space pool and deleting its task control block. The Deactivate module then exits to the Dispatcher, which selects a new running task. Note that the STOP SVC is not a HALT instruction. Its meaning, to the task which issues it, is merely equivalent to that of a HALT.

An I/O SVC conveys, to the I/O Initiation module, sufficient information to define the desired I/O operation. The I/O Initiator begins by checking this information, to ensure that the request is a valid one. [Each task may be assigned, for example, a specific set of tracks on one of the system's disks. (If so, the track numbers assigned to a task are likely to be part of the data contained in its task control block.) The validity check ensures that one task does not erroneously access another task's peripheral storage space.] If the I/O SVC is found improper, the I/O Initiator does not start the I/O operation. Rather, it exits to the Deactivate module, which terminates the erroneous task. If the I/O SVC is valid, however, the Initiator prepares the proper I/O program and then issues the START I/O instruction that begins the I/O process. The calling task's state is then marked as WAITING, and control is passed to the Dispatcher to select another task to run. Note that the I/O SVC does not actually initiate the I/O operation. It merely requests this service. Observe also that a single I/O SVC may correspond to a complex I/O sequence, as set up by the I/O Initiator module.

A task is assumed activated by a request from the computer operator, which generates an interrupt. The Supervisor's Activate module responds by creating (and properly initializing) a new task control block and assigning to the new task an available memory area. For simplicity, we assume that adequate memory space is always available. Similarly, we assume that each task is relocatable, employing a relative addressing mode throughout. After issuing the I/O to load the new task, the Activate module finally exits by marking it as WAITING, since it does not yet actually reside in memory.

The initial PC value for a task is assumed to point to the first word in its assigned space. This address value is placed in the PC slot of every new task control block. Note that the currently running task is not "preempted" by the task-activation process. That is, the task that resumes, when the Activate module exits, is the same as the one that was originally interrupted.

Whenever an I/O process completes, its interrupt is handled by the I/O Termination module. This routine identifies the WAITING task to which the completed I/O belongs and promotes that task to the READY state. Normally, the currently running task is then resumed, having been interrupted only for a relatively simple table-lookup procedure. However, if the currently running task happens to be the *idle* task, a different action is taken. The idle task is not resumed. Rather, the task just made READY is permitted to continue. This is accomplished by returning the idle task to the READY state and then re-entering the Dispatcher.

Figure 9.4 contains a simplified, hypothetical example illustrating the interaction of three competing tasks over an arbitrary time period. Each key event, which generates an interrupt, is marked appropriately. The example assumes that the time taken by each Supervisor intervention is negligible. A more realistic analysis would include the Supervisor's running time.

The execution of an I/O SVC transfers a block of data between a calling task's I/O memory area and an external storage element. Consequently, each I/O SVC must supply (either directly or indirectly) a data flow direction, a memory address, and the identity of the participating external storage element. The Supervisor may require that the caller provide specific device, track, and sector numbers to physically locate that portion of the secondary storage medium which will be accessed during the operation. Alternatively, a sufficiently sophisticated Supervisor will relieve the caller of this burden, asking only that it be provided with the *name* of the *file* that will participate in the I/O operation, no matter *where* it is stored physically. The file is a so-called *logical* or *virtual* I/O "device," whose actual physical location in the secondary storage system is known only to the Supervisor. Such a Supervisor assumes full responsibility for managing all files for users, by properly allocating secondary storage space.

A file is a sequence of lines or records, each consisting of a sequence of characters. A file may contain either data or a program. A *source* program is

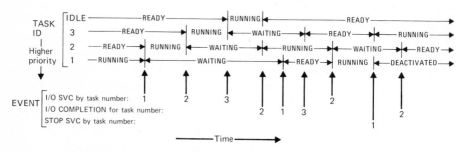

Figure 9.4   Example of task switching in a multiprogramming system

one created by a programmer, according to the rules of a specific programming language. A language translator program, known as an assembler or a compiler, converts a source program file into a separate, but equivalent, *object* program file, in the machine language of a specific processor. To run a program, its object file is first loaded into memory.

To manage a system of files, a Supervisor maintains a set of *directories*. A directory is a table, each of whose entries associates a file name with a corresponding physical location on the secondary storage medium. Other control information (defining, for example, the conditions under which file access is permitted) may be included in each entry as well. A directory may itself comprise a special file, in a known location on the secondary storage medium.

When a virtual I/O system is employed, a program may be given *random* or *sequential* access to the records in a named file. In the first case, each access to a record must be accompanied by a record number or index, identifying the desired record within the file. In the second case, the Supervisor maintains a pointer to the *current* record in the file. This pointer increments implicitly, after each record access, so that it will select the next sequential record on the next access. Normally, a RESTART command is available to reposition the pointer to the first record in the file.

Some of the files that are accessible to the Supervisor constitute a basic library of system programs. While the detailed structure of each of these software components (in particular, that of the Supervisor) is beyond the scope of this text, the functions of three of the most prominent system programs are briefly summarized here. An *Editor* is a program that makes it easy to manually create and modify files. Most of the rudimentary Supervisory features (described earlier), which permit the user to manually create, verify, store, and load programs, form the basis of an elementary Editor. A typical Editor significantly extends these facilities, by providing convenient means to insert, delete, replace, move, copy, and search for text strings of arbitrary length.

The symbolic equivalent of a machine-language program is an assembly-language program. Most of the program examples in this book are expressed in an assembly-language form. An *Assembler* is a program that converts an assembly-language source file into an object file, ready for loading and execution. Each address in an assembly-language program is expressed as a name or "symbol." The most fundamental function of an assembler is to maintain a *symbol table*, which assigns, to each programmer-defined symbol, an actual memory address. While a typical assembly-language program statement is the symbolic equivalent of *one* machine instruction, a statement in a "higher-level" language, which requires a *Compiler* for translation, is normally equivalent to a sequence of *several* machine instructions. A higher-level language is *machine-independent*. That is, a program written in such a language is *portable* because it may be run on any machine whose library contains a Compiler for that language.

9.2 INTERPRETERS

A program that simulates the behavior of a processor is known as an *interpreter*. While an interpreter runs, it behaves as if it were *another* machine whose instruction set is arbitrary, generally totally different from that of the "host" processor (the one that is executing the interpreter program). The apparent processor, produced by an interpreter, is known as a *virtual* machine. Thus, an interpreter program *itself* fetches and executes instructions. However, the meaning it assigns to any code that is presented to it for execution is completely different from that which the host hardware would assign to the same code.

One may *tailor* an instruction set to match a specific class of applications by designing a proper interpreter. Thus, an interpreter converts a *given* computer into a *desired* computer. It enables you to "produce" the desired computer, without actually physically constructing it in hardware. An interpreter may be used to simulate a new computer, whose fabrication and testing are not yet complete. In other words, an interpreter permits software to be developed for a machine that does not yet physically exist.

The "machine" language of an interpreter may be a higher-level language. That is, an interpreter may be designed to execute *source* code *directly*, without any intervening translation process. While use of such an interpreter has the advantage of combining interpretation and execution in a single program, it has the disadvantage of much slower execution speed, because the time taken to interpret each source statement and to define its equivalent sequence of host-machine instructions is always part of the execution process. When a Compilation phase *precedes* actual execution, the "work" generating the object program is expended only *once*. All subsequent executions of the same program need not duplicate this translation process.

The speed of a virtual machine, realized using an interpreter, is normally two or three orders of magnitude slower than that of the same machine realized directly in hardware. Since an average register transfer in the *simulated* machine consists of a sequence of host instructions, each of which entails the execution of several host register transfers, a speed reduction factor in the vicinity of 100 is normally easy to account for. This factor increases directly with the degree of disagreement between the characteristics of the virtual

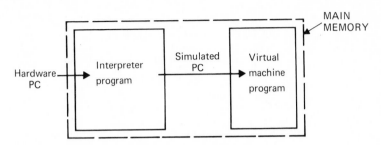

Figure 9.5 Representation of an interpreter and a program that runs on the virtual machine that it simulates

processor and those of the host. For example, if the word lengths of the two machines are not compatible, the amount of processing required in the interpreter, to execute every virtual register transfer, increases significantly.

Figure 9.5 depicts an interpreter and a program that it is interpreting, both resident in separate areas of the host system's main memory. The interpreter is the program running on the hardware (the host processor). Hence, the hardware PC points within it, as it executes. The interpreter program, in turn, maintains a *separate* register, which we may call the "simulated PC," which selects the current instruction in the virtual machine program. Note that, for each elementary step in the *simulated* PC value, the *actual* PC normally makes very wide excursions within the interpreter. That is, each single virtual instruction execution corresponds to many hardware instruction executions.

A real processor is sometimes called a "hardware interpreter"—i.e., an interpreter fully realized in hardware. While we may use the term "software interpreter" to describe a program that simulates a processor, the word "software" is normally implicit. In this regard, there is another type of interpreter—namely, a *microprogram*—which we should consider. Normally resident in the Read-Only control memory of a processor, a microprogram implements that processor's instruction set. (Recall the discussion in Section 7.4.) When a microprogrammed controller is employed, for each elementary step in the hardware PC, the μPC value makes wide excursions within the microprogram. Because a microprogram facilitates the implementation of hardware, it is sometimes called a "firmware" component, to distinguish it from a conventional program, which is customarily called "software."

Figure 9.6 pictures a portion of a program in the process of execution by an interpreter. The simulated Program Counter, denoted by PC1, selects the current instruction. Whenever the interpreter fetches a new instruction, PC1 is incremented past it.

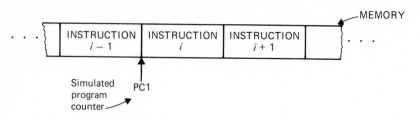

Figure 9.6   A portion of a virtual machine program

A listing of a very elementary interpreter is given in Table 9.1. It is written in a simplified assembly language. All of the names in the program (excluding the opcode mnemonics) represent memory addresses. In the left-hand column, each symbol (followed by a colon) identifies or labels a word in memory. All numeric values are assumed to be expressed in hexadecimal notation. The first six words in memory are *data* registers, used by the interpreter program, which consists of the remaining words. The opcode mnemonic WORD merely causes the assembler to allocate one word of memory, labeled with the name specified. If a value appears in the operand portion of the statement, the word is initialized with that value. Otherwise its initial value is arbitrary.

Each statement in the program represents a one-word instruction, having one or two operand fields. Those which are jump destinations are labeled with convenient symbolic addresses. The *host* processor's instruction set is assumed to contain all of the operations listed in the opcode column. MOVE transfers the contents of the first address into the register denoted by the second address. INCR and DECR appropriately step the contents of the specified memory register. JUMP unconditionally jumps to the destination specified. AND logically ANDs the two specified operands, leaving the result in the first-addressed memory cell. TEST selects a specified hex digit of a specified register and stores it in an *implicit* cell, for testing by subsequent IF instructions. An IF instruction conditionally jumps to a specified address only if the saved hex digit matches a value specified in the instruction. Finally, the notation "(I)" indicates that the corresponding instruction address field should be marked as *indirect*.

The simulated processor incorporates four registers, named PC1, IR1, SP1, and AC1. For simplicity, all virtual machine instructions are assumed to be one word long. Each contains an opcode, in its upper hex digit, followed by an address field. Eight operations, corresponding to opcode values 0 to 7, are recognized. The names in the left-hand column, beginning at PUSH, identify the entry points of the eight execution routines.

The Comments (preceded by . . .'s) explain the program's operation. Beginning at entry point FETCH, the first two interpreter instructions fetch the *virtual* instruction. The next two interpreter instructions save the OP field of the virtual instruction and clear its portion of IR1, leaving only the instruction's address field in IR1. ["IR1(3)" identifies the upper hex digit of the instruction. The mask hex value of 0FFF indicates an assumption of 16-bit

Table 9.1   An Elementary Interpreter Program Listing

Memory Address	Contents of that Address		Comments
	Opcode	Operands	
PC1:	WORD	0	... Simulated Program Counter
IR1:	WORD		... Simulated Instruction Register
SP1:	WORD		... Simulated Stack Pointer
AC1:	WORD		... Simulated Accumulator
MASK:	WORD	0FFF	... Used to clear OP field in IR
ZERO:	WORD	0	... Used to execute CLEAR instr.
FETCH:	MOVE	PC1(I) IR1	... Get next instruction
	INCR	PC1	... Advance PC1 past it
	TEST	IR1(3)	... Move OP field for IF tests
	AND	IR1 MASK	... Address field remains in IR1
	IF	0 RETURN	... Multi-way
	IF	1 POP	... Branch
	IF	2 CALL	... Based
	IF	3 BRANCH	... On
	IF	4 LOAD	... OP
	IF	5 STORE	... Code
	IF	6 CLEAR	... Value.
PUSH:	INCR	SP1	... Point to an available slot
	MOVE	AC1 SP1(I)	... Store Accumulator there
	JUMP	FETCH	... Get next instruction
RETURN:	MOVE	SP1(I) PC1	... Pop top stack item to PC1
POP:	DECR	SP1	... Discard top stack item
	JUMP	FETCH	... Get next instruction
CALL:	INCR	SP1	... Point to an available slot
	MOVE	PC1 SP1(I)	... Store PC1 there
BRANCH:	MOVE	IR1 PC1	... Address in instr. to PC1
	JUMP	FETCH	... Get next instruction
LOAD:	MOVE	IR1(I) AC1	... M(address) $\rightarrow$ AC1
	JUMP	FETCH	... Get next instruction
STORE:	MOVE	AC1 IR1(I)	... AC1 $\rightarrow$ M(address)
	JUMP	FETCH	... Get next instruction
CLEAR:	MOVE	ZERO AC1	... Clear Accumulator
	JUMP	FETCH	... Get next instruction

words.] The succeeding seven IF instructions comprise an eight-way branch based on the current OP value. The comments explain the executions, which are conventional. Note that each execution terminates with a return to the beginning of the FETCH sequence.

The interpreter program in Table 9.1 naturally divides into two parts. The first performs the virtual instruction fetch and exits with a multi-way branch based on the opcode value. The second contains the collection of execution routines that implement the virtual instruction set. A more sophisticated interpreter is similarly organized, with one added modification to provide more generality and flexibility. Its fetch sequence reads, and advances past, only the *opcode* field. It then exits by selecting the proper execution routine based on the opcode value. The fetch routine assumes that all *subsequent* fields of the instruction, if any exist, will be processed properly by the individual execution routines. In other words, each execution routine is responsible for advancing the simulated Program Counter past any in-line fields that *it* processes. Thus, at the culmination of any execution, the simulated PC is left pointing at the opcode field of a new instruction. Such an approach permits a wide variety of acceptable instruction formats, including the possibility of many "zero-address" instructions (which use a stack for implicit operand storage).

The fetch routine reads the current opcode and *vectors* to the execution routine that it selects. In other words, the opcode is *mapped* into the entry address of the proper execution routine. (Recall a similar mapping process in conjunction with the use of a microprogrammed controller, in Section 7.4. In that case, the instruction opcode was mapped, via an encoder, into the address of an execution microroutine.) If the host hardware has the proper facilities, the code that implements the interpreter's fetch process may be expressed in very concise terms. We proceed by examining some of these alternatives.

Consider a host processor that permits a combined indexing-indirect addressing mode. Assume that it uses an index register named X and that the entry addresses of all of the execution routines are stored, in order, in a table whose base address is represented by the symbol TABLE. Under these conditions, the fetch sequence may be expressed as:

```
FETCH:   LOADX   PC1(I)
         INCR    PC1
         JUMP    TABLE,X(I)
```

The first instruction places the opcode in the index register. The last instruction executes by performing the indexing operation *before* the indirect addressing operation. You will recall that the interrupt vectoring scheme, discussed in Section 8.1, provided a similar linkage mechanism.

Since the simulated Program Counter is such an active register, it is preferable to assign its function to a *processor* register, if one is available. Let us call this pointer register "PTR". Assuming that the processor is equipped with an auto-increment addressing mode, the same fetch sequence may be expressed as:

```
FETCH:   LOADX   @PTR+
         JUMP    @(TABLE,X)
```

where the "@" symbol is a common assembly-language indirect-addressing indicator, and where the "+" character is the auto-increment symbol. (PTR is incremented after index register X is loaded.)

Rather than use the opcode as an index into a table, which maps it into an address value, consider the *direct* use of the opcode as a field in the JUMP's destination address, in which case, the mapping table is no longer needed. Assume, for example, that the host processor is capable of executing "LD" and "LDA" instructions, each of which transfers the contents of a first specified register into a second specified register. LDA merely increments the source pointer after the transfer takes place. Under these conditions, the sequence:

```
FETCH:   LDA   @PTR,TEMP
         LD    TEMP,PCF
```

will also perform the desired function. TEMP is a processor register used for temporary storage. We are assuming that its length is shorter than that of the host PC. PCF stands for an appropriate field in the host PC. When this field is loaded from TEMP, any lower PC bits are cleared. Note that the single instruction LDA @PTR,PCF replaces the pair above.

We may generalize this idea by *equating* an opcode with the address of its execution routine. To do this, let us appropriately widen the opcode field, to the length of the PC, and accept the fact that many possible opcode values will go unused. Under these conditions, the single instruction

```
FETCH:   MOVE   @PTR+   PC
```

also accomplishes the desired operation.

You are reminded that each execution routine is responsible for advancing the PTR value past any in-line fields that it processes, and that it returns via a JUMP FETCH instruction, to reinitiate the next fetch.

Having defined a system in which an opcode *is* an address, must we limit the number of possible address values only to those that the interpreter considers valid? In particular, since one of the most fundamental instructions (which is almost entirely an address) is a CALL, suppose we permit the virtual machine programmer to specify *any* address, with the understanding that it may point *either* to a basic virtual instruction execution routine (implemented by the interpreter) *or* to a programmer-defined *subroutine*. Such a scheme is feasible if the interpreter is able to *distinguish* between the two. In the first case, it must transfer control to the routine that executes the virtual instruction. In the second case, it must push the current PTR value on a stack and then point it at the CALLed subroutine.

While a distinguishing "mark" may be included in the op-address field (using a single bit, for example), such a scheme limits the range of express-ible addresses. Another possibility, which we employ below, is to begin each user-defined subroutine with a unique marker word, which is known *not* to be found at the beginning of any conventional execution routine. (For exam-ple, an execution routine will never begin with a HALT instruction.) We designate this special constant by the name SUBMARK. It precedes every user-defined subroutine.

A modified fetch routine, which includes the capability to execute the CALL, is listed in Table 9.2. The first instruction moves the current op-address to a temporary processor register and advances PTR past it. The next instruction compares the word it *points* to with the special marker value. The BEQ exits (to location NEST) if a subroutine starting mark was found. If not, the fourth instruction completes the conventional fetch by transferring con-trol to the execution routine. Thus, the first four instructions are equivalent to a simple MOVE @PTR+ PC when the address does not point to a subroutine.

The four instructions beginning at location NEST constitute execution of the CALL. First, the pointer value is advanced past the dummy marker word. The current simulated PC value is then pushed on a stack. A virtual machine jump to the beginning of the subroutine is then executed. Finally, the last instruction reinitiates the fetch phase. Note that every subroutine must end

Table 9.2 An Interpreter FETCH/CALL Sequence, Assuming that Each Opcode Is the Address of its Execution Routine

Label	Opcode	Operands		Comments
FETCH:	MOVE	@PTR +	TEMP	. . . Get the current op-address
	COMPARE	@TEMP	SUBMARK	. . . Does it point to a subr?
	BEQ	NEST		. . . Skip out if yes.
	MOVE	TEMP	PC	. . . No. It's a virtual instr.
				. . . Jump to execute it.
NEST:	INCR	TEMP		. . . Step past the marker word
	PUSH	PTR		. . . Save the return address
	MOVE	TEMP	PTR	. . . Point to first subr. instr.
	JUMP	FETCH		. . . and execute it.

with a virtual RETURN instruction, which is mechanized with the following execution routine:

```
RETURN:  POP   PTR
         JUMP  FETCH
```

In other words, while every basic interpreter execution routine (including that which mechanizes the RETURN instruction) ends with a JUMP FETCH, every user-defined subroutine begins with a special marker word and ends with the virtual RETURN.

9.3 PROTECTION

Protection mechanisms are employed to defend against erroneous use of a computer's hardware and software resources. The sample Supervisor, discussed in Section 9.1, for example, checked the validity of an I/O SVC before activating its corresponding I/O program. This ensured that a task did not erroneously access, and possibly modify, the files belonging to another task. The issue of protection and its implementation is a complex one, particularly in a system having many users. We will limit ourselves to examining two of its aspects, namely, memory protection and the use of privileged instructions. In both of these cases, hardware enhancements are employed to protect against erroneous access to, and especially modification of, system registers and files.

Consider the situation in which two programs, simultaneously resident in the main memory, are alternately executing on the same processor. One may be a Supervisor, and the other, a task. Both may be independent application programs. One may be an interpreter, and the other, the program which it is interpreting. (Strictly speaking, this last example does not conform to the given circumstances, because the interpreter always executes instructions *for* the virtual machine program. Nevertheless, since the host processor and the virtual processor share the same memory, it is applicable.)

The consequences of a task's unintentional access to the memory area allocated to another program may be damaging. An erroneous write is the most serious fault, because it normally renders the altered program unusable. An erroneous transfer of control is usually just as serious, because the results are totally unpredictable. An erroneous read is the least damaging (assuming that the information read is not "secret"), because it affects only the behavior of the defective running task. We discuss below means by which such access errors may be detected and prevented.

A processor may be equipped with one or more special *limit* registers, whose contents are compared with the address value presented to the memo-

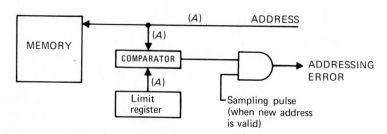

Figure 9.7   Typical application of a limit register

ry. Figure 9.7 illustrates the use of such a register. The comparator is de-signed to detect when the address value exceeds the threshold value stored in the limit register. (It is assumed that an instruction is available, in the machine's repertoire, to control this boundary value.) The comparator may detect when the memory address is above or below the threshold. The asser-tion of the comparator's output signal, at the instant in the memory cycle when the new address is known to be valid, indicates an addressing error.

This error signal has at least two purposes. First, it may be used to pre-vent the erroneous access. For example, if the memory's WRITE input is conditional on the quiescence of the addressing error signal, an erroneous write will be inhibited. Similarly, the memory's overall ENABLE may be withdrawn whenever an addressing error occurs. Second, the error signal may cause an *interrupt* (commonly known as a "trap"), whose accompanying identifying code indicates that an addressing error has occurred. Typically, the Supervisor responds to this interrupt by terminating the run of the task that caused it.

A single limit register is adequate when a single boundary between two programs is to be maintained. More generally, a pair of limit registers, defin-ing the upper and lower bounds of the space allocated to the currently run-ning task, may be employed. Typically, the Supervisor changes the limit val-ues whenever it dispatches a new task. (Using the example discussed in Section 9.1, the Supervisor would find the proper boundary values in the current task's Task Control Block.) While allocated memory areas are nor-mally nonoverlapping, it is conceivable that two adjacent resident tasks may want to *share* a common area (for example, a data block). Under these re-stricted conditions, the lower bound of the upper task may extend *below* the upper bound of the lower task.

Several common memory protection schemes operate by logically divid-ing the memory space into an array of blocks or *pages* of equal size. As discussed in Section 4.3, an appropriate upper address field (for example, the upper eight bits, if the memory is divided into 256 blocks) specifies the page number of the addressed register. Each block is allocated a *protection code*—also called an "access key"—by the Supervisor. The protection codes for all pages are stored in a special auxiliary memory whose capacity and access time are small compared to those of the main memory. On each access, the page number is applied to the special protection memory, as shown in Fig. 9.8. It is the address of a register in the auxiliary memory. The value read from the protection memory (the contents of that register) is the protection code for the addressed page. This code is used to decide whether or not the access should be granted. If it is not granted, an addressing error interrupt is generated.

A protection code may merely define the types of access that are permitted. For example, it may contain three bits, specifying whether or not the addressed page is write-protected, read-protected, and execute-protected, respectively. Typically, a write-protect violation inhibits the assertion of WRITE, while a read-protect violation prevents the read. An execute-protect violation may be detected by sensing when a read has been attempted during a *fetch* sequence. (You will recall, from the discussion in Chapter 7, that signals are available whose assertion indicates when a fetch is occurring.) Preventing an erroneous fetch access defends against an incorrect transfer of control into a data area.

A more sophisticated protection code includes a field *identifying the task* to which access is granted. An access attempt by any other task generates an interrupt. Normally, the task number of the currently running task is stored in a special register, not shown in Fig. 9.8. This register is loaded by the Supervisor whenever a new task is dispatched. The hardware compares the contents of this register with the assigned task ID in the protection code to decide whether or not an access is authorized. The assigned protection code may be considered as a "lock" and the current running task number as a "key." Access is permitted only when they match.

The auxiliary protection memory permits a fast table lookup, during every memory access. Since its capacity is small, its access time need not signif-

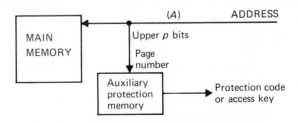

Figure 9.8 Use of a small, auxiliary memory
containing a table of assigned protection codes

icantly reduce the speed of the composite system. For simplicity, Figs. 9.7 and 9.8 do not show the paths by which the Supervisor *loads* the protection control registers (using appropriate instructions in the processor's repertoire).

If instructions are available to load the protection control registers, what prevents a task from erroneously (or maliciously) issuing such instructions itself? Certainly, a system of locks is not very secure if the burgler (or bungler) has the means to alter the lock combinations. Similarly, using the example discussed in Section 9.1, while a single I/O SVC normally initiates a complex I/O process (via the services provided by the Supervisor), what is to prevent a task from rejecting this built-in facility and *directly* issuing its own (possibly incorrect) I/O instructions? For that matter, even though a task is required to exit via the STOP SVC, what is to prevent it from simply issuing a HALT, bringing the system to a sudden standstill?

These questions are representative of protection issues which have led the designers of some processors to define a special class of instructions—not normally available to conventional application programs—called *privileged* instructions. The instruction set of a machine that provides such instructions is divided into two parts. Conventional instructions, such as those discussed in Section 6.5, comprise the predominant portion. A small set of special, privileged instructions are "reserved" for execution only by the Supervisor.

The hardware control network of such a processor contains a special flip-flop whose state defines whether or not privileged instructions may be executed. While the Supervisor is running, it is set. Otherwise, it is reset. The set state is known as the "privileged" or "Supervisor" state, while the reset state is known as the "user" or "problem" state. If a task attempts execution of a privileged instruction, an interrupt is generated, indicating the violation.

The setting of this control flip-flop must not be controllable by instruction execution. If the instruction that sets the privileged mode is *itself* privileged, how is this mode established in the first place? If the instruction is not privileged, all of our protection efforts fail, because a task may declare itself privileged and then proceed to be arbitrarily destructive. For these reasons, the transition to the privileged state is controlled implicitly by hardware. Typically, it is set *whenever an interrupt is taken.* That is, the TAKE INTERRUPT hardware sequence includes not only the saving of key registers and the disabling of further interrupts but also the setting of the mode control flip-flop. If the TAKE INTERRUPT sequence *sets* the privileged mode, it is logical to include, in the execution of the RETURN FROM INTERRUPT instruction, the *resetting* of the mode control flip-flop. Alternatively, a separate SET USER MODE instruction may be made available.

Thus, the typical processor capable of assuming a privileged state is designed by assuming an "interrupt-driven" Supervisor, of the type described in Section 9.1. Every entry to the Supervisor is via an interrupt, whether synchronous or asynchronous. Every exit from the Supervisor is via a RE-TURN FROM INTERRUPT instruction, which resumes a task and re-establishes the user mode. [Note that it is not absolutely necessary that a simple, *nonprivileged* Supervisor be interrupt-driven. Supervisors to which all interrupts are transparent also exist.]

The questions which initiated this discussion suggest some of the instruction types that are normally included in the privileged class. Generally speaking, if a system is considered *vulnerable* to the execution of a specific instruction, then that instruction should be part of the reserved class. Consequently, typical privileged instructions include:

1. I/O instructions;
2. Instructions that control memory-protection parameters;
3. Instructions that control address-mapping parameters (see Section 9.4);
4. Instructions that control interrupt masks, priorities, and other key program-status registers;
5. HALT instructions.

9.4 VIRTUAL MEMORY

While a program runs, its references to memory are *localized*. Over any short time interval, only a few relatively small areas in the memory are active, no matter how large the program is. Most of the addressable memory space remains dormant, most of the time. Figure 9.9 illustrates a typical situation in which a program loop is presently engaged in processing an array of input data and generating an array of output data. The shaded areas indicate the current patches of activity within the memory. All of the rest of the space occupied by the program is temporarily inactive.

The speed of a memory is an *inverse* function of its capacity. Those technologies that yield the largest storage capacities (for example, magnetic disk

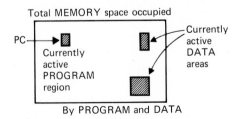

Figure 9.9 Representation of patches of program activity during a short time interval

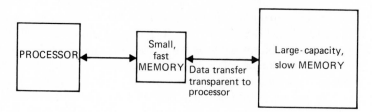

Figure 9.10   Simplied structure of a two-level memory hierarchy

technology) also provide the longest access times. Conversely, the cost-per-bit for extremely fast memories is sufficiently high that only small capacities are economically feasible. With this in mind, consider a configuration of two memories, one a large, slow memory, and the other a small, fast memory, organized as indicated in Fig. 9.10. The processor interfaces with the faster memory. The path between the two memories is employed to execute data transfers that are transparent to the processor. (It is not aware that they are taking place.) Suppose it were possible to ensure that all of the current patches of activity in the large memory were always found in the small memory. Under such ideal circumstances, we would realize a composite memory whose capacity is that of the large memory, but whose access time is that of the fast memory.

Since the time to transfer data between the memories is not negligible, this ideal is not achievable. However, sufficient performance improvement may be realized, for programs having appropriate memory-access statistics, to make such a two-level memory hierarchy desirable. It is called a *virtual memory* because it behaves as if it were a single, composite memory system. In operation, it requires an *address-mapping* control network, not shown in Fig. 9.10. The function of this network is explained below.

Both memories are divided into register blocks of equal size. Every address is interpreted as consisting of two parts: a *page number*, which selects a specific block of registers, and a *displacement* value, which selects one register within the selected page. (This concept was first introduced in Section 4.3.) At any given instant, the small memory contains *copies* of some of the large memory's pages. On each access, the processor presents to the composite system a *virtual address*, consisting of a v-bit page number field and a d-bit displacement field. (The capacity of the large memory is therefore 2^v pages.) For each such access, the control system that regulates the composite memory must determine whether or not the addressed virtual page *resides* in the small memory and, if so, in *which* page of the small memory it can be found.

To do this, the memory's control system must maintain a *table*, stored either in a special auxiliary memory (like the one used to store protection codes, in Section 9.3) or in a portion of the small memory itself. This table is referenced on *every* access. (Note that, if the table resides in the small memory, an immediate time penalty of one access time is paid just to find out whether or not the referenced page is immediately accessible and, if so, where it is.) Such a table is known as a "page table," because it maps a virtual page number into a *physical* page number, which selects a page in the small memory. (The capacity of the small memory is assumed to be 2^p pages. By definition, p is less than v. Note that we call a page that is immediately accessible to the processor, a "physical" page.)

Several different organizations for the page table are possible. We consider two of the most common arrangements. First, the table may contain one entry per *virtual* page. The entry contains a "presence" or "availability" bit, signifying whether or not the corresponding virtual page resides in the small memory, and a field that specifies its physical page number, which is valid only when the presence bit is asserted. This second field may have a totally different use when the availability bit is not asserted. For example, if the secondary memory is a disk, this field may specify the virtual page's assigned track and sector numbers (if such information is not immediately implied by the virtual page number).

Figure 9.11 illustrates this organization. We are assuming that the page table resides in a special, auxiliary memory, whose access time is sufficiently

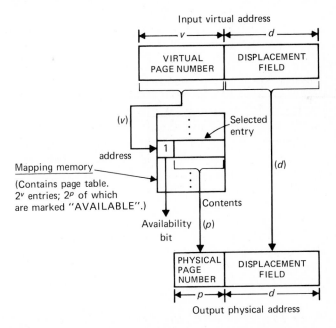

Figure 9.11 Virtual-to-physical address mapping using a page table containing as many entries as there are virtual pages

small. The given virtual page number is employed as the *address* of a table entry. Assuming that the addressed page has an asserted availability bit, the p-bit physical page number, which is read out of the mapping memory, is concatenated with the d-bit displacement field to assemble the proper small-memory address. If the presence bit is not asserted, the access must be temporarily postponed. We will consider this issue later.

A page table that contains as many entries as there are *physical* pages is also feasible. Each entry in it contains the virtual page number of the page currently occupying the corresponding physical page. While the number of entries in such a table is distinctly smaller than that in the table proposed earlier, the means of finding the physical page number, which corresponds to a given virtual page number, is not as direct. The table must be *searched*, item by item, until an entry is found that matches the input argument. Since a *serial* search of all table entries on every memory access is too time-consuming, a means must be devised to search all of the items stored *in parallel*.

Fortunately, a special type of memory, known as an *associative* memory, is specifically designed to permit parallel searches. It consists of an array of registers, each of which includes an internal comparator. One possible structure is illustrated in Fig. 9.12. The input "interrogation code" is applied, along a bus, to every cell in the memory. The same field, in every stored

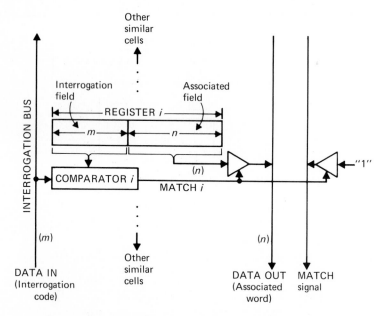

Figure 9.12   One cell of a simplified associative memory. (The write mechanism is omitted.)

word, is compared with it. If a match is found in word *i*, a local MATCH*i* signal is asserted, gating the remaining contents of word *i* to the DATA OUT bus. All MATCH*i* signals are logically ORed together, along an additional one-bit bus, whose output signal indicates whether or not a match was found. (For simplicity, we are ignoring the mechanism by which information is written into the memory. We also assume that, at most, *one* match will be found.)

We may employ an associative memory, having as many registers as there are physical pages, in a structure like that shown in Fig. 9.13. Each word in it contains the virtual page number and the corresponding physical page number of one of the immediately available pages. Thus, the memory fulfills the same function as that of the mapping memory in Fig. 9.11. Note that the *absence* of the MATCH assertion indicates that the addressed virtual page does not reside in the small memory.

The discussion above ignores two key issues. First, it implicitly assumes that every virtual-memory access by the processor is a *read* access. When a write occurs, the *original copy* of the accessed page must be updated proper-

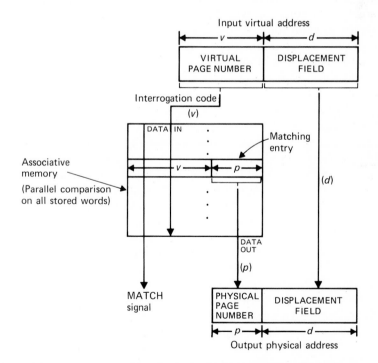

Figure 9.13 Virtual-to-physical address transformation using an associative memory for the mapping function

ly. Second, it does not explain what procedure is followed when a page is *not* found resident in the fast memory. Normally, such a page must be *made* resident, under the assumption that subsequent accesses will also reference it. We must consider how this is accomplished. In particular, *which* page in the small memory is chosen for replacement?

To help answer these questions, let us compare two of the most common virtual-memory implementations. One of these contains a conventional main memory, having an access time in the vicinity of one microsecond, as the primary store (the one accessed by the processor), and a magnetic disk, whose access time is approximately 50 milliseconds, as the secondary store. The other contains a conventional main memory as the *secondary* store, while the primary store is a smaller, faster memory, having an access time in the vicinity of 100 nanoseconds, commonly known as a *cache* memory. Note that the primary-to-secondary speed ratio is approximately 10 in the second case, while it is between 10^4 and 10^5 in the first case. This striking difference is responsible for several important implementation distinctions.

Consider the disk system first. When a desired page is not found in the main memory (i.e., when the presence bit is "0" or when an associative match does not occur), that page must be brought in from secondary storage. The time to execute the page transfer is sufficiently long that (assuming a multiprogramming environment exists) the currently running task should be suspended in favor of another ready task. Normally, the signal that indicates that the addressed page is not in main memory is also the one that generates a special interrupt, known as a *page fault* interrupt. This interrupt is another example of a synchronous interrupt caused by an *exception* condition. The Supervisor responds to it by issuing the proper I/O instructions which replace one of the resident pages with the newly addressed page.

First, the Supervisor must select a currently resident page for replacement. The possible algorithms it may use to make this decision are briefly discussed below. Having chosen a page for replacement, the Supervisor then determines whether or not that page was *written into*, during the time it was resident in the primary store. Typically, each entry in the page table includes a "page modified" flag bit, which is set by the hardware whenever a write to that page takes place. If the page was not modified, a faithful copy of it already exists in secondary storage, and its copy in the primary memory can be overwritten immediately. If its written-into bit is set, this page must be copied out to secondary storage first, before it is replaced, to update its copy there. Thus, bringing a new page in may entail writing an old page out. Such a process has sometimes been termed a page "swap." Whenever a swap is executed, the Supervisor updates the page table appropriately, to reflect the new contents of the primary store.

A cache system, on the other hand, does not exhibit such a wide discrepancy between the speeds of the primary and secondary stores. Consequently, it does not need to resort to a Supervisor to execute the page swap. Rather, the "page-not-found" condition invokes a built-in *microroutine*, which executes the page transfer. Since the cache page size is much smaller than that in a typical disk system, this microroutine merely performs the equivalent of one or two MOVE instructions. In addition, because the speeds of the two memory components are more nearly comparable, the composite system may adopt a so-called "write through" policy, in which every write access is automatically directed to the secondary memory copy, as well. Such an arrangement makes it unnecessary to ever write a page from cache back to secondary storage. Since most of the accesses during a typical program run are reads, this policy is a sound one. Note that it is also possible to make a requested word available to the processor as soon as it is read out of the secondary store, even before the transfer of its block to the cache has been completed.

The question of which page to select for replacement remains a difficult one to answer. Several algorithms are possible. One may make a strong case for replacing the *least recently accessed* page, on the grounds that those pages which have been referenced recently are the most likely to be accessed in the immediate future. Using this "LRU" (least recently used) algorithm, a count field in each page table entry is employed to keep track of recent access activity. For example, if every access to a page clears its counter, while *all* counters are incremented on a periodic basis, the page with the *highest* count is the one least recently accessed. An alternative algorithm selects for replacement the page that has spent the most time in the primary memory. Using this "FIFO" (first-in-first-out) algorithm, nothing special has to be kept track of, on each memory access. Surprisingly, experimental test data suggests that neither of these strategies is very much better than selecting a *random* page for replacement.

In summary, a virtual memory is best suited to programs whose memory-access patterns are not "erratic." It works well when the statistics of page reference are such that, once a page is addressed, it continues to be accessed many times. As memory references become scattered and page boundaries are crossed frequently, a virtual memory, which operates according to the rules described above, becomes less effective.

Note that, once a system has been equipped with a special auxiliary memory to store the page table, the *same* memory may be employed for memory *protection* purposes. That is, any of the protection codes discussed in Section 9.3 may be stored in the page table and accessed while address-mapping operations are taking place. Observe also that the magnetic-disk virtual-memory implementation is an excellent example of one that employs an appropriate combination of hardware *and* software components.

9.5 PROGRAM DEBUGGING

A language translator program (e.g., a compiler or an assembler) has no conception of the *purpose* of the source program it is translating. Its function is merely to re-express the statements of the source program in a form directly executable by a real machine. In the process, it does detect certain programmer errors. For example, it will reject as unacceptable any expression in which each left parenthesis character is not properly matched by a corresponding right parenthesis character. Similarly, it will flag as an error any attempt to assign to the same symbol two or more different values. However, the fact that a source program has been accepted by a compiler or an assembler is no guarantee that it will execute properly. That is, it may be *syntactically* correct but not *functionally* correct. We examine here some of the techniques that are employed to isolate program errors, called "bugs," during program execution. The removal of these errors is termed "debugging."

If a program is *stopped* in the midst of execution, its progress up to that point may be examined. Most program errors are found by this process. Such a stop is known as a "break," and its location in the program is called a "breakpoint." We determine how the program has progressed by examining the contents of the registers it has been manipulating. They carry the information indicating whether or not an error has occurred and, if so, what the nature of the error is. That is, they permit us to *diagnose* the error.

A break may be only momentary. For example, a programmer may intentionally insert into a program instructions whose sole purpose is to output (e.g., print or display) diagnostic information. The mere fact that such an instruction is executed provides information about the *flow* of the program, by indicating that the Program Counter did reach that instruction's location, while engaged in a specific computational sequence. Instructions having only diagnostic purposes are normally removed from a program, after it has been tested sufficiently. Although the program doesn't actually halt when one of these is encountered, it does pause momentarily, for a sufficient time to output the diagnostic data "snapshot."

One of the most common diagnostic snapshots continues to be the memory "dump"—a printout or display of the contents of a selected memory area. Unfortunately, such a presentation usually overwhelms the user with a great deal of information, only a small part of which is actually useful. A preferable debugging environment provides the user with a mechanism to examine selected register values, one at a time, while tracking down the cause of an error. A memory dump of the processor's *stack* area in memory is particularly useful. The data and address values that were most recently pushed on the stack are often very helpful in diagnosing an error.

A processor may be designed to detect certain errors that occur during program execution. Normally, it will use its *interrupt* facility to break into the erroneous process, once an error has been discovered. A sufficiently comprehensive processor is equipped with several internal interrupts that trap *exception* conditions. The opcode trap, which signifies detection of an invalid opcode, and the addressing error interrupt, which traps an invalid memory address, are two of the most prominent internal interrupts. Others that are useful in stopping a misbehaving program include interrupts generated by arithmetic overflow, memory-protection violation and attempted privileged-instruction execution. Any one of these error conditions normally causes the Supervisor to respond by terminating the erroneous task. The termination is usually accompanied by the output of diagnostic data (e.g., processor register values and selected memory values) to help the task programmer determine the cause of the problem.

An interpreter routine may similarly incorporate helpful debugging aids. Since it executes every instruction for the program it is interpreting, it has the opportunity to check for errors that are not normally detected by hardware. For example, an interpreter may be designed to maintain a log of all of the changes to the contents of one or more selected registers. Similarly, it may be able to record all of the branches taken within a specified program segment. Each list provides valuable diagnostic information to the programmer. The first describes the detailed behavior of selected variable values, as the program runs. The second traces the *flow* within a portion of the program.

Program debugging is a highly *interactive* process. Typically, it involves several test runs of the program under test, each of which employs one or more *implanted* stops. When a stop occurs, selected registers are examined. Since the programmer cannot always predict, at the time a program is created, *which* breakpoints will be the most judicious to select and *which* registers will be the best to examine, he needs a facility that permits such choices after the program has been coded. Such a facility is provided by a special utility program, commonly known as a "debugger." It is specifically designed to facilitate the interactive testing of another program. The program under test need not include any explicit diagnostic instructions. We consider some of the fundamental features of a debugging routine below.

Figure 9.14 illustrates the interface of a typical interactive debugging utility program. While it is in control, it communicates with the programmer via a conventional keyboard/display terminal. Under specified conditions (for

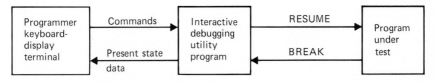

Figure 9.14 Typical interactive debugger interface

example, on command from the programmer) it transfers control to the program under test and, sometime later, receives control back, when the test program reaches an implanted breakpoint. Whenever it is re-entered in this fashion, the debugger first preserves all key registers of the program under test, so that it may be later resumed properly from the point of the break. Conversely, whenever the debugger exits to the test program, it restores this saved program state (possibly with some of its register values intentionally changed by the programmer). Thus, from the test program's point of view, the debugger resembles an *interrupt-response routine* whose execution time may be exceptionally long (because a resumption of the test program may not occur until the debugger has had a chance to converse with the programmer).

This description suggests the most likely means by which a debugger may implant a breakpoint in a test program—namely, by the *insertion of a special instruction, whose execution will return control to the debugger.* The programmer specifies the location of the breakpoint. Since a small portion of the test program is overwritten by the inserted instruction, the debugger must *save* the original contents of this area, before it is modified. Whenever the breakpoint is later removed, either temporarily or permanently, the original contents of this area is restored. A *software interrupt*, if such an instruction is available, is a logical means by which a breakpoint may be established. So is a *CALL* to an appropriate entry point in the debugger. All key information not preserved during the execution of the implanted instruction is immediately saved by the debugger, when it is re-entered.

Note that *several* breakpoints may exist simultaneously. This explains why an inserted JUMP back to the debugger is usually an insufficient breakpoint implementation. The debugger has no means of identifying from *which* breakpoint it received control.

A test program run begins with the debugger in control. On command from the programmer, the debugger sets one or more breakpoints in the test program, and then initiates execution of the test program at a point specified by the programmer. When a break occurs, the debugger provides the programmer with facilities to examine, and possibly modify, the contents of all registers accessible to the test program. Copies of the processor register values, at the time of the break, are available in a special register-save area in memory. The processor registers are later restored from this area, when the test program is resumed. Before resuming execution, the programmer may delete existing breakpoints and insert new breakpoints. After doing so, he reinitiates execution of the test program at a new arbitrary location. In particular, this location may be the *same* as that of the last break. If the break has not yet been removed, such a resumption requires a temporary restoration of the overwritten instruction at the breakpoint. Typically, after this instruction has been executed, the break instruction is automatically re-established to permit subsequent breaks at the same spot.

Several other debugging aid implementations implicitly utilize the break-point mechanism. For example, a common (though sometimes laborious) debugging mode executes one instruction at a time. The programmer is able to examine the effects of each instruction immediately after it is executed. Such a *single-step* mode implicitly implants a temporary breakpoint immediately after each next instruction to be executed. The location of this temporary breakpoint steps as execution proceeds.

A debugger may give the programmer the option of specifying the *number* of instructions to be executed before the next break is taken. Typically, such a mode is mechanized as an automatic sequence of single steps, where each intermediate break includes an increment and a test of a counter value, followed by an immediate resumption if the count has not yet reached a prescribed limit.

A *trace* is a valuable debugging tool whose implementation may also utilize the break mechanism. It may be defined as a continuous sequence of single steps, which automatically outputs, at each intermediate breakpoint, a prearranged (usually programmer-controlled) packet of diagnostic data. As soon as this data is recorded, the test program is immediately resumed. Each information packet is a diagnostic snapshot of the state of the system between two successive instructions. It specifies the contents of selected key registers. A trace of the PC value, for example, describes the flow of the program. A trace of the contents of a memory location tracks all changes in the value of the variable assigned to that location.

A debugger may provide the user with several trace options. Typically, the programmer may specify when a trace should be activated and when it should be deactivated. In addition, the debugger may permit the user to select those registers that should be traced and the conditions under which their values should be recorded.

Note that the operation of a debugger resembles that of a Supervisor. It is the basic program in control. Under appropriate conditions, it temporarily relinquishes control to another program, which ultimately returns control to it. Observe also that the memory area in which the debugger saves the register values of the program under test when a break occurs, has a function very similar to that of a Task Control Block (see Section 9.1).

The behavior of a debugger operating in the *trace* mode also resembles that of an interpreter. In fact, a trace routine is often defined as an interpreter simulating a machine that is *identical* to the host processor. Such an interpreter employs the host hardware to directly execute each of the instructions in the program under test. It may operate by fetching the next instruction and then directly transferring control to it. (The instruction residing in the location immediately following the one where the just-fetched instruction has been staged returns control to the trace routine.) Such an arrangement operates properly provided that the current instruction is *not a branch*. If a branch instruction is directly executed and the branch is *taken*, the trace routine *loses* control. This may be remedied by a trace-program structure such as that illustrated in Table 9.3.

We assume a host processor similar to that employed for Tables 9.1 and 9.2. The trace program is assumed stored in RAM. The first instruction calls a subroutine (not shown) that outputs the current diagnostic data snapshot. The next four instructions deposit in locations INSTR1 and ADDRESS, respectively, the opcode and address fields of the current instruction. The sixth instruction actually executes the fetch, advancing the simulated Program Counter, called PTR, past it. Note that the staging area for the current instruction, at location INSTR, is within the trace routine.

The COMPARE instruction tests whether the opcode of the current instruction matches that for a conditional branch. [This segment of code is normally extended to test for *all* possible branch opcodes. We assume, for simplicity, that there is only one (even though the tracer program itself shows that there are at least two others).] If the current instruction is not a branch, the BNE (Branch if Not Equal) instruction skips to location INSTR, where the current instruction is executed directly. This is followed by a return for a new fetch.

If the current instruction *is* a conditional branch, the OR command assembles a *substitute* instruction, with the same opcode, whose address field points instead to location JENTRY, within the tracer. (Memory location HERE contains a constant which is the address value that has been assigned to symbolic address JENTRY.) The MOVE that follows stages this substitute instruction. Now, when INSTR is executed, if the jump is not taken, control is returned properly for the next fetch. If the branch *is* taken, control is transferred not to the branch's real destination but to JENTRY instead. At that point, the original branch destination is placed in the simulated Program Counter, and a new fetch is initiated.

The above discussion suggests one possible mechanism by which a debugger may ensure that a break will occur immediately *after* a branch instruction is executed. (This issue was not adequately covered earlier. You will recall that a resumption at an active breakpoint may begin with an implicit single step executing the original instruction at that point, after which the break is re-established. Similarly, the explanation of the single-step mode implies that the break following each instruction is *always* reached. How does one ensure this, if the current instruction is a branch?) When a branch is encountered, the debugger may modify the branch's destination (after having saved its original value) to point to an appropriate point within the debugger. If the branch *is* taken, the code at that point will store the original branch-destination address *in the PC slot* within the debugger's register-save area.

An alternative mechanism, which will ensure a break after one executed instruction whether or not the instruction is a branch, is to arrange for an

Table 9.3 An Elementary Trace Program Listing

Label	Opcode	Operands	Comments
FETCH:	CALL	SNAPSHOT	. . . Record current program state
	MOVE	@PTR	. . . Get copy of next instruction
	AND	INSTR1	. . . Mask out the address field
	MOVE	@PTR	. . . Get another instruction copy
	AND	ADDRESS	. . . Mask out the opcode field
	MOVE	@PTR+	. . . Fetch the next instruction
	COMPARE	INSTR1	. . . Is it a conditional branch?
	BNE	INSTR	. . . Skip to execute it if not
	OR	INSTR1	. . . Combine opcode with address
			. . . of the "jump taken" entry.
INSTR:	MOVE	INSTR1	. . . Replace real instr. with dummy
	WORD	FETCH	. . . Current instr. executed here
	JUMP	ADDRESS	. . . Return to fetch next instr.
JENTRY:	MOVE	PTR	. . . Entered if branch is taken.
			. . . Move real branch address into
			. . . Simulated Program Counter
			. . . and return for a new fetch.
PTR:	JUMP	FETCH	. . . Simulated Program Counter
INSTR1:	WORD	0	. . . Instr copy. Ends with opcode
ADDRESS:	WORD		. . . Instr copy. Ends with address
OPMASK:	WORD	F000	. . . AND mask to leave opcode
ADMASK:	WORD	0FFF	. . . AND mask to leave address
BRANCH:	WORD	N000	. . . N is the cond. branch opcode
HERE:	WORD	A[JENTRY]	. . . Address assigned to JENTRY

external interrupt to occur *during the execution* of that instruction. An elapsed time clock or *timer* (described in Section 8.1) is specifically designed to generate an external interrupt after waiting for a prescribed amount of time. If properly initialized by the debugger, it will interrupt *while* the subject instruction is executing. Such a facility, if available, is a preferable means to implement single-step operation and other debugging operations, such as trace, that are based on it, because it does not require special instruction insertion or branch address modification.

Implicit throughout the entire discussion above is the assumption that the programmer converses with the debugger using a hexadecimal (or octal) notation. In particular, addresses were assumed to be expressed in absolute (e.g., hexadecimal) form. A more sophisticated debugger, known as a *symbolic* debugger, has available to it the symbol table generated by the assembler that assembled the test program in the first place. This table contains all of the symbolic addresses in the source program, each assigned a corresponding absolute address value. Such a debugger permits identifying memory locations *by name*, as they appear in the *source* program. While it is clearly more convenient to use, its basic operations remain the same as those described above.

9.6 MICROPROCESSORS

Very little has been said, in the preceding chapters, about the *cost* or the *size* of a processor—two factors that clearly influence its suitability to specific applications. In the last decade, the development of one element—known as a *microprocessor*—has dramatically expanded the number of areas in which computers are employed. A microprocessor is a very small and very inexpensive processor. While a computer used to be regarded as a million dollar instrument, carefully maintained in a special environment, and operated only by white-coated scientists, the same element is now found in a multitude of devices, never before thought eligible for computer control, from implanted heart pacemakers to children's toys.

The dramatic growth in integrated-circuit technology, in the last ten years, has made it possible to fabricate, on a single "chip" of silicon (a very thin, quarter-inch square wafer), an array of as many as 10,000 interconnected gates. Some devices now exist that include not only a sophisticated processor but also a portion of the main memory that it addresses. (The term "microcomputer" is used to describe a combination of a microprocessor, a main memory, and a complement of I/O ports.) As a result of these developments, computer engineers who, not so long ago, designed devices using only gate and register elements, now treat the microprocessor as the basic, general-purpose component, applicable to a wide variety of possible functions. We discuss below the interface and the characteristics of a typical, one-chip microprocessor. By treating it as a single component, we tie together many of the implementation details discussed in preceding chapters.

As the sophistication of integrated-circuit technology has grown, the number of constraints faced by microprocessor designers has diminished. When the number of gates realizable on a single chip was measured in the hundreds, the microprocessor's word length and its complement of internal registers were severely limited. So was its instruction set, whose control implementation consumed a significant number of gates. Similarly, when the number of pins (signal-carrying terminals) per chip was less than 40, it was necessary not only to limit the word length but also to employ bidirectional terminals, to multiplex two (or more) signals on the same terminals, and even to use serial data transmission. Short word lengths also meant short instructions, and a short instruction means that much more about its execution is implied. While current restrictions are not nearly as severe, they have not yet totally vanished.

A typical microprocessor contains a reasonable number of internal general registers. A 16-register scratchpad, for example, is now quite common. While the most prevalent word length still remains as eight bits, 16-bit machines are much more plentiful, and 32-bit machines are now in the research stage. All of the instruction types described in Chapter 6 are available in current microprocessors. So are all of the addressing modes described in Section 6.6. While the typical eight-bit machine outputs a 16-bit memory address (permitting a maximum main-memory size of 65,536 words), some versions of the newer 16-bit machines include virtual addressing.

It is convenient to list the signals that comprise a typical microprocessor interface assuming that an unlimited number of pins is available for use. Then, given the constraint of a specific number of pins, various economies in pin usage, some of which were described earlier, are possible. The most likely of these will be pointed out as we proceed. Figure 9.15 will serve as a graphic summary of the discussion below.

Like any other integrated circuit, a microprocessor requires allocation of at least two of its interface pins for connection to a source of electrical power. It usually has an additional input to receive an externally generated, periodic CLOCK signal (i.e., a square wave), whose frequency defines its basic cycling rate. In addition, it has a general RESET signal input, whose assertion initializes the device, ensuring that it begins running from a well-defined state. Thus, to be *operable*, the device needs an initial allocation of at least four pins.

Most of the interface pins comprise its data and address ports. Typically, the data port is *bidirectional*. It interfaces with a system data bus, whose width is equal to the machine's word length. The address port may have several purposes. Fundamentally, it supplies to the memory an address value

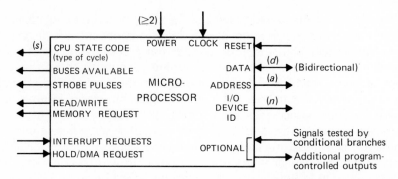

Figure 9.15 A typical microprocessor interface

for the next access. However, whenever a processor memory access is not taking place, this port may serve other purposes. For example, during execution of a programmed I/O data transfer to or from a *processor* register, the memory remains dormant and the address lines may be used to supply an I/O device identifying code. Alternatively, the microprocessor may have a separate output port, whose code identifies the selected I/O device. If the microprocessor is designed assuming a *memory-mapped* I/O system, no special I/O identification mechanism is needed. Since the number of address pins is so large, at least one microprocessor has been designed to supply the address value as a serial sequence, in two parts, permitting half of the address pins to be made available for other purposes.

Note that special output control signals, not yet discussed, are implied by the descriptions given above. For example, the microprocessor must make it clear, to external devices, whether its bidirectional data port is currently transmitting or receiving. Similarly, if a code is transmitted serially, signals must exist to make it clear, to external devices, which part is currently being transmitted. Such control signals are discussed further below.

Virtually all of the other pins in a microprocessor interface are allocated to control signals. *Output* control signals define the present *state* of the element. External devices know when to respond properly by reading these signals. For example, several output pins convey a state code, which defines the *type of cycle* presently occurring. By this means, external devices are able to identify when fetch, execute, interrupt, and DMA cycles are taking place. An interrupting device is informed that its interrupt request has been honored when it sees the interrupt cycle state code. A device desiring direct memory access knows that it may proceed to use the memory access buses when it sees the DMA state code. (Sometimes, a single signal is made available whose assertion indicates that the microprocessor has decoupled from its data and address buses.) Other output signals, identifying specific timing instances within cycles, are known as "strobe" or timing pulses. An external device uses a time pulse as an indication that a data or address output code is valid and may be latched.

Signals defining the *direction* of data transmission, typically named READ and WRITE, are also available from the microprocessor. If these signals are used for I/O data transmission as well as for memory access, an additional control signal, commonly named MEMORY REQUEST, defines whether or not the data transfer is directed to the memory.

Many of the microprocessor's *input* control signals are "requests for service." Specifically, one or more *interrupt* requests normally exist. The CPU may permit both "maskable" and "nonmaskable" interrupts. A request for the latter always receives an immediate response. DMA or HOLD requests permit external devices to temporarily freeze the CPU state. While the CPU is decoupled from the memory-access buses, they are free for other uses.

The number of possible interface variations is clearly large. A microprocessor may permit one or more digital input signals whose values are tested by conditional branch instructions. (Recall the FLAG signal in Section 6.2.) Similarly, one or more general-purpose, program-controlled output signals, separate from those appearing on the data bus, may be available.

Some microcomputers, having elementary higher-level language interpreters resident in "on-chip" ROM, already exist. Other current experiments lead us to expect the future development of machines whose instruction repertoires will be much more compatible with existing higher-level languages.

PROBLEMS

9.1 How should the flow chart in Fig. 9.3 be modified to permit a high-priority WAITING task, whose I/O completes, to resume immediately, *preempting* an already-running lower-priority task?

9.2 What hardware or software components may be added to the multiprogramming system described in Fig. 9.3, to protect against an "infinite loop" in a (high-priority) running program? (Without intervention, such a task will run indefinitely, totally monopolizing the CPU.)

9.3 Using the system described in Fig. 9.3, define a situation in which a low-priority READY task may *never* have a chance to run, even though each of the other tasks with which it competes exhibits a significant amount of I/O activity. To remedy this situation, propose a modification that does away with the priority rule. Specifically explain all changes that you make to the flow chart in Fig. 9.3.

9.4 Redraw a portion of the diagram in Fig. 9.4 to demonstrate how the running time of the Supervisor may be shown explicitly.

9.5 A typical elementary "time-sharing" system includes a Supervisor like the one illustrated in Fig. 9.3. However, every time the Supervisor dispatches a task to run, it allocates to it a specific amount of CPU time. If the task is still running after its time allocation has expired, it is preempted in favor of another READY task. Tasks are serviced by the CPU in a "round robin" fashion. Make the simplest alterations to the diagram in Fig. 9.3 to include such a "time-sharing" feature. Draw only those portions of the diagram that are new or modified.

9.6 A computer has a *range* of undefined opcodes (for example, from hex E0 to hex FF). Its instruction set includes neither a Supervisor Call nor a Software Interrupt. We wish to use the opcode trap for this purpose. Each illegal opcode will invoke a corresponding Supervisor service. Using a notation resembling that employed in Tables 9.1 through 9.3, write a program for that portion of the Supervisor which receives control when an illegal opcode interrupt occurs. It responds by activating the proper service routine. Make any plausible assumptions about the instruction set of the host CPU.

9.7 Assume that each instruction in the interpreter program in Table 9.1 is one word long. If symbolic location FETCH corresponds to memory address 50 (decimal), write down the sequence of hardware PC values (in decimal) as the interpreter FETCHES and EXECUTES a virtual BRANCH instruction.

9.8 Briefly compare the function of an interpreter FETCH routine with that of an interrupt analyzer.

9.9 The interpreter routine in Table 9.1 does not check for the undefined opcodes "8" to "F". What does it presently do when it encounters any of these codes? Modify the interpreter program so that it treats each illegal opcode as if it were a NO-OP.

9.10 Using the advanced interpreter whose FETCH/CALL sequence is given in Table 9.2, and assuming that its virtual instruction set includes all of the operations implemented in Table 9.1, write down the symbolic code for a virtual *subroutine* that PUSHes and then CLEARs the simulated accumulator. You may find it convenient to use the notation employed in the last instruction of the program in Table 9.3.

9.11 Draw the block/logic diagram of a hardware network that will WRITE PROTECT the lowest 256 words of memory. An attempted WRITE into this area should be prevented and should cause an internal interrupt. Label the diagram to indicate where all inputs come from and where all outputs go to.

9.12 Under what conditions is a PRIVILEGED MODE FLIP-FLOP *set*? Under what conditions may it be *reset*?

9.13 Draw a logic/block diagram of a network that will prevent a nonprivileged program from executing a privileged instruction. The network should generate an appropriate interrupt when the attempt is detected. Assume that each of the lowest eight, out of a total of 64 opcodes, is privileged. For simplicity, you may assume processor-control logic similar to that employed in Fig. 6.9. Properly label all inputs and outputs in your diagram, to indicate the points to which they are connected.

9.14 Assuming a time-sharing Supervisor as introduced in Problem 9.5, explain why the SET TIMER instruction should be a privileged instruction.

9.15 Assume a disk-oriented virtual-memory system in which an addressed virtual page is *not* in the physical main memory. Describe the sequence of events, step by step, from the instant when the access is first attempted until the time when the access is finally granted. Pay particular attention to the contents of the page table.

9.16 Define an algorithm that will develop the information needed to permit an "LRU" page-replacement policy to be employed.

9.17 To which system components is the AVAILABILITY signal generated in Fig. 9.11 (or the MATCH signal, generated in Fig. 9.12) directed?

9.18 Briefly explain how a debugger may identify from which of several breakpoints it received control. How does it find the value that it places in the PC slot in its register-save area?

9.19 We wish to utilize the interrupt facility of a processor to implement a TRACE function. An interrupt response routine, which records all necessary "snapshot" information, is made resident in memory. Assume that the following two control signals are available from the processor: FETCH·IE indicates that an instruction fetch is occurring, with interrupts enabled. INTERRUPT ACKNOWLEDGE indicates that an interrupt is being taken. Assume further that the interrupt response routine runs with interrupts disabled. Draw the logic, external to the processor, that will implement the TRACE mode.

9.20 Assuming that the symbol FETCH, in Table 9.3, corresponds to address zero, specify the sequence of PC values and the corresponding values for memory word PTR, while the program traces a conditional branch instruction residing at location 50. (Use decimal values throughout. Ignore PC values while subroutine SNAPSHOT is executing.) Assume that the branch (to location 100) is *taken*.

9.21 We wish to evaluate the percentage of total computation time that a system spends executing any part of its Supervisor program. (This number is sometimes called the "overhead" of the system.) Briefly describe one hardware and one software mechanism for accomplishing this. You may postulate any plausible components in your solution.

Solutions to Problems

CHAPTER 1

1.1 JJJ JJQ JJK JQJ JQQ JQK JKJ JKQ JKK QJJ QJQ QJK QQJ QQQ QQK QKJ QKQ QKK KJJ KJQ KJK KQJ KQQ KQK KKJ KKQ KKK

A total of 27 possible combinations or codes.

1.2 ....− ..−. ..−− .−.. .−.− .−−. .−−− −... −..− −.−. −.−− −−..
−−.− −−−. −−−−

A total of 16 possible combinations or codes.

1.3 We require at least a three-bit code. Using three bits, there are several possible assignments, all of which include two unused or unassigned codes. One of these is:

> excellent . . . 000, very good . . . 001, good . . . 010,
> fair . . . 011, bad . . . 100, and worthless . . . 101,

leaving codes 110 and 111 unassigned.

1.4 A 14-bit string may be used to describe one clothing item in the inventory. A two-bit field specifies the department number (0, 1, 2, or 3). A six-bit field defines the style or type of the clothing item (since $2^6 = 64$). An encoding table would normally be provided here. Finally, two three-bit fields permit eight possible sizes and eight color variations, respectively.

1.5 A 14-bit string identifies a single apartment in the complex. Three bits specify the building number (0 to 7). Six bits identify the floor number (0 to 63). Two bits define the corridor number (0 to 3), and three bits locate an apartment within the selected corridor.

1.6 Octal: 132. Hexadecimal: 5A.

1.7 631 (base 8).

1.8 91.   12774.   19414.

1.9 48 61 70 70 79 20 42 69 72 74 68 64 61 79 21. 15 bytes.

1.10 No differences should be discernible. A signal originating at the output terminal travels with the speed of light over all wiring paths available to it. If the wire lengths are reasonably short, a signal's propagation time is negligible, and all of the input terminals receive the same signal simultaneously, no matter which wiring pattern is chosen.

1.11 The possible W,T combinations are as follows:

$$1,32 \text{ (pure serial)};\quad 2,16;\quad 4,8;\quad 8,4;\quad 16,2,$$
$$\text{and}$$
$$32,1 \text{ (pure parallel)}.$$

1.12

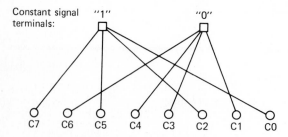

Figure S1.12

1.13

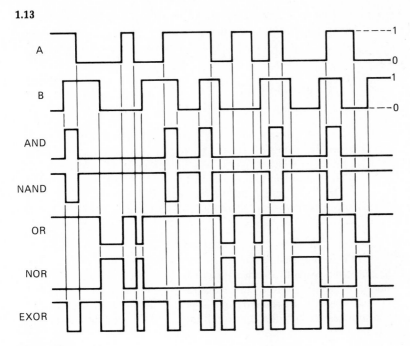

Figure S1.13

1.14

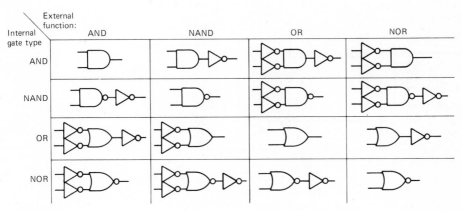

Figure S1.14

1.15 (See Fig. S1.15) While arrangement a (or c) is often more convenient, b (or d) is sometimes preferable because it minimizes the electrical "loading" on the A output terminal.

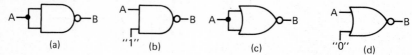

Figure S1.15

1.16 There are four smaller complete sets, containing, respectively, the following gate types: (1) ANDs plus INVERTERs; (2) ORs plus INVERTERs; (3) only NANDs; (4) only NORs. The solution to Problem 1.15 shows that an INVERTER may be realized using a NAND or a NOR. The solution to Problem 1.14 shows that *any* of the basic gate functions may be realized by employing INVERTERs and only *one* of the gate types.

1.17 The solution that often comes to mind first is to NAND A and B together and then to INVERT the resulting signal. An alternative is to develop $\overline{A}$ from A (using an INVERTER) and then to NOR $\overline{A}$ and B together, to achieve the same function. The *second* solution is usually preferable, because it is quite likely that the signal $\overline{A}$ will be required elsewhere in the same design. One has the greatest freedom of design choice when one has the complements of all input signals available for use.

1.18

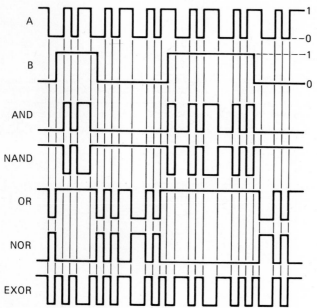

Figure S1.18

1.19

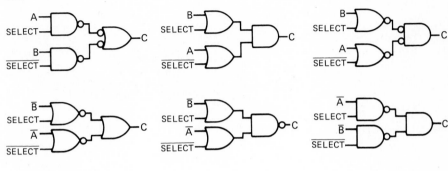

Figure S1.19

1.20

$X + \overline{X}Y$	Given.
$X \cdot 1 + \overline{X}Y$	Theorem 5a, in reverse.
$X(1 + Y) + \overline{X}Y$	Theorem 4b, in reverse.
$X + XY + \overline{X}Y$	Theorem 3a, in reverse.
$X + Y$	Theorem 8a.

$(X + Y)(\overline{X} + Z)(Y + Z)$	Given.
$(X + Y)(\overline{X} + Z)(Y + Z + 0)$	Theorem 5b, in reverse.
$(X + Y)(\overline{X} + Z)(Y + Z + X\overline{X})$	Theorem 7a, in reverse.
$(X + Y)(\overline{X} + Z)(X + Y + Z)(\overline{X} + Y + Z)$	Theorem 3b, in reverse.
$(X + Y)(X + Y + Z)(\overline{X} + Z)(\overline{X} + Y + Z)$	Rearranging terms.
$(X + Y)(\overline{X} + Z)$	Theorem 9b, applied twice.

1.21 $f = [\overline{AB} + C][(\overline{D + E})F + \overline{G}]$

1.22

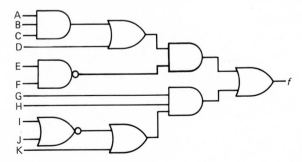

Figure S1.22

1.23 ABC **f**

000	0
001	1
010	0
011	1
100	1
101	1
110	0
111	0

1.24 a) $(\overline{A} + \overline{B})\,C$

b) $\overline{A}\overline{B} + C$

c) AB

d) $A\overline{B}$

e) $(A + \overline{B}C)\,D$

1.25

Figure S1.25

1.26 a) $\mathbf{f} = (\overline{A} + B)\,\overline{C} + DEF$

b) $\mathbf{f} = (\overline{A} + B)\,(\overline{C} + DE)\,F$

c) $\mathbf{f} = (A + \overline{B})\,(\overline{C} + D) + EF(G + \overline{H}(I + J))$

1.27 For each of the 16 combinations of A, B, C, and D, **f** will be 0, because, when $CD = 1$, **f** is forced to be 0 (via the output NOR gate), and when $CD = 0$, **f** is *also* forced to be 0 (via the NAND gate).

1.28 $Q = 1$ for DATA [3 : 0] values in the range "A" through "F".

1.29 a) $\mathbf{f} = \overline{A}B + BC + B\overline{D}$; $\mathbf{f} = B(\overline{A} + C + \overline{D})$

b) $\mathbf{f} = \overline{B}\overline{D} + \overline{A}\overline{B}C + \overline{A}C\overline{D}$; $\mathbf{f} = (\overline{A} + \overline{B})\,(\overline{A} + \overline{D})\,(\overline{B} + C)\,(\overline{C} + \overline{D})$

c) $\mathbf{f} = \overline{A}\overline{B}\overline{D} + \overline{A}\overline{B}C + AB\overline{D} + AB\overline{C}$;

  $\mathbf{f} = (A + B + \overline{D})\,(A + \overline{B} + \overline{C})\,(\overline{A} + \overline{B} + \overline{D})\,(\overline{A} + B + \overline{C})$

d) $\mathbf{f} = \overline{C}D + \overline{A}B\overline{C} + \overline{A}BD$; $\mathbf{f} = (\overline{A} + \overline{C})\,(\overline{A} + D)\,(B + \overline{C})\,(B + D)\,(\overline{C} + D)$

e) $\mathbf{f} = BD + \overline{B}\overline{D} + (\overline{A}B$ or $\overline{A}\overline{D})$; $\mathbf{f} = (B + \overline{D})\,(\overline{A} + \overline{B} + D)$

f) $\mathbf{f} = AC + \overline{B}C + \overline{A}\overline{B}D + ABD$; $\mathbf{f} = (A + \overline{B})\,(C + D)\,(\overline{A} + B + C)$

CHAPTER 2

2.1

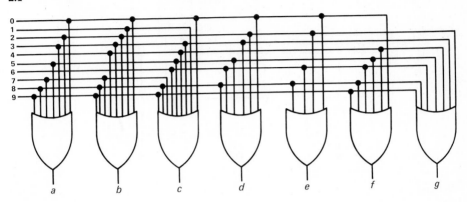

Figure S2.1

2.2

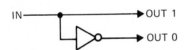

Figure S2.2

2.3

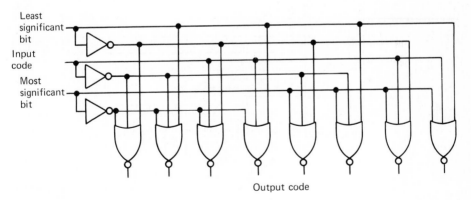

Output code

Figure S2.3

2.4

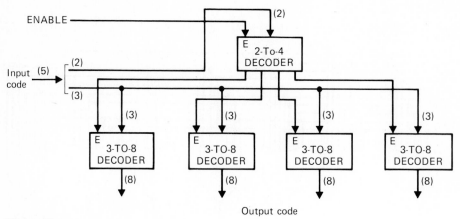

Figure S2.4

2.5

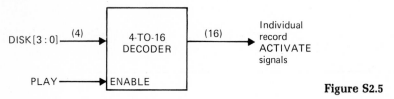

Figure S2.5

2.6

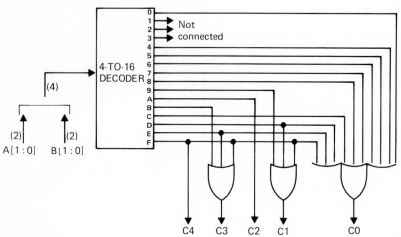

Figure S2.6

2.7

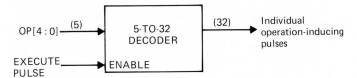

Figure S2.7

2.8 Binary: 11111111; BCD: 001001010101.

2.9

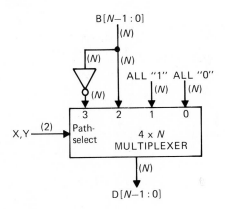

D[N−1:0]   **Figure S2.9**

2.10

Answer
switches
at student
desk number

0 ─(k)──►
1 ─(k)──►
2 ─(k)──►
.
.
.
N − 1 ─(k)──►

$N \times k$
MULTIPLEXER

Path-
select

(k) ─► SELECTED
ANSWER
LIGHTS

TEACHER
DESK

(a)   SELECT
DESK NUMBER
switches

Figure S2.10

(Note: $N=2^a$)

2.11

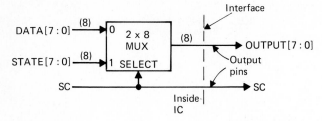

Figure S2.11

2.12

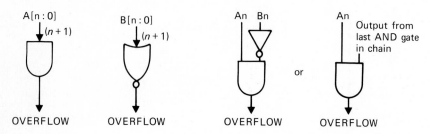

Figure S2.12

2.13

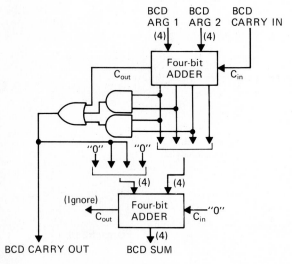

Figure S2.13

2.14 $+80 = 01010000$; $-80 = 10110000$; $+270 = 000100001110$; $-270 = 111011110010$.

2.15 $+14 = 001110$; $-14 = 110010$; $+15 = 001111$; $-15 = 110001$; $+25 = 011001$;
$-25 = 100111$.

    a) Result = 011101 (+29). Final CARRY = 0. Correct.

    b) Result = 101000 (wrong sign). Final CARRY = 0. Overflow.

    c) Result = 110110 (−10). Final CARRY = 0. Correct.

    d) Result = 001010 (+10). Final CARRY = 1 (ignore). Correct.

    e) Result = 011000 (wrong sign). Final CARRY = 1. Overflow.

    f) Result = 100011   (−29). Final   CARRY = 1   (ignore). Correct.

2.16

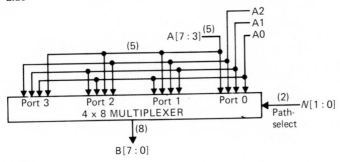

Figure S2.16

2.17

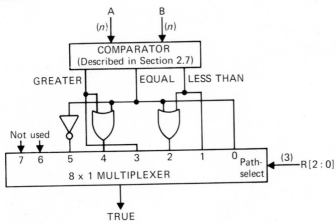

Figure S2.17

2.18

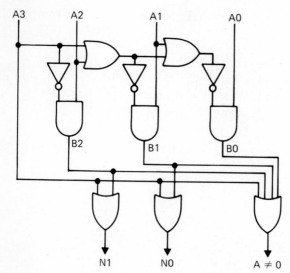

Figure S2.18

2.19

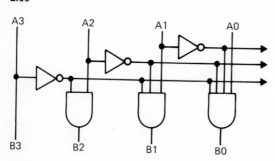

Figure S2.19

2.20

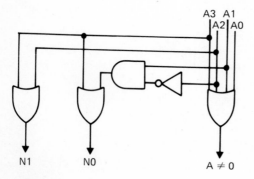

Figure S2.20

2.21 80; EF; 6F.

2.22 a) OR it with hex 80.

b) EXCLUSIVE OR it with hex 3C.

c) AND it with hex F0.

2.23 If $A \oplus B = A\bar{B} + \bar{A}B$, then $A \oplus \bar{B} = AB + \bar{A}\bar{B}$. $A \odot B = \overline{\bar{A}B \oplus A\bar{B}}$, which is $(\bar{A} + B)(A + \bar{B})$ (by application of Theorem 14), which reduces to the same $AB + \overline{AB}$ when it is "multiplied out" (Theorem 3a, in reverse).

2.24

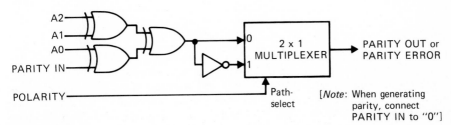

Figure S2.24

CHAPTER 3

3.1

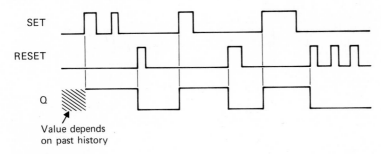

Figure S3.1

3.2

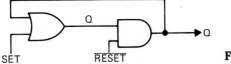

SET $\overline{RESET}$

Figure S3.2

3.3

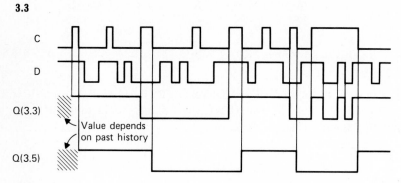

C

D

Q(3.3)

Value depends
on past history

Q(3.5)

Figure S3.3

3.4 The real INVERTER may be replaced by an ideal one followed by a *delay* element whose present output signal is always the same as what its input signal was *t* seconds earlier. Since there is always a contradiction between the present and future values of any signal in the circuit, the network must be *unstable*. All of its signals continually oscillate between 0 and 1. A signal stays at either level for exactly *t* seconds, before making a transition to the other level. The *period* of oscillation (the duration of the square waveform which constantly repeats) is therefore 2*t* seconds.

3.5   See Figs. 3.3 and 3.5.

3.6

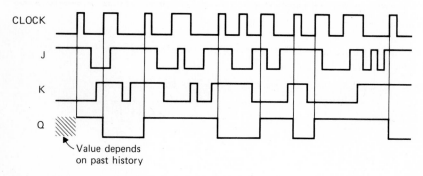

CLOCK

J

K

Q

Value depends
on past history

Figure S3.6

3.7   Its behavior is identical to that of a JK FLIP-FLOP, where J = A and K = B.

3.8

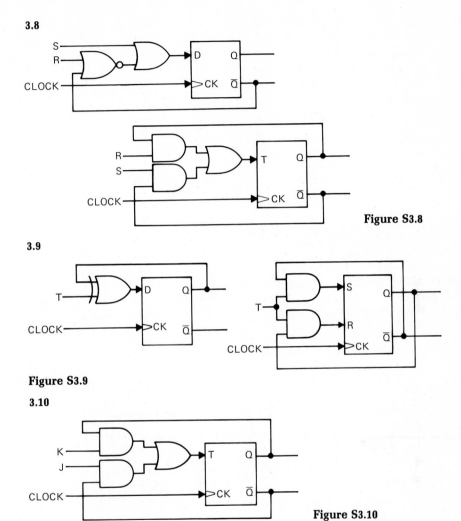

Figure S3.8

3.9

Figure S3.9

3.10

Figure S3.10

3.11 Since a FLIP-FLOP is a *symmetrical* circuit, both of its states are equally likely when electrical power is turned on. A register's ini'al contents, when power is first applied, is totally arbitrary (i.e., any stored code is possible), since each of its FLIP-FLOPs is just as likely to start with 1 as with 0.

3.12 (See Fig. S3.12.) The A and B negative pulses are extremely short, having a duration comparable to the delay through a single gate.

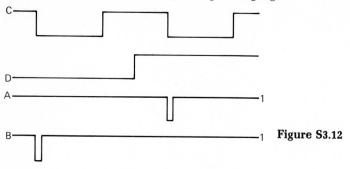

Figure S3.12

3.13 It is a negative edge-triggered JK FLIP-FLOP, where J = A, K = B, and CLOCK = C.

3.14 On the first X = 1 sample, the network generates a standard Z pulse whose width is equal to the time between two adjacent CLOCK pulses, *no matter how wide the X pulse is*. Any X = 0 sample resets the circuit so that it may respond again, in a similar fashion, to the first X = 1 sample detected subsequently.

3.15

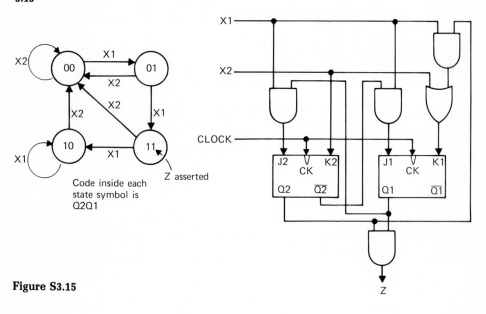

Code inside each state symbol is Q2Q1

Figure S3.15

3.16 If A = 0, FLIP-FLOPs Q1 and Q0 *swap* bits whenever a P pulse occurs. If A = 1, FLIP-FLOPs Q1 and Q0 *load* the values D1 and D0, respectively, whenever a pulse P occurs.

3.17 a) The contents of register N. (N[1:0] = 0, 1, 2, or 3.)

b) Register N *loads* the value DIN[k:1].

3.18 If A = 0, Q[2:1] *increments* whenever a CLOCK pulse occurs. If A = 1, Q[2:1] *decrements* whenever a CLOCK pulse occurs.

3.19

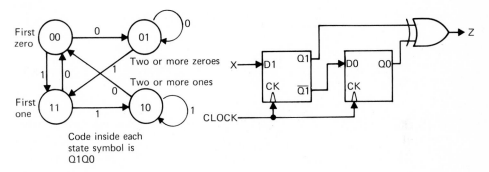

Figure S3.19

3.20 The new Z[1:0] value, after a CLOCK pulse occurs, is the binary *sum* (mod 4) of its old value and D[1:0]; here "mod 4" indicates that only the lower two result bits are retained.

3.21

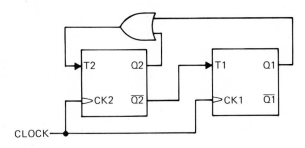

Figure S3.21

3.22

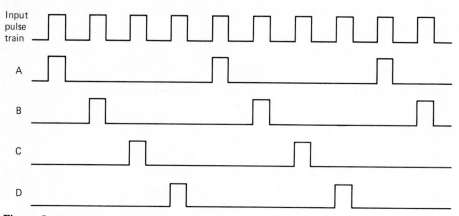

Figure S3.22

3.23 $(2^N!)/(2^N - S)!$.

3.24 With D_{IN1} connected to D_{OUT4}, the contents of the register will ROTATE left on every LOAD pulse. With D_{IN1} connected to "0", the contents of the register will SHIFT LEFT (with 0 inserted into the rightmost position) whenever a LOAD pulse occurs.

3.25 The contents of the register will *increment* whenever a LOAD pulse occurs (11 increments to 00).

3.26

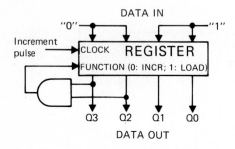

Figure S3.26

3.27

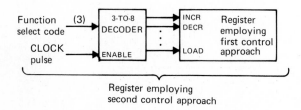

Figure S3.27

CHAPTER 4

4.1

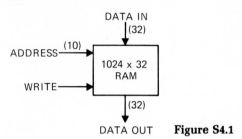

Figure S4.1

4.2

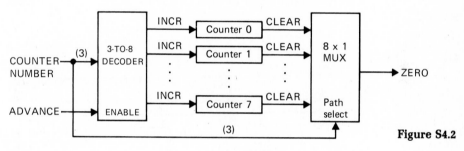

Figure S4.2

4.3

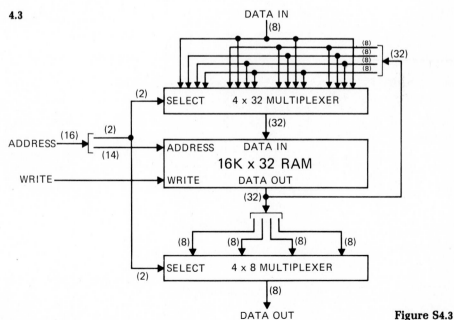

Figure S4.3

4.4

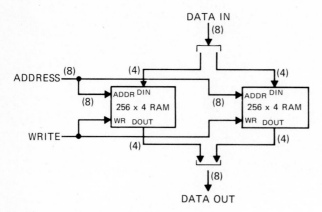

Figure S4.4

4.5

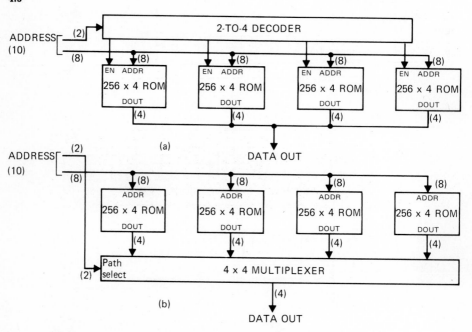

Figure S4.5

4.6

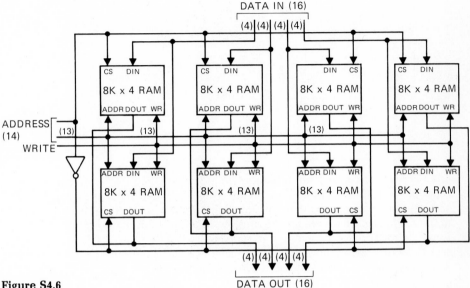

Figure S4.6

4.7   a) 010010   d) 010XXX
         b) 1XXXXX   e) XXX010
         c) XXXXX0   f) 1100XX

4.8

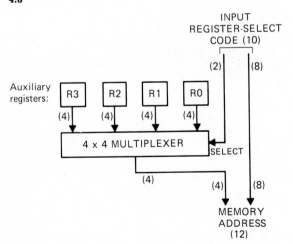

Figure S4.8

4.9

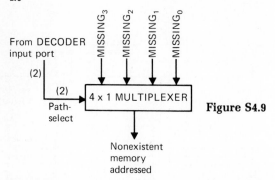

Figure S4.9

4.10 For each 1K-byte page, beginning with the first, the program *writes* a special code into one of its registers (for example, the first), then *reads* the same cell and compares the read value with the written value. If they match, the program proceeds to the next page. The written code must be *different* from the quiescent value that would be read from a nonexistent memory cell. Address value XXXXXX0000000000 selects the first register in a page. The X field increments, starting at zero. A good test data value, which "mixes" ones and zeroes, is a hex AA.

4.11 Three registers contain the value zero. Seven contain the value one. The remaining six registers are divided into six sets of one register each. Their respective contents are the values 2, 3, 4, 8, 9, and 27 (decimal).

4.12 a) 0, F, 0, F, 0, F, . . .
b) F, 0, F, 0, F, 0, . . .
c) 0, 1, 2, 3, 4, 5, . . . , E, F, 0, 1, 2, . . .
d) 0, 0, 0, 0, 1, 1, 1, 1, 2, 2, 2, 2, . . . , F, F, F, F, 0, 0, 0, 0, 1, 1, . . .

4.13

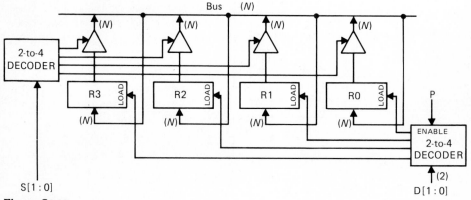

Figure S4.13

4.14 C ← C + M(A + B).

4.15 M(R2) ← M(R2) + R1.

4.16

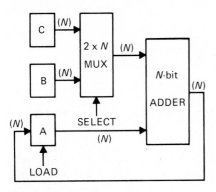

Figure S4.16

4.17

	LD1	LD2	LD3	S1	S2	CLEAR
a	0	0	1	X	X	0
b	1	1	0	0	0	0
c	1	1	1	1	1	0
d	0	0	1	X	X	1

4.18

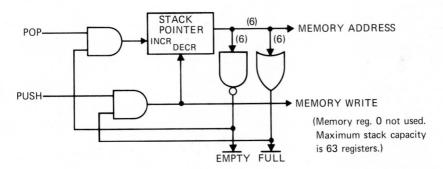

Figure S4.18

4.19   a) R1 ← S; S ← R1; S ← R1
        b) R1 ← S; R2 ← S; S ← R1; S ← R2
        c) R1 ← S; R2 ← S; S ← R2; S ← R1; S ← R2

4.20 When pulse P1 is activated, the control signal to the multiplexer is no longer a level, and the multiplexer's output is no longer guaranteed valid while C is being loaded. If the register happens to be *trailing* edge-triggered, and the width of P1 is greater than the response time of the multiplexer, the circuit will operate as desired. However, if the register happens to be *leading* edge-triggered, the network will fail to operate properly.

4.21

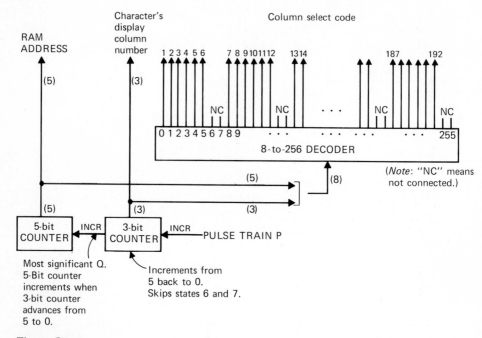

Figure S4.21

4.22 $A \leftarrow A \oplus B$
$B \leftarrow A \oplus B$
$A \leftarrow A \oplus B$

CHAPTER 5

5.1

A8:	7043.10 Hz	A7:	3521.55 Hz	A6:	1760.77 Hz
A5:	880.39 Hz	A4:	440.19 Hz	A3:	220.10 Hz
A2:	110.05 Hz	A1:	55.02 Hz	A0:	27.51 Hz

("Hz" = cycles per second)

5.2   a) 00, 04, 08, 0C, 10, 14, 18, 1C
b) 02, 06, 0A, 0E, 12, 16, 1A, 1E
c) (14, 15, 16) or (14, 15, 17) or (14, 16, 17)

5.3   Change the *one*-stage counter (which divides its input frequency by two) into a *two*-stage counter (which divides its input frequency by four).

5.4   Four.

5.5   2, 8, 4, 8, 2, 0, 4, 0, 2, 0, 4, 0, 2, 0, 4, 0
2, 8, 4, 8, 2, 0, 4, 0, 3, 0, 4, 0, 3, 0, 4, 0

5.6   One

5.7   PP contents after each pass = 00, 16, 42, 42.

5.8

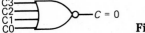
C3
C2
C1
C0
$C = 0$

Figure S5.8

5.9   PP contents after each pass: 06 (start), 03, 59, 84, 42.

5.10   C PP.1 PP.0 = 09 00 00, 08 00 93, 07 55 49, 06 7F A4,
05 3F D2, 04 1F E9, 03 64 F4, 02 32 7A,
01 19 3D, 00 61 9E

5.11

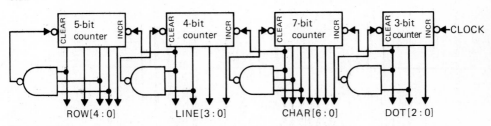

Figure S5.11

5.12   Dot time = 94 nanoseconds. Character scan-line-segment time = 564 nanoseconds. Line scan time = 63.1 microseconds. Time for a row of characters = 757.6 microseconds. Frame time = 16.7 milliseconds.

5.13   1XXXXXXXXXXXXXXXXXX;   XXXXX1XXXXXXXXXXXXX;
XXXXXXXXX1XXXXXXXXX;   XXXXXXXXXXXXXXXX000;
XXXXX0000XXXXXXXXXX   (The ROM outputs zeroes here.)

5.14   Disabling the AND gate forces the X input to the corresponding shift register to be zero. This causes the register to *shift* whenever it receives a CLOCK pulse. Since the shift-in bit is a constant "0", the register remains cleared as it continues to shift, in which case, its shift-out bit remains zero.

5.15 It has no effect. It is not used.

5.16 Add an EXCLUSIVE OR gate in the VIDEO signal path, as shown in Fig. S5.16.

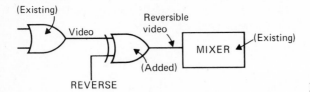

Figure S5.16

5.17 Refer to Fig. S5.17. First, the conditions under which the GRAPHICS mode is established must be modified. One added AND gate is used to cause GRAPHICS to be asserted only when holding register bits 7 and 6 are 1 and 0, respectively. (The complements of all signals needed are assumed available.) The added six-input AND detects when bits 7 and 6 are both 1, for LINE NUMBER 9, provided that the display is not blanked. The added D FLIP-FLOP loads this output bit at the same time that the upper shift register loads its next six-bit output pattern. The ADDED VIDEO signal is ORed with the two other video signal sources.

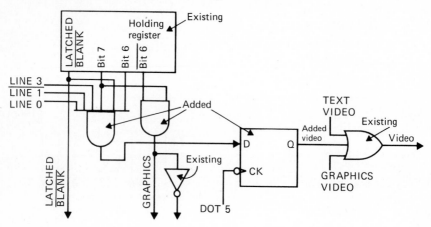

Figure S5.17

CHAPTER 6

6.1 Simple, "straight-line" code would not require any modification. However, all *branch destination addresses* would need to be reduced by one. Skip instructions would not need to be modified. The PC, however, would have to be initialized, before a program run, to point to the location *before* the program's first instruction.

6.2 BRANCH or JUMP, SKIP, CALL, and RETURN. PUSH, POP, CALL, and RETURN.

6.3

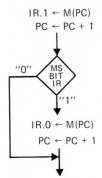

IR.1 ← M(PC)
PC ← PC + 1

"0"

MS
BIT
IR

"1"

IR.0 ← M(PC)
PC ← PC + 1

Figure S6.3

6.4 See Fig. S6.4. An erroneous JUMP into a data area will cause the fetch of a data word.

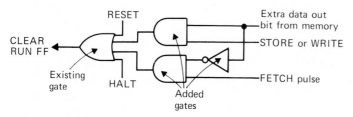

RESET

Extra data out
bit from memory

CLEAR
RUN FF

STORE or WRITE

Existing
gate

HALT

Added
gates

FETCH pulse

Figure S6.4

6.5 All those instructions, whose corresponding D bits are set, will be executed *simultaneously*.

6.6 If the EXTERNAL DEVICE contains a register receiving the DATA IN code (the value of Y), and if that register's LOAD control input is connected to the STROBE input terminal, then the transfer EXT REG ← Y will be executed whenever a STROBE pulse is generated.

6.7 Disconnect the SUB wire, presently directed to the five-input OR gate that generates Y's LOAD input signal. Connect it instead, as an extra input, to the OR gate that generates PC's INCR input signal.

6.8 If the leading edge of the RUN signal occurs during a clock pulse, the first pulse, which clocks the FETCH-EXECUTE flip-flop and enables the pair of AND gates associated with it, will be *narrower* than usual. If it is so narrow that *none* of the devices that receive it respond to it, then it is merely ignored, in which case, the very *next* pulse will start the run. If it is sufficiently wide that *all* devices that receive it respond to it, then it acts as a normal first pulse. However, if it is exactly at the threshold where some devices respond to it while others do not, an error condition exists. For example, if IR and PC respond to the narrow FETCH PULSE, while the FETCH-EXECUTE flip-flop does *not* toggle, the first instruction will be skipped.

6.9 IF ADD and SUB are reassigned opcodes 1 and 2, respectively, the control logic is simplified somewhat, as shown in Fig. S6.9. The five-input OR that generates Y's LOAD pulse becomes a two-input gate. The 3-to-8 OP decoder becomes a 2-to-4 decoder. An additional 1-to-2 decoder (a pair of ANDs and an INVERTER), which steers the EXECUTE pulse based on the value of OP2, is needed, however.

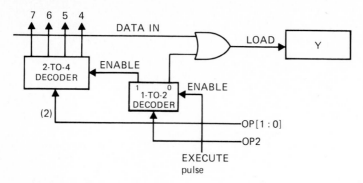

Figure S6.9

6.10 There is a specific instant during the execution of the first instruction (the JUMPFL) at which the FLAG signal is tested. If FLAG = 0 at that instant, the *next* instant, at which the same test is made, occurs *two* instruction times later. Therefore, to ensure that it will be detected, the FLAG pulse width must be greater than the time between successive tests. If its leading edge occurs after one test, while its trailing edge occurs before the next test, it will not be detected.

6.11 From -1.7×10^{38} to $+1.7 \times 10^{38}$ (which is 2^{127}). The smallest nonzero magnitude is 1.47×10^{-39} (which is 0.5×2^{-128}).

6.12 Each 32-bit word holds a sequence of four eight-bit line segment fields, each of which is composed of a three-bit direction field, a four-bit length field, and a one-bit visibility field. Strictly speaking, the format is not defined until tables are constructed, assigning a specific meaning to each possible value in each field.

6.13 An unconditional BRANCH to itself.

6.14 All *addresses* in the program that reference locations *after* the insertion point must be incremented by one.

6.15 Refer to Fig. S6.15. Replace the instruction just before the insertion point with an unconditional JUMP to the unused memory area. At the JUMP's destination, copy the replaced instruction, followed by the sequence of instructions to be inserted, followed by an unconditional JUMP back to the instruction immediately after the insertion point.

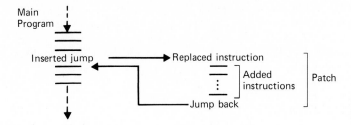

Figure S6.15

6.16

Stack contents:				5 3 1	3 1	6 3 1	9 6 3 1	6 3 1	6 3 1	3 1	1
PC value:	0	2	4	7	5	8	10	9	6	3	1	2
	(START)										

Figure S6.16

6.17 The accumulated gate delay, to develop a *path* to or from a memory register, is larger than that to implement a path to a processor register. Similarly, there is a larger accumulated gate delay, in a memory, before a control signal (such as WRITE) is known to be directed to the selected register. (Electrically speaking, signal propagation in a memory is further delayed by "capacitance" and "inductance" distributed along its lengthy paths.)

6.18 RUN, FETCH, PC[A:1], OP[2:0], Z, D, SIGN, and FLAG. [Note that each of these signals (except FLAG, whose source is unspecified) is a FLIP-FLOP Q signal.]

6.19

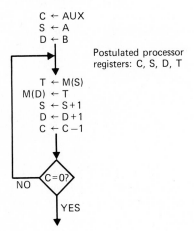

C ← AUX
S ← A
D ← B

Postulated processor
registers: C, S, D, T

T ← M(S)
M(D) ← T
S ← S + 1
D ← D + 1
C ← C − 1

C = 0?
NO
YES

Figure S6.19

6.20 a) During a FETCH or the execution of a SKIP.
      b) During execution of a BRANCH or CALL.
      c) During execution of a CALL.
      d) During execution of a PUSH, POP, CALL, or RETURN. It depends on the direction of stack growth.
      e) During execution of LOAD ACC.
      f) During execution of PUSH ACC.
      g) During execution of POP ACC.

6.21 The MOVE instruction in Problem 6.19 is a good example of the first variation. A SEARCH or FIND instruction, which scans a memory area for a specific code and terminates execution when it reaches that code, is a good example of the second variation.

6.22 $C \leftarrow C - 1$
      If C not zero, $PC \leftarrow PC + A$

This instruction is useful as the last instruction in a *loop* that is executed a fixed number of times. Register C is initialized with this number before the loop is entered.

6.23

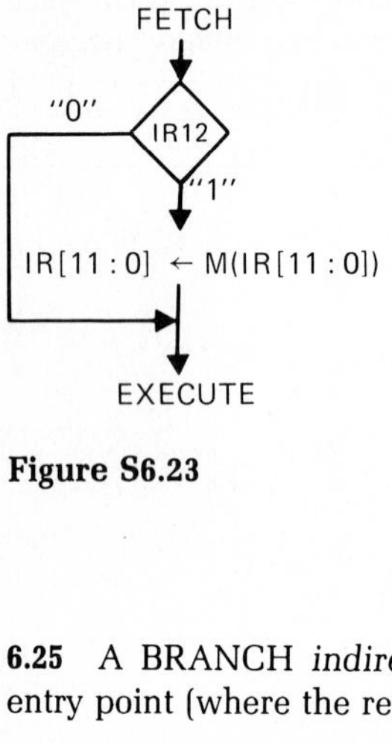

FETCH

$IR[11:0] \leftarrow M(IR[11:0])$

EXECUTE

Figure S6.23

6.24

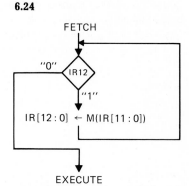

Figure S6.24

6.25 A BRANCH *indirect* to the location immediately preceding the subroutine's entry point (where the return address is stored).

6.26 5, 15, 30, 20, 40, 10, 25

6.27 The four-bit field may be subdivided into three subfields. A one-bit field specifies the shift direction (left or right). Another one-bit field defines the end conditions (shift in zero or rotate). The remaining two-bit field specifies the shift distance. Only three of the four possible values are assigned meanings.

6.28 First, 15 three-address instructions, having the format OP3 ADDR1 ADDR2 ADDR3, for OP3 values from 0000 to 1110 (1111 is used as an "escape" code). Then, 15 two-address instructions, having the format 1111 OP2 ADDR1 ADDR2, for OP2 values from 0000 to 1110. (Again, 1111 is an escape value.) Next, 15 one-address instructions, having the format 1111 1111 OP1 ADDR, for OP1 values from 0000 to 1110. Finally, 16 zero-address instructions, having the format 1111 1111 1111 OP.

CHAPTER 7

7.1 $m(0)$ and $m(1)$. $m(0)$ is used as the Program Counter. It is not directly accessible to the programmer. $m(1)$ is used as the Stack Pointer. It is implicitly modified during the execution of CALL and RETURN instructions.

7.2 The STORE operation. When it executes, the destination of the ALU/SHIFTER result is not $m(R2)$—as you would expect. Rather, it is the memory location from which OPERAND1 came. The STORE instruction was included to provide a mechanism for storing scratchpad values back into the main memory. Since a unary operation modifies an operand "in place," it cannot be used to move a word from one place to another. While a binary operation can be used to transfer *from* memory *to* the scratchpad (by having the ALU merely pass OPERAND1), it needs a special variation to transfer in the *other* direction. The STORE instruction provides this variation.

7.3 The CALL and BRANCH instructions. In the first case, the source is H concatenated with the CALL ADDRESS (IR[14:0]). In the second case, it is the BRANCH OFFSET (IR[9:0]), with its sign bit extended to bit position 15.

7.4

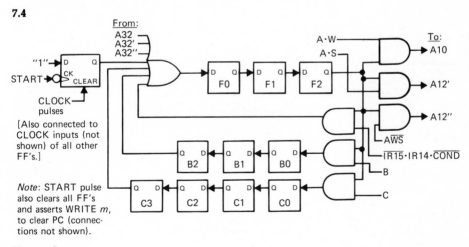

Figure S7.4

7.5

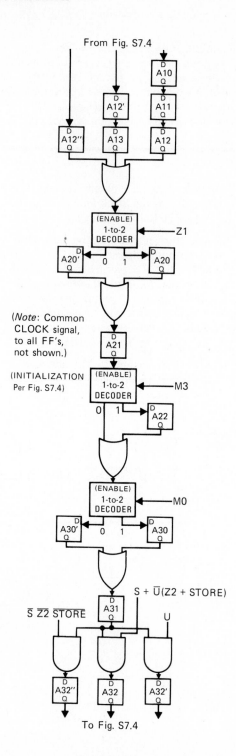

Figure S7.5

7.6 Add the following entries to Table 7.5:

A10   READ m, LOAD MAR, LOAD X
A11   GATE RESULT, WRITE m
A12   READ M, LOAD Y
A12′   GATE R2, READ m, LOAD X, LOAD Y
A12″   LOAD Y
A13   GATE RESULT, GATE R2, WRITE m
A20′   GATE R1, READ m, LOAD X
A22   READ M, LOAD MAR
A30   GATE MAR, LOAD X
A30′   READ M, LOAD X
A32′   GATE OP, GATE RESULT, GATE R1, WRITE m
A32″   GATE OP, GATE RESULT, GATE R2, WRITE m
C0   SELECT SP, READ m, LOAD MAR, LOAD X
C1   SELECT SP, GATE RESULT, WRITE m
C2   READ m, WRITE M
C3   GATE ADDRESS, WRITE m
B0   READ m, LOAD X
B1   GATE OFFSET, LOAD Y
B2   ADD, GATE RESULT, WRITE m

7.7 It would halt. No FLIP-FLOP would remain activated.

7.8 (See Fig. S7.8.) Assume the system is initialized with all registers cleared and with the first output word already available at the DATA OUT port of the paper tape reader. All clocked devices are assumed triggered on the trailing CLOCK pulse edge. Before the START pulse, all ENABLE signals are zero, and READY = 1. The START pulse sets control FLIP-FLOP Q1, which, in turn, asserts LOAD A ENABLE. This causes A to load and Q2 to set (asserting ADVANCE) on the very next CLOCK pulse. In response, signals "A = 0" and READY both drop, causing LOAD A ENABLE and Q1 to drop as well; Q1 will remain reset until another START pulse is received.

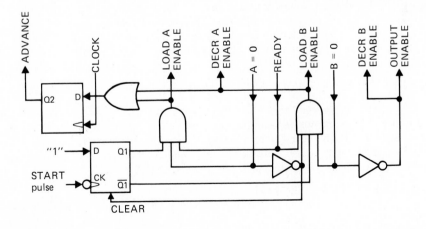

Figure S7.8

ADVANCE will drop at the CLOCK pulse that follows. When the next paper-tape character is valid, READY is re-asserted, which activates LOAD B ENABLE and DECR A ENABLE. Thus, on the very next CLOCK pulse, B loads and A decrements. Simultaneously, ADVANCE is re-asserted for one CLOCK period, causing the paper-tape reader to begin moving the tape to the next character. The load of B causes "B = 0" to drop, which, in turn, asserts DECR B ENABLE and OUTPUT ENABLE. These signals permit the first burst of N output pulses, where N is the initial value loaded into B from the tape. Each output pulse also decrements B. When B reaches zero, the system stops until READY is raised again. At that time, since Q1 is zero, B will again load (and A will again decrement), causing a new burst of pulses. This process continues until A reaches zero, at which time a final pulse burst occurs while a new paper-tape character is fetched. Thus, when the system stops, the new paper-tape character is available for the next run, which is initiated when the START button is depressed again.

7.9 The network assembles a *serial* sequence of four hex digits into a *parallel* 16-bit output code. If the counter increments on the trailing edge of the DATA STROBE, the decoder is disabled while the counter is advancing, and spurious output "spikes" are prevented. By including the R3 register as shown, an output code value remains valid while the *next* output code value is being assembled. The assertion of A indicates, to the device with which this element communicates, that a new 16-bit DATA item is READY. The signal B is a DATA RECEIVED signal, which causes A to drop until the next 16-bit word has been assembled.

7.10 R1 = SP, R2 = PC, R3 = IR, and R4 = ACC.
   a) R2 to ABUS; DOUT to DBUS; LOAD R3; INCR R2.
   b) R3 to ABUS; DOUT to DBUS; LOAD R4.
   c) R1 to ABUS; R4 to DBUS; WRITE; DECR R1.
   d) R1 to ABUS; R2 to DBUS; WRITE; DECR R1; then R3 to ABUS; ABUS to R2; LOAD R2.
   e) INCR R1; R1 to ABUS; DOUT to DBUS; DBUS to R2; LOAD R2.

7.11 For each of the control signals listed on the right side of Table 7.5, enumerate all those ACTIVATE signal names that induce it. (For example, READ m is induced by F0, A31, A10, A12′, A20′, C0, C2, and B0.) Convert this list into a sum-of-products logical expression, where a single numeric digit n converts to "E1Tn", while a pair of numeric digits mn converts to "EmTn". (Using the example above, we would derive

$$\text{READ } m = \text{FT0} + \text{AE3T1} + \text{AE1T0} + \text{AE1T2} + \text{AE2T0} + \text{CE1T0} + \text{CE1T2} + \text{BE1T0.})$$

For each of the terms on the right side of each equation, check its corresponding box in Fig. 7.4 to see if its execution is *conditional* on any *other* signals, and, if so, add (AND) these signals into the corresponding term. (Using the same example, A10 is also conditional on W, A12′ is also conditional on S, and A20′ is also conditional on $\overline{Z}1$. Thus, the equation above becomes:

$$\text{READ } m = \text{FT0} + \text{AE3T1} + \text{AWE1T0} + \text{ASE1T2}$$
$$+ \text{A}\overline{Z}1\text{E2T0} + \text{CE1T0} + \text{CE1T2} + \text{BE1T0,}$$

which is the same as the corresponding equation in Table 7.6.)

7.12

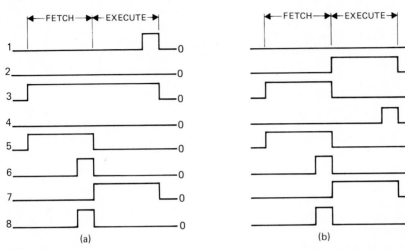

Figure S7.12

7.13 a) A path from the Q field of the IR to the PC and a LOAD control input to the PC. The LOAD PC signal must be derived from a *multiplexer*, whose path control code comes from the F field of the IR. The individual branch condition signals are multiplexer inputs.

b) In addition to the facilities described in (a), we require an SP register, having an ADVANCE (INCR or DECR, as appropriate) control input and a gated path from SP to the Address Bus, activated by an "SP to ABUS" control signal. Further, a gated path from the PC to the DATA BUS (activated by a "PC to DBUS" control signal) must exist to permit the PC value to be stored.

c) In addition to the facilities described in (b), we require a path from the DATA BUS to the PC. Since a path to the PC from the IR already exists, a two-way multiplexer, at the DATA IN port of the PC, is required. It has a single path-select control input.

7.14 Answers, in order, from 1 to 36: F0, ZERO, REG5, FIELD, Q, RESULT, MEM, F1, $\overline{QC}$, MEM, RESET, QB, F10, F2, QC, RESET, START, PULSES, RESET, FIELD, T, QC, $\overline{QC}$, MUX8, F2, QC, F10, MUX5, QC, F2, F1, F0, REG8, F0, REG8, MEM.

7.15 MAP is asserted for one special TEST field value. This TEST code is employed in the microinstruction that executes the multi-way branch based on the just-fetched OP value. One of the multiplexer's internal decoder outputs is brought out as the MAP signal. When MAP = 1, the other MUX output is also 1. In Table 7.8, the TEST code corresponding to the symbol "NONE" is also guaranteed to generate a 1 output.

7.16 05, 0B, and 10.

7.17 0, 1, 2, 3, 4, 10, 11, 19, 1A, 1B, 1C, 1D, 1E, 1F, 21, 22, 23, 24, 25, 26, 28, 29, 2A, 2B, 2E, 2F.

7.18

ADDRESS	MICROINSTRUCTION		
	TRANSFER	AUX	C
	TRANSFER	A	S
	TRANSFER	B	D
LOOP	TRANSFER	S	MAR
	TRANSFER	M	T
	TRANSFER	D	MAR
	TRANSFER	T	M
	INCR	S	
	INCR	D	
	DECR	C	
	JUMP	C	LOOP
	JUMP	NONE	FETCH . . . To fetch next instr.

7.19 If the branch CONDition is not met, the machine will sequence through three execution cycles (E1, E2 and E3), doing *nothing*, before the next fetch starts. This oversight in the design is remedied by adding the term PDFT3 to the FETCH NEXT expression in Table 7.6 (where D is the first logical combination marked with an asterisk in Table 7.4). With this modification, the fetch of a BRANCH, which is not taken, will be *immediately followed* by the fetch of the next instruction (eliminating three time-wasting execution cycles).

CHAPTER 8

8.1 A RETURN restores information saved during execution of a CALL. Normally, its execution consists only of the single transfer PC ← STACK. A RETURN FROM INTERRUPT, on the other hand, "undoes" everything that was executed during a previous TAKE INTERRUPT sequence. In addition to restoring the PC, its execution normally includes IE ← 1 *plus* the restoration of any other registers whose values were saved. (If execution of a CALL were defined to be *identical* to that of a TAKE INTERRUPT sequence, a single RETURN could serve both purposes. A software interrupt is, in fact, such a special "CALL".)

8.2 If an interrupt is pending when the SET IE completes execution, the interrupt will be taken *before* the RETURN is fetched. The previously saved PC value will remain on the stack until the RETURN is ultimately executed. If a sufficiently long sequence of overlapping interrupt requests develops (in which interrupt request $i + 1$ occurs while interrupt i is being serviced), and if the stack has a *limited* capacity, the stack capacity may be exceeded before the string of unresolved RETURNs is finally unraveled.

8.3 See Fig. S8.3. An Interrupt Enable flip-flop is required. In addition, a gated path to the VALUE output port (in Fig. 7.3) is needed. When an interrupt is taken, this port carries the value LOC to the central data bus.

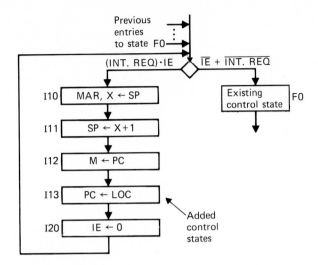

Figure S8.3

8.4   Change the transfer in control state I13 to read:

$$PC \leftarrow 00(ID[3:0])0 \text{ (zeros are hex digits)}.$$

8.5   Since $m(0)$ has already been pushed, the response routine must save $m(2)$ through $m(15)$. [We assume that they are saved on the stack, in which case, $m(1)$ is jointly used by all programs. If the interrupt handler expects to use *another* stack, it must preserve $m(1)$ as well.] Note that X, Y, MAR, and IR are all temporary registers. They need not be saved. In addition, the contents of the FLAG register (Fig. 7.3) must be preserved, because the interrupted program may later execute a branch which is conditional on its value. Similarly, the contents of the H flip-flop must be saved, because the interrrupt response program may change it. Therefore, instructions such as PUSH FLAGS and POP FLAGS must be added to the processor's repertoire. (For simplicity, we assume that the H value is processed as part of the flag code.)

8.6   In addition to having explicit control over the value in the Interrupt Enable flip-flop (via ENABLE INTERRUPTS and DISABLE INTERRUPTS instructions), the programmer may have available a SET INTERRUPT MASK instruction, which permits explicit control over the program's interruptibility to each of the possible interrupt sources, on an individual basis. A sophisticated interrupt system may provide the programmer with an instruction that modifies the interrupt priorities.

8.7   (1) Immediately after the higher-priority response routine RETURNs, but before the main program resumes. (2) Immediately after the main program instruction that *unmasks* that interrupt.

8.8   See Fig. S8.8. Whenever a SET TIMER instruction is executed, the value on the data bus (typically, derived from an immediate field in that instruction) is loaded into the counter. While the contents of the register are nonzero, it continually decrements at a rate determined by the frequency of the clock oscillator. When it reaches zero, the leading edge of the "CONTENTS = 0" signal sets an interrupt request flip-flop. The counter is prohibited from decrementing past zero. When the interrupt is taken, the ACKnowledge signal resets the flip-flop. A SET TIMER instruction, which initializes the timer to a minimum value (for example, 1) may be able to induce an interrupt request *before* the very next instruction is fetched, if the rate at which clock pulses are generated is sufficiently high. Under these conditions, the SET TIMER instruction acts as if it were a software interrupt instruction.

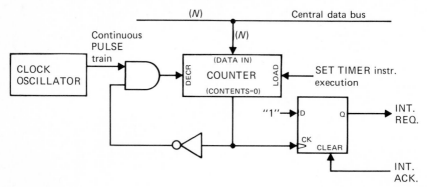

Figure S8.8

8.9 If the interrupt handler, which receives control on an opcode trap, uses the illegal opcode value to *vector* to a corresponding response routine, which executes a function not available in the hardware's repertoire, programs may be written as if these functions *were* mechanized in hardware.

8.10 a) "Here is another unit of data for you."
  b) "Please send me your next unit of data."

8.11 See Fig. S8.11. The logic is identical to that of the priority network in Fig. 2.26, once we recognize that BUS GRANT*i*, being an *enable* signal, is the *complement* of DISABLE*i* in Fig. 2.26.

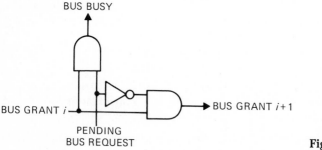

Figure S8.11

8.12 See Fig. S8.12. The D LATCH is transparent (i.e., it merely passes its input signals) when its LOAD control input is "1".

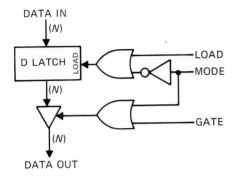

DATA IN
(N)

D LATCH

(N)

LOAD
MODE

GATE

(N)

DATA OUT

Figure S8.12

8.13 a) "I am ready to accept a new unit of data."
b) "Here is a new unit of data for you to dispose of."

8.14

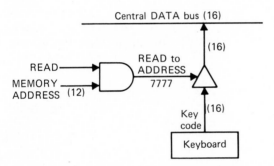

Central DATA bus (16)

(16)

READ to
ADDRESS
7777

READ

MEMORY
ADDRESS (12)

Key
code (16)

Keyboard

Figure S8.14

8.15 (50 to 100 microseconds)/(1 microsecond) = 50 to 100.

8.16 a) A "program-controlled" I/O process.
b) An "interrupt-driven" I/O process.
c) An I/O process employing Direct Memory Access.

8.17 Each is initiated by the execution of a special instruction. Each operates *in parallel* with the other computation. Each makes its termination known by generating an interrupt. While the timer's operation is totally independent of the CPU, the DMA controller must compete with the CPU for memory access.

8.18 The initial PC value is conveyed either in a field of the START I/O instruction or as the contents of an auxiliary register (either assigned to the I/O processor or selected by a field in the START I/O instruction). An I/O termination interrupt indicates completion of the I/O program.

8.19 See Fig. S8.19. The two waveforms differ only in the position of a single pulse. The receiver measures time beginning with the leading edge of the START bit. If its internal clock does not agree with that of the transmitter (because either or both have inadequate timing accuracy), a transmission error may develop.

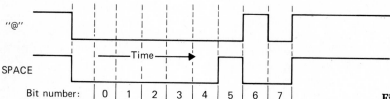

Figure S8.19

CHAPTER 9

9.1 Eliminate the RESUME path from the I/O Termination Module to the currently running task box. Change the second and third sentences in the I/O Termination Module description to read: "Mark current task as READY" (whether or not the current task is the IDLE task). Retain the exit path to the dispatcher.

9.2 A hardware timer may be employed to prevent such a situation. Suppose each Task Control Block includes a "maximum CPU time" allocation, specifying how long its task may run between I/O SVC's. The Supervisor may utilize the timer to keep track of each task's accumulated CPU time since its last I/O. When this value exceeds the prescribed limit, the task is deactivated.

9.3 As long as one higher-priority task is always READY, the low-priority READY task will never run. Several patterns of activity will yield such a situation. For example, there may be only two other tasks, one running and the other waiting for I/O completion. If the current I/O operation always completes before the running task issues a new I/O SVC, there will always be a higher-priority READY task. While such a situation is not likely to last indefinitely, it is more plausible as the number of higher-priority tasks increases.

If we eliminate the priority system and treat the READY LIST on a First-In-First-Out (FIFO) basis, the task that has spent the most time in the READY LIST will be the one dispatched next. The IDLE task should be dispatched only if the READY LIST is empty. Specific changes needed in the flow chart are as follows: (1) Change the first sentence in the description of the I/O Termination module to read: "Add the corresponding task to the end of the READY list". (2) In the same module, omit the "Mark it READY" operation. (3) Change the description of the Dispatcher module to read: "Select the oldest task in READY list and mark it as RUNNING. If the READY LIST is empty, dispatch the IDLE task".

9.4

Shaded regions represent Supervisor's running time.

Task states: R = READY; W = WAITING; E = EXECUTING.

Figure S9.4

9.5 In addition to the changes listed in the solution to Problem 9.3, add to the Dispatcher's description the following: "Initialize timer for a new time slot". Also, add to the flow chart the Timeout module shown in Fig. S9.5.

(To DISPATCHER)   **Figure S9.5**

9.6

Opcode	Operands	Comments
POPX		. . . Get saved PC value into X.
PUSHX		. . . Restore the stack.
DECRX		. . . Point X at the trapped instruction.
LOADX	@X	. . . Get the instruction itself into X.
ANDX	FF00	. . . Leave only the opcode in X.
SWAPX		. . . Swap the two bytes of X. This
		. . . leaves the opcode on the right.
SUBX	00E0	. . . Leaving only the index in the
		. . . illegal opcode range.
JUMP	@(TABLE,X)	. . . Exit to the called routine via
		. . . an address table.

A processor register X is assumed. The value in the illegal opcode range is isolated in X and used as an index into a table containing the entry addresses of the Supervisor service routines. Each service routine terminates with a RETURN FROM INTERRUPT instruction.

9.7 50, 51, 52, 53, 54, 55, 56, 57, 69, 70.

9.8 Each *vectors* to a specific "handler" program based on a given code value. An interrupt analyzer is given a code identifying the interrupt just taken. An interpreter FETCH routine is given a code identifying the instruction to be executed next.

9.9 It executes a PUSH instruction. To remedy this situation, insert, before symbolic location PUSH, the following pair of instructions:

```
IF      7       PUSH
JUMP    FETCH
```

9.10 WORD SUBMARK
WORD A(PUSH)
WORD A(CLEAR)
WORD A(RETURN)

where the virtual RETURN is mechanized with:

RETURN: POP   PTR
           JUMP   FETCH

9.11

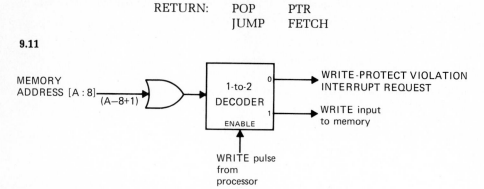

Figure S9.11

9.12 Set whenever an interrupt is taken. Reset when either of the following instructions is executed: RETURN FROM INTERRUPT or SET USER MODE.

9.13

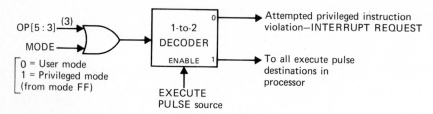

Figure S9.13

9.14 If SET TIMER were not privileged, any task could allocate itself an arbitrarily long time slice.

9.15 The address-mapping hardware (which contains the page table) detects that the addressed virtual page is not in the main memory. It generates a "page fault" interrupt request. When the interrupt is taken, the Supervisor responds by temporarily suspending the running task and issuing the disk I/O instructions to bring in the addressed virtual page. This may necessitate first writing out the page that will be replaced (if it has been modified). Some other READY task is then dispatched. When the I/O completes, the Supervisor responds to its completion interrupt by appropriately updating the page table in the memory-mapping hardware and by marking the task as READY. The Supervisor may then resume the suspended task at any time. When it does, the original access request is finally granted.

9.16 Maintain a counter, in the page table, for every physical page. Increment all counters periodically. Whenever a page is accessed, clear its counter. The counter with the highest count is therefore the least recently accessed.

9.17 Its complement (properly timed) is directed to the SET input of the "page fault" interrupt flip-flop. The signal may also be directed to the memory's ENABLE input terminal, so that an erroneous access, on a page fault, will be prevented.

9.18 Whether the debugger receives control via a CALL or via an interrupt, the address just past the breakpoint instruction will be found on top of the stack. Since the debugger maintains a table listing the addresses of all of the implanted breakpoints, it is able to identify the breakpoint. The value that it places in the PC save-slot is the value from the stack, properly decremented.

9.19

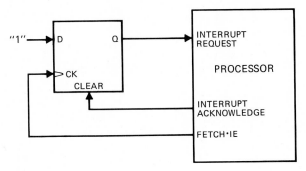

Figure S9.19

9.20
PC:	0	1	2	3	4	5	6	7	8	9	10	12	13
PTR:	50	50	50	50	50	50	51	51	51	51	51	51	100

9.21 Assuming that the Supervisor occupies a single, contiguous memory area, suppose we monitor the address presented to the memory on every instruction fetch. If we maintain an external counter, which is incremented on every fetch whose address is inside the Supervisor area, we develop a count of the total number of Supervisor instructions executed within a specified time period. Knowing the average instruction execution time permits a simple calculation of the overhead. Alternatively, if the system is equipped with an elapsed time clock having sufficient resolution, the Supervisor may keep track of its own CPU time by computing the elapsed time, between each Supervisor entry and its corresponding exit, and by adding this value to an accumulator. This gives the total CPU time used by the Supervisor within a specified time period. (The time take by the Supervisor to record this information must be negligible compared to its normal computation time.)

Index

DATE DUE

OC 22'84			
MAR 18 '86			
OCT 28 '86			
GAYLORD			PRINTED IN U.S.A.